INSIGHT GUIDES

ALASKA

APA PUBLICATIONS L

Part of the Langenscheidt Publishing Group

★ INSIGHT GUIDE
ALASKA

Editorial

Managing Editor
Siân Lezard
Art Director
Ian Spick
Picture Manager
Steven Lawrence
Series Manager
Rachel Fox

Distribution

United States
Langenscheidt Publishers, Inc.
36–36 33rd Street 4th Floor
Long Island City, NY 11106
orders@langenscheidt.com

UK & Ireland
GeoCenter International Ltd
Meridian House, Churchill Way West
Basingstoke, Hampshire RG21 6YR
sales@geocenter.co.uk

Australia
Universal Publishers
1 Waterloo Road
Macquarie Park, NSW 2113
sales@universalpublishers.com.au

New Zealand
Hema Maps New Zealand Ltd (HNZ)
Unit 2, 10 Cryers Road
East Tamaki, Auckland 2013
sales.hema@clear.net.nz

Worldwide
**Apa Publications GmbH & Co.
Verlag KG (Singapore branch)**
7030 Ang Mo Kio Ave 5
08–65 Northstar @ AMK
Singapore 569880
apasin@signet.com.sg

Printing

CTPS – China

©2009 Apa Publications GmbH & Co.
Verlag KG (Singapore branch)
All Rights Reserved

*First Edition 1988
Eighth Edition 2009
Reprinted 2010*

CONTACTING THE EDITORS

We would appreciate it if readers
would alert us to errors or out-
dated information by writing to:
**Insight Guides, P.O. Box 7910,
London SE1 1WE, England.**
insight@apaguide.co.uk

www.insightguides.com

ABOUT THIS BOOK

The first Insight Guide pioneered
the use of creative full-color
photography in travel guides in
1970. Since then, we have
expanded our range to cater for our
readers' need not only for reliable
information about their chosen destination but also for a real understanding of the culture and workings
of that destination. Now, when the
internet can supply inexhaustible
(but not always reliable) facts, our
books marry text and pictures to
provide those much more elusive
qualities: knowledge and discern-
ment. To achieve this, they rely
heavily on the authority of locally
based writers and photographers.

Insight Guide: Alaska is structured to
convey an understanding of the
region and its people as well as to
guide readers through its numerous
attractions:

◆ The **Features** section, indicated
by a pink bar at the top of each page,
covers the natural and cultural history of the region as well as providing illuminating essays on a range of
subjects, from visiting Alaska's
Natives and surviving in the wilderness to the rapid growth of cruising.
◆ The main **Places** section, indicated by a blue bar, is a complete
guide to all the sights and areas
worth visiting. Places of special
interest are coordinated by number
with the maps.
◆ The **Travel Tips** listings section,
with a yellow bar, provides full information on transportation, hotels,
activities, from culture to shopping
to sports, a guide to useful contacts,
and an A–Z section of essential
practical information. An easy-to-
find contents list for Travel Tips is
printed on the back flap, which also
serves as a bookmark.

LEFT: sunrise at low tide, Glacier Bay National Park.

based Sherwonit has probably traveled through more of the state's national parks than most veteran rangers, and his advice here on surviving in Alaska's wilderness is based on experience, not theory.

Bill Bjork and **Debby Drong-Bjork** wrote the chapters on Fairbanks and the Interior. **Mike Miller** wrote on Juneau, Misty Fiords National Monument and the Panhandle communities; **Jeff Brady**, the editor and publisher of the *Skagway News*, wrote on Skagway. **Kris Capps** covered Alaska's Native villages and artifacts. **Douglas Ward**, author of the renowned *Berlitz Complete Guide to Cruising and Cruise Ships*, covered developments in Alaskan cruising.

Among those who have written about Alaska's national parks are **Leslie Barber**, a member of the Citizens' Advisory Commission on Public Lands, **Rick McIntyre**, a naturalist and park ranger at Denali and **Diane Brady**, a commercial pilot for an air taxi service.

Other contributors to the guide included **Chris Blackburn**, **Chris Carson**, **Kathy Hunter**, **Katy Korbel**, **Kyle Lochalsh**, **Gloria Maschmeyer** and **Mark Skok**. The book was proofread by **Leonie Wilding** and indexed by **Helen Peters**.

The contributors

The latest edition of this long-time Insight bestseller, meticulously updated by Alaskan **Elizabeth Linhart**, has been structured to reflect the changing face of Alaska. Edited by **Brian Bell**, one of Insight Guides' founding editors, who made his first trip to Alaska in the 1970s to report from Prudhoe Bay on the construction of the trans-Alaska oil pipeline, the book builds on earlier editions produced by **Janie Freeburg**, **Diana Ackland**, **Pam Barrett** and Anchorage-based **Nancy Gates**.

Bill Sherwonit wrote the chapters on Chugach, Lake Clark and Wrangell-St Elias national parks, McNeil River State Game Sanctuary, Southwest Alaska, The Arctic, Arctic National Wildlife Refuge, and several of the one-page background features. As author of a guidebook on Alaska's parks, Anchorage-

Map Legend

▬ ▬ ▬	International Boundary
▬ ▬ ▬	State Boundary
▬ • ▬	National Park/Reserve
▬ ▬ ▬	Ferry Route
✈ ✈	Airport: International/Regional
🚌	Bus Station
ⓘ	Tourist Information
✝ † ⊕	Church/Ruins
†	Monastery
∴	Archeological Site
⛫	Castle/Ruins
☾	Mosque
✡	Synagogue
∩	Cave
1	Statue/Monument
★	Place of Interest
▪	Lodge/Ranger Station

The main places of interest in the Places section are coordinated by number with a full-color map (eg ❶), and a symbol at the top of every right-hand page tells you where to find the map.

Contents

LEFT: a team competes in the Iditarod Trail Sled Dog Race.

Travel Tips

THE BEST OF ALASKA: TOP ATTRACTIONS

Bears, birds, totems, train travel, skiing down glaciers, camping in the wilderness... Alaska can still astonish the most jaded of travelers

△ The **Iditarod Trail Sled Dog Race** – "the last great race on earth" – is run over 1,150 miles (1,850km), involves more than 1,200 dogs, and takes from 10 to 17 days to complete. *See pages 302–3.*

▽ Getting close to **brown bears** allows you to recognize their individuality – some are aggressive by nature but other are mild-mannered or even timid. Areas such as McNeil River State Game Sanctuary create safe conditions for bear watching. *See page 335.*

△ **Totem poles**, tall and elaborately carved, are comparable to family crests and are used to tell a story or recall an event. The totemic symbols are often animals or birds – typically bears and eagles. *See page 295.*

△ Trains such as the **McKinley Explorer**, with glass domes or open-air viewing platforms, penetrate deep into Alaska. *See page 346.*

◁ Prime **fishing** in pristine waters offers anglers a sporting chance of reeling in massive king salmon, leaping trout, halibut, and northern pike. *See page 359.*

△ With eight **national parks** and a **state parks** system of over 3.2 million acres (1.3 million hectares), Alaska has tremendous appeal to outdoor enthusiasts. *See page 183.*

△ **Mount McKinley** is North America's highest peak, and is surrounded by one of the world's greatest wildlife sanctuaries, Denali National Park and Preserve. *See page 223.*

△ The **Northern Lights** can be viewed most clearly in winter in the area around Fairbanks, which calls itself an "auroral zone." *See page 70.*

◁ The **trans-Alaska pipeline** moves oil 800 miles (1,300km) from the North Slope to Valdez, across three mountain ranges and 800 rivers and streams. *See page 53.*

▷ Alaska is the stronghold of **bald eagles**, which congregate in places where fish are plentiful. *See page 74.*

THE BEST OF ALASKA: EDITOR'S CHOICE

Setting priorities, discovering secrets, the best wildlife viewing, the top sporting events, unique attractions... here, at a glance, are our recommendations plus some tips and tricks that even the locals won't always know

ONLY IN ALASKA

● **Denali National Park and Preserve**
A memorable trip to see North America's highest peak and one of the world's greatest wildlife sanctuaries. *See pages 223–33.*

● **Glacier Bay National Park and Preserve**
Sixteen massive tidewater glaciers flow down from snow-capped mountain peaks and plunge into ice-choked fjords – a dramatic backdrop for viewing wildlife, including bears, seals, humpback whales, and eagles. *See pages 140–3.*

● **Aurora Borealis Displays** (Northern Lights)
Although these heavenly light shows can be viewed only in the darkened autumn or winter skies, in Anchorage, that begins in late August. *See page 70.*

● **Alaska's Thermal Resort** (Chena Hot Springs)
Soak away your preconceived notions about a "frozen wasteland" in outdoor and indoor steaming-hot thermal pools, in summer or winter. *See page 258.*

● **Land of the Midnight Sun**
Communities throughout Alaska celebrate the summer solstice each year with parties and barbecues and, in Fairbanks, midnight tee time for golfers in natural light. *See page 242.*

ALASKA'S BEST-KEPT SECRETS

● **Exit Glacier**
This spectacular glacier, located in Seward, is the only portion of the Kenai Fjords National Park which is accessible by road. A great place to take close-up glacier photographs, but watch out for falling ice! *See page 200.*

● **Lake Clark National Park and Preserve**
A short flight from Anchorage or the Kenai Peninsula, this offers boundless recreational opportunities for wildlife viewing, river running, kayaking, hunting and angling, yet it is among Alaska's least known, and least visited, national parks. *See pages 320–25.*

● **Richardson Highway**
This scenic road from Fairbanks to Valdez provides spectacular views of Worthington Glacier, the many waterfalls of Keystone Canyon, and Thompson Pass. *See page 253.*

● **Ship Creek**
This salmon-laden stream, within casting distance of downtown Anchorage hotels, is a favorite fishing hole for locals during lunch hour. *See page 167.*

● **Surf Yakutat**
Said by some to be one of the top, and certainly most unusual, surf beaches in the US. A great spot for serious surfing enthusiasts. *See page 157.*

LEFT: the bar at the Ice Museum, Chena Hot Springs.

BEST SPOTS FOR BEAR VIEWING

● **Brooks River and Camp**
Located in Katmai National Park and Preserve. Safe viewing platforms allow you to watch bears feed on spawning salmon near the Brooks Falls. Visitors may stay at Brooks Lodge, or fly out on a day trip from Anchorage. *See page 326.*

● **Denali National Park and Preserve**
Shuttle bus tours present visitors with excellent

opportunities for spotting bears. *See pages 223–33.*

● **Kodiak Island**
Famous for its healthy population of large brown bears. Bear-viewing tours will take you to see them in the Kodiak National Wildlife Refuge. *See page 316.*

● **McNeil River State Game Sanctuary**
Created for the world's largest concentration of brown bears. Access is limited: visitors are selected by lottery. *See pages 331–34.*

● **Pack Creek**
Admiralty Island National Monument in Southeast Alaska also offers bear viewing from platforms, and is accessible by air from Juneau. *See pages 75, 110.*

BEST FOR FAMILIES

● **Alaska Zoo**
A guaranteed, safe, close-up look at Alaska wildlife. *See page 170.*

● **Crow Creek Mine**
Try your hand at panning for gold at Southcentral's richest goldmine. *See page 174.*

● **Imaginarium**
This award-winning hands-on science center features touch tanks, a planetarium and reptiles. *See page 169.*

● **Alaska SeaLife Center**
A "window to the sea", this is the place for

people of all ages to get up close to puffins, sea lions, octopus, and more. *See pages 199–200.*

● **H2Oasis**
Alaska's indoor answer to the outdoor water parks in the lower 48 states. Includes a water-coaster ride. *See page 171.*

ABOVE: a brown bear.
RIGHT: panning for gold.

ABOVE: walruses are plentiful in the Bristol Bay area.

THINGS TO DO FREE AROUND ANCHORAGE

● **Drive to Hatcher Pass**
You can have a family picnic on the tundra, take a hike, or pick fresh berries on stunning alpine slopes. *See page 214.*

● **Navigate the Coastal Trail**
Whether you travel by bike, in-line skates, (or skis, in winter) or your own two feet, the 11 miles (18km) of the Tony Knowles Coastal Trail, from downtown Anchorage to Kincaid Park, makes for a delightful afternoon. *See page 171.*

● **Eagle River Nature Center**
This center offers free nature pro- grams, hiking trails, a viewing telescope, and natural history displays. Parking fee. *See page 172.*

● **Anchorage Coastal Wildlife Refuge**
A broad, open expanse, just south of Anchorage, which provides an excellent wetland habitat for a variety of resident and migratory birds. You may also see salmon spawning. *See page 173.*

● **Windy Corner and Beluga Point**
At Miles 107 and 110 on the Seward Highway, there are pull-outs that will allow you to safely park and look for Dall sheep, which are often standing on nearby craggy ledges, apparently watching the traffic go by. Telescopes help spot the inlet's beluga whales. *See pages 173, 182.*

● **Climb Flattop Mountain**
Panoramic views of Anchorage, the Alaska Range, and the Cook Inlet reward the sweaty hiker. *See page 181.*

UNIQUE SPORTING EVENTS

● **Iditarod Trail Sled Dog Race**
Known as "The Last Great Race," mushers and their dogs dash 1,150 bone-jarring miles (1,850km) from Anchorage to Nome, crossing two mountain ranges, following the Yukon River for about 150 miles (240km), then traversing the pack ice of Norton Sound. *See pages 302–3.*

● **World Eskimo Indian Olympics**
Hundreds of Native athletes from Alaska and the circumpolar nations *(above)* gather each July in Fairbanks to compete in many exotic, and often painful, athletic events. These competitions are patterned after the traditional Native hunting, fishing and gathering culture. Endurance, observation and a spirit of cooperation are all key ingredients in events like the ear pull, the knuckle hop, the Eskimo stick pull and the blanket toss. *See pages 250–1.*

● **Great Alaska Shootout (Anchorage) and Top of the World Classic (Fairbanks)**
Hosted yearly in November by the University of Alaska, these invitational college basketball tournaments have gained national prominence. *See pages 176, 358.*

● **Baseball Under the Midnight Sun**
During Fairbank's yearly summer solstice festivities, you can watch a baseball game (which has been played on June 21 for more than 100 years). It begins around 10.30pm and is played without any need of artificial light. *See page 242.*

ABOVE: bald eagles at Chilkat Bald Eagle Preserve.

BEST FOR BIRDWATCHING

● **Alaska Chilkat Bald Eagle Preserve (Haines)**
This preserve is home to the world's largest gathering of bald eagles, and hosts a festival each November. *See page 147.*

● **Kachemak Bay (Homer)**
Hundreds of thousands of shorebirds from as far away as Asia, Hawaii, and South America visit the picturesque hamlet of Homer during spring migration. The city hosts the Katchemak Bay Shorebird Festival each May. *See page 205.*

● **Pribilof Islands**
These tiny islands 300 miles (480km) off the west coast are a nesting ground for nearly 200 species of seabirds. You can also spot "accidental" Asian migrants. *See page 339.*

● **Creamers Field (Fairbanks)**
Originally a dairy farm, this migratory waterfowl refuge now plays host to sandhill cranes, Canadian honkers, and ducks every spring and fall. *See page 245.*

● **Copper River Delta (Cordova)**
The delta is a birder's paradise, home to the entire population of dusky Canada geese, and Cordova hosts a lively festival during May's migration. *See page 189.*

LEFT: a sled dog musher in the Yukon Quest race.

BEST RAIL TOURS

● The **Spencer Glacier and Grandview Tour** from Anchorage aboard the Alaska Railroad is a chance to see gorgeous landscapes, close-up glaciers – even take a float trip – and be back in Anchorage in time for dinner. *See page 346.*

● The **Hurricane Turn Train**, part of the Alaska Railroad, is used by locals to reach remote cabins. Passengers may get off the train at any point along the 55-mile (90-km) trip to fish, hike or enjoy a float trip, then flag it down on its return trip to Talkeetna. *See page 346.*

● **The Anchorage to Seward** route also

passes the Spencer Glacier and Grandview areas, but continues on to Seward, where you can take a day cruise into Kenai Fjords National Park. *See page 346.*

● Traveling to **Denali National Park and Preserve** via train offers several good opportunities to view Mount McKinley, weather permitting. *See page 346.*

● **Aboard the White Pass and Yukon Route Railroad.** You can retrace the steps of the historic Klondike Trail of '98, from Skagway to the White Pass Summit (elevation nearly 3,000ft.) *See pages 149–50.*

ABOVE: the White Pass and Yukon Route Railroad.

ABOVE: some of the crafts produced by Native artisans.

MUST-SEE MUSEUMS

● **Alaska Native Heritage Center (Anchorage)**
This is the place to learn about Alaska's incredibly rich Native culture, art, and traditional customs and see Native artists at work. *See page 170.*

● **UAF Museum of the North (Fairbanks)**
The University of Alaska museum has long been considered to be one of the top museums in the state. Exhibits include cultural artifacts, a huge mummified bison, a giant copper nugget, and more. *See page 244.*

● **Sitka National Historical Park**
Wind your way through a beautiful, old-growth coastal forest, view an excellent collection of totem poles, visit a museum and watch Native artisans at work. *See pages 130, 363.*

● **Alaska State Museum (Juneau)**
Exhibits range from a Native community house to Inuit ivory carvings and gold-rush memorabilia, all illustrating Alaska's varied history. The most notable feature is a model of a towering, two-story "eagle tree". *See page 135.*

FANTASTIC FESTIVALS

● **Talkeetna Moose Dropping Festival**
July. Score a bullseye with moose poops. www.talkeetnachamber.org

● **Polar Bear Jump-Off Festival**
Seward, January. Locals in bear costumes jump into Resurrection Bay. www.sewardak.org

● **Bering Sea Ice Golf Classic**
Nome, March. Six-hole course on ice with bright orange golf balls. www.nomealaska.org

● **Fur Rendezvous**
Anchorage, February. A week of winter fun and contests to celebrate Alaska's fur-trapping and trading heritage. www.furrondy.net

● **World Ice Art Championships**
Fairbanks, March. People come from miles around to carve their masterpieces in ice. www.fairbanks-alaska.com

● **Bear Paw Festival**
Eagle River, July. A parade, teddy

bears' picnic, and lots of family fun. www.cer.org

● **Anderson Bluegrass and Country Music Festival**
Anderson, end July. Camping and country music with great views.

● **Pelican Boardwalk Boogie**
Pelican, May. A craft and folk fair, with live bands and original goings-on like the filthy song contest and the underwear race. www.pelicanboardwalkboogie.com

THE LAST FRONTIER

Some people say there are no more frontiers
to explore without leaving the planet.
But they're forgetting about Alaska

Alaska: the Great Land, the Last Frontier – more than 580,000 sq miles (1½ million sq km) that taunted early explorers and still challenges modern-day researchers. It also provokes a fascination that attracts more and more travelers looking for something that a conventional vacation cannot give them. The hint of urban sophistication in Anchorage and Juneau rapidly gives way to the frontier, where outdoor survival skills are among the most useful attributes a resident can possess.

America's 49th state is so broad, so unpeopled, and so roadless that small airplanes are more common than cabs in other states. There are more private pilots than truck drivers and cabbies combined. Men outnumber women (though women have coined the phrase "The odds are good, but the goods are odd"). The population numbers just over 670,000, almost half of whom live in one city, Anchorage. Nearly the entire state is raw, wondrous wilderness.

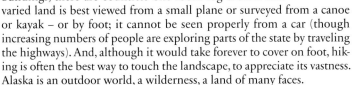

Alaska has lush rain-drenched forests and fragile windswept tundras. There are lofty mountains, spectacular glaciers, and still-active volcanoes, as well as 3 million lakes and endless swamps. Along with a handful of modern high-rise buildings, there are countless one-room log cabins. This varied land is best viewed from a small plane or surveyed from a canoe or kayak – or by foot; it cannot be seen properly from a car (though increasing numbers of people are exploring parts of the state by traveling the highways). And, although it would take forever to cover on foot, hiking is often the best way to touch the landscape, to appreciate its vastness. Alaska is an outdoor world, a wilderness, a land of many faces.

The Alaskan experience includes the sheer wonder of finding what hides beyond the horizon or over the next ridge. No one person has ever seen it all; no one person ever will. Therein lies the essence of Alaska. Its huge, untamed spaces, it has been said, are the great gift Alaska can give to a harrassed world.

PRECEDING PAGES: viewing melting glaciers from a cruise ship; mountain house on the Ruth Glacier, south of Mount McKinley; after the photographer had retreated.
LEFT: many parts of Alaska are accessible only by air.
ABOVE: the mail arrives by floatplane; Native Alaskans.

When to go

Springtime (or "breakup") to an Alaskan is a hopeful time of dwindling snow berms, widening streets, emerging lawns and, most exciting of all, lengthening daylight hours. But to a visitor in the here-and-now of Alaska spring, it may look like dirty snow melting to reveal accumulated trash, huge puddles trapped by still-frozen drains on winter-ravaged roads and fickle weather conditions. March, April and early May are months of renewal for Alaskans, but visitors would be wise to allow sufficient time for the state to wake up, spruce up and set up for tourist season.

Just before the first cruise ship arrives, store merchants bring out lovely hanging flower baskets and the cities seem to "bloom" overnight. Gift shops, which may have been closed over the winter, are re-opened, swept out, shelves stocked and windows polished. The visitor season runs from mid-May to mid-September. During those months, all tours, parks, campgrounds, trains, buses, ferries, restaurants, hotels, B&Bs and other service-related facilities are running at full speed. Many offer bargain rates for the "shoulder seasons" of late May and early September. Summer in Alaska boasts mild temperatures and, in most areas, seemingly endless daylight.

If springtime is when Alaska showers and shaves, and summer is open house, fall feels like a time for getting together with a few close friends. Like spring, the timing of autumn in Alaska is a fickle business, and one can miss it altogether. Generally it begins to feel like fall in late August and continues through mid-September. The trees and grasses turn golden, the spent fireweed magenta, and the mountains,

below the "termination dust" of newly snow-capped peaks, a warm russet. Fall brings darkness back to the night sky of most of Alaska, and with it displays of the aurora borealis, or Northern Lights.

There are far fewer tourists in autumn – but fewer options, too. The favorite tourist destinations, lodgings, restaurants, transportations and other amenities taper off as suddenly as they gear up in late spring. The use of a private or rental car greatly increases sightseeing options. Careful research and planning is needed for a rewarding autumn visit to Alaska – but are well worth the effort.

If skiing, snowboarding, sled dog races and other winter sports appeal, a wintertime visit to Alaska is an excellent option. The Fur Rendezvous, held in Anchorage in February, is a yearly celebration that includes the World Champion Sled Dog Race, fireworks, art exhibits, fur auctions, a winter outdoor carnival (dress warmly), and much more. Fairbanks also celebrates winter with festivals, fireworks displays, sled dog races and the incredible sculptural masterpieces of the World Ice Art Championship. ❑

ABOVE: canoes are versatile transportation; floatplane meets cruise ship in the Gulf.
RIGHT: the Northern Lights are best seen between late September and early April.

PRESERVING THE FRAGILE WILDERNESS

It's thrilling to visit pristine areas unchanged for a thousand years. But how can more people enjoy the experience without endangering that very wildness?

You don't really know what wild means until you've been to Alaska. With one-fifth of the land area of the contiguous United States and more shoreline than all the other states combined, Alaska includes 150 million acres (60 million hectares) of national parks and forests, wildlife refuges and other designated preserves. Its 38 mountain ranges, 3,000 rivers and 3 million lakes fall within climate ranges from temperate rainforest to arid arctic. Much of this territory is barely charted, let alone touched by the human foot.

Of Alaska's 15 national parks, preserves and monuments, only five can be accessed by road. Glacier Bay National Park (3.2 million acres/1.3 million hectares), for example, can be reached only by boat or floatplane. North America's premier mountain wilderness and its largest national park, Wrangell-St Elias National Park and Preserve (13.2 million acres/5.3 million hectares), is home to nine peaks of more than 14,000ft (4,270 meters), including the 18,010ft (5,490-meter) Mount St Elias, the continent's fourth-highest peak (and the second-tallest in the United States).

It also has the largest collection of glaciers in North America, the Bagley Icefield, numerous wild rivers, and multitudes of wildlife. Yet only two unpaved roads, best negotiated by four-wheel-drive vehicles, penetrate the park boundaries.

Exploring the arctic

The Gates of the Arctic National Park, the northernmost of all the state's parks, is a remote

LEFT: watching a calving glacier in Tracy Arm Wilderness Area, Juneau.
RIGHT: camping with a low environmental impact.

and undeveloped 8.4 million acres (3.4 million hectares) of crags, fragile alpine meadows, crystal clear mountain streams, and sweeping arctic valleys. Without roads or trails, backpacking, mountaineering, river floating, and dogsled excursions are the best ways in which visitors can explore these arctic expanses.

Besides its federal parks and refuges, Alaska has state-managed parks and sanctuaries that are among the nation's finest, from 1.55-million-acre (630,000-hectare) Wood-Tikchik – the country's largest state park – to the Alaska Chilkat Bald Eagle Preserve and McNeil River State Game Sanctuary, where dozens of brown bears, some weighing 1,000 pounds (450kg) or more, gather each summer to fish for salmon.

Whether bears or birds, wildlife is abundant throughout much of the state's wilderness. Hundreds of thousands of caribou roam across sweeping tundra, Dall sheep graze in high alpine basins, seals sun themselves on ice floes, wolves howl from the tops of ridges, golden eagles spiral through blue skies and clouds, whales ply turquoise fjords.

When federal geographer Henry Gannett, a founder of the National Geographic Society, surveyed Alaska's expanse in 1904, he set the tone for today's ecotourism: "Its grandeur is more valuable than the gold or the fish or the timber, for it will never be exhausted." Alaska is a land where inhabitants and travelers sense that they can do no better.

Low-impact tourism

Unfortunately, the traditional tourist industry in the state often bypasses its great wilderness areas in favor of organized tours that take visitors by bus, train or airplane to cities, towns and developed parks. The majority of tourists see sights that are reached by road (such as Portage Glacier, Denali National Park and Preserve, and cities such as Anchorage, Juneau and Fairbanks) – but rarely step into untouched wilderness.

GEOLOGICAL YOUTH

Alaska is a young country, geologically speaking. Composed of fragments of the earth's crust that rafted from the Pacific area on the backs of crustal plates and then "docked" together, the entire region is still in the process of coming together. Tracing the ridgeline along the Aleutians and Alaska Range, it is easy to see where the Pacific plate rammed into the North American.

Its youth and place on the globe are responsible for much of Alaska's diversity. America's largest state has arctic tundra, 5,000 glaciers, mountain ranges, coastal rainforests, fjords, active volcanoes, 3 million lakes and countless islands.

Only one road goes into 6-million-acre (2.4-million-hectare) Denali National Park – a 90-mile (145km) strip that bars most private vehicles. While this road channels more and more visitors into the park each year via bus tours – which cause minimum disturbance to the landscape and wildlife – only 31,000 of the park's 404,000 visitors in one recent year registered for backcountry permits.

Guides such as Bob Jacobs, owner of St Elias Alpine Guides in McCarthy, feel that visitors to Alaska should see a lot more, but, at the same time, the land should be protected. "Alaska is a wonderful classroom," Bob says. But, unlike school, "you don't need a schedule. In summer you can hike until 2am and sleep until noon."

On Jacobs' trips into the heart of the Wrangell-St Elias National Park you climb unnamed peaks, raft down swift, milky rivers and backpack

> Alaska's a whole new experience once you've touched the 1,000-year-old ice of a massive glacier, rafted a raging river and heard wild creatures calling across unpeopled lands.

for weeks at a time. Jacobs helped pioneer ecotourism, comprising environmentally-friendly outdoor adventures such as sea kayaking, moun-

The Alaska Travel Industry Association reports that in one recent summer around 1.6 million non-resident visitors spent nearly $1.5 billion, or about $930 a person. About half of these visitors said they did some wildlife viewing – although only an estimated 10 percent strike out away from traditional tourist areas into the pristine wilderness.

Protecting the land

Essentially, ecotourism means using the tourist industry as a tool to protect and enhance Alaska's natural beauty. "It's important to understand that we're a part of nature and a part of

taineering and wildlife watching. Though the great majority of travelers continue to see Alaska by car, tour bus, or cruise ship, ecotourism – defined as low-impact vacations that allow people to learn about, enjoy, and help preserve the natural environment while disturbing local people as little as possible – has helped a growing number of people see wild and pristine areas of Alaska inaccessible to the masses. Traveling at nature's pace in a land that offers adventure and asks for respect, tourists gain an intimate awareness of life as it was 1,000 years ago.

LEFT: a bus stops for a grizzly sow and her cubs to cross the road, Denali National Park.
ABOVE: a humpback whale makes a splash.

the plan," says Penney Hodges, who helped direct the Alaska Center for Coastal Studies in Homer. "We need to learn how to get back into balance with nature." By opening its doors to travelers in summer and to parties of schoolchildren in spring and fall, the center works to foster responsible human interaction with our natural surroundings and to generate knowledge of the marine and coastal ecosystems of Kachemak Bay through its environmental education and research programs.

Ecotourism in Alaska was initiated by a handful of small, independent operators and outfitters that led groups into the outback, while the mainstream industry concentrated on marketing developed resort areas. Now some large-scale organizations have developed policies and principles that depart significantly from traditional commercial concerns and lean toward low-impact tourism. Nevertheless, ecotourism largely remains the domain of smaller businesses that emphasize small groups.

The guidelines of the American Society of Travel Agents spell out the ecotourism ethos: visitors should support local cultures; avoid littering; walk only on designated trails; support conservation-oriented programs; learn about local customs; avoid disturbing local habitats or buying products which utilize any part of endangered animals.

Eco-friendly options

Dozens of outfitters offer river rafting, tundra trekking, mountain climbing, birdwatching, whale cruising, wildlife photography safaris, and sea-kayaking adventures, ranging from easygoing to incredibly strenuous. Some tour operators offer ecotours geared specifically toward senior citizens. Although some of these trips hark back to the days of the pioneers, they are usually made comfortable enough. Visitors can take advantage of experienced guides without having to acquire all the necessary skills themselves; and many of the backcountry meals approach gourmet quality.

NATURAL WONDERS

When it comes to counting the most and the biggest, Alaska can amass some amazing statistics. Measuring 2,400 miles (3,860km) from east to west, Alaska covers more than twice the land area of its closest competitor, Texas. It has 33,900 miles (54,500km) of sea coast – 50 percent more than the contiguous United States. Its mountains include 19 that are over 14,000ft (4,270 meters), and 17 of them are among the 20 highest peaks in the United States.

The state also has over 5,000 glaciers and more than 3 million lakes. The largest of these, Lake Iliamna, in Southwest Alaska, encompasses 1,100 sq miles (2,850 sq km).

Wildlife viewing is a major draw, especially for those hoping to see the monarchs of the land: the grizzly and its coastal cousin, the brown bear. One of the most notable areas is the McNeil River State Game Sanctuary, but visitors are strictly regulated by permit; only 10 people a day, accompanied by sanctuary staff, can visit the bear-viewing areas. This close supervision means that visitors have to apply in advance, and names are randomly drawn (by computer, nowadays). You have a better chance of getting to Brooks Camp, another top bear-viewing area, within Katmai National Park.

Other renowned bear-viewing areas include Denali National Park and Preserve, home to 200–300 bears; many can be seen grazing on plants or digging for ground squirrels near the Park Road. Kodiak National Wildlife Refuge, designated a refuge by President Franklin D. Roosevelt in 1941, is home to the largest bears on earth (they can reach 1,200 pounds/540kg). As much as 10 percent of Alaska's grizzlies live on Kodiak Island. "Big bears fill big hotels," said the controversial grizzly activist Timothy Treadwell, who was mauled to death by a bear in Katmai National Park in 2003. "People go to Alaska to see wilderness, to be part of what Earth used to be like. That's good for tourism. If you protect grizzly habitat, you protect your bread and butter."

impact scale. Currently, no such system exists, but Bob Jacobs has some suggestions to enable would-be visitors to pick the right company to travel with. "Do your homework. Look for organizations that go beyond making money. Talk to them. Get a feeling for their philosophy. Ask for references. That's the best policy."

Following some guidelines will help make your trip ecologically friendly. Check to see if an operator limits the number of people it takes into fragile areas. Does the company practice low-impact camping and hiking and vary the location of campsites from trip to trip in order to avoid scarring the ground in certain areas?

Besides bears, people come from around the world to see other wildlife: Dall sheep, moose, caribou, wolves, bald and golden eagles, and all manner of songbirds, shorebirds, and seabirds, as well as marine mammals *(see pages 73–7)*.

Ethical guidelines

Although ecotourism industry operators generally follow environmental ethics, they don't all abide equally by the unwritten code of minimal impact. Some people are now advocating a "green rating" system to distinguish between good and poor operators on an ecological

Does it supply a reading list about the area and the type of activities you will be pursuing?

Top ecotourism companies are staffed by experienced naturalists who accompany their guests on journeys and offer extensive information along the way. Such specialists help minimize impact on wildlife by keeping groups at unobtrusive, safe distances. The companies should also be committed to energy conservation and recycling, as this helps preserve the environment that you have come here to enjoy.

Even if you're traveling on your own, you can do your bit by following the guidelines that come with backcountry permits. It makes sense to preserve the grandeur of Alaska's wilderness for the benefit of future generations. ❏

LEFT: setting up camp in Glacier Bay.
ABOVE: flowers add color in the high tundra.

AN INDEPENDENT PEOPLE

Nearly a quarter of Alaska's population has moved
to the state within the past few years. So how
do you define a "typical" Alaskan?

Before Alyson Rigby Ronningen, who grew up in England, traveled to Alaska for the first time, she thought she had a pretty clear idea of what Alaskans were like: "They all wore flannel shirts, had big bushy beards, and they owned guns and big dogs," she recalled. Alyson eventually married an Alaskan and moved to the Far North. Once there, she looked around at her Fairbanks neighbors and smugly told a friend, "I was right."

But Alyson was not a "typical" visitor, or even a run-of-the-mill new Alaskan. She spent her first winter living in a wall tent with her husband and new baby. While her husband worked as a carpenter nearby, she used a tiny wood stove for both warmth and cooking. Temperatures plummeted as low as –30° or –40°F (–34° to –40°C) but Alyson stayed toasty by baking on her trusty wood stove. She conformed to what many believe to be an unspoken code of the north: be independent and self-sufficient.

In that way she was a "typical" Alaskan, yet it is difficult to generalize about what is typical, because it depends so much on where you choose to settle and under what circumstances you live. Alaska is so huge and the various parts of the state are so different from each other that the residents are bound to differ widely as well.

Anchored down in Anchorage

The hub of the state is its largest (although not its capital) city, Anchorage. Rural Alaskans often joke that Anchorage is only 20 minutes from the real Alaska. That may well be true, but many

LEFT: as part of an intensive ecology program, a radio-tagged eagle is being released into the wild.
RIGHT: Alaskans enjoy the phenomenal outdoor life.

urban Alaskans make the best possible use of those 20 minutes.

In a state where the median age is 34, Anchorage (with 42 percent of the population) is a city of young – but aging – professionals (the population's average age in increasing). They include active outdoor-sports lovers, such as rock climbers, mountain bikers, whitewater kayakers, and runners. Many people bring their outdoor toys to work with them, and at the end of the day, they head for the hills, the city's biking trails and parks, or nearby streams. In summer they don't have to worry about running out of daylight, either, because from late May through early August the sky never fully darkens.

People in Anchorage also spend a lot of time getting out of town. Lake Hood, a float-plane base in the city, is the largest and busiest such base in the world, with more than 1,000 take-offs and landings recorded on a peak summer day.

Where do they all go? Just peek out of a plane window as you fly into Anchorage and you will see hundreds of little getaway cabins tucked into the surrounding wilderness and the more remote areas. Those without their own cabins may fly to public-use cabins, developed campgrounds, or backcountry destinations where they set up their own campsites.

No water, no problem

John Power, a long-time Alaskan who became a "big city" resident in his early 40s, thought about getting one of those backcountry cabins when he first moved to Anchorage, but instead bought a 30ft (9-meter) sailboat, which he keeps in Prince William Sound. Power, a geophysicist with the Alaska Volcano Observatory, moved to Anchorage from Fairbanks, where for many years he had lived on the town's outskirts in a little cabin with no running water and, like Alyson, just a wood stove for heating.

"I liked it," he says. "I liked living in a place where I didn't really have any neighbors. I liked

JACK LONDON AND THE YUKON

The prolific San Francisco-born novelist Jack London (1876–1916) joined the fortune hunters in 1897's Klondike Gold Rush and later created a romantically adventurous portrait of Alaska in such novels as *White Fang* and *The Call of the Wild*. In both books, sled dogs fight to survive in Alaska's unforgiving wilderness.

London developed scurvy from a lack of fresh food in winter, and, having failed to strike it rich, worked as a laborer back in San Francisco until a newspaper published his account of his trip down the Yukon. Today a log cabin in Dawson City is a Jack London Interpretive Center (tel: 867-993-5575).

not having to worry about it when I left in winter, which I frequently did when I was traveling. It was inexpensive. I first got into that lifestyle when I was a student and I never really changed. I didn't have to worry about house-sitters, or about the plumbing freezing or the heat being on when I was gone." He misses his reliable little wood stove most of all. "I used to like getting up in the morning, building my fire and cooking pancakes in the kitchen with the wood stove roaring away," he says nostalgically.

There are several thousand Fairbanks-area residents who still embrace the wood-stove, no-running-water lifestyle with enthusiasm. These people usually fill 5-gallon (22-liter) water jugs at the laundromats in town, or at their places of employment. Showers are also available for use at the laundromats of many communities.

> In communities along the Alaskan coast, life revolves not only around the weather, but around the fishing season. When the fishing is poor, the whole town suffers and the economy of the whole community is in trouble.

When winter settles in and the mercury begins to drop, conversation generally revolves around the weather, particularly the frigid tem-

The Russian community

Some Alaskans came here long ago as visitors and stayed on. Typical among them are the descendants of Russian immigrants in the Kenai Peninsula, Kodiak and Sitka. The first Russians came to Alaska in the late 18th century (see page 45) and established communities first in Kodiak, then in present-day Sitka, which became the headquarters of the fur trading Russian-American Company.

Both towns retain strong Russian influences, but it is on the Kenai Peninsula that a strict Russian Orthodox community survives, based around their "Island of Faith" near Anchor

peratures endured in the Interior and Arctic regions. Eventually, someone will complain about water pipes freezing and bursting, and those who have no running water try not to look too self-satisfied.

In Kodiak and other fishing communities, extra-Tuf rubber boots and heavy-duty raingear are the fashion *du jour*. Since many students and some teachers fish, the school calendar is based on fishing openings and closures. The population swells in the summer when people arrive to fish, then contracts when they leave again at the end of the season.

LEFT: the Tlingit Indian owner of a fishing boat.
ABOVE: wolf and friend, Valdez.

Point. Survivors of persecution by the Orthodox Church, the government, and later the Stalinist purges, they call themselves "the Old Believers."

Today they work in local businesses, or operate companies of their own, and manage their own fishing fleet. But their lives revolve around their religious beliefs. The study of holy books is mandatory during periods of fasting before Christmas and Lent. They wear traditional clothes: the women and girls always cover their heads with scarves, and men dress conservatively, often sporting close-trimmed beards.

Yet they are no less Alaskan than the man who lives in the bush and calls the Lower 48 states "America," as if he inhabited a separate country; or the Anchorage college graduate, rushing from his downtown office to the mountain tops at weekends.

Bush pilots

Life in Alaska can be tough, and it has always attracted people who are not easily daunted. Among the most intrepid of Alaskans are the bush pilots. Their history begins in the 1920s, when Alaska and the airplane became partners in a relationship best described as complicated bliss. Despite an obvious need, Alaska wasn't equipped for airplanes. There were lots of places to go, but there was no place to land once you

got there. This created a special breed of flyer: the bush pilot.

Alaska entered the aviation age courtesy of James V. Martin, who had contracted to fly an airplane over Fairbanks in honor of the 4th of July in 1913. He loaded his disassembled airplane on a steamship and sailed it to Skagway. There he transferred it to the White Pass and Yukon Railroad for the 125-mile (200km) trip to Whitehorse, Yukon Territory, in Canada.

Finally, Martin loaded his plane on a sternwheeler and steamed 800 miles (1,300km) down the Yukon River, then 100 miles (160km) up the Tanana and Chena rivers to Fairbanks. In

PAYBACK FOR THE PEOPLE

Because Alaska depends to such an extent on its natural resources, its citizens argued they should benefit directly from the exploitation of those riches rather than trust politicians to spend the money. In 1976, as the potential of the North Slope oilfield became apparent, voters passed a constitutional amendment creating the Alaska Permanent Fund. This trust fund invests a proportion of revenues from mineral sales and each October pays out a dividend to every qualified Alaskan resident. The sum has varied from $331.29 a person in 1984 to $1,963.86 in 2000. It is valued income, particularly for the poor, and it tends to lessen local opposition to further oil drilling in wilderness areas.

Fairbanks, Martin reassembled the plane. It flew in exhibition for 11 minutes, and was then carted out of the territory.

Conditions are easier today, but pilots must still turn out in all weathers and people still rely on them to turn up in emergencies, and to deliver the mail if not – they hope – the babies. And, although many people now take commuter planes between Alaska's larger communities, hundreds of flyers continue the bush pilot tradition, as they transport passengers and supplies to tiny villages and into remote backcountry, where they may land on glaciers, lakes, or tundra, just as pioneering pilots did a century ago.   ❑

ABOVE: meeting the mail plane in Chefornak.

A Trapper's Life

Fur for fashion's sake is out, but Alaskans still consider trapping a part of their heritage and a way of life in the far north.

For many, fur is an integral and critical part of life in the Alaskan bush. Not only does it provide more warmth than wool or other synthetic material, trapping is one of the few ways for those living off the land to make money to pay for their most basic provisions.

Life in the bush has changed little over the years. Most trappers maintain two or three traplines, each about 40 to 60 miles (65–95km) long. Checking them on a routine basis is essential to ensure that no animal is caught for long periods of time, causing excessive pain and suffering. While nearly all Alaska's small mammals, from the Arctic fox to the tiny weasel, are valued for their fur, lynx and beaver are particularly prized.

Working with dogs

Some have started to use snow-machines, but for many, dogsleds are essential to a trapper's life. Not only do they provide companionship, dogs do not break down like machines, a factor in these remote areas that can mean the difference between life and death. Still, a trapper must be able to control a sled drawn by a dozen huskies, capable of doing some 60 miles (100km) a day on a good trail, in temperatures dipping as low as −50°F (−45°C). Many things can go wrong on a trip: a sled could clump a sapling in its careening descent of a slope; there could be a dog fight, or a threat from runaway dogs; a last-minute repair job might be needed, or the towline can disconnect from the sled, sending the dogs flying in formation without their driver. And sometimes a 1,500-pound (700kg) bull moose can challenge the team's right to use the trail.

Because there's always something to watch out for, the trapper must work in close unison with the team. The dogs are guided verbally, with commands to tell a leader which trail to take, to order slack dogs to speed up, or to encourage the team as a whole when they begin to tire. By watching the dogs' ears, eyes and attitudes, an experienced trapper can determine whether the team scent a moose or an animal in a trap ahead, if they want to fight or balk, if they're happy, discouraged, or over-tired.

The seasons are important in the remote Alaskan bush – for those working with machines as much as for those still using dog teams. In the summer, many trappers concentrate on fishing, picking berries and cultivating gardens. Fish nets must be run daily and the dogs fed with cooked whitefish or salmon and rice. Any extra fish are cut and dried for next winter.

In the summer months, trappers may take the opportunity to build dog houses and sleds, sew sled bags, dog booties and harnesses. Some trappers

tan and sew furs from the winter's catch, making hats and mitts which they can sell for extra cash.

When fall arrives, there are cranberries to be picked, jam to be made. And when the annual fish run begins, whitefish are netted and frozen whole for the dogs' food. With winter comes the trapping season, and the truly hard work: snowshoeing through deep snow; skiing miles to set trails; and cutting cord after cord of firewood.

So it goes. The yearly cycle of putting food up in summer and fall, and trapping and woodcutting in winter and spring. The weekly cycle, measured by the mail plane and the trapline rounds, and the daily cycle of mushing dogs, maintaining equipment and feeding fires. It's a hard life but, for many, a happy and fulfilled one. ❑

RIGHT: at the Anchorage Miners' and Trappers' Ball.

Decisive Dates

The Early Alaskans

30–10,000 BC

The migration of tribes from Asia occurs across a land bridge, which at the time linked Siberia and Alaska.

10,000 BC

The Aleuts settle in the Aleutian Islands. The name Alaska derived from their word "Alaxsxag" meaning "the object toward which the action of the sea is directed." Other tribes disperse throughout North and South America but the Aleuts, the Eskimos (Inupiats and Yup'iks) and the Indians, which include the Athabascans and the

coastal Tlingits and Haidas, settle in Alaska.

The Russian Invasion

1741

First Russian ships arrive. Vitus Bering turns back after his crew made one brief landing in what is now called Prince William Sound, and dies before he could reach home, while Alexei Chirikof lands on Prince of Wales Island, where some of his crew mysteriously vanish. The fur trade is established, and the Natives forced to hunt on the Russians' behalf.

1778

Captain James Cook visits the Aleutian Islands. His brief visit prompts English interest in the fur trade the Russians have developed.

1784

Grigor Ivanovich Shelikof arrives on Kodiak Island. He enslaves and ill-treats the Natives, then sets up the first permanent Russian settlement on Three Saints Bay where he builds a school and introduces the Russian Orthodox religion.

1790

Alexander Baranof takes over the fur enterprise. He treats the Natives more humanely than his predecessors, and moves the Russian colony to the site of the present city of Kodiak.

1799

The Russian-American Company is formed.

1802

The Tlingits raze to the ground the Russian town of Mikhailovsk, built near the site of present-day Sitka, on land they had sold to Baranof. Later, the Russians destroy the Tlingit village and establish the town of New Archangel, capital of Russian America.

1812

Russia finally reaches a settlement with America over hunting rights in Alaska, but the agreement doesn't last.

The White Pass and Chilkoot Trail to the gold fields are tackled by thousands and Skagway becomes a thriving center.

1899
Gold is discovered at Nome in the far northwest. Many prospectors who had been unsuccessful in the Yukon move west to try again.

1902
Felix Pedro strikes gold in the Tanana Hills.

1903
The town of Fairbanks, near Pedro's strike, is founded on the site of a trading post set up by entrepreneur E.T. Barnette and named for a senator who had given him financial support.

1833
The British Hudson's Bay Company establishes a fur-trading outpost in Alaska.

Mid-19th century
Russian power diminishes. British and Americans undermine the fur monopoly and the Tlingits wage guerrilla war.

1866
A Western Union expedition under William H. Dall produces the first scientific studies of Alaska and the first map of the Yukon River.

AMERICA TAKES OVER

1867
US Congress, at the instigation of Secretary of State William Seward, buys Alaska from the Russians for $7.2 million.

1870s–80s
Fish canneries established around Nushagak Bay to exploit the huge runs of

salmon. In the Aleutians, fur seals and otters are slaughtered ruthlessly. Whalers pursue their quarries to the high Arctic.

THE GOLD RUSH

1880
Gold is discovered at Silver Bow Basin, and the town of Juneau is founded.

1882
The Treadwell Mine, across the Gastineau Channel from Juneau, flourishes.

1896
Gold is discovered in the Klondike, a tributary of the Yukon, and the easiest route to it is by ship to Skagway.

Early 1900s
Prospectors flock to Alaska from all over North America and Europe.

1910
Kennicott, the richest copper mine in the world, starts operations in the Wrangell-St Elias mountains.

PRECEDING PAGES: a train reaches the summit of White Pass, 1899. FAR LEFT TOP: an inhabitant of Unalaska Island in his canoe, 1811. FAR LEFT: a Native bearing arms. LEFT: Natives trade their furs for nails, 18th century. ABOVE: miners on Snake River. RIGHT: workers on the Alaska Highway, here only two days old.

WORLD WAR II

1942

The Alaska Highway – the Alcan – is built *(see picture on page 37)* in under nine months as both a means of defense and an overland supply route to America's Russian allies, after sea routes are cut off following the Japanese attack on Pearl Harbor. The Japanese land on the islands of Kiska and Attu. The villagers are interned in Japan for the remainder of the war. Aleuts living in the Pribilofs and Aleutian Islands' villages are evacuated.

1943

After a two-week battle the Americans re-take Attu in May. In July the Americans bomb Kiska and the Japanese retreat.

STATEHOOD AND OIL

1957

Oil is discovered at the Swanson River on the Kenai Peninsula.

1959

Alaska becomes the 49th US state in January, and is welcomed into the union by President Dwight D. Eisenhower.

1964

The Good Friday earthquake hits Southcentral Alaska. Over 100 people are killed, mostly by tidal waves. Valdez, Seward, Cordova, Kodiak, and several small villages suffer the worst effects.

1968

Oil is found at Prudhoe Bay.

1971

The Alaska Native Claims Settlement Act (ANCSA) gives Natives title to 44 million acres (18 million hectares) of land, and $963 million, distributed among specially formed Native corporations.

1971–77

The construction of the trans-Alaska pipeline to Valdez creates thousands of jobs and transforms Anchorage and Fairbanks into bright, modern cities.

1976

The Alaska Permanent Fund is created to ensure long-term benefits from oil revenues.

1977

The trans-Alaska pipeline is completed. Oil begins to flow and the state economy booms.

1980

In one of the 20th century's landmark conservation successes, President Jimmy Carter signs the Alaska National Interest Lands Conservation Act (ANILCA), which adds 106 million acres (43 million hectares) of conservation lands, in national parks, wildlife refuges, and forests.

1989

The Exxon Valdez tanker hits Bligh Reef and spills 11 million gallons (42 million liters) of oil into Prince William Sound. A huge clean-up operation is launched. Thousands of miles of coastline are inundated by oil and thousands of birds and mammals are killed. Litigation follows.

1990

A new decade sees the logging and fishing industries in steady decline but the cruise industry starts to boom.

1992

The oil industry retrenches, causing big job losses.

1995
Canadian fishermen protest about access to Southeast Alaska's troll king salmon fishery.

1996
A fierce debate begins over the question of whether rural residents – particularly Native peoples – should be granted a subsistence priority for the harvest of Alaska's fish and wildlife.

1998
The moose is adopted as the state's official land mammal.

1999
The Alaska Native Heritage Center opens in Anchorage.

2000
A census puts the population at 626,932, a rise of 14 percent in just 10 years.

LEFT TOP: scene showing earthquake destruction, Anchorage, 1964. FAR LEFT: President Eisenhower shakes hands with Alaska Governor after Alaska became 49th state, 1958. LEFT: trying to clean up after *Exxon Valdez* disaster, 1989. ABOVE: bull moose feeding on spring grass. TOP: cruising through the fjords. RIGHT: trademark wink from Republican vice-presidential candidate and former Alaska governor, Sarah Palin, October 2008.

2001
A fierce debate continues over the future of the Arctic National Wildife Refuge's Coastal Plain; developers want it to be opened to oil and gas exploration and development; environmentalists fight to have it preserved as wilderness, while Alaska's Native peoples are split on the issue. There is talk of building a new pipeline, to ship Alaska's rich reserves of natural gas to the Lower 48 states.

2002
A fall of 28.6 inches (73 cm) of wet snow in March breaks all records.

2003
Bears maul to death author Timothy Treadwell, famous for approaching them upclose, in Katmai National Park.

2004
A record 708 fires burn more than 6.7 million acres (2.7 million hectares).

2006
An oil leak in August means Prudhoe Bay Oil Field is shut down until 2007.

2008
Sarah Palin becomes the first Alaskan to appear on the ticket of a major political party for the presidential race. Ultimately, she and John McCain were defeated by Barak Obama and Joe Biden. Ted Stevens, the longest serving US Senator, is convicted on corruption charges.

2009
Mount Redoubt, a volcano 100 miles (160km) southwest of Anchorage, starts erupting, spreading ash over a wide area. Sarah Palin announces her resignation as governor of Alaska.

BEGINNINGS

Alaska was inhabited for thousands of years by various Native groups, each with their own culture and language. But the discovery that the territory was rich in furs attracted the attention of Russian traders, and changed the lives of the Native people for ever

Who were the people who first thrived in such an unforgiving environment? Anthropologists believe the ancestors of the Alaska Natives migrated in several waves over a land bridge which joined Siberia and Alaska thousands of years ago.

When Europeans first encountered Alaska Natives in the early 18th century, there were dozens of tribes and language groups throughout the region, from the Inupiat Eskimos in the Arctic region to the Tlingits in the Southeast. Today, these first Alaskans are divided into several main groups: the southeastern Coastal Indians (the Tlingits and Haidas), the Athabascans (Interior Indians), the Aleuts, the Alutiiqs, the Eyak, and the two groups of Eskimos: Inupiat and Yup'ik. What follows is a look at their early, traditional subsistence lifestyles, before their (sometimes forced) transition into modern, western culture.

The Coastal Indians

These were probably in the first wave of immigrants to cross the land bridge, although many initially settled in Canada. The Tlingits were the most numerous; they claimed most of the coastal Panhandle, leaving only a small southern portion to the less populous Haidas. (In the late 1800s they were joined by the Tsimshian, Coastal Indians who emigrated from Canada to Annette Island off the southeastern coast. The Tsimshian live on the only federally recognized Indian reservation in Alaska.)

The Tlingits were excellent navigators, and were known to travel more than 1,000 miles

(1,600km) south to trade with Native peoples in the Pacific Northwest. The standard of currency was "blanket value," based on blankets made of cedar bark, dog and goat hair.

The Coastal Indians had great respect for the natural world, which provided them with all they needed. They believed that fish and animals gave themselves willingly to humans, and strove to acknowledge and honor that sacrifice. A bear killed for meat might be brought to the house, greeted with a welcome speech and placed in a seat of honor for a day or two. The bones of a consumed salmon were always returned to the river where it had been caught, to allow for reincarnation.

LEFT: Native Alaskans have a long history.
RIGHT: a Tlingit woman in traditional dress.

The Coastal Indians lived in a capitalist society that allowed private ownership. Each household owned economic goods, such as weapons, utensils, and clothing – anything they had made themselves – while the clan owned religious titles and objects, for example, the right to perform a certain dance or practice a profession such as seal hunting.

In the social organization of the Tlingits and Haidas, status was determined by wealth. To maintain position, a person of power demonstrated wealth by giving a ceremonial potlatch when he would give away, destroy or invite guests to consume all his food and possessions.

Those who received goods at one potlatch had to reciprocate and better their host in the future. Another important feature of the potlatch was the recitation of family histories and bloodlines.

The Athabascans

The Athabascan Indians of Alaska's harsh Interior were hunters and inland fishermen. Most lived in small nomadic bands along the region's rivers. If game was scarce, they might travel for days without food; in deepest winter they survived temperatures of –50°F (–45°C) or less, sometimes without shelter or fire. Endurance and

Lith par Chorus.   *Lith de l.*

COASTAL CULTURE

The mild climate and plentiful resources of the Panhandle allowed the Coastal Indians to develop a rich culture over many years. They had leisure time to devote to social pastimes, travel, and trade. They enjoyed ceremony and drama, and the traditional recitation of family histories and bloodlines kept an accurate account of the generations.

The painted designs developed by the Coastal tribes feature fish and animals, often in bold patterns of black and red. They decorated their crafted goods: domestic utensils, clothing, masks, canoes, ritual objects, and the characteristic totems that marked family residences.

physical strength were prized; game was often run down on foot over difficult terrain.

Athabascans hunted salmon, hares, birds, caribou, moose, and bear with the help of snares, clubs, and bows and arrows. Because they were semi-nomadic and hunted on foot, footwear was very important, and the Athabascans designed efficient snowshoes made of birch.

Some Athabascan groups inhabited permanent winter villages and summer fishing camps. Most bands consisted of a few nuclear families, and had limited internal organization. Leadership was acquired by great warriors or hunters.

Athabascans also gave potlatches for a variety of reasons: to mark a death, to celebrate a child's first successful hunt, as a prelude to marriage.

Those who aspired to leadership were expected to host especially memorable potlatches, at which the would-be leader would give away all his possessions then prove his prowess by providing for himself and his family for an entire year without outside help.

The Aleuts

This group settled the windswept islands of the Aleutian chain 10,000 years ago. Although their location allowed them to harvest the sea's bounty, they also had to contend with harsh and often unpredictable weather, as well as earthquakes and volcanic eruptions.

skin boots. Waterproof overgarments made from the intestines of sea lions were also worn.

> The Aleuts made ingenious skis by drying hair-seal skins over wooden frames. Going uphill the hair would dig into the snow and act as a brake; downhill the hair would lie flat and the skis would slide along.

Because of a ready supply of grass in the summer, Aleut women became skillful at basketry – their baskets were so closely woven that they

Aleut fishing technology included fish spears, weirs, nets, hooks, and lines. Various darts and nets were used to obtain sea lions and sea otters. Whales were usually killed with a poisoned, stone-bladed lance. The job of women and children was to gather shellfish at low tide.

Aleut society was divided into three categories: honorables (usually respected whalers), common people and slaves. At death the body of an honorable was mummified, and sometimes slaves were killed to honor the deceased.

In winter Aleuts wore hoodless, knee-length parkas; in colder weather they added knee-length

could even hold water. Mats and some kinds of clothing were also made in this way.

The Alutiiqs

Close relatives of the Aleuts, Alutiiq peoples settled on the Alaska Peninsula, Kodiak Archipelago, and parts of the Kenai Peninsula and Prince William Sound. Sites dating back 7,000 years suggest the Alutiiqs were skilled maritime hunters and fishers. They paddled *bidarkas* while hunting sea lions, seals, sea otters, and whales. They fished for halibut, cod, and salmon and harvested sea birds and their eggs. Occasionally, they hunted bears and caribou.

The people collected all manner of items to make their clothes and build their homes and

LEFT: Natives from the Aleutian Islands.
ABOVE: young women show off their best furs.

tools: animal skins, feathers, bones, sod, drift-wood, grasses. Most houses were made of sod and dug partly into the ground; these semi-subterranean dwellings were often reinforced with whale bones or driftwood. Seal oil was used as a fuel to light their lamps.

The Eyak

The tribe's oral history suggests that the Eyak people traveled south through Alaska's Interior, then down the Copper River, to the Gulf of Alaska coast, where they finally settled. Though their language has links to both Athabascan and Tlingit, linguists believe it began to develop as a separate language some 3,500 years ago.

A relatively small group, the Eyak were some-times raided by other coastal tribes, particularly the Alutiiq residents of Prince William Sound. They had friendlier relations with the Tlingit tribes of Southeast Alaska, who had similar social structures. The two groups regularly traded goods and even intermarried. Over time, much of the Eyak population was assimilated by the Tlingit's larger and more dominant soci-ety. (Today the Eyak tribe is Alaska's smallest Native group, with a little more than 100 survi-vors.) The Eyak, like other coastal tribes, depended heavily on the ocean's abundance.

The Eskimos

Eskimos, the Native group most familiar to non-Alaskans, were originally divided into two sub-groups. The Inupiat Eskimos settled in Alaska's Arctic region, while the Yup'ik lived in the west. Life was a constant struggle against hunger and the cold. Seasonal food was stored against future shortage and for the long dark winter; and even though his own family might be wanting, a hunter always divided a fresh kill evenly throughout the community. Status was determined by hunting ability.

The Eskimos used boats called *umiaks* to hunt larger sea animals. They also used smaller, one-man craft, called kayaks. Both were made of a frame of wood covered with skins or hides.

Sleds and dog teams were used for winter travel, and in summer dogs were used as pack animals.

Eskimo villages were sited near food sources. The Arctic coast people depended on seal, walrus and whale, while the inland Eskimos – known as the Nunamiut – lived on a diet of caribou, birds and other small game animals.

Women were skilled in basketry and sewing. They stitched and fitted waterproof garments made of animal intestine and fish skins. The Eskimos' everyday clothing of trousers, boots, and coats were sewn from skins and fur, sometimes in complex geometric designs. The coats (parkas) featured an attached hood and ruff.

Eskimos are renowned for their fine carving, especially their small ivory pieces. In early times household utensils and weapons were beautifully ornamented. Using wood, bone, baleen (bony plates that line the mouths of baleen whales), walrus ivory, and fossil mammoth tusks, Eskimos crafted dishes and knives, oil lamps, small sculptures and game pieces, and goggles to protect their eyes from the glare of snow and ice. The *ulu*, or woman's knife, is found in tourist shops today and is appreciated for both its beauty and its utility.

The Russian invasion

The story of Russia's invasion of the land long inhabited by Alaska Natives begins in 1741, when two tiny vessels, the *St Peter* and the *St Paul*, captained respectively by a Dane, Vitus Bering, and a Russian, Alexei Chirikof, set sail from Russia.

When Chirikof sighted land, it was probably the west side of Prince of Wales Island in Southeast Alaska. He sent a group of men ashore in a long boat. When the first group failed to return, he sent a second. Eerily, that group also vanished. Most likely, the men drowned or were killed by Indians. Chirikof pulled anchor and moved on.

In the meantime, Bering and the crew of the *St Peter* sighted a towering peak on the Alaska mainland – Mount St Elias, which at 18,000ft (5,500 meters) is second only to Mount

McKinley among Alaska's highest mountains. Turning westward, Bering anchored his vessel off Kayak Island, in Prince William Sound, while crew members went ashore to explore and find water.

Alerted by these explorers to the riches represented by the fur-bearing marine life and mammals, Russia threw itself wholeheartedly into setting up hunting and trading outposts.

For the Native populations, the coming of the Russians was an unprecedented disaster. Rather than hunting the marine life for themselves, the Russians forced the Aleut people to do the work for them. Hostages were taken,

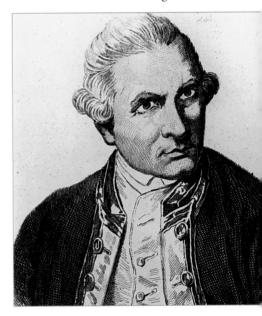

families split up, individuals forced to leave their villages and settle elsewhere. Eighty percent of the Aleut population was destroyed by violence and European diseases, against which they had no defenses, during the first two generations of Russian contact.

Other Europeans

About this time, the British were continuing their search for the Northwest Passage, the fabled water route between the Atlantic and the Pacific. In 1778 Captain James Cook sailed north from Vancouver Island, through the Inside Passage and then along the Gulf Coast, to the Aleutians. Along the way, he explored a narrow embayment that would later be given

---

LEFT: traditional Native headdresses.
RIGHT: Captain James Cook, who arrived in 1778.

his name: Cook Inlet. The Russians tried to impress him with the extent of their control over the region, but Cook saw how tenuous was the position of this ragtag group of hunters and traders stationed 3,000 miles (4,800km) from home.

Although Cook died in Hawaii after visiting Alaska, his crew continued on to Canton, China, where they sold their Alaskan sea otter pelts for outlandishly high prices. Britain became interested and increased its sailings along the northwest coast. Then came the Spanish, already well established on the coast of California, who founded the towns of Valdez and Cordova.

Gaining a foothold

The Russians were determined to dig in and keep Alaska's fur wealth for themselves. One particularly ruthless individual, Grigor Ivanovich Shelikof, arrived in Three Saints Bay on Kodiak Island in 1784 with two ships, the *Three Saints* and the *St Simon*. Fearing the foreigners, the island's Alutiiq residents tried to drive off the Russians, but failed. Shelikof responded by killing hundreds and taking hostages to enforce the obedience of the rest.

Having established his authority on Kodiak Island, Shelikof founded the first permanent Russian settlement in Alaska on the island's Three Saints Bay, built a school to teach the Natives to read and write Russian, and introduced the Russian Orthodox religion.

In 1790, Shelikof, back in Russia, hired Alexander Baranov to manage his Alaskan fur enterprise. Baranov moved the colony to the northeast end of Kodiak Island, where timber was available: the site is now the city of Kodiak. Russian members of the colony took Alutiiq wives and started families whose names survive today.

Colonial powers

The Hudson's Bay Company, formed by the British in 1821, set up a post on the southern edge of Russian America in 1833. The British firm, which was more organized and better run than the Russian, began siphoning off trade. Baranov began to depend heavily on American supply ships, since they came much more frequently than Russian ones. Also, Americans could sell furs in Canton (then closed to the Russians).

The downside of the US presence was that

THE RISE AND FALL OF RUSSIA'S TRADE

In 1795, Alexander Baranof, concerned by the presence of non-Russian Europeans trading with Natives in southeast Alaska, established Mikhailovsk 6 miles (10km) north of present-day Sitka, on land he bought from the Tlingits. For a while, the Russians and Tlingits peacefully co-existed. But in 1802, while Baranof was away, Tlingits from a neighboring settlement attacked and destroyed Mikhailovsk. Intent on revenge, Baranof returned in 1804 with a Russian warship and razed the Tlingit village. He then built the settlement of New Archangel, which became the capital of Russian America.

Meanwhile, as Baranof secured the Russians' physical presence in Alaska, back in Russia the Shelikof family continued to seek control of Alaska's fur trade. In 1799, Shelikof's son-in-law, Nikolay Petrovich Rezanov, had acquired a monopoly on the American fur trade from Tsar Paul I. Rezanov then formed the Russian-American Company. As part of the deal, the Tsar expected the company first to establish new settlements in Alaska and then carry out an expanded colonization program.

By 1804, Alexander Baranof had consolidated the company's hold on fur trade activities in the Americas. But despite all these efforts, the Russians never fully colonized Alaska; for the most part they clung to the coast, shunning the rugged inland. By the 1830s their monopoly on trade in the region was weak enough to allow in the Hudson's Bay Company.

American hunters and trappers encroached on territory the Russians considered theirs. In 1812 a settlement was reached giving the Russians exclusive rights to the fur trade above 55°N latitude, the Americans to that below. The agreement didn't settle matters, however, and with Baranov's retirement in 1818 the Russian hold on Alaska was further weakened.

When the Russian-American Company's charter was renewed in 1821, it stipulated that the chief managers from then on be naval officers. But most naval officers did not have any experience in the fur trade, so the company suffered under a string of incompetent "governors."

Although the mid-1800s were not a good time for the Russians in Alaska, for those coastal Alaska Natives who had survived contact – primarily the Aleuts, Alutiiqs and Tlingits – conditions improved, if only slightly.

The Tlingits were never conquered, and continued to wage guerrilla warfare on the Russians into the 1850s. The Aleuts, many of whom had been removed from their home islands and sent as far south as California to hunt sea otter for the Russians, continued to decline in population during the 1840s. For them, the naval officers of the Russian-American Company were a blessing: they established schools and hospitals for the

The second charter also tried to cut off all contact with foreigners, especially the competitive Americans. But this strategy backfired, since the Russian colony had become used to relying on American supply ships, and the United States had become a valued customer for furs. Eventually the Russian-American Company entered into an agreement with the Hudson's Bay Company, which gave the British rights to sail through Russian territory. Pacts were also signed in the mid-1820s that allowed both British and US vessels to land at Russian ports.

LEFT: Grigor Ivanovich Shelikof, who founded the first permanent Russian settlement in Alaska.
ABOVE: William Seward (seated) buying for the US.

Aleuts, and gave them jobs. Russian Orthodox clergy moved into the Aleutian Islands. Slowly, the Aleut population began to increase.

An American buy-out

By the 1860s the Russians were considering ridding themselves of Russian America. Overhunting had severely reduced the fur-bearing animal population, and the difficulties of supplying and protecting such a distant colony caused interest to wane.

A Russian emissary approached the US Secretary of State, William Henry Seward, about a possible sale, and in 1867 the US Congress, at Seward's urging, agreed to buy Russian America for $7.2 million – just under 2 cents an acre. ❑

THE MAKING OF MODERN ALASKA

People regarded the new possession as a wild land,
producing nothing but furs, until the discovery of
gold in 1896 made the world sit up and take notice.
In the 20th century the discovery of oil would
change Alaska's fortunes yet again

America wasn't sure what, exactly, it had acquired when it bought Alaska. The interior had been little touched by the Russians, who had stayed in the coastal areas. US exploration, too, had been limited. In 1865, Western Union had decided to lay a telegraph line through Alaska across the Bering Strait to Siberia, where it would connect with an Asian line. William H. Dall took charge of the Western Union expedition, conducting the first scientific studies of the region and producing the first map of the entire Yukon River.

That same year (1866), workers finally succeeded in laying an Atlantic undersea telegraph cable, and the Alaskan overland project was abandoned. Dall returned to Alaska many times, recording many geographical features. A breed of sheep and a type of porpoise bear his name.

The Alaska Commercial Company also contributed to the growing exploration of Alaska in the last decades of the 1800s, building trading posts along the Interior's many rivers. Small parties of trappers and traders entered the Interior.

1885 Allen and four others left the Gulf of Alaska, followed the Copper River to its headwaters, crossed the Alaska range and traveled down the Tanana River to the Yukon, portaged to the Kanuti and then the Koyukuk rivers. Allen went up the Koyukuk, then back down to the Yukon, crossed over to the coastal village of Unalakleet, and then made his way to Saint Michael. In all, his team explored about 1,500 miles (2,400km) of Interior Alaska.

Whether the US knew what it had or not, the territory still needed to be governed. Unfortunately, back in Washington, DC, legislators had their hands full with post-Civil War reconstruction issues. As a result, a US Army officer, General Jefferson C. Davis, was put in charge.

> *Many Americans thought that even at its low purchase price, the territory of Alaska was a waste of money, and initially the Natives were allowed to administer their own affairs.*

Exploring the Interior

Army officers sometimes undertook their own explorations. In a four-month journey, Lt Frederick Schwatka and his party rafted the Yukon from Lake Lindeman in Canada to Saint Michael near the river's mouth on the Bering Sea. Lt Henry T. Allen made an even more remarkable journey. In

The gold strike

It was the discovery of gold in the Yukon in 1896 that finally made the world sit up and take notice of America's northern possession. A wave of fortune hunters clamored for passage to the Klondike.

The Klondike was in Canada's Yukon Territory, not in Alaska, but the easiest route was by ship to Skagway, in Southeast Alaska. Once in Skagway, miners had the choice of two brutal passes across the mountains to the Yukon gold fields: White Pass, also called Dead Horse Trail, because it was littered with corpses of pack animals, or the Chilkoot Trail, a route used by Natives.

1901 drew to a close, Pedro and his partner prepared to embark on a 165-mile (265km) walk to Circle City for supplies. Plans changed when the men met E.T. Barnette, who had been forced to disembark from the steamer *Lavelle Young* *(see panel below)* with his entire load of supplies – some of which he was happy to sell to Pedro.

It was a match made in heaven: Pedro and his partner were delighted to be spared the long walk to Circle City, and Barnette was equally delighted to see his first customers walking out of the wilderness. Replenished with supplies, Pedro resumed prospecting and finally struck gold in July 1902. Shortly afterwards Barnette's

Alaska, in fact, had plenty of gold of its own, and many who didn't make their fortunes in the Klondike strike came back to look for it. An earlier strike had established Juneau in Southeast Alaska, and gold was found in Nome in 1899. A combination of fortune and misfortune led to a gold strike and the birth of Fairbanks in the early 1900s. For several years a prospector called Felix Pedro had been searching the Tanana Hills of Alaska's Interior for a gold-rich creek he had stumbled upon years earlier but had been forced to abandon. As the summer of

LEFT: troughs were constructed to separate gold from soil during the Klondike Gold Rush.
ABOVE: the Commerce Saloon in Nome, *c.*1900.

BARNETTE'S GAMBLE

In 1901 E.T. Barnette had been trying to get thousands of dollars' worth of supplies up the Tanana River to Tanana Crossing, a point on the proposed Valdez-to-Eagle trade route. He convinced the captain of the steamer *Lavelle Young* to take him, his wife, his partner and the supplies to where the Chena River entered the Tanana.

The captain agreed to take Barnette farther if he could work the *Lavelle Young* through the shallow river channel, but if not the party would be put ashore. The channel proved impassable, and that was how Barnette ended up on a slough off the main Tanana River.

outpost was transformed into a booming town. Named Fairbanks in honor of a US senator, the settlement grew as more miners and new businesses arrived. Fairbanks had shanties on the fringes, but the center offered many of the conveniences to be found in more "civilized" settings. Traffic came and went on the river, and an overland route to Valdez cut days off a trip to the Lower 48.

Eventually the Tanana Mining District became a huge gold producer, and a powerful magnet for Americans and Europeans alike.

Of course, not everyone in Alaska was a gold miner. Many more found ways to profit from

The coming of canneries

The more traditional ways of life – fishing, in particular – also provided a livelihood for many Alaskans, particularly after canning was introduced. In 1878 the first two canneries were built in Southeast Alaska. In 1883 the Arctic Pack Company established a cannery at Nushagak Bay in Southwest Alaska, where they were able to exploit the immense runs of salmon.

Two years later the Alaska Packing Company opened a cannery across the bay, and by 1908, 10 canneries ringed Nushagak Bay. Kodiak's first canneries were built in the late 1800s, when word of phenomenal fish runs became widespread.

the gold rushes without actually panning for the metal themselves. At Ruby Creek, for example, gold strikes in 1907 and 1910 brought the predictable rush of miners to the area, giving birth to the town of Ruby. Newcomers arrived, some by small riverboats, others on large paddlewheelers. The steamers required large quantities of wood to keep them moving, and locals along the river bank were only too happy to sell them the wood.

Ruby grew from a tent city in 1911 to a bustling river port. With running water in summer, a theater, shops and cafés, it sought to provide all the amenities of its rival, Fairbanks. By 1917, at the height of the rush, creeks south of Ruby had yielded $875,000 worth of gold.

By the turn of the 20th century, commercial fishing had gained a foothold in the Aleutian Islands. But, before long, overhunting became a serious threat (*see panel on opposite page*).

World War II

On June 3, 1942, the Japanese launched an air attack on Dutch Harbor, a US naval base on Unalaska Island, in the Aleutians. US forces held off the planes, and the base survived this attack, and a second one, with minor damage. But on June 7 the Japanese landed on the islands of Kiska and Attu, overwhelming Attu

ABOVE: the Newens & Glandon grocery store, Nome.
RIGHT: the Flying Tiger, used in Alaska in World War II.

villagers. The villagers were taken to Japan and interned for the rest of the war. Aleuts from the Pribilofs and Aleutian villages were forcibly evacuated by the United States to Southeast Alaska, where they too were interned.

In the fall of 1942, the US Navy began constructing a base on Adak, and on May 11, 1943, American troops landed on Attu, determined to retake the island. The bloody battle wore on for more than two weeks. The Japanese, who had no hope of rescue because their fleet of transport submarines had been turned back by US destroyers, fought to the last man.

The end finally came on May 29 when the Americans repelled a banzai charge. Some Japanese remained in hiding on the small island months after their defeat. When discovered, they killed themselves rather than surrender.

The taking of Attu was the second bloodiest battle of the Pacific theater; only Iwo Jima was more costly in terms of human lives. The US then bombed the other occupied island, Kiska. But the Japanese, under cover of thick Aleutian fog, escaped via transport ships. After the war, the Native Attuans who had survived internment in Japan were resettled to Atka by the federal government, which considered their home villages too remote to defend.

World War II affected Alaska in unexpected ways. One was the construction of the Alaska–Canada Military Highway (Alcan), which was completed in 1942 at great speed (nine months) and great cost ($20 million) to form an overland supply route to America's "last frontier" – and northwesternmost line of defense. Running from Great Falls, Montana, to Fairbanks, the

1,420-mile (2,280km) road – the work of 9,000 soldiers and 12,000 civilians – was the first stable link between Alaska and the rest of America.

New military bases also contributed to the growth of some cities. Anchorage almost doubled in size, from 4,200 people in 1940 to 8,000 in 1945. And two other catalysts were just around the corner: statehood and oil.

The push for statehood

After its purchase by the US in 1867 Alaska was governed by the US Army, the US Treasury Department and the US Navy. Finally, in 1884, the federal government declared the territory

THE THREAT FROM OVERHUNTING

Whaling, a traditional marine occupation, continued well into the 20th century with no regard for overhunting. Bowhead whales, the awesome behemoths of northern seas, attracted a parade of whale hunters to the high Arctic. Following routes they had used since the end of the Pleistocene Age, the bowheads migrated twice yearly through the Bering Strait on their run from the southwestern Bering Sea to summer feeding areas in the Beaufort Sea. Weighing a ton per foot and reaching lengths of 60ft (18 meters), bowheads carry huge quantities of oil in their tissue.

Whalers seeking the oil pursued the bowhead to the edge of extinction, but their numbers have now recov-

ered to the point that Native whale hunters are able to harvest a limited number each year for subsistence purposes without affecting the population.

The American fishing, canning and whaling operations, as well as walrus hunting, were as unchecked as the Russians' hunting. The Aleuts soon suffered severe problems due to the depletion of the fur seals and sea otters which they needed for survival. As well as requiring the flesh for food, they also used seal skins to cover their boats, without which they couldn't hunt. The American newcomers also expanded into Interior and Arctic Alaska, exploiting the fur-bearers, fish and other game on which Natives depended.

the District of Alaska, and a civil government was appointed by President Chester Arthur.

By the turn of the 20th century, a movement pushing for Alaska statehood had begun. But in the Lower 48, legislators were worried that Alaska's population was too sparse, its location too distant and isolated, and its economy too unstable for the territory to become a state.

World War II and the Japanese invasion of Attu and Kiska highlighted Alaska's strategic importance, and the issue of statehood was taken more seriously. Anticipating their home would eventually become a state, residents organized a constitutional convention in 1955.

After 75 days, the participants drafted and approved a 14,400-word document that the National Municipal League called "one of the best, if not the best, state constitutions ever." That same year, a poll showed that 82 percent of Americans favored Alaska's becoming a state.

The discovery of oil at Swanson River on the Kenai Peninsula in 1957 helped the statehood movement, because it made Alaska less dependent on federal assistance. On January 3, 1959, President Dwight D. Eisenhower formally admitted Alaska to the union as the 49th state. William A. Egan was sworn in as the first governor, and Juneau continued to be the capital.

Disaster strikes

It was not long before the young state underwent its first trial. On March 27, 1964, the Good Friday earthquake struck Southcentral Alaska, churning the earth for four minutes. At an estimated 8.7 on the Richter scale – later revised upward to 9.2, under the current scale used to measure earthquake intensities – the Good Friday quake is the most powerful ever recorded in North America. The earthquake and its aftermath killed 131 people, including 115 Alaskans; most were drowned by the tidal waves (tsunamis) that tore apart the towns of Valdez and Chenega (*see panel below*).

Oil and land

Despite the extent of the catastrophe, Alaskans rebuilt many of the devastated communities. Four years later, the state experienced a different sort of upheaval. In the mid-1960s Alaska Natives had begun participating in state and

HOW THE 1964 EARTHQUAKE WREAKED HAVOC

Throughout the Prince William Sound region towns and ports were destroyed, land uplifted or shoved downward, islands tilted. The uplift destroyed salmon streams, as the fish could no longer negotiate waterfalls and other barriers to reach their spawning grounds. Ports at Valdez and Cordova were beyond repair – what land and mud slides didn't claim, ensuing fires did.

At Valdez, an Alaska Steamship Company ship was lifted by a huge wave over the docks and out to sea. Amazingly, most hands survived. Witnesses on shore swore that at one point they could see daylight all the way under the ship. There were very few witnesses, however, because most of those who had been waiting on the

dockside to greet the ship were swept to their deaths.

Along Turnagain Arm, off Cook Inlet, the incoming water destroyed trees and caused cabins to sink into the mud. In Anchorage, huge chunks of road asphalt piled on top of each other like shingles and many buildings were destroyed. At Seldovia, near the junction of Kachemak Bay and Cook Inlet, fish processing facilities and an active fishing fleet were laid waste, along with Seldovia's harbor.

On Kodiak, a tidal wave wiped out the villages of Afognak, Old Harbor and Kaguyak, and damaged other communities. Seward, a thriving port town at the southern terminus of the Alaska Railroad, also lost its harbor.

local government and flexing their electoral muscles. More than 200 years after the arrival of

> *The 1971 settlement officially compensated Natives for the invasion of their lands. It also opened the way for all Alaskans to profit from the state's tremendous natural resource – oil.*

the first Europeans, Natives from all ethnic groups united to claim title to the lands wrested from them. The government responded slowly until, in 1968, the Atlantic-Richfield Company

struct the pipeline, which would cross lands involved in the Native land claims dispute, depended on those claims being settled.

With major petro dollars on the line, there was new urgency for an agreement, and in 1971 the Alaska Native Claims Settlement Act (ANCSA) was signed, under which the indigenous peoples relinquished aboriginal claims to their lands. In return they received title to 44 million acres (nearly 18 million hectares) of land and were paid $963 million. The land and money were divided among regional, urban and village corporations. Some have handled their funds wisely; others have not.

discovered oil at Prudhoe Bay, and catapulted the ownership issue into the headlines.

Prudhoe Bay is on Alaska's Arctic coast, along the Beaufort Sea. Drilling at such a remote location would be difficult enough – but transporting the resulting crude to refineries in the Lower 48 seemed impossible. The answer seemed to be to build a pipeline to carry the oil hundreds of miles to the port of Valdez (rebuilt a few miles from the ruins of the previous town). At Valdez the oil would be loaded onto tanker ships and sent by water to the Lower 48. The plan was approved – but a permit to con-

LEFT: a Native Alaskan bark house.
ABOVE: Anchorage after the 1964 earthquake.

The pipeline

After ANCSA was signed, there remained the challenge of building a pipeline that would stretch from Arctic Alaska to Valdez. Between the two points were three mountain ranges, active fault lines, miles and miles of unstable *muskeg* (boggy ground underlain with permafrost) and the migration paths of wildlife, particularly caribou. The pipeline was designed with all these factors in mind. To counteract the unstable ground and allow animal crossings, half the 800-mile (1,280km) pipeline is elevated on supports. The supports hold the pipe – and its cargo of hot oil – high enough to keep it from melting the permafrost and destroying the natural terrain. To help the pipeline survive an earthquake, it was laid out in a zigzag pattern, so that it would roll with the earth instead of breaking up. That construction was tested on November 3, 2002, when a magnitude 7.9 quake struck Alaska and the ground ruptured along a fault that ran beneath the pipeline. Many of the supports collapsed and the pipeline was temporarily shut down, but it withstood fierce shaking without any serious damage or leakage of oil.

The first oil arrived at Valdez in 1977. The cost of the pipeline and related projects, including the tanker terminal at Valdez, 12 pumping stations and the Yukon River Bridge, was $8 billion.

against inflation; and it provides funds to the state legislature.

The fund, worth nearly $30 billion, is the largest pool of public money in the US, and a major source of income to Alaska's state government. Since 1993, the fund has produced more revenue than the Prudhoe Bay oil fields, where production has halved from its peak in the late 1980s. Prudhoe Bay oil may dry up, but the fund should continue to benefit the state.

Tourism and the environment

In the second half of the 20th century, Alaska discovered another important source of reve-

During the years of pipeline construction, Anchorage and Fairbanks blossomed into bright, modern cities. As the oil bonanza took shape, per capita incomes rose throughout the state, with virtually every community benefitting. State leaders were determined that this boom would not end like the fur and gold booms – in an economic bust as soon as the resource had disappeared.

To this end, the Alaska Permanent Fund was created in 1976. Into the fund is deposited 25 percent of all mineral lease proceeds (including oil and gas). Income from the fund is divided in three ways: it pays annual dividends to all residents who apply and qualify; it adds money to the principal account to hedge

nue. Although visitors had been lured north by Alaska's natural wonders since at least the late 19th century, tourism got a big boost after World War II when men stationed in the region returned home praising its natural splendor. The Alcan Highway, built during the war, and the Alaska Marine Highway System, completed in 1963, made the state more accessible than before.

Tourism is now very big business in Alaska: more than 1½ million people visit the state every year. Once there, they flock to the top

ABOVE: pipeline technology in Alaska led the world.
RIGHT: tourists cruise into Misty Fiords.
FAR RIGHT: cleaning up the mess after an oil spill.

attractions: Denali National Park, Katmai, Glacier Bay, and other destinations within the Inside Passage, and the Kenai Peninsula. Wildlife watching is a main attraction, although only a small proportion of visitors go deep into the wilderness.

With tourism ever more vital to the economy, environmentalism has also risen in importance *(see page 59)*. Alaskans are working to balance the needs of their remarkable land with the needs of its residents. Much is already well protected – the Alaska National Interest Lands Conservation Act (ANILCA) of 1980 added 53.7 million acres (22 million hectares) to the national wildlife refuge system, parts of 25 rivers to the national wild and scenic rivers system, 3.3 million acres (1.3 million hectares) to national forest lands, and 43.6 million acres (17.5 million hectares) to national park land. As a result of the lands act, Alaska now contains two-thirds of all American national parklands.

The oil spill

Nothing better illustrates Alaska's struggle to protect the environment, and to benefit from the state's natural resources, than the *Exxon Valdez* disaster. The huge tanker ran aground on March 24 1989, in Prince William Sound,

THE AFTERMATH OF THE OIL SPILL

During the summer of 1989, 12,000 workers descended on the soiled shores of the sound. They bulldozed blackened beaches, sucked up petroleum blobs with vacuum devices, blasted sand with hot water, polished rocks by hand, raked up oily seaweed, and sprayed fertilizer to aid the growth of oil-eating microbes.

For Alaska's tourism industry, the *Exxon Valdez* spill strained an already uneasy relationship with the state's petroleum interests. Not only did it generate horrendous international publicity but the influx of clean-up workers filled to capacity virtually every hotel and campsite in the Valdez area – which was bad news for the tourist industry, but very good for the Valdez economy.

Exxon continued its clean-up efforts into the early 1990s. In some areas, such as Smith Island, an oil-soaked wasteland after the spill, winter storms did more to wash the shore clean than any human efforts.

Government studies show the oil and the cleaning process itself caused long-term harm to the ecology of the Sound, interfering with the reproduction of birds and animals in ways that still aren't fully understood. Some fishermen, particularly those dependent on shellfish, worry about hard-to-measure impacts on their catch. Prince William Sound has largely bounced back, but some species still haven't recovered and scientists dispute the extent of the recovery.

releasing 11 million gallons (42 million liters) of crude oil into the water. The oil eventually spread along 1,100 miles (1,760km) of formerly pristine shoreline.

It was an ecological disaster of unprecedented proportions *(see panel on page 55)*. At least 300,000 sea birds, 2,000 otters and countless other marine animals died as a result of the spill. Exxon spent $2 billion on cleaning up in the first year alone.

Today's issues

One of the biggest changes in Alaska recently has been the economy's shift from one almost

entirely dependent on resource extraction (and government employment) to a "new economy" that depends much more heavily on the service

> *The past two decades have seen a decline in Alaska's traditional industries, like oil, timber and commercial fishing, and a search for new sources of revenue from service industries such as tourism.*

industries, from tourism to shopping. Oil fields on Alaska's North Slope continue to be the primary fuel that drives Alaska's economy and state government programs, but even oil production has slipped dramatically, to half of what it was during Prudhoe Bay's late 1980s peak. The timber and commercial fisheries industries have suffered even greater losses.

Centered in the Panhandle's Tongass National Forest, Alaska's timber industry has been on the skids since the 1980s; its two largest mills (one in Ketchikan, the other in Sitka) shut down in the 1990s due to changing Forest Service policies and decreased demand for wood pulp, causing hardships for many Southeast Alaska communities. Nowadays timber cutting and milling is done on a much smaller scale, but the widespread economic crisis predicted by many in the timber industry hasn't been realized, largely because there's been something of a tourism boom in the Panhandle.

Increased numbers of cruise ships travel the Inside Passage, bringing thousands of visitors to spend money in Southeast communities.

THE BRIDGES THAT WENT NOWHERE

In Alaska, the saying goes, corruption flows like crude oil. Federal conspiracy, bribery, tax evasion, influence-peddling, and self-dealing… all these charges and more have been leveled against Alaska's senators, congressmen and government officials, and the frequency of scandals encourage Senate committees in faraway Washington, DC, to regard it as one of the most ethically challenged states.

At the heart of many federal investigations have been the close ties between Alaska lawmakers and the powerful oil industry. Oil money doesn't talk, say cynics, it shouts. But the state's relatively small population and its remoteness from the rest of the nation can all too easily tempt vote-hungry politicians into all manner of pork-barrel spending. One notorious example was the 2005 saga of the "bridge to nowhere," a proposed $230 million span higher than the Brooklyn Bridge intended to connect Ketchikan (population 8,900) with Gravina Island (population 50). The 15- to 30-minute wait for the ferry was inconvenient, argued local advocates, and it cost too much ($6 per car). A second, similarly priced proposal envisaged a bridge connecting Anchorage to the town of Knik (population 22).

Congress torpedoed both schemes, though it didn't reduce the amount of money allocated to Alaska in the particular appropriations bill.

Smaller ecotour businesses are also thriving in some portions of the region. Much of the area's fishing industry, however, has been struggling to stay in business.

Hard times for fishermen

Commercial fishing has been steadily declining – in some areas, precipitously – since the early 1990s. The fisheries most in trouble are those that harvest salmon. Declining numbers of fish, particularly in western Alaska waters, have severely hurt rural residents who depend on commercial (and in some cases, subsistence) fishing for their livelihood. Several years

fishing fleet has had some disastrous seasons.

While salmon fishermen have struggled, commercial fishermen who ply the Gulf of Alaska and Bering Sea for bottomfish have so far continued to thrive. The North Pacific and Bering Sea bottomfish fleet continues to be the nation's richest. But many of the boat owners and fish processors are non-residents, who live in Washington and Oregon. To ensure that more of the fisheries' profits remain in Alaska, the federal agency that oversees the bottomfish industry has enacted a plan whereby Alaskan communities share a percentage of the earnings.

in a row, the governor declared a state of emergency for parts of the state, because the salmon returns were so poor that people in many villages didn't earn enough money for necessities such as food and fuel.

Some areas, most notably Bristol Bay, have been hard hit by a double whammy: smaller numbers of fish and lower prices, brought on by a worldwide glut of salmon attributed to the rise of farmed salmon in countries like Chile, Canada, and Norway. Though Bristol Bay remains Alaska's biggest salmon fishery, its

LEFT: salmon fishermen have experienced hard times.
ABOVE: horse and buggy tours of Skagway indicate the growing importance of tourism in the state.

The retail chains arrive

Though slowed somewhat by the September 11, 2001 terrorist attacks on the United States, Alaska's tourism industry continues to play an important and ever-enlarging role in the state's economy. Also playing an expanded role are national chains: huge "box stores" have been built in communities from the Panhandle to the Interior, from WalMart to Office Max, Barnes & Noble to Best Buy. New restaurants and hotel chains have been popping up, particularly in Alaska's urban centers. A high and steadily growing percentage of people now work in the tourism and retail industries, where the jobs don't pay nearly as well as those in resource extraction.

Alaska's Native culture, too, has undergone some major changes. There's been a strong push for tribal sovereignty and both the federal and state governments have recognized a limited authority of tribal governments in Alaska's Native communities. Alaska's Native peoples continue to deal with the challenge of living "in two worlds" – their traditional culture, which stretches back generations, and the modern, Western culture that has so greatly influenced Native communities throughout the state, in ways that have been both helpful and harmful. Few Native Alaskans would choose to return to a life without electricity, modern plumbing, snowmobiles, computers, and TV; but technological advances have also disrupted the family and community lives in many villages and Native leaders are fervently seeking a way to balance old and new.

A cultural revival begun in the late 20th century has continued to flourish as more and more people celebrate their roots and long-lived cultural values, celebrations and art, from dancing to mask making and storytelling.

A cultural clash

One tradition that Native tribes continue to fight for is subsistence. Though it centers on the harvest of animals and plants, subsistence is about more than hunting, fishing, and gathering; it's a way of life that has spiritual and emotional importance to Native residents, particularly in rural areas beyond the road system. For more than 15 years, there's been a cultural clash over Native "subsistence rights." Some Alaskans – mostly white, urban sportsmen – insist that all residents must have equal access to fish and wildlife resources. However, most Alaskans – both Native and non-Native, urban and rural – agree that some sort of subsistence priority must be recognized, if the Native culture is to thrive.

There's been a strong push to change the Alaska constitution, so that it guarantees a rural subsistence preference, but the Alaska Legislature has so far resisted enacting legislation that would allow a statewide vote. The federal government, meanwhile, has recognized a rural subsistence priority since the passage of ANILCA in 1980. Because the policies differ, the US government took over fish and wildlife management on Alaska's federally managed lands and waters during the 1990s. This dual management system is unique to Alaska and complicates hunting and fishing regulations throughout the state.

Most Alaskans seek to heal urban vs. rural and Native vs. non-Native tensions. They also seek to find new sources of revenue to improve their lifestyles, while also protecting the magnificent wildness and scenic splendor that makes Alaska such a unique place to live in – and to visit. ❑

A YOUNG STATE

Alaska has a particular appeal for young people. Many of them have moved here from outside, probably because the state attracts those who both like and can cope with an active and not always easy life. According to the 2000 census, the average age of the population was 32.4.

Although the population is increasing rapidly, there are only about 664,000 permanent residents – very low compared with most other states in the union. Most of them live in urban areas, and more than half live in and around Anchorage.

According to the most recent estimates, Alaska Natives make up 12 percent of the population.

ABOVE LEFT: Mina Weyliouanna holds a portrait of her grandparents by the family home collapsed by melting permafrost. Climate change has forced villagers to abandon Shishmaref, in the far north.

Economy and Ecology

Almost every dollar that flows through Alaska's economy originates from its land or water – or from government expenditures.

Natural resources are the primary fuels that drive Alaska's economy. The oil and mining industries extract vast wealth from under the ground, fishermen harvest much of the nation's seafood from the water, and loggers and tourism operators exploit the landscape itself.

Oil is by far the largest industry; fishing is second and employs more people, but has suffered a downturn, largely because of competition from fish-farming operations in other parts of the world. Tourism also is a big employer. The logging industry has shrunk under the pressure of new environmental concerns. The government employs more people than any other industry, and state government is largely funded by oil. The service industry employs a sizeable portion of Alaska's workers.

Oil and the environment

It's not surprising that most Alaskans support more resource development. Every new oil field discovered on the North Slope creates jobs and new revenue that affect every citizen. When the salmon season is good, coastal towns thrive. And the flow of summer visitors employs thousands.

But many Alaskans also advocate environmental protection, and not only because they tend to be young and to spend time outdoors enjoying the beauty of the place. Fishermen know that oil spills damage the waters from which they draw their livelihood. Tourism operators know their clients aren't interested in visiting areas that have been clear-cut for logging (poor logging techniques can also threaten salmon-spawning streams).

When, in 1989, the tanker *Exxon Valdez* spilled 11 million gallons (42 million liters) of crude oil in Prince William Sound, both industries worked as hard to clean up the image of their products as Exxon did to scrape the oil off the shore *(see page 55)*. The fishing industry has largely recovered, but some species – herring and pink salmon, for instance – have not fully rebounded. Visitors to the Sound still see abundant wildlife, but again there's

RIGHT: the Prudhoe Bay oil refinery.

evidence that some species, including orcas, have not yet recovered from the spill's toxic effects.

Large-scale logging has altered the environment in ways that affect other industries. Besides the ruined vistas, fishermen worry about logging near streams, which can harm or even destroy the habitat critical to spawning salmon and other fish.

Yet tourism and fishing, if unchecked, can harm the environment as well. In Glacier Bay National Park, environmental groups sued the National Park Service to stop it granting more permits for cruise ships to enter the bay, contending that they are scaring away the humpback whales. Cruise ship companies have also drawn criticism – and large fines – for

polluting the waters and air in southeast Alaska. There are worries about noisy helicopter sightseeing in wilderness areas, a proposal for a new road in Denali National Park, and large-scale tourism.

As for fishing, environmentalists blame large-scale factory trawlers operating in the Bering Sea for reducing marine mammal populations by taking too many fish from the food chain. There are also concerns that bottomfishing trawlers wreak havoc on the ocean bottom with their gear.

Only a fraction of 1 percent of Alaska's landmass is privately owned. The federal government controls more than half, and the state government about a third. It is therefore government's job to ensure that Alaska's lands, waters, and air are protected, even as companies exploit its natural resources. ❑

VISITING ALASKA'S NATIVES

Tourists are a useful source of income as they experience
Alaskan Native cultures, but the people don't want
to be treated simply as a visitor attraction

Many Native Alaskans live a subsistence lifestyle that still depends upon collecting meat and fish during the abundant summer months and preparing it for storage to sustain them over the long winter. In the southern part of the state, Natives depend upon deer, salmon and other food from the sea. In the Interior, the Athabascans fish on the rivers and hunt caribou, moose, black bears, and waterfowl. Farther north, Eskimos hunt whales and seals, caribou and polar bears, geese and seabirds.

Villages welcome visitors

An international fascination with indigenous people has spread to Alaska, and village residents from Saxman Native Village in Southeast Alaska to Gambell on St Lawrence Island in the Bering Sea are cautiously opening their doors to visitors. Visiting an Alaska Native village can be a great adventure for people who are both flexible and open-minded. Organized tours are now offered to more than a dozen villages.

Until the early 1990s, about the only outsiders who spent any time in villages were friends, relatives, healthcare workers or teachers. Now the list is growing.

In these encounters, both the visitors and the visited learn from each other. Visitors learn how Natives live in various parts of the state and

along the way they discard stereotypes about igloos, wardrobes of animal skins and rubbing noses. "Visitors come with an expectation that they're going to go back in time," says the Alaska Native Tourism Council, an organization formed in 1992 to promote rural tourism and help Native groups who operate tours. "They find out that visually it's very familiar in terms of clothing – people wearing Nike tennis shoes – but the culture and life of the people haven't changed a lot. Value systems are still deeply rooted in the past and in their culture."

In recent years, as an increasing number of young people leave villages for life in the cities, Natives have worked to keep their culture and

PRECEDING PAGES: Yup'ik Natives ice fishing.
LEFT: an Inupiat walrus-skin blanket toss to celebrate a good spring whaling season.
RIGHT: Alaskan Native woman, Chena Indian village.

their language alive. Tourism now provides an impetus for them to do so. Young Natives learn the dances and stories of old, passing them on to their own children and to the rest of the world.

Selling ancient rights

The 20th century brought numerous changes to the Native communities. Thirteen regional, four urban and 200 Native village corporations were formed to manage money and land received from the government as a result of the 1971 Alaska Native Claims Settlement Act. The measure approved the transfer of 44 million acres (nearly 18 million hectares) and $963 mil-

lion to corporations in exchange for giving up their aboriginal rights to the land.

Some of these corporations have been phenomenally successful, parlaying the oil, mineral and other natural resource wealth of their lands into large annual dividends for members. Others made bad investments, and some were tainted by corruption. There has been increased debate as to whether the corporations serve the best interests of Alaska's Native peoples.

Although snow-machines have largely replaced sled dog teams as a means of winter travel and boats with motors are preferred to the skin boats that their ancestors used for fish-

THE BEST WAY TO VIEW NATIVE VILLAGES

Contact the village council before you show up, to make sure that residents are happy to see visitors, or find a tour operator that includes Native villages on its itineraries. One company that arranges customized tours around the state is Explore Tours, 1415 East Tudor Road, Anchorage, AK 99507, tel: 907-786-0192 or 800-523-7405; www.explore tours.com. In the Southeast, Keet Gooshi Tours combines wildlife viewing along the Chilkat Trail and a visit to a traditional Tlingit village; PO Box 997, Haines, AK 99827, tel: 907-766-2168 or 877-776-2168; www.keetgooshi.com.

The Northern Alaska Tour Company does ecotours that emphasize both natural and Native cultural history; PO Box 82991-W, Fairbanks, AK, 99708, tel: 907-474-8600 or 800-

474-1986; www.northernalaska.com. Another good resource is the book Nae'da (meaning "Our friends"), which includes contact information for all of the state's village tribal councils; for more information, go to www.theciri foundation.org/publications.

Some residents worry about tourists walking into their houses unannounced, as if they were strolling into a Disneyland attraction, or indiscriminately snapping photographs. It is common courtesy to ask before taking pictures of people. Some villages, such as Gambell, prefer that you ask before taking any photographs at all. And the travel brochure publicizing Arctic Village specifically prohibits the use of video cameras.

ing and hunting, Natives still follow traditional ways. Now, however, they must have money to buy gasoline for their snow-machines and bullets for their guns. Their subsistence way of life requires modern tools. It's a delicate balance.

The modern world, which lures away younger Natives, has also brought its share of ills to Native communities and many struggle to overcome high rates of alcoholism, suicide, and domestic strife. A number of villages have voted to stay dry, with no alcohol allowed.

Yet modern conveniences have also made life a little easier. Under her fur parka, an Eskimo woman may be wearing a dress bought through

of Land Management had been hiring young villagers to fight summer forest fires, but a series of rainy seasons put a damper on that. To employ the young people, the village decided to try tourism. The first season, only a dozen people visited; the second, over 20 arrived. Instead of steady growth, the number of visitors has remained small at Huslia and many other small villages, which are remote and expensive to reach. In some ways that's a blessing: small communities would find it hard to handle large crowds of tourists. On the other hand, tourism hasn't brought the economic boom that many villagers anticipated. ❏

a mail-order catalog. Her whaler husband and friends stay in touch with short-wave radio as they track movements of their prey through ocean waters, and when the meat is consumed raw, as in the old days, they may supplement that meat with store-bought foods.

Tourism disappoints

For many remote communities, welcoming tourists is a step prompted by an increasingly gloomy economic outlook. In the Interior village of Huslia, for example, the Federal Bureau

LEFT: sleds remain a practical means of transport.
ABOVE: an Inuit man and child contemplate a gray whale trapped in ice off Barrow.

TIPS FOR TRAVELERS

A big hurdle for villagers is the fear of losing their privacy. Indeed, outsiders who show up unescorted in some villages receive a chilly reception.

Whether you are visiting as part of an organized tour or on your own, remember that what happens in Native villages is real life, not a tourist attraction: day-to-day community life takes precedence over visitors' needs. Read up on the people and their culture and learn as much as you can about Native values before you reach a village. Show your respect for Native culture by the way you behave. Don't ask personal questions. Observe for a while first, then ask a question respectfully.

LIFE IN WINTER

Sled dog racing, skiing, seasonal festivals, and
the Northern Lights all help Alaskans
get through the long, cold winters

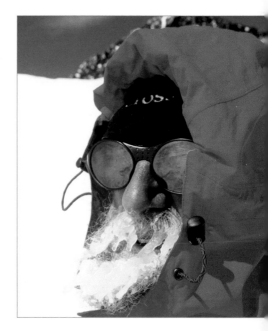

Winter is Alaska's longest season, and its quietest – at least from a tourism perspective. Most visitors explore the state between the end of May and the beginning of September, when daylight hours are long and temperatures warm – though, in some parts, warm may mean only 50 or 60°F (10 or 15°C).

By mid-September, most tourists have gone south with the waterfowl and locals have begun preparing for the winter, which in most of the state will last seven or eight months. Yet Alaska is not a frozen wasteland, and unlike bears, its human residents do not go into hibernation.

The lowest temperature

As would be expected, Alaska's Interior and Arctic regions experience the most severe and prolonged winter conditions.

Temperatures bottom out in February, which has average daily lows of –25°F (–32°C) and highs of –12°F (–24°C). But Barrow isn't just

The coldest temperature ever recorded in Alaska was –80°F (–62°C), at Prospect Creek Camp in January 1971. Barrow, the nation's northernmost outpost, averages sub-zero temperatures from December through March.

frigid in winter – it's also very dark. The long winter night begins at noon on November 18 and lasts through January 24. That's 67 days from sunset until the next sunrise.

LEFT: year-round cabins need to be well insulated.
RIGHT: protection against the cold is essential.

Winter in Anchorage

By comparison, Anchorage is downright bright and balmy. The city's shortest day (the winter solstice, December 21) has 5 hours and 28 minutes of daylight, plus a couple of hours of twilight. Its coldest month, December, has average daily highs and lows of 20° and 6°F (–7° and –15°C). Even more moderate conditions are experienced in Southeast Alaska. Ketchikan, near the Panhandle's southern tip, has 7 hours, 6 minutes of daylight on the winter solstice and even its coldest month, January, averages above-freezing temperatures of 34°F (1°C).

For further evidence of Alaska's winter extremes, consider that the state's record snowfall for one season is 974.5 inches (2,475cm), at Thompson Pass (near Valdez) during the winter of 1952–3; nearly 300 inches (760cm) fell in a single month, February. The one-day record, also at Thompson Pass, is 62 inches (1,600cm) in December 1955. Barrow holds the state record for the least snowfall in one season: 3 inches (7.5cm), in 1935–6.

The darkness and cold produce a variety of malaises, from cabin fever to seasonal affective disorder (SAD). To combat winter woes, residents around the state participate in a variety of activities and special events – some strenuous and skillful, others just plain fun.

Sled dog racing

Among the most popular cures for seasonal blues is sled dog racing, Alaska's official winter sport. And the best known of the mushing events is the incredible Iditarod Trail Sled Dog Race, also known as "The Last Great Race" *(see pages 302–3).*

The Iditarod is billed as a 1,150-mile (1,850-km) race but in reality mushers and dogs often travel much further. The race celebrates the "mushers" who helped open up the state in the early 1900s and also commemorates a frantic dash in 1925 to get diphtheria vaccine to Nome, which was on the verge of an epidemic.

RIDING THE IRON DOGS

While some Alaskans choose to explore the winter landscape behind a team of sled dogs, many others prefer "iron dogs." Snowmobiles, also locally known as snow-machines and sno-gos, have replaced sled dogs as the primary means of winter transportation in most of rural Alaska, where roads are minimal. Though commonly used by bush residents for work, or simply "getting from here to there," snow-machines are also popular for recreation and racing in both urban and rural Alaska.

The most challenging snowmobile race by far is the Iron Dog Gold Rush Classic, a long-distance event along the Iditarod Trail from Wasilla to Nome, then on to Fairbanks (a distance of nearly 2,000 miles/3,200km).

Another intriguing race is the Arctic Man Ski & Sno-Go Classic ("The Ultimate Adrenaline Rush"), which is staged in April in the Hoodoo Mountains near Paxson; on uphill stretches, a snowmobile pulls a skier at speeds of up to 86mph (138kmh).

It's relatively rare to see skiers and snow-machiners enjoying each other's company in the backcountry. Some recreational areas popular with both user groups – for instance, Chugach State Park in the mountains just east of Anchorage, Hatcher Pass in the Talkeetna Mountains and Turnagain Pass on the Kenai Peninsula – have designated snowmobile corridors, to minimize conflicts between these motorized and "quiet" human-powered activities.

The trail follows an historic freight-and-mail route established during the gold rush of the early 1900s. It crosses two mountain ranges, runs along the Yukon River for about 150 miles (240km) and crosses the pack ice of Norton Sound. From its ceremonial (and noisy) start in

> A growing number of Alaskans also run dog teams purely for recreation, and several companies now offer sled dog rides and trips that range from a few hours in urban Alaska to a week or more in the state's remote wilderness.

years later the inaugural race from Anchorage to Nome was staged.

The mushers are the glamour figures in sled dog racing and the top contenders are household names. But many would agree that the dogs are the true heroes, the athletic stars, of this and other mushing events. They're specially bred, raised, trained and conditioned to race.

Speed and stamina

While the Iditarod is unquestionably Alaska's best-known sled dog race, dozens – perhaps hundreds – of other competitions are staged around the state. Another major long-distance

Anchorage – the first Saturday in March – until the final musher has reached the finish line in Nome, the Iditarod is given center stage throughout Alaska.

A contest in which men and women compete as equals – four titles were won by the late Susan Butcher, another by Libby Riddles – the Iditarod not only pits competitors against each other, but also against the raw wilderness and brutal winter weather. But most importantly, the Iditarod celebrates Alaska's frontier past. The first Iditarod took place in 1967, as a two-day event that covered 50 miles (80km). Six

LEFT: high noon in Fairbanks in mid-winter.
ABOVE: a spectacular entry for an ice-carving contest.

IS SLED DOG RACING CRUEL?

Sled dog races, especially the Iditarod, have come under pressure in recent years from animal rights organizations who claim that, although most dogs are treated well, too many die or are injured. Figures are hard to come by, but causes of death include strangulation in towlines, internal hemorrhaging after being gouged by a sled, heart failure, and pneumonia.

Some sled mushers are alleged to abuse their dogs. In 1990 the Iditarod's winner was given a lifetime ban for hitting a dog with a metal snow hook (although he was allowed back 10 years later). Similar allegations against a musher in 2007 prompted the Iditarod's organizers to offer an independent investigation.

event is the 1,000-mile (1,600km) Yukon Quest, staged each February between Fairbanks and Whitehorse, in Canada's Yukon Territory. At the other end of the mushing spectrum are the so-called "speed races," or sprints.

The two most prestigious speed races are the North American Open, a three-day event staged each March in Fairbanks, and the Fur Rendezvous World Championship, another three-day affair (teams run 25 miles/40km each day), and the main attraction of Anchorage's mid-February winter festival. While Iditarod champions such as Butcher, five-time champion Rick Swenson, and four-time winner Doug Swingley of Montana (the first "outsider" to win the Iditarod) have achieved far greater acclaim outside Alaska, several of the premier speed racers – George Attla, Charlie Champaine and Roxy Wright-Champaine among them – are every bit as famous within the state.

Nordic and alpine skiing

Skiing is especially popular in and around the main towns. Anchorage has one of the nation's premier cross-country ski-trail systems: more than 100 miles (160km) of trails wind through a variety of terrain, with opportunities for both traditional diagonal striders and skate skiers.

THE NORTHERN LIGHTS

Alaska is the best place in the USA to view the aurora borealis, or Northern Lights. Literally meaning "dawn of the north," this is a solar-powered light show that occurs in the earth's upper atmosphere when charged particles from the sun collide with gas molecules.

The Northern Lights occur most intensely in an oval band that stretches across Alaska (as well as Canada, Greenland, Iceland, Norway and Siberia). All the state, except parts of the southwest and the Aleutian Chain, are within the "auroral zone," with the best light shows visible north of the Alaska Range. One of the best views to be had is in Fairbanks, which calls itself an "auroral destination," in an attempt to lure winter visitors.

The aurora occurs throughout the year, but can be seen only on clear nights when the sky has darkened. In Alaska that means from fall through spring, with peak viewing in winter. Colors vary from pale yellowish green – the most common shade – to red, blue and purplish-red. Northern Lights often begin as long, uniform bands, stretching along the horizon, but may develop vertical bars or rays, that give the appearance of waving curtains.

Some people claim they can not only see the aurora but can hear it as well. Scientists at the University of Alaska, Fairbanks, who have been studying the Northern Lights for years, are interested in such reports, but have yet to confirm them.

The city's best-known Nordic center, at Kincaid Park, has hosted several national championship races, as well as the Olympic Trials. For those who want backcountry solitude, Chugach State Park – Anchorage's "backyard wilderness" – has dozens of valleys and ridges to explore.

Other popular Nordic backcountry destinations within a half-day's drive of Anchorage include the Talkeetna Mountains, Chugach National Forest on the Kenai Peninsula, and the Peters Hills, the foothills of the Alaska Range.

While most of Alaska's lodges shut down for winter, a few cater to cross-country skiers. The three most popular Nordic retreats are Hatcher world-class facility in Girdwood, about 40 miles (65km) south of Anchorage, to the single-run volunteer operation at Salmonberry Hill outside Valdez.

The most unusual of Alaska's eight downhill sites (which include three in the Anchorage area, two near Fairbanks and one on Douglas Island, 12 miles/20km from Juneau) is the Eyak Ski Area, near the coastal community of Cordova. The tiny, single-seat Prince lift here used to operate at Sun Valley until it was replaced in 1969 by a triple-seat chair. Eventually the lift made its way north to Cordova, where it has been in operation every winter since 1974. ❏

Pass Lodge, in the Talkeetna Mountains; Sheep Mountain Lodge along the Glenn Highway; and Denali View Chalet – also known as Sepp Weber's Cabin, after its builder and owner – in the Alaska Range foothills. Each of the lodges offers groomed trails, wood-fired saunas, heated rooms, home-cooked meals and other amenities. Both Hatcher Pass and Sheep Mountain are accessible by road, while Denali View is about 2 miles (3.2km) from the nearest road.

Though not known as a magnet for alpine skiers, Alaska nonetheless offers a wide variety of downhill ski areas. They range from Alyeska's

LEFT: ski contestants in winter at Summit Lake.
ABOVE: traditional cross-country skiers near Nome.

WINTER FESTIVALS

Many communities host festivals to chase away winter doldrums. In December, there's the Barrow Christmas Games, followed in January by Kodiak's Russian New Year and Masquerade Ball celebration.

Things begin to pick up in February, with the Anchorage Fur Rendezvous, the Wrangell Tent City Winter Festival, Cordova Ice Worm Festival and Kodiak's Annual Seafood Extravaganza. March brings the North Pole and Fairbanks winter carnivals and the Bering Sea Ice Golf Classic tournament in Nome.

For more details of winter events, contact the Alaska Travel Industry Association, tel: 907-929-2842 or 800-862-5275; www.travelalaska.com.

WILDLIFE

Far from being a wasteland permanently covered
with snow and ice, Alaska is a world teeming
with wildlife, from birds to bears

More than 400 different species of birds have been officially documented in Alaska. With few exceptions, these species inhabit the state only during spring and summer and then migrate south. They come north to take advantage of the eruption of life which occurs on the tundra each spring, when a multi-colored explosion of flowers covers the ground and clouds of insects fill the air. The tundra offers an almost unlimited banquet of foodstuffs – plants, insects, and small animals – for birds attempting to raise their hungry young.

Long-distance flyers

The Arctic tern is the world's record holder for migration distances. These gull-like birds breed and nest on the shores of Alaskan tundra ponds. In late summer, the terns and their young start a migration that will eventually take them all the way to the Antarctic. Summer is just beginning in the Southern Hemisphere as the terns arrive. The round-trip flight from Alaska to the Antarctic and back is approximately 25,000 miles (40,000km).

Alaska's state bird, the willow ptarmigan, was chosen by a vote of the state's schoolchildren. During extremely cold weather, ptarmigans keep warm by burrowing into snow drifts.

Other long-distance commuters include the American golden plover, the surfbird, the long-tailed jaeger, and the Arctic warbler. Along with its close relatives, the rock ptarmigan and the white-tailed ptarmigan, the willow ptarmigan lives in Alaska year-round. A ptarmigan is brown in summer and white in winter, changing to blend with the surroundings, and is usually found on high ground: look for them in willow thickets and on the open tundra.

While near tundra ponds, look for loons, grebes, geese, ducks, phalaropes, yellowlegs, and sandpipers. On the tundra, watch for long-tailed jaegers, golden plovers, whimbrels, snow buntings, wheatears, sparrows, and water pipits. Owls, woodpeckers, gray jays and chickadees are common in forested areas, as are goshawks, the large, handsome birds of prey

LEFT: gray woves are watchful but keep out of sight.
RIGHT: the great gray owl.

which swoop down through the trees and catch their prey completely unawares. Gulls, terns, murrelets, auklets, shearwaters (known for their highly developed powers of navigation), cormorants, and puffins are found along the coastlines.

Mammals

The premier wildlife-viewing area in Alaska is Denali National Park *(see pages 223–33)*. Grizzly bears, moose, Dall sheep, caribou, red foxes, snowshoe hares, beavers, Arctic ground squirrels, and hoary marmots are seen by almost everyone who visits Denali. The park's shuttle

bus system is designed to maximize wildlife sightings. The only vehicles allowed in the park are the buses, which cause comparatively little disturbance, and many animals, including grizzlies, can be photographed within 300ft (90 meters) of the road.

If you are lucky, you may also spot wolves in Denali. Ranging from black to white, but more commonly gray in color, they are usually not fond of human company and are more likely to be heard than seen. At Denali they have become habituated to the presence of vehicles and are sometimes spotted near the Park Road – or even trotting along it.

WHERE EAGLES DARE

Alaska is the stronghold of the bald eagle, the national bird of the United States. More of them live in Alaska than in the other 49 states combined. White heads, white tails and 8ft (2.4-meter) wing-spans make them easily identifiable, even at a great distance. They are most often seen where fish are common, especially along the coastal areas of southern Alaska, from the Aleutians to the southernmost Panhandle.

The best place to see large gatherings of bald eagles is near Haines, during October and November. A late run of chum salmon into the Chilkat River, just north of town, attracts thousands of bald eagles, which feed on the dead or spent salmon. A single tree may contain dozens of

roosting eagles – an extraordinary sight. Because fish are available throughout the winter in coastal areas, these bald eagles have no need to migrate from Alaska. You can visit the American Bald Eagle Foundation in Haines *(see page 147)* for attractive displays and useful information about the birds, which are no longer classified as an endangered species.

Golden eagles, the darker cousins of the bald eagle, are normally found in Alaska's Interior and Arctic regions, soaring above tundra and mountainous areas. They hunt rodents, such as the Arctic ground squirrel, rather than fish. The Polychrome Pass area of Denali National Park is an excellent place to see golden eagles.

Denali and other Alaskan national parks are textbook examples of what wilderness parks were meant to be. A half-dozen or more protect entire ecosystems in a condition nearly identical to their original state. The population levels of wildlife such as Dall sheep, moose, caribou, hares, and marmots are controlled not by human intervention, but by the area's natural predators: grizzly and black bears, lynx, wolverines, foxes, wolves, and raptors. If you are lucky enough to see a grizzly dig out a ground squirrel from its burrow or a wolf pack chase a caribou herd, you will be witnessing a scene which could have taken place during the last Ice Age.

the peak of the sockeye salmon run. The McNeil River State Game Sanctuary, just outside the park, provides the ultimate bear-watching experience, but you literally have to enter a lottery to get in (see page 334). A third option is to do guided day trips from Anchorage, Soldotna or

Confusingly, black bears are sometimes brown in color; and brown bears can appear black. The best way to distinguish them is by looking for the hump which the brown/grizzly variety has at the back of its neck.

Alaska's bears

Katmai National Park *(see pages 326–9)* is the most popular place to closely observe brown bears. At one time, grizzlies and browns were classified as different species but they are now known to be the same animal *(Ursus arctos)*. Grizzlies are residents of Alaska's inland regions, while brown bears inhabit the coast. Partly because of the almost unlimited supply of salmon, adult male brown bears can grow to weights of more than 1,200lbs (540kg).

The best place to see them is at Brooks River and Camp, in Katmai, and the best time is in July,

Homer to view bears on the west side of Cook Inlet. Another excellent region to see brown bears is the Tongass National Forest in Southeast Alaska, especially Admiralty Island where there's a bear-viewing program at Pack Creek. Admiralty's Native name is Kootsnoowoo, which translates to "fortress of the bears." Much of Kodiak Island *(see page 311)* is home to a particularly large variety of brown bear, which has long tantalized trophy hunters. Black bears also inhabit much of Alaska. Smaller and more timid than grizzlies and brown bears, they tend to prefer forested areas.

Polar bears live along the Arctic coastline. They are among the largest land carnivores in the world, with some of the older males weigh-

LEFT: a migrating herd of caribou.
ABOVE: polar bears are fiercer than they look.

ing over 1,500lbs (680kg). Spending most of their lives on the ice floes of the Arctic Ocean, they can swim long distances in these frigid waters and survive on a diet of seals and other marine mammals. Because they live in the remote Arctic, they are seldom seen by visitors.

Moose and other species of deer

It is sometimes said that a camel is a horse designed by a committee, and much the same could be said of the moose: its legs are too long and its nose is too big. But if you watch these lumbering creatures running or swimming you will realize that nature got it right after all. The best places to see them are in Denali Park and the Kenai National Wildlife Refuge. The Athabascan Indians once relied on the moose for their survival, eating the meat and using the skins for clothing, blankets and boat making. The animals are still hunted extensively in the fall.

Denali is, again, the best – or at least the most accessible – place to see caribou, though its herd is among the state's smallest, with just a couple thousand animals. In all, more than half a million caribou migrate through the state, including two huge herds (the Porcupine and Western Arctic herds) each with more than 100,000 members. Like other varieties of deer, caribou

STREAMS OF SALMON

The lives of brown bears and salmon are inextricably linked, since salmon are the bears' favorite food. The fish come in five varieties (sockeye, king, chum, coho, and humpback) and are as popular with fishermen as with bears – understandably so, since their flesh has so much more flavor than the farmed variety. Witnessing a salmon run (from June to mid-September), when thousands of the fish cram the streams and leap the waterfalls, as they swim upstream to spawn, is a wonderful experience, as is watching the bears who come to prey on them, though access to prime venues such as McNeil River State Game Sanctuary is limited *(see pages 331–5)*.

are herbivores and will eat the available grasses and berries as they travel the very long distances between their calving grounds and their overwintering areas.

Reindeer, the domesticated version of caribou, were introduced into northern Alaska in 1892 as a dependable source of food and clothing. Today, there are approximately 30,000 reindeer in Alaska. The largest herd lives near Nome on the Seward Peninsula. A small herd can be seen at the Reindeer Research Station in Cantwell, south of the entrance to Denali National Park.

Sitka black-tail deer are distributed throughout the Southeast and also on the Kodiak Archipelago, southwest of Anchorage: these small, rusty-brown animals (their coats turn gray in the winter) are most likely to be seen in Misty Fiords National Monument *(see page 114)*, Admiralty Island National Monument *(see page 110)*, and on Kodiak Island. Other island residents are the Roosevelt elk and mountain goats.

The musk ox

Nunivak Island, off Alaska's Southwest coast, is inhabited by a most extraordinary native animal: the musk ox, a stout, shaggy, creature which appears to be the result of an amorous encounter between a prehistoric ox and a mountain sheep. Musk oxen are rare, and shy in

Arm south of the city. Though their numbers have declined in the past decade, Cook Inlet's beluga population is believed to be stabilized.

A state-managed walrus-viewing program has been established at Round Island, in Bristol Bay, where thousands of bull walrus haul out every summer. Large numbers of walrus can also be seen in the Togiak National Wildlife Refuge and near Kotzebue and other northern communities. Harbor seals, sea otters, and sea lions are frequently sighted in the Gulf of Alaska and Prince William Sound. In fact, Alaska's coasts, like its inland areas, offer opportunities for wildlife watching which are difficult to match. ❑

the wild, but small herds roam the Arctic and some are held captive in research stations, particularly in the Large Animal Research Facility, part of the University of Alaska-Fairbanks.

Sea creatures

Alaska is rich in marine life: humpback, killer and minke whales can be seen in Glacier Bay and Kenai Fjords national parks, as well as other coastal regions. Belugas – small, white whales – inhabit Cook Inlet and can sometimes be seen from Anchorage's coastal fringes, or the Seward Highway, as it winds along Turnagain

LEFT: brown bears go fishing; a caribou in the tundra.
ABOVE: harbor seal, Kenai Fjords National Park.

THE ALASKA SEALIFE CENTER

Accessible by highway from Anchorage, the Alaska SeaLife Center *(see pages 199–200)* is a fascinating introduction to the plants and animals you might see on a guided boat trip in the waters of nearby Kenai Fjords National Park. The center re-creates habitats for harbor seals, Steller sea lions, and seabirds including tufted puffins, common murres, and pigeon guillemots. Aquariums along one wall show the complete spectrum of local marine life.

Visitors can peer through scopes on the observation deck for a look at wild sea otters and harbor seals. In late spring, humpback whales sometimes enter the bay and can be seen from the center.

SURVIVING IN THE WILDERNESS

The most successful explorers are those who take sensible precautions against threats, which can come from unexpected directions

Sean Penn's 2007 movie *Into the Wild* captured Alaska's breathtaking beauty – and its deadliness. The film was based on the story of a 24-year-old Virginian, Christopher McCandless, who in 1992 starved to death near the Teklanika River, at the eastern edge of Denali National Park, after living in the wilderness for four months in an abandoned bus. Opinions vary about whether McCandless was mentally unstable or a victim of circumstances, but it is beyond argument that Alaska is an unforgiving environment unless proper precautions are taken.

Due to the latitude and varying weather conditions, travelers must have the appropriate equipment and be physically prepared for the activities they wish to pursue. Because there are so few roads and distances are so great, clear and precise communication is also vital.

Variations in weather

Coastal and Southcentral Alaska: The word to remember when selecting equipment for coastal Alaska is rain. Some of this area receives up to 200 inches (508cm) annually. If you plan to be outside for long periods, a waterproof suit (jacket, pants, and hat) and a synthetic pile or fleece jacket will be used frequently. Tents must be able to withstand long wet spells. Sleeping bags filled with synthetic materials are better than down because they retain more of their insulating qualities when wet.

The Interior: The Interior has dramatic seasonal contrasts. Summer temperatures are pleas-

antly warm while in winter the mercury can dip below –40°F (–40°C).

Even in summer, visitors should expect nighttime temperatures sometimes to dip below 40°F (4°C). A hat and gloves and at least one heavy long-sleeved shirt, plus the usual jacket and rain gear will be useful, as will a mosquito headnet, which takes up little luggage space.

The extreme cold of winter demands the best quality equipment. A good down jacket, a hat, mittens, and warm boots are essential. Camping in winter requires a sleeping bag that is comfortable at –40°F (–40°C) or colder.

Spring is the finest time, by far, to ski in the mountains. Temperatures may allow people to

---

LEFT: camping in the clouds usually requires the services of an experienced guide or outfitter.
RIGHT: taking a rest, Gates of the Arctic National Park.

ski without shirts – although the sensible ones cover themselves in sunblock. But snow-blindness is a painful reality for unprotected eyes; mirrored sunglasses are best, but dark sunglasses will suffice. And there's always the chance of springtime blizzards and avalanches.

The North Slope: If the key word for coastal Alaska is rain, the equivalent for the North Slope is wind. The area is technically an arctic desert with less than 5 inches (13cm) of annual precipitation. But this meager amount should not be disregarded as it may fall as snow or freezing rain and be driven by gale force winds. Travelers to the North Slope need clothes that

What happens if the plane crashes while you are in it? There is a legal requirement for all planes to carry emergency equipment. The required list includes food for each person for two weeks, an ax, first-aid kit, a knife, matches, mosquito headnets, gill net, fishing tackle, and a pistol or rifle with ammunition. A sleeping bag, snowshoes, and a wool blanket are added to the list for winter travel.

It's a good idea to check the survival gear before taking off. If you decide to bring your own, keep as much of it on your person as possible. In winter fill your pockets; in summer, use a small waist pack.

are windproof and warm and camping equipment that can withstand heavy winds.

Getting there

Charter flights: Check first to see if there is a regular air service – there is to some small villages and communities, and this will save you a lot of money. But if you are bound for the wilderness, a charter flight is necessary.

Before departure, be sure someone knows where you are going. If you have no alternative, inform the Alaska State Troopers and land managers of your destination and expected return date. Make firm arrangements to be picked up. Be certain that someone besides the pilot knows where you are going.

LEARNING THE RULES

Taking the trouble to learn a few basics could save your life if you were stranded in the wilderness. There is a record of one man in a desperate situation who spotted an Alaska State Troopers airplane flying over his campsite. He frantically waved both his arms over his head. When the plane flew over a second time, he waved again. The plane flew off.

It was only much later that the man realized his mistake; when he studied his hunting license, he saw that he had signaled, "Everything OK, don't wait." Sadly there was no happy ending: this information was recorded in a diary found when the man's body was discovered.

Every plane in Alaska is also required to carry a downed aircraft transmitting device (Emergency Location Transmitter, or ELT). Learn how to operate this device before you set off. If the pilot becomes incapacitated, you can activate the ELT and be rescued more quickly. Don't be deterred by these dire warnings: these precautions pertain only to the 0.5 percent of flights during which an inflight problem does occur.

Automobile travel: There is no Alaska law which governs what survival equipment should be kept in a motor vehicle, yet far more cars than planes break down while traveling. In sub-freezing weather, a breakdown can be life-

operating engine heater, and ample electrical cord to reach a power source.

When renting a car, inform the rental agency of your proposed route and confirm that maintenance is available along the way. Anticipating problems before traveling will avoid misunder-

Alaska may have been spared snakes, skunks and termites but this has been more than compensated for by the mosquito. Thick clothing will reduce the number of bites, but sometimes a headnet is the only means of relief.

threatening as well as inconvenient. The Alaska State Troopers recommend the following survival kit: down coat, boots, mittens, hat, snowpants, sleeping bag, flare, candles, extra spark plugs, extra belts, shovel, chain, flashlight, and high-energy food.

Automobile maintenance is vitally important. Even if you come to no real harm, it is expensive and time-consuming to break down on the road – towing charges can be very costly, especially in remote areas. Check the car carefully before leaving the city, and remember winter essentials: snow tires or studded tires, an

standings later. Most agencies have stringent rules about driving on gravel roads – and many road-accessible destinations require some driving on gravel.

Encountering bears

For all the worries that people have about bears, humans are in fact a much greater danger to them than bears are to us. Many Alaskans have stories about encountering bears at close quarters, but there are few tragic accounts. Most bears turn tail and run upon encountering people, but in some instances the bear will stand its ground. Or charge.

If you do meet a bear, stay as calm as possible. Talk to the bear, to identify yourself as a human,

LEFT: well-equipped hiker in Denali National Park.
ABOVE: Mt McKinley makes a dramatic backdrop.

but don't yell. And *don't run*. Running is usually the worst possible strategy, because it will likely trigger the bear's predatory instincts. Back away slowly and give the bear an escape route. Avoid getting between a female and her cubs. Some experts suggest that you raise your arms above your head and wave them slowly. If you're in a group, stand side by side, to increase your apparent size.

Should a bear attack and make contact with you, it's usually best to fall to the ground and "play dead." Protect your head and neck and try to lie on your stomach, but do not struggle. If you're wearing a pack, leave it on. Once a bear

feels there's no longer a threat, it will likely end its attack. The exception to this rule is when a bear shows predatory behavior. Instead of charging in a rush, such a bear will show intense interest and may circle or stalk you. If you think a bear is treating you as prey, fight it off. Such behavior is extremely rare and most often involves black bears. It would be almost impossible to fight off an adult grizzly.

Some important strategies should be used to minimize chance meetings with bears. It's most important to avoid surprise encounters, which lead to the vast majority of bear attacks. Make plenty of noise while walking in the wilderness.

TOOT HORN ONLY IF BEAR IN CAMP

THE THREAT FROM TIDES

There are large tidal variations in Southeastern Alaska, Prince William Sound, Cook Inlet, and Bristol Bay. The extreme diurnal variation occurs in spring in Cook Inlet near Anchorage where high tide can be 38ft (11.5 meters) above low tide. Such tides present two dangers for those traveling through or near the water: swift incoming tides and strong currents, which are magnified in island areas.

Obtain a tide book from a fishing tackle shop, a hardware store, a bar or gas station. All too frequently, the fisherman standing on a rock working the incoming tide waits too long to retreat. This can be life-threatening. People traveling along beaches in vehicles must also be

aware of the tides or they risk losing their transportation – or worse.

Large tides create swift currents in constricted areas such as inlets, which can be a danger to those in small boats; avoid traveling in kayaks, skiffs, and other small watercraft at these times – it's perilous.

The mudflats surrounding Anchorage are particularly dangerous. Made of glacial silt, they have a quicksand-like quality and trap would-be strollers. The danger is then compounded by the quickly rising tide, drowning those trapped in the mud. Still, from a safe distance, the Cook Inlet's changing tide, which advances in two-foot (60-cm) high waves, is a thing to behold.

Some people tie "bear bells" to their shoes or pack, but talking or singing is better. Human voices carry farther than tinkling bells. If bears hear your approach, there's less chance they'll be surprised and they're likely to leave.

Stay alert and look for signs of bear, such as tracks, scat, partially eaten salmon. Choose your

> Some bear researchers now recommend that any black bear attack should be fought off, because they are smaller, less aggressive animals than grizzlies and more easily intimidated.

store them in airtight containers. If you are flying, notify the pilot; a leak inside the plane could disable the pilot and lead to a crash.

Hiking with moose

More dangerous than bears are moose, and unlike bears, a moose never bluffs. Killing more people annually, moose can charge, kick and stomp anyone too close to them or their young. Therefore, always give moose a wide berth. If one does charge, run and quickly get behind something, like a tree, and if you are about to be stomped, curl into a ball, protecting your head with your hands.

tent site carefully and avoid trails, streams with spawning salmon, and berry patches. And don't attract bears with your food. Cook well away from your tents and store food far from your campsite. Keep all food and garbage in air-tight, bear-proof containers. These can be purchased at any outdoor store and are often available at park visitors' centers for a small deposit.

Finally, carry a firearm only if you know how to use it. (Guns are forbidden in some wilderness areas.) Pepper spray is another option. Because the cans sometimes leak, it's best to

---

LEFT: various ways of repeling bears and insects.
ABOVE: remembering the bear's favorite food, it's best not to pitch a tent near a salmon stream.

Avoiding hypothermia

Beware of hypothermia, the sub-normal lowering of the body temperature. It is caused by exposure to cold, but aggravated by exhaustion, wind, and wet clothing. Left untreated, a person suffering from hypothermia may become disoriented, incoherent, then unconscious, and may finally die. Never ignore shivering, it is the body's way of signaling for help. The time to prevent hypothermia is during the initial period of exposure.

The following suggestions may help prevent an emergency:

● *Try to stay dry*. Wet clothing loses most of its insulating value. Functional raingear is vitally important. Ponchos are almost useless.

● *Avoid the wind*. Wind carries body heat away much faster than still air; it also refrigerates wet clothing by evaporation. If you feel yourself getting chilled, look for shelter from the wind.

● *Understand the cold*. Most people die of hypothermia when the temperature is between 30° and 50°F (–1° and 10°C). The majority of hikers underestimate the severity of being wet in Alaskan waters. Many rivers are fed by glaciers and their temperatures, even in mid-summer, aren't much above the freezing mark. Getting soaked can be fatal, and first-aid measures must be taken immediately *(see panel below)*.

● *End the exposure*. If someone shows any signs of hypothermia, or if it becomes impossible to keep dry with your existing clothing and conditions, make camp or end the trip.

● *Avoid over-tiredness*. Don't be too ambitious. Make camp before you get exhausted, and bring high-energy food to replenish your reserves.

Surviving avalanches

These pose a serious threat to winter mountain adventurers. Research has shown that most avalanches involving humans are triggered by people traveling through avalanche-prone terrain.

A snow-covered slope is especially prone to sliding when its gradient ranges between 27°

TREATING HYPOTHERMIA

If a member of your party develops hypothermia while in the wilderness – one of the first signs is violent and uncontrollable shivering – there are emergency measures you can take. Handle a victim gently, replace wet clothing with dry, and warm the core area of the body with hot liquids. Do not give a victim any alcohol as this could prove fatal; forget stories about a sip of brandy being restorative.

Avoid the mistake of rapidly warming the extremities, as it takes much-needed blood away from the core area and can result in unconsciousness. If the condition worsens, put a victim in a sleeping bag with another person, who will help warm the bag.

and 45°. On steeper slopes, the snow usually won't accumulate, and on shallower slopes, the angle is usually not sufficient to release snow. Avoid disaster by careful route selection and trip planning.

Don't ski through a likely avalanche zone – make sure you pass above or below it. Choose the route carefully to avoid steep mountain faces, especially after a fresh snowfall. And remember, spring is an especially dangerous season for avalanches, as the snow melts and the weight of the snowpack increases. If possible, take an avalanche-awareness class to learn more about safe winter travel in the mountains. ❏

ABOVE: pitching camp in Tongass National Forest.

Public-Use Cabins

Between posh wilderness lodges and tent camping, there's a third way for travelers to spend the night in Alaska's backcountry.

Given Alaska's often cool and wet weather, it can make all the difference to return to a roomy, dry, and heated shelter at the end of a day's explorations. Public-use cabins provide an economical way of doing this. For as little as $15 a night, you can spread out your soaked clothing, pull up a chair, and read a book beside an oil- or wood-burning stove while your hiking or paddling partner grabs fresh greens from the cooler and prepares a gourmet meal on your camp stove.

Essentials to bring

You don't have to worry about crowding, leaky tents, or a wild critter getting into your food supplies, which can be safely stored inside the cabin. All public-use cabins include heating stove, bunks or other platforms for sleeping, table, chairs, counter tops or shelves, and outhouse. Some also include propane-fueled lights, burner plates, stainless steel sinks, picnic tables with benches, wash area, and more. Visitors are generally responsible for bringing their own food, heating and cooking fuel, utensils, water, cook stove, and bedding.

Frontier etiquette demands that, where possible, you attempt to leave cabins in better condition than you found them. You are encouraged to chop firewood, clean up the place, and leave canned goods for the next occupants.

Where to find them

Balancing these "comforts of home" is the wildness and solitude to be found outside your shelter. Many public-use cabins are located in remote wilderness areas that can be reached only by boat or plane. Others can be easily reached from the road system. Many, particularly more modern cabins, have been built to blend with their surroundings, so they have a minimal impact on the environment or wilderness aesthetics.

More than 250 such cabins are available for rent throughout much of the state, in state and

RIGHT: the path leads to a public-use cabin in Kenai Fjords National Park.

national parks, wildlife refuges, Bureau of Land Management lands, and Alaska's two national forests. Some are along trails, others are on lakes, rivers, forested coastlines, or alpine meadows.

Their nightly costs range from around $15 to $65 – a bargain for those seeking dependable protection from Alaska's unpredictable weather as well as some degree of comfort. Some can be rented only in summer, while others can be used year-round.

How to reserve a cabin

Most cabins are available on a first-come, first-served reservation system and can be reserved up to six months in advance. In nearly all cases, the

length of stay is limited. Check for specifics, as details vary from agency to agency. These include the National Park Service, Alaska State Parks, the US Fish and Wildlife Service, the US Forest Service, and the Bureau of Land Management (BLM).

Information on public-use cabins throughout Alaska and details on how to apply and pay for cabin rentals are available from Alaska Public Lands Information Centers in four locations: Anchorage (tel: 644-3661); Fairbanks (tel: 459-3730), Tok (tel: 883-5667) and Ketchikan (tel: 228-6234). Information is also accessible from the website www.nps.gov/aplic/cabins/index.html.

A good reference is *55 Ways to Wilderness in Southcentral Alaska* (Mountaineers Books, 2002), by Helen Nienhueser and John Wolfe. ❑

CRUISING'S IRRESISTIBLE GROWTH

Douglas Ward, the world's foremost authority on cruising, reveals the best ways of getting an up-close but comfortable view of Alaska's ice fields and glaciers

Alaska's cruise season is short, from May to September, and it can be misty, wet, and chilly in early and late summer. But the lure of the state's dramatic wilderness scenery, invigorating clean air, wildlife, and fascinating shore excursions have led to a phenomenal growth in cruise traffic. Indeed, about 60 percent of Alaska's visitors are now cruise passengers, served by more than 40 vessels. Ships have become larger, with more balcony cabins and more dining options, while fares have fallen. Docks and quayside facilities have been renovated and expanded to cope with the growth.

The early days

The first organized cruises to Alaska took place when a young Chuck West, originally a bush pilot, formed a travel company called Westours. In 1954, he pioneered Alaska cruising using two small ships, the 1,835-ton *Yukon Star* and sister ship, the 1,833-ton *Glacier Queen*. Both ships carried 148 passengers in a one-class arrangement.

Larger ships were acquired in 1968 and 1971, and in the 1970s the company itself was acquired by Holland America Line. In 1973 Chuck West started a company dedicated to *small* ship travel: Alaska Sightseeing, which later changed its name to Cruise West.

The majors arrive

Soon major cruise brand names such as Cunard Line, Holland America Line, and Princess Cruises became interested in the region. But most of their vessels operated in the Caribbean and, to reach Alaska, had to go through the

THE MOST POPULAR CRUISE ROUTES

● Inside Passage Route from Vancouver to Skagway, with visits to tidewater glaciers, such as those found in Glacier Bay's Hubbard Glacier or Tracy Arm (just two of the 15 active glaciers along the 60-mile/100km Glacier Bay coastline). Ports of call might include Juneau, Ketchikan, Skagway and/or Haines.

● The Glacier Route, which usually includes the Gulf of Alaska during a one-way cruise between Vancouver and Seward or Whittier (the ports for Anchorage). Typical ports of call might include Haines, Sitka, and Valdez. Of special interest is the marine life of Hubbard Glacier and Prince William Sound.

LEFT: approaching Hubbard Glacier in Glacier Bay.
RIGHT: a buffet lunch during a shore excursion.

Panama Canal and northward along the American west coast to get to Vancouver – the Canadian port became the base of cruise operations because of restrictive US legislation *(see box on page 90)*. Alaskan cruising thus did not develop significantly until the 1970s, when the majors dedicated ships exclusively to the state.

Around the same time, Cunard had the idea of extending the standard cruise. Instead of sailing back to Vancouver, the company introduced one-way voyages from Vancouver to Whittier, the port for Anchorage. At Whittier, a train would take passengers to Anchorage, for a stopover, with a bus connection to the airport for their flights home. This was followed by even more extensive "Cruise 'n' Stay" vacations, which included a 7-day cruise, a hotel stay in Anchorage, from where passengers could head out to the surrounding areas and wildlife lodges. While Cunard no longer cruises in Alaska, their "Cruise'n'Stay" concept has been adopted by most cruise companies and has evolved into the popular "cruise-tour".

Economic benefits

Alaska cruising has evolved into a big money-maker for the cruise companies, and provides income and work for local Alaskans who operate some of the land-based tourism infrastructure and cruise-related services. The government is happy too, as it collects taxes not only from visiting cruise ships, but also from every passenger carried, and through certain services on shore.

In fact, the impact the cruise industry has had on the local economy is immense. For each passenger carried, the cruise lines pay between $65 and $80 in fees and taxes to cover state and local governments' cruise-related expenses, from port maintenance to emergency services and tourism infrastructure. Then there are the sums spent by passengers: $74 million in Juneau, for example, and $54 million in Ketchikan.

The cruise industry also donates money to local communities, the most consistent givers being Holland America Line, and Princess Cruises (both owned by Carnival Corporation). For example, Holland America Line recently donated $200,000 in educational grants to the University of Alaska state-wide system, including a grant to fund a new writer-in-residence

WHEN CROWDS ARE A NUISANCE

With almost 1 million cruise passengers a year visiting Alaska and several large resort ships likely to be in port on any given day, there is so much congestion in many small ports that avoiding crowded streets can be difficult. And, with more people around, wildlife is harder to spot

These high volume bursts of tourists have also been blamed for the "Disneyfication" of many towns in the Southeast. Often filled with over-priced trinket shops, lots of fudge hawkers (why fudge?), and diamond jewelry stores (many of which are also found in Caribbean destinations), they can feel like brightly painted parodies of the downtowns frequented by locals, which are usually only a couple of blocks away.

Sitka is the one city in Alaska to prohibit cruise ships docking in town and it shows, but places like Ketchikan and Juneau can feel as if the real and imagined versions of the city sit side-by-side. However, a quick stroll will take you beyond these sometimes-tacky tourist zones into the sloped residential neighborhoods, where narrow streets yield to lush staircases, giving you a sense of daily life in the Southeast.

The more adventurous might consider one of the more unusual Alaska cruises to the far north, around the Pribilof Islands (superb for bird watching) and into the Bering Sea. Or you can create your own cruise tour by taking to the ferries *(see page 113)*.

program. Holland America Line also hires an artist in residence for each of its Alaska cruise ships, a program that included a $250,000 gift to the Alaska Native Heritage Center. They are also one of the state's largest private employers.

New taxes

Still, the cruise industry has plenty of critics. In 2006, Alaskans voted to institute a $50 "head tax" for each cruise-ship passenger. New measures tax all corporate and gambling earnings gained while in Alaskan waters, and impose stricter regulations on wastewater treatment and discharge. Now, a ship must obtain specific

cent. Despite the companies' claim that the tax deters would-be passengers, proponents blame

> While cruise ships provide an opportunity to see wild landscapes for those who might not otherwise, the ships themselves have a significant environmental impact.

the economy for reduced bookings and insist that the tax is essential to protect the environment and maintain the infrastructure necessary to accommodate the high impact industry.

wastewater permits while in Alaska, and is subject to stiff fines for any violation. The head tax alone brings in $50 million a year, and is used for the maintenance of the ports and harbors that house the ships each season.

Since passing, there has been considerable pressure to overturn the legislation. The cruise industry has even threatened to sue the state and pull some of its ships. In the spring of 2009, they made good on the latter by announcing steep cuts to their Alaskan fleet, with Holland America and Princess reducing their sailings by 10 per-

LEFT: souvenir hunting on a shore excursion.
ABOVE: smaller vessels make it possible to view seal colonies at close range.

Environmental concerns

It is estimated that a 3,000-passenger ship produces 50 tons of trash; generates and releases 210,000 gallons of untreated sewage every week; and emits diesel exhaust equal to thousands of automobiles, a third of which are given off while idling in port. Reasons like these give many a reason to view the boom in the cruise industry as a mixed blessing.

Over the years, the state has worked to lessen the impact of these floating cities. Today, cruise ships use power from Alaska's grid instead of idling in port, and can only release sewage, waste, or grey water three miles (5km) offshore or away from ecologically sensitive areas. Some popular destinations have imposed their own rules. For example, Glacier Bay, an important feeding ground for the endangered humpback whale, restricts the number of vessels entering its waters each day. To do so, a cruise line needs an entry permit from the Glacier Bay National Park and Preserve. A limited number of permits are issued for the "prime season" (June 1–August 31). Only two cruise ships (over 100 gross tons) are allowed in each day, plus three ships of under 100 gross tons (such as the ships of Majestic America Line, Cruise West, Lindblad Expeditions, and American Safari Cruises).

In a typical summer season, the National Park Service issues more than 220 cruise-ship permits to enter Glacier Bay. Although these are spread around the industry, Holland America and Princess Cruises receive the greatest number because of their pioneering role in Alaska cruising.

Despite attempts to lessen the effects of large cruise ships, their sheer size and copious number of amenities (pools, patios, restaurants, barbers, stores, and theaters) keep cruising from being a low impact way to travel.

Cruise tours

Cruise tours have become an increasingly popular way to see more of Alaska, particularly by

WHY CRUISES LEAVE FROM CANADA

The US Passenger Services Act of 1886 requires that only US-flag and US-built vessels can be used to carry passengers between two US ports, but it allows foreign-flag vessels to pick up or drop off passengers while calling at a single US port. Since most large cruise ships are registered not in the US but with a foreign-flag nation (such as the Bahamas, Bermuda, Liberia, Panama, and the UK), most cruises to Alaska start and end in Vancouver, British Columbia.

This has the effect of keeping business away from ports in the Pacific Northwest, such as Seattle. Canada has clearly been the major beneficiary of the US Passenger Services Act.

those who have time and may only visit it once. This usually involves a cruise plus land stay in a hotel, or a cruise plus an extended trip usually via train. Although the most popular cruises to Alaska last for seven days, extending a vacation by taking a cruise plus an escorted land tour can stretch to 18 days.

Popular destinations include Denali National Park and the Yukon. All trips are neatly packaged by the cruise lines, include a variety of luxurious amenities, and some lines, like Princess, own a network of hotels and lodges, so that

ABOVE: the specially constructed domed railcars of cruise trains offer fine paroramic views.
RIGHT: a Celebrity ship gets up close to the ice.

travelers never have to sleep in a bed not made by a cruise line staffer.

For added adventure and sightseeing opportunities, the major cruise companies feature special domed railroad cars. These are part of the trains operated by the Alaska Railroad, which is owned by the State of Alaska. The railway extends northwards, from Seward through Anchorage to Fairbanks, a distance of 470 miles (756km). Smaller cruise lines also offer a variety of land extension tours. However, these depend on local transportation and accommodations, while providing a more intimate look at the state. (For details, see page 365.)

Pre- and post-cruise stays

The cruise lines have many options of pre- and post-cruise stays ashore to extend Alaska vacations. However, it is easy enough to create and book your own "cruise tour". Staying a few extra days in Anchorage allows you to rent a car and explore nearby attractions such as Portage, Girdwood, or the Matanuska Valley. The railroad also offers "tours" of the Kenai Peninsula and the Interior, turning a delayed plane ticket home into a Seward, Denali, or Fairbanks adventure. ❑

Douglas Ward is author of the annual Berlitz Complete Guide to Cruising and Cruise Ships.

THE BEST SHORE EXCURSIONS

Shore excursions have increased in number (and cost) over the years; Holland America Line alone offers more than 100 optional excursions. These include flightseeing (by floatplane or helicopter), salmon fishing, hiking, glacial ice treks, mountain biking, train rides, jeep safaris, and whale watching. Here are some of the best:

● On cruises to Skagway, a trip on the White Pass & Yukon Route Railroad is recommended. This narrow-gauge track, built in 1898, now provides Alaska's most popular shore excursion. The railroad operates 19 diesel locomotives and one steam locomotive.

● Flightseeing excursions depart from Juneau and land on Mendenhall Glacier, which has signed trails and interpretive panels. Most floatplanes fly at around 2,000ft, and all passengers have window seats.

● Tours to Denali National Park can be made by helicopter, tour bus or self-drive jeep. Wildlife includes moose, caribou, brown bears, Dall sheep, and golden eagles.

● Prudhoe Bay provides close-ups of the trans-Alaska oil pipeline and sightseeing along the Dalton Highway.

● A ride on the Mount Roberts tramway above Juneau, with great views across Gastineau Channel.

● Top-class salmon fishing expeditions to the Ninilchik River and Deep Creek, plus deep-sea charters for halibut.

● A walking tour of historic Ketchikan, with a trip to nearby Saxman Totem Park for fans of intricately carved poles.

Big ships vs small ships

Choosing a ship is a lot like buying a car. Big or small? Classic or modern? Luxurious or functional? Assess what you really want.

The difference between so-called "big ships" and "small ships" could hardly be more stark, and it isn't simply a matter of tonnage or floor space, but what they have to offer. These days, large mainstream ships tend to be very big indeed, carrying 3,000 passengers or more, soaring 14 stories above the water, and stretching to lengths of nearly 1,000ft (300 meters).

By contrast, small ships in Alaska tend to be very small, measuring around 100ft (30 meters) in length and carrying between 12 and 140 passengers. Some are closer to yachts in size and appearance, others have the utilitarian feel of expedition ships, and still others look like the miniaturized cruise ships that they are.

A choice of entertainment

In examining whether a big or small ship would best suit your needs, you need to consider three main variables: the onboard experience you should expect during your cruise, the kinds of itineraries and ports of call offered by each, and the cost.

By design, most big ships are busy places, with activities, entertainment, and meals programmed so that, if you cared to, you could be occupied during every waking moment you were on board. As such, they're ideal for families, allowing parents and children to pursue their own interests and stay out of each other's hair. They're also the better choice for people who, although they want to see the natural wonders of the 49th state, don't expect that glaciers, whales, and mountains will be able to hold their interest every minute of the day.

These people want a show in the evening, multiple restaurants for dinner, sports options (of both the active and couch-potato varieties), maybe a casino, and they might even like to take a dip in the ship's pool – if only for the kick of doing so within sight of an iceberg. For these people, Royal Caribbean, NCL, and Carnival are the top choices.

Those looking for a slightly more refined version of this same experience should check out tradition-minded Holland America or stylish Celebrity line, while those with the money to go with their refine-

ment should opt for the luxury lines Crystal and Radisson, which feature much enhanced service, cuisine, and facilities.

Accommodations

Accommodations run the gamut from smallish inside cabins to outside ones with private balconies, to palatial suites with butler service. Balcony cabins offer the pleasant option of landscape- and wildlife-viewing in the privacy of your own room, but if you're just as happy watching from public areas you can save by opting for an inside cabin (if you're not claustrophobic) or an exterior one with a small window.

Eating at sea

Dining is another area of great choice on the big ships. Whereas a decade ago the most you could expect to find would have been a main restaurant with two seatings and a buffet option at breakfast and lunch, today's mega-ships are being built with multiple main dining rooms, casual options for every meal, specialty coffee-and-pastry cafés, and multiple, reservations-only restaurants serving Asian, Italian, French, steakhouse, and other menus, at an extra cost of around $5 to $25 per person per meal.

And if you want to work off the calories you are likely to pack away at those restaurants, the mega-ships all have sprawling gym complexes, jogging tracks, and varying sports amenities, from the almost ubiquitous golf-driving nets and basketball/volleyball courts to Royal Caribbean's rock-climbing walls. In essence, sailing aboard a mega-ship in Alaskan waters is like checking into a smart, big-city hotel and then taking that hotel with you to the wilderness.

Small ships for watching wildlife

Across the board, small ships offer exactly the opposite kind of experience, with onboard dining, activities, and entertainment taking a backseat to the natural world outside. All meals are served in a single, simple dining room (with a small buffet also set out in a lounge at lunch and dinner times), while

modations on these vessels is limited, tending toward cozy outside cabins with few amenities.

Ports of call

Itinerary-wise, ships both large and small tend to visit the popular Alaska ports of Juneau, Ketchikan, and Skagway, where all passengers get exactly the same experience, although big ships tend to offer a wider range of shore-excursion options. One advantage small ships do have here is that, with fewer passengers, it takes less time to get on and off the ship, so you have more time in port and less frustrating waiting time. Small ships also have the advantage when it comes to visiting smaller port

the only entertainment you might expect is, perhaps, a crew talent show or an informal lecture by the ship's onboard naturalist.

Instead of inside-oriented activities, passengers spend their time out on deck with binoculars scanning for whales, bears, sea otters, and other wildlife – which they're much more likely to see from these ships than from the big ones, since small vessels are less obtrusive, can therefore sail closer to shore, and have passenger decks that begin only a few yards above the waterline. These same factors also mean you get a more intimate experience of Alaska, which is the main reason people choose this type of cruise. Typically, the range of accom-

ABOVE: smaller ships get closer to the glaciers.

towns like Petersburg and Metlakatla and sailing narrow wilderness passages like Misty Fiords National Monument – places from which the big ships are barred by their sheer bulk.

Counting the cost

Small ships, which cost more to operate, are more expensive than the big mainstream lines. Consider your priorities and your budget. For the same cost, you could sail with a mainstream line and take all the best optional shore excursions (helicopter glacier treks, sport fishing, dogsledding); sail with a luxury line and find your own way around ports of call; or sail with a small-ship adventure line, where most off-ship wilderness activities are included in the cost. In the end, it's all a matter of taste. ❑

ALASKA FROM THE AIR

Even long-time Alaskans are awestruck by the view from the air. Flightseeing, a growing industry, provides two guarantees: the view will be incomparable, and there's not a bad seat in the house

Flying through the Knik Valley in South-central Alaska, a Cessna 185 descends into the Gorge, a canyon with a glacier on one side and a sheer rock face on the other. The landscape dwarfs the buzzing aircraft, giving passengers the sense that they're riding inside the hull of a fragile flying insect. They drink in the astonishing view. Pastel-blue cracks on the face of the glacier are deep enough to swallow a 17-story building. No one speaks. It's a wondrous sight.

Wild places stretch from horizon to horizon, untouched by human hands. From the lush rain forest of the southeastern Panhandle to the delta wetlands of the western coast and the tapestry of the far northern tundra, much of Alaska is accessible only by air. And it may never look more spectacular than it does from above.

Travel by airplane

A plane trip in Alaska is almost always a breathtaking journey, but it's also a crucial mode of transportation. Beyond the cities and towns, many communities can't be reached by road. Most bush villages appear on the map like disconnected specks without the usual web of asphalt connecting them to the outside world. Almost everything that goes in or comes out – people, mail, groceries, medicine – travels by air.

Given the importance of air travel, Alaska has been dubbed the "flyingest" state in the Union. One out of 58 Alaskans is a registered pilot, and one out of 59 owns an airplane. Lake Hood in Anchorage is the largest and busiest seaplane base in the world, averaging 234 landings and take-offs a day; 800 per day are not uncommon in summer. Merrill Field, also in Anchorage, is also home to hundreds of small aircraft.

How to arrange a flight

This is a fairly straightforward matter. Air taxi and bush operators are listed in the Yellow Pages of any Alaskan telephone directory. Some companies offer a regular schedule of flights and destinations. Others operate on a charter basis and will take you just about anywhere you want to go. Still others specialize in flightseeing tours of the region's most scenic places. Want to spend a day or two fishing in complete solitude at a remote mountain lake,

ABOVE: pilot Rebecca Fisher by her K2 ski plane at Mount McKinley base camp.
RIGHT: a Cessna floatplane negotiates the Neacola Mountains above Lake Clark National Park.

or perhaps spend a few hours trekking across an otherwise inaccessible glacier? If so, these are the people you need to see.

Bush planes range in size from a two-person Piper Super Cub to a 20-passenger DeHavilland Twin Otter. They are remarkably versatile aircraft designed to operate in the most rugged settings. Depending on season and terrain, they may be equipped with pontoons, skis, or tundra tires. Pontoons on an aircraft make convenient landing strips of coves, lakes, and streams; skis are used on ice and snow; and tundra tires, like big rubber donuts, cushion landings on gravel bars or soft, spongy tundra. Helicopters are also an option for backcountry travel, especially for close-up views of the terrain and extremely tight landings.

Legendary pilots

Bush pilots are a rugged and colorful bunch. Their courageous, comic, and sometimes tragic stories are the stuff of legend. Take Paul Claus, one of Alaska's most celebrated bush pilots. He's been known to land on a glacier so steep that he had to anchor the plane with an ice screw to keep it from sliding off the edge. To take off, he leaned out the window, cut the tether with a knife, and throttled off the slope. ❏

A CHECKLIST FOR PASSENGERS

Before you plan to fly into the wilderness, there are a few things you should keep in mind. First, air taxis aren't cheap. Cost varies widely depending on the destination, amount of gear, and the number of passengers, and is usually based on flight hours. Even a relatively short hop in the outback can cost as much as a flight from the Lower 48 states to Alaska.

Second, patience is a virtue. Bad weather and mechanical problems often delays flights for hours or days, so bring extra provisions, a deck of cards, and a sense of humor. Impatience, known by some pilots as "get-home-itis," is a leading factor in small aircraft accidents.

Finally, put safety first. Don't hesitate to ask your pilot if he or she has insurance and a commercial license, which requires a higher standard of training and aircraft maintenance than a private license. And be sure the plane has life vests, an emergency locator transmitter (ELT), and other essential safety equipment.

Never challenge a pilot's decision to cancel a flight; the sun may be shining where you are, but the weather at your destination could be dramatically different – and unsafe. Nor should you pressure a pilot to carry more people or gear than the aircraft can handle. Weight and balance are critical for safe flying.

Taking to the air in Alaska should be enjoyable. The experience is routine here, but it is very seldom boring.

PLACES

A detailed guide to the entire state, arranged
by region and with main sites clearly
cross-referenced by number to the maps

Given that its landmass amounts to one-fifth the size of the combined Lower 48 states, it's not surprising that Alaska has six distinct geographic areas.

● **Southeast Alaska** (also known as the Panhandle) is a narrow, 400-mile (640km) strip of land sandwiched between the Pacific Ocean and Canada, and cut off from the rest of Alaska by the towering St Elias range. It is covered by huge temperate rainforests nurtured by a mild climate: readings of 60° or 70°F (15° or 21°C) are not uncommon in the summer, and winter temperatures don't often dip much below freezing.

● **Southcentral Alaska** lies along the Gulf of Alaska. A region of mountains, fjords, tidewater glaciers, and forested lowlands, it includes Prince William Sound, the Kenai Peninsula, Cook Inlet, and Kodiak Island, as well as the fertile Matanuska Valley. Temperatures vary from –20°F (–29°C) in winter to 60–70°F (15–21°C) in summer.

● **Alaska's Interior** is a broad lowland cradled between the Brooks and Alaska mountain ranges. It encompasses the mighty Yukon, Tanana and Kuskokwim rivers. In some areas, birch and spruce thrive; others support only vast reaches of tundra. Temperatures can fall to below –50°F (–45°C) in winter and climb to 70–80°F (21–26°C) or higher in the summer.

● **Arctic Alaska** stretches north from the southern edge of the Brooks Range to the Arctic Ocean. Huge stretches of tundra flower spectacularly in the night-less summer. Mid-summer temperatures may exceed 80°F (26°C), while mid-winter temperatures can sink to –40°F (–40°C) or below. The minimal rainfall of 5 inches (13cm) a year qualifies it as a desert.

● **Southwest Alaska** is the home of the Alaska Peninsula and Aleutian Islands, which stretch 200 miles (320km) west into the Bering Sea. A warm current from Japan meets the icy northern air over the Aleutians, creating the rain and fog that enshroud them. Temperature range: 0°F (–17°C) to 50–60°F (10–15°C).

● **Western Alaska** and the Bering Sea coast stretch from the Arctic Circle to Bristol Bay. Much of the land is treeless tundra underlain with permafrost. Temperature range: 0°F (–17°C; with wind-chill) to 60°F (15°C). ❑

PRECEDING PAGES: a traditional winter sled dog train; grizzly bears at Hallo Bay in Katmai National Park and Preserve.
LEFT: an Alaskan pilot. **ABOVE:** glacier in Prince William Sound.

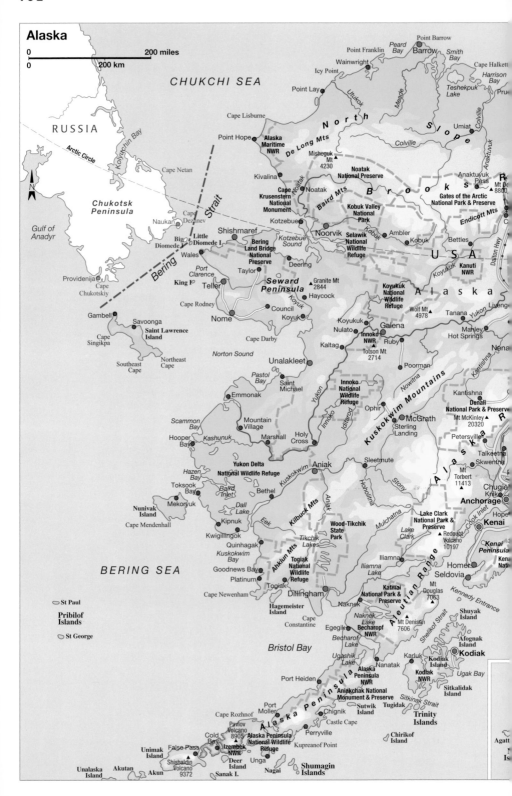

Alaska

0		200 miles
0	200 km	

CHUKCHI SEA

RUSSIA

Arctic Circle

Kolyuchin Bay

Chukotsk
Peninsula

Gulf of
Anadyr

Naukan

Cape
Dezhnev

Providenija

Cape
Chukotskiy

Gambell

Savoonga

Cape
Singikpa

Saint Lawrence
Island

Southeast
Cape

Northeast
Cape

Scammon
Bay

Hooper
Bay

Kashunuk

Hazen
Bay

Toksook
Bay

Mekoryuk

Nunivak
Island

Cape Mendenhall

BERING SEA

St Paul

Pribilof
Islands

St George

Point Barrow
Peard
Bay
Point Franklin   Barrow   Smith
Bay
Wainwright   Cape Halkett
Icy Point   Harrison
Bay
Point Lay   Teshekpuk   Pru
Lake

Cape Lisburne   North   Slope
Umiat

Point Hope   Alaska
Maritime   Colville
NWR

Misheguk
Mt
4230

Kivilina   Noatak
National Preserve   Anaktuvuk
Pass
Cape   Noatak   Mt De
Krusenstern   8800
National   Baird Mts   Brooks   Gates of the Arctic
Monument   National Park & Preserve
Kobuk Valley
National   Endicott Mts
Kotzebue   Park

Shishmaref   Noorvik Selawik Ambler   USA
Kotzebue   National   Kobuk   Bettles
Big   Little   Sound   Wildlife
Diomede Diomede I   Refuge   Dalton Hwy
Wales   Koyukuk
Port   NWR
Clarence   Deering
Taylor

King I   Teller   Granite Mt   Koyukuk   Alaska   Kanuti
Seward   2844   National   NWR
Peninsula   Wildlife
Cape Rodney   Haycock   Refuge   Wolf Mt
Council   4978   Tanana   Yukon Liveng
Nome   Koyuk

Koyukuk   Mahley
Nulato   Galena   Hot Springs
Innoko Ruby
Cape Darby   NWR
Kaltag   Totson Mt
Norton Sound   2714   Nena

Unalakleet   Poorman

Pastol
Bay   Saint
Michael   Kantishna

Emmonak   Yukon   Nowitna   Denali
National Park & Preserv
Innoko   Ophir
National   Mt McKinley
Mountain   Wildlife   20320
Village Marshall Refuge   McGrath
Holy   Sterling
Cross   Landing   Petersville

Yukon Delta   Aniak   Sleetmute   Talkeetna
National Wildlife Refuge   Skwentna

Bethel   Mt
Bald   Kuskokwim   Hoholitna   Torbert
Inlet   Killbuck Mts   11413   Chugia
Dall
Lake   Eek   Aniak   Anchorage
Kipnuk
Wood-Tikchik   Mulchatna Lake Clark   Hope
Kwigillingok   State   Lake   National Park &   Kenai
Tikchik Park   Iliamna Clark   Preserve   Kenai
Quinhagak   Lakes   Redoubt   Peninsula
Kuskokwim   Ahklun Mts Togiak   Iliamna   Volcano Kena
Bay   Goodnews Bay National Iliamna   10197   Nati
Platinum   Wildlife Lake   Homer
Togiak   Refuge   Seldovia

Cape Newenham   Katmai   Mt
Dillingham   National Park & Douglas
Hagemeister   Naknek   Preserve   7063   Kennedy Entrance
Island   Naknek Mt Denison   Shuyak
Cape   Lake   7606   Island
Constantine Egegik Becharof
NWR   Afognak
Becharof   Island
Lake
Bristol Bay   Ugashik   Karluk   Kodiak
Lake   Nanatak   Island Kodiak
Port Heiden   Alaska   Kodiak Ugak Bay
Peninsula   NWR
NWR   Sitkalidak
Aniakchak National   Island
Monument & Preserve Sitkinak Strait
Port   Sutwik Tugidak   Trinity
Cape Rozhnof Moller Chignik Island   Islands
Pavlov   Castle Cape
Volcano   Chirikof
Cold   8905 Alaska Peninsula Perryville Island
False Pass Bay National Wildlife   Kupreanof Point
Unimak   Izembek Refuge   Agatt
Island   NWR   Unga
Shishaldin Deer
Unalaska Akutan Volcano Island Nagai   Shumagin   Is
Island   9372 Sanak I.   Islands
Akun

Cape Netan

Cape

Bering Strait

Little
Diomede I

De Long Mts

Noatak

Kobuk

Koyukuk

Kuskokwim Mountains

Alaska Range

Alaska Peninsula

Aleutian Range

Shelikof Strait

Cook Inlet

Knik

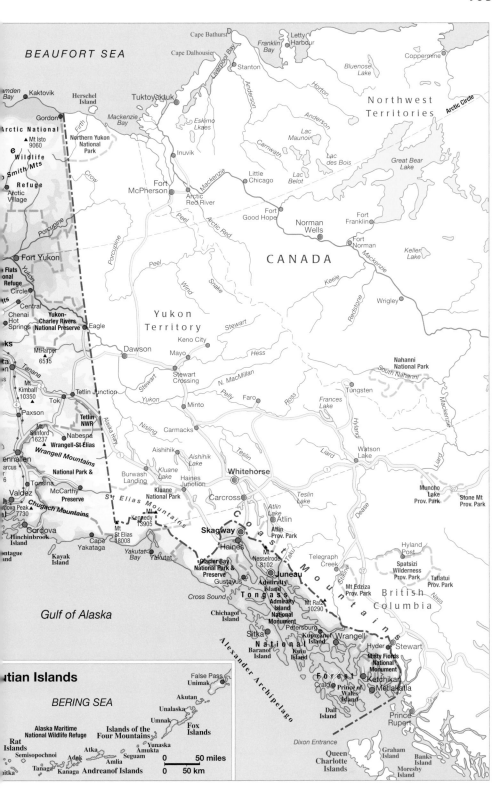

BEAUFORT SEA

Cape Bathurst
Cape Dalhousie
Liverpool Bay
Franklin Bay
Letty Harbour
Stanton
Coppermine

Bluenose Lake

Herschel Island
Kaktovik
amden Bay
Gordon

Mackenzie Bay
Eskimo Lkaes
Anderson

Northwest Territories
Arctic Circle

Arctic National
Mt Isto 9060
Northern Yukon National Park
Inuvik
Anderson
Carnwath
Lac Maunoir
Lac des Bois
Great Bear Lake

e
Wildlife
Smith Mts

Refuge
Arctic Village
Crow
Fort McPherson
Arctic Red River
Little Chicago
Lac Belot

Mackenzie

Porcupine
Peel
Arctic Red
Fort Good Hope
Norman Wells
Fort Franklin

Fort Yukon
Porcupine
CANADA
Fort Norman
Keller Lake

Flats onal Refuge
Yukon
Circle
Peel
Wind
Snake
Keele
Redstone
Mackenzie
Wrigley

ts
Central
Chenai Hot Springs
Yukon-Charley Rivers National Preserve
Eagle
Yukon Territory
Stewart
Nahanni National Park
South Nahanni
Tungsten

MtHarper 6515
Dawson
Mayo
Keno City
Hess

Tanana
Mt Kimball 10350
Tetlin Junction
Stewart Crossing
Yukon
N. MacMillan
Pelly
Faro
Frances Lake
Mackenzie

Tok
Paxson
Minto
Carmacks
Ross
Hyland

Mt Sanford 16237
Nabesna
Tetlin NWR
Nisling
Aishihik
Aishihik Lake
Teslin
Liard
Watson Lake

Wrangell-St Elias
Wrangell Mountains
Kluane Lake
Burwash Landing
Haines Junction
Whitehorse
Muncho Lake Prov. Park
Stone Mt Prov. Park

ennallen
arcus
6
Tonsina
McCarthy
National Park &
Kluane National Park
Carcross
Teslin Lake
Dease

Valdez
Cova Peak 7730
Preserve
St Elias Mountains
Atlin Lake
Atlin
Atlin Prov. Park

Cordova
Chugach Mountains
Mt Kennedy 13905
Mt St Elias 18008
Skagway
Coast
Hyland Post
Telegraph Creek
Spatsizi Wilderness Prov. Park

Hinchinbrook Island
ntague nd
Kayak Island
Cape Yakataga
Yakutat Bay
Yakutat
Haines
Mt Nesselrode 8102
Mt Edziza Prov. Park
Tatlatui Prov. Park

Glacier Bay National Park & Preserve
Gustavus
Juneau
Mt Ratz 10290
British Columbia

Gulf of Alaska
Cross Sound
Chichagof Island
Tongass
Admiralty Island
Petersburg

Sitka
Baranof Island
National
Kuiu Island
Kupreanof Island
Wrangell
Hyder
Stewart

Misty Fiords National Monument
Craig
Forest
Ketchikan
Metlakatla
Prince of Wales Island

Alexander Archipelago

utian Islands

BERING SEA

False Pass
Unimak
Akutan
Unalaska
Umnak
Fox Islands
Dall Island
Prince Rupert

Alaska Maritime National Wildlife Refuge
Islands of the Four Mountains
Yunaska
Amukta
Seguam
Dixon Entrance
Queen Charlotte Islands
Graham Island
Banks Island

Rat Islands
Semisopochnoi
Adak
Atka
Amlia
Andreanof Islands
Tanaga
Kanaga

0   50 miles
0   50 km

Mt St Elias
18008
Wrangell-St Elias
National Park &
Preserve
*Malaspina
Glacier*

Mt Vancouver
15700

Mt Kennedy
13905

St Elias Mountains

Hubbard Glacier

Russell Fjord

Mt Aylesworth
9310

Yakutat
Bay
Ocean Cape
Yakutat **12**

Cordova, Valdez

Dry Bay

Mt Hay
8870

Fairweather Range

Mt Fairweather
15300
Cape
Fairweather

Lituya Bay

Icy Point

Cape Spencer

Alsek

Tetlin

Canyon
Creek

Haines
Junction

Champagne

Klukshu

Dezadeash
Lake

Kluane
National Park

Chilkat Pass
7300

Porcupine

Klukwan

Muir Glacier

Glacier Bay
National Park
and Preserve **8**

Gustavus

Cross Sound

Elfin
Cove

Pelican

Point
Theodore

Portage

Alaska Hwy

Takhini

Lake
Laberge

Whitehorse

Yukon Territory

Squaw
Creek

Kusawa
Lake

Marsh
Lake

Carcross

Bennett

Klondike Gold Rush
National Historic
Park **11**

Dyea **10**

Glacier

Skagway

Alaska Chilkat
Bald Eagle
Preserve **9**
Haines
Port Chilkoot

Chilkat

Chilkat Range

Excursion
Inlet

Auke Bay

Mendenhall
Glacier

7

Juneau

Douglas

Hoonah
Hawk
Inlet

Tongass

Admiralty
Island
National
Monument

Chichagof
Island
Tenakee
Springs

Chatham

White Pass
2890

Klondike Hwy

Taku Arm

Lynn Canal

Funter

Klondike Hwy

Johnsons
Crossing

Wolf
Lake

Teslin

Atlin
Lake

Atlin

Surprise

Ben-My-
Chree

Atlin
Provincial
Park

Mt Nesselrode
8102

Inklin

Taku

Tulsequah

Lemieux

Galbraith

Nakina

C A N A D A

British
Columbia

Sheslay

Mt Ogden
7482

Inklin

Nahlin

Tahtian

Alaska Hwy

Teslin
Lake

Swift
River

Teslin

Wolf

Nisutlin

Jennings

Stephens Passage

Cobol

Todd

Baranof

Kruzof
Island
St Lazaria
NWR **6**
Sitka

Mount
Edgecumbe
Island

Goddard

Alexander Archipelago

Whale
Bay

Chatham Strait

Baranof

Tyee

Admiralty
Island
Angoon

Pack Creek

Seymour Canal

U S A
Alaska

Frederick Sound

Kake

Kuiu
Island

Kupreanof
Island
Petersburg **4**

Mitkof
Island

Sumdum

Windham

Cape
Fanshaw

Maury Peak
5575

Baird
Glacier

LeConte
Glacier **5**

Coast Mountains

Mt Ratz
10290

Stikine

Mt Ediza
Provincial
Park

Glenora

Telegraph
Creek

National

Tebenkof Bay
Wilderness

Pott
Alexander

Cape Pole

Coronation
Island

Edna
Bay

Warren
Island

Sumner Strait

Point
Baker

Tokeen

Zarembo
Island

Wrangell **3**

Etolin
Island

Wrangell
Island

Stikine

Iskut

Mt Whipple
5745

Unuk

G u l f o f

A l a s k a

Noyes
Island

Baker
Island

Waterfall

Hydaburg

Klawock

Craig

Hollis

Prince
of Wales
Island

Dall
Island

Kaigani

Cape Muzon

Cordova
Bay

Thorne
Bay

Meyers
Chuck

Salt
Chuck

Kasan

Ward
Cove

Gravina
Island

Saxman

Annette
Island

Metlakatla

Forest

Cape
Chacon

Duke
Island

Cape Fox

Bell Island

Loring

Revillagigedo
Island

Ketchikan **1**

Behm Canal

Rødyerd Bay-
Punchbowl Cove

Misty
Fiords
National
Monument **2**

Stewart

Hyder

Kincolith

Arrandale

Dixon Entrance

Dundas
Island

Port
Simpson

Portland Inlet

Prince George

Queen
Charlotte
Islands

Stephens
Island

Prince
Rupert

Port
Edward

Porcher
Island

N

Southeast Alaska: The Panhandle

| 0 | 100 miles |
| 0 | 100 km |

TOURING THE SOUTHEAST PANHANDLE

A cruise or ferry tour of the Panhandle is a good introduction to Alaska, giving the visitor a taste of the scenery and the culture

Ever since it emerged from the melting of the last great Ice Age 15,000 years ago, the great island-studded, 1,000-mile (1,600km) passage of water that stretches from present-day lower British Columbia to the top of the Southeast Alaska Panhandle has been one of Earth's treasures. The first Europeans to visit a portion of what is now called the Inside Passage did not get a friendly reception from the locals, however. In 1741 Alexei Chirikof, captain of *St Paul*, set sail from Russia. With his commander, Vitus Bering (who also was captain of the vessel *St Peter*), he left the Kamchatkan Peninsula in Siberia and headed east on a voyage of exploration and discovery.

The two captains were separated in a storm which struck soon after leaving port, and never saw each other again. Bering died after being shipwrecked on his voyage home. Chirikof and his crew sighted the high wooded mountains of what we now call Prince of Wales Island in Southeast Alaska on July 15, 1741. Two days later they dropped anchor near the present-day city of Sitka. It was there that tragedy struck, when two boatloads of sailors put ashore to reconnoiter disappeared without trace *(see page 45)*.

These days, it is not often that visitors to the Panhandle fail to return to ship. When it does happen, it is probably because they lose track of time while hiking to the top of Deer Mountain in Ketchikan, get carried away in the pursuit of pleasure at the Red Dog Saloon in Juneau, or simply decide the fishing is too good to be hurried.

Lifestyles along the Inside Passage

The sights along the Inside Passage are surprisingly varied and seldom boring. There are two capital cities, one Canadian (Victoria) and one American (Juneau), where life and lifestyle revolve largely around politics and bureaucracy. And there are tiny Native villages where the food on most residents' tables still depends on the skills of the hunters and fishermen.

The geography and the geology of the Inside Passage varies greatly as well. At its southernmost end, the passage is protected by Vancouver

ABOVE: a contemporary gold panner; fishing boats in Wrangell harbor.

Island, a large, elongated landmass that begins near the northern border of the continental United States and stretches almost 300 miles (480km) northwest, nearly half the distance up the British Columbia coast to Southeast Alaska. Then comes the seaward protection of the Queen Charlotte Islands, not as large as Vancouver Island but a number of them – especially Graham and Moresby islands – quite sizeable nonetheless.

And finally, about where US jurisdiction resumes and Southeast Alaska begins, there's the Alexander Archipelago, a 400-mile (645km) long maze of 1,000 islands which, along with a 30-mile (48km) wide sliver of mainland, make up the Southeast Alaska Panhandle.

If the size and national colors of the islands of the Inside Passage vary, there is this commonality all along the way: lush green forests of spruce, hemlock, cedar, fir, and other conifers cover whole islands and mountains except for snow-capped peaks, ice fields feeding glaciers, and gravel beaches. Generous bays and exquisite little coves rival one another for attention, and major rivers course through great glacier-carved valleys, while waterfalls plunge from mountainside cliffs to the sea.

The islands' allure

Everywhere along the way are watercraft: seine boats with crews of half a dozen or more; small trollers and gillnet fishing craft with a skipper and, maybe, a single helper; tugs pulling rafts of logs or barges of commercial goods; exotic yachts and simple open boats; cruise-ships; state ferries; freighters; even sailboats and kayaks. The reason for this concentration of watercraft, of course, is protection. The same islands which

provide evergreen beauty to visitors along the way provide buffers from North Pacific winds and weather that could otherwise threaten all but the toughest vessels.

The islands also protect and nurture a wide variety of wild creatures. Ashore, and beyond the gaze of spectators, numerous animals make their homes within the forests and even atop the mountains of the Southeast Alaska Panhandle. Charter a light aircraft at Yakutat, near the very top of the Panhandle, and you are likely to see moose and perhaps brown bear as well. Near Juneau or Ketchikan or any of the other cities in the region, there is a good opportunity to spot groups of white mountain goats.

Take one of the kayak excursions in **Glacier Bay National Park** in the northern Panhandle *(see pages 140–3)*, and you just might see the rare "Glacier Blue" – a subspecies of black bear. Cruise or fly to Pack Creek on **Admiralty Island** *(see pages 110 and 119)* during the salmon spawning season and you can easily view dozens of huge, lumbering brown bears.

Spotting wildlife

Throughout the Panhandle, and down the coast of British Columbia as well, Sitka black-tail deer are numerous. This is one species of land animal you may be able to spot along the beaches from a cruise ship.

Sea mammals are easier to see from a boat, of course. Humpback and killer whales, cavorting porpoises in twos and fours, and sea lions, seals and sea otters by the dozen are frequent sights, much appreciated by vessel-borne visitors along the Inside Passage.

Eagles are everywhere – the white-headed, white-tailed bald eagle, symbol of the United States. You see them diving and swooping from the heights to grab unwary fish swimming near the water's surface, you witness the strength of their powerful talons as they rip salmon carcasses to shreds alongside spawning streams, and you see them high in the spruce trees, standing guard over heavy nests that are lodged in the forks of great branches.

Besides the eagles, there are huge black ravens, tiny gray wrens, and black-capped Arctic terns (which come here from as far south as Antarctica), plus hundreds of different waterfowl, shorebirds, sea birds, and upland species.

The fishing here is world-class. Perhaps your goal is to haul in a lunker king salmon of 50lbs (23kg) or more. Or maybe you want to test your skill against diving, dancing, and frothing steelhead trout. Whatever your heart's desire, the fishing in this region is simply unbeaten anywhere else. In addition to kings and steelheads, there are coho (silver) salmon – considered by many to be, pound for pound, the gamest fish in salt water – plus sockeye salmon, halibut, rainbow trout, Dolly Varden, and eastern brook trout (these latter two are actually chars).

With this concentration of fish, wildlife, and scenic beauty, it's easy to see why increasing numbers of people choose to settle in this region.

Getting there

Only three of the many Southeast Alaska communities are located on any road system; therefore travel to and within the area is generally by air or water. Nearly 60 percent of all visitors to Alaska arrive by cruise ship.

The second most common mode of arrival is by air. Alaska Airlines offers by far the most comprehensive coverage of the state, with regularly scheduled jet service to every major community (and some incredibly minor ones – *see Yakutat, page 156*).

Regional airlines, air taxis and charter services (using small planes on wheels, skis or floats) provide transportation to any and all locations within the state, including Southeast. For information on local air carriers, check the visitor information website of the community nearest your destination *(see Travel Tips, page 343)*.

The Alaska Marine Highway System ferries are the most common (and economical) option for travel between Southeast communities *(see page 113)*. Cross-sound ferry service, connecting Southeast routes with those in Southcentral and Southwest, is available twice monthly in summer. For schedules and rates, contact the AMHS directly (tel: 800-642-0066; www.dot.state.ak.us/amhs). ❏

LEFT: Chilkat dancer in Haines; Skagway excursion. **ABOVE:** abundant sealife.

KETCHIKAN

Creek Street's brothels have turned into restaurants and boutiques, but the area's frontier past is commemorated in shows and exhibitions highlighting totems, eagles, and lumberjack skills

The city of **Ketchikan** ❶ tumbles down the densely-forested, mountainous, southwestern side of Revillagigedo Island until it reaches its distinctive angle of repose: stacks of steep-roofed houses cling to the wooded slope, while the business district, apparently unable to halt the momentum, surges forward onto pilings in the Tongass Narrows. Located near the southernmost boundary of Alaska, Ketchikan is a major port of entry for Southeast Alaska and is generally the first stop for Alaska-bound cruise ships and Alaska Marine Highway System ferries.

Salmon capital

The "First City", or the "Salmon Capitol of the World" as it is referred to by locals, has adapted through several economic "boom-and-bust" cycles. Many of the 7,600 residents (14,000, counting the surrounding areas) work in commercial fishing, fish processing, tourism, or logging.

The earliest inhabitants of the area were Tongass and Cape Fox Tlingit Indians, who established a fish camp by Ketchikan Creek and called it "kitschk-hin", or "thundering wings of an eagle". The region's mild, maritime climate and rich natural resources, primarily timber and fish, eventually drew non-Native adventurers. As more settlers moved into the area, the majority of the Tlingit population relocated to nearby Saxman.

In 1885, a founder of Ketchikan, Mike Martin, bought 160 acres of land from Tlingit Chief Kyan – a parcel that later became the town site. The first cannery was soon built along the creek and, by 1936, a total of seven canneries were operating in the area.

Following the discovery of gold and copper in the region, the City of Ketchikan (incorporated in 1900) became an important mining supply center. As the city grew, so did the demand for lumber. Ketchikan Spruce Mills opened its doors in 1903, and the

Main attractions
CREEK STREET
DOLLY'S HOUSE
SOUTHEAST DISCOVERY CENTER
DEER MOUNTAIN TRIBAL HATCHERY
& EAGLE CENTER
TONGASS HISTORICAL MUSEUM
POTLATCH PARK
SAXMAN
TOTEM HERITAGE CENTER

LEFT: Totem Heritage Center.
BELOW: Ketchikan.

A guide at Dolly's House.

BELOW RIGHT:
Creek Street,
Ketchikan.

city became the hub for logging activities and supplies. In 1954, the Ward Cove pulp mill was constructed nearby, and the operation provided many years of economic growth and stability for Ketchikan residents. The U.S. Forest Service eventually canceled its 50-year contract with the company, however, and the pulp mill closed in 1997.

There were other reasons for fishermen, miners and loggers to flock to Ketchikan in the early 1900s. The town's infamous **Creek Street ⓐ** enjoyed a booming alcohol trade at the time of the territory's Bone Dry Law of 1917, the National Prohibition Act of 1920 and for many years to follow. Rowdy crowds gathered for the music, dancing and "social opportunities" of the notorious Star dance hall and the several houses of prostitution nearby. In 1953, this era ended as city officials permanently closed the doors of the brothels.

From brothel to museum

Today the wooden walkway of a chastened Creek Street leads tourists through a colorful array of gift shops,

galleries, restaurants, coffee shops (featuring a delicious, locally roasted brew) and **Dolly's House,** a popular brothel-turned-museum. While in the Creek Street area, take a ride on the **funicular tram** (charge), which travels up the steep mountainside to the lobby of the beautiful Cape Fox Lodge Hotel. The brief ride will afford a good view of the city and a chance to enjoy fine dining at the hotel restaurant.

A stop at the **Ketchikan Visitors Bureau ⓑ** (131 Front Street; tel: 800-770-3300 or 225-6166; www.visit-ketchikan.com; summer daily 6am–6pm, year round Mon–Fri 8am–5pm), located on the cruise ship dock, will help you plan your visit. The staff will hand you a walking tour map as well as the *Ketchikan Art Guide.*

The Bureau's **tour center,** located in the same building, provides public restrooms, pay phones, an ATM (cash machine), a phone card dispenser and bicycle or scooter rentals. You may also purchase tickets at the center for local attractions (like the popular **Great Alaskan Lumberjack Show**) or to tour Ketchikan and surrounding areas

Remote Adventuring in the Southeast

In addition to the major communities along the Inside Passage, there are countless other settlements worth a day's or a week's visit. Near Ketchikan, on Prince of Wales Island, a colorful old cannery has been converted into **Waterfall Resort** (www.waterfallresort.com), what the owners call "the most civilized resort in Alaska." It's within easy reach of some of Southeast Alaska's hottest salmon angling.

Angoon is the only settlement in **Admiralty Island National Monument**, a largely wilderness preserve that can be reached by air or sea from Sitka or Juneau, and that is famous for its salmon and large numbers of brown bears. **Kake**, which has the tallest totem pole in the state, is the jumping-off point for trips to **Tebenkof Bay Wilderness**, where experienced kayakers can spend days paddling the waters around the bays and coves of many tiny islands. **Hoonah**, the largest Tlingit village in Southeast Alaska, has some good hiking trails and a Cultural Center and Museum, which exhibits Tlingit art.

Small commercial fishing centers, like **Elfin Cove**, **Tenakee Springs**, with its hot thermal baths, and **Pelican**, though never touted as tourist towns, provide visitors with indelible memories of a very contented part of Alaska. Pelican can be visited on a day trip from Juneau through the **Icy Strait**, where you may well see humpback whales.

via horse-drawn trolley, motorcycle, ATV, tour boat, kayak, semi-submersible or amphibious craft, aerial zip-line, or floatplane (to name a few).

The tour center can also help you arrange for a fishing charter from one of many local operators. Public transportation and taxi stands are close by for those who prefer to strike out on their own.

Be sure to visit the **Southeast Discovery Center** G (50 Main Street; tel: 228-6220; www.fs.fed.us/r10/tongass/districts/discoverycenter; May–Oct Mon–Fri 8am–5pm, Sat–Sun 8am–4pm, Oct–May Tue–Sat 10am–4pm; charge in summer only, 15 years and younger free). This excellent interpretive facility, operated by the US Forest Service, will give you an overview of the Tongass National Forest, its history, wildlife, and various recreational opportunities including hiking, boating, kayaking, fishing, camping, and remote cabin rentals. The center also features authentic totems, Native artists in residence, cultural exhibits, and a gift shop.

In addition to the Discovery Center and the Creek Street shops, the **Deer**

Mountain Tribal Hatchery and Eagle Center D (1158 Salmon Road; tel: 228-5278; www.kictribe.org; May–Sept daily 8am–4.30pm; charge, 12 years and younger free) is an easy stroll from the downtown area, and offers a chance to see an active salmon and steelhead hatchery, visit a fish ladder, and watch live bird of prey demonstrations.

The small, but interesting **Tongass Historical Museum** E is also nearby (629 Dock Street; tel: 225-5900; May–Sept daily 8am–5pm, Oct–Apr Wed–Fri 1–5pm, Sat 10am–4pm, Sun 1–4pm; charge in summer). Its photographic collection is a particular strength.

Potlatch Park

Among the Native peoples of North America's northwest coastal communities, a potlatch is a ceremony that includes not only a sumptuous feast of traditional Native dishes, but also the giving of gifts (often lavish) by the potlatch host. Ketchikan's newest totem site, **Potlatch Park** F (9805 Totem Bight Road; www.potlatchpark.com; daily 7.30am–approximately 6pm) was dedicated in August 2006 as a tribute to the

TIP

The best way to see Ketchikan is on foot, as part of an organized tour or an independent ramble. But be prepared for rain. The town "enjoys" a yearly average of 13.5ft (4 meters) of precipitation, so the chances of getting wet are excellent. Fortunately, most of the attractions are within a short walk.

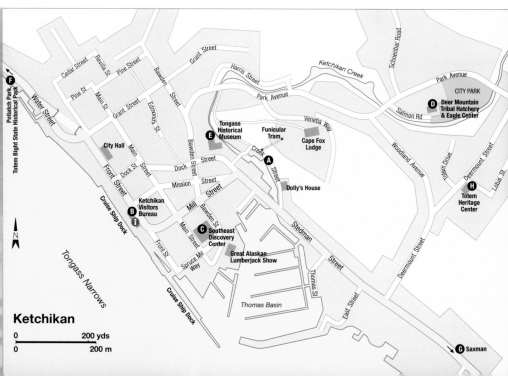

Ketchikan

0   200 yds
0   200 m

Traditional totems captured a family's heritage in their design, and the pole's height was often an indication of wealth and power.

BELOW RIGHT: demonstrating traditional skills at the Great Alaskan Lumberjack Show.

major tribal ancestors of the Native villages of the Ketchikan area. The 5-acre (2-hectare) park, located 10 miles north of downtown, is situated in a wooded area facing the Tongass Narrows – the site of ancient Tlingit fishing grounds. It features 12 full-sized totems (the tallest measuring 42ft/12.8 meters in height), five intricately carved tribal houses, a busy carving center, an antique car museum, an antique Alaskan firearm museum, interesting Native art displays, an expansive gift shop, and free coffee.

The main tribal house is an exact recreation of an 18th-century dwelling, which would have housed up to 50 people, and is held together by gravity, as opposed to nails and bolts.

Inside the nearby carving center, master Native carvers are busy chiseling family stories into elaborate totems made from 36ft (11-meter) cedar logs. Potlatch Park, owned by Kanoe Zantua, of the Eagle Frog Clan of the Haida Nation of Ketchikan is well worth visiting by those interested in Native culture, as it "…stands in tribute to the souls of Alaska coastal communities."

Saxman

Just 2 miles (3km) south of Ketchikan is the Native village of **Saxman** ⑤ (actually an incorporated city, with a population of about 400 – primarily Tlingit – residents). The Cape Fox Corporation (www.capefoxtours.com) offers an interesting tour of the **Saxman Totem Park**, which includes a tribal house, carving center (where you can watch Native artisans at work), dance exhibitions, and a gift shop.

Other Cape Fox offerings include a trip to the historic George Inlet Cannery site, or an opportunity for fly-fishing in a remote river valley.

More totems are on show at the **Totem Heritage Center** ⑪ (601 Deermount Street; tel: 225-5900; www.city. ketchikan.ak.us; May–Sept daily 8am–5pm, Oct–Apr Mon–Fri 1–5pm; charge in summer), at the **Totem Bight State Historical Park** (10 miles/16km north of town on North Tongass Highway).

Ketchikan is also the jumping-off point for **Misty Fiords National Monument** *(page 114)*. The monument, 40 miles (64km) south of Ketchikan, is accessible by boat or floatplane. ❑

RESTAURANTS

Annabelle's Keg and Chowder House
326 Front Street
Tel: 225-6009 **$–$$$**
www.gilmorehotel.com
In the historic Gilmore Hotel, this eatery serves lunch and dinner in the heart of downtown.

Burger Queen
518 Water Street
Tel: 225-6060 **$**
Burgers, breaded halibut, grilled chicken, salads and more served up in generous portions. Tiny seating area, so consider take-out or the free delivery.

Heen Kahidi Dining Room (Cape Fox Lodge)
800 Venetia Avenue
Tel: 225-8001
www.capefoxlodge. com **$–$$$$**
Take a scenic tram ride up from the downtown shops to have breakfast, lunch or dinner while enjoying the view. Extensive menu, full bar.

Ketchikan Coffee Company
207 Stedman Street
Tel: 247-2326 **$–$$**
Coffee, soups, and sandwiches served in the popular New

York Hotel. Dinner specials nightly; beer and wine.

Oceanview Restaurant
1831 Tongass Avenue
Tel: 225-7566
www.oceanviewmex. com **$–$$$**
Eclectic menu featuring many delicious Mexican and Italian dishes. Beer and wine.

Price is for dinner excluding tax, tip, and beverages:
$ = under $15
$$ = $15–20
$$$ = $20–30
$$$$ = over $30

Getting Around by Ferry

Alaska Marine Highway System ferries are the main means of travel around this region, but you need to plan ahead in the summer months.

For independent travelers with the luxury of time, cruising the Inside Passage aboard one of the 11 state-run Alaska Marine Highway System (AMHS) ferries is a relaxing, comfortable and reasonably convenient option for seeing the coastal communities of Southeast, Southcentral and Southwest Alaska. Since driving between these communities is, generally speaking, not an option, locals rely on ferry travel as a primary mode of transportation.

If you're traveling in spring or fall, you'll likely see school athletes, debate teams or spelling bee contestants bound for competitions in neighboring (or far-flung) coastal communities. Residents of more remote towns travel for doctor visits, shopping, business, and countless other reasons.

US Forest Service interpreters are onboard the ferries during the summer months to give informative lectures and to point out the interesting sights along the way. Additionally, visitors generally have no problem getting Alaskans onboard to talk about their state.

The AMHS ferries offer clean, comfortable staterooms (for most ships, advance reservations are important), tasty, reasonably priced cafeteria-style food service, a bar, clean restrooms, hot showers (towel rental available), and various lounges (some with recliners) featuring large windows for easy viewing of the passing landscape. Should the captain see a whale (or other notable wildlife) en route, he'll usually make a public announcement and try to maneuver the ship to allow for a good view.

Traveling aboard the Alaska ferries is also a great option for families with children. There's plenty of wiggle room, and most ferries have a play area for toddlers, a video game room, a movie room and, if you pay extra for a stateroom, a good place to nap. Those without staterooms spread out sleeping bags onto the carpeted floors at night, stretch out in one of the many recliners, or pitch a tent up on the top deck near the solarium.

The downside of ferry travel is that if you bring a vehicle aboard the cost jumps considerably. You must make reservations early because the car decks fill up quickly for the summer months. The price for traveling non-stop from one end of Southeast to the other is not hugely different from that of breaking up your trip with stopovers at various communities along the way. But it may be a day or two (much more in some instances) before another ferry traveling in the desired direction comes along.

Information, routes, ship descriptions, fares, and scheduling information are all available online at www.dot.state.ak.us/amhs, or telephone: 800-642-0066 or 465-3941.   ❏

ABOVE: backpackers use a ferry as a dormitory.
RIGHT: a ferry docks at Ketchikan.

MISTY FIORDS NATIONAL MONUMENT

Alaska
Anchorage●

The southernmost of Alaska's national monuments is a magical place, carved out by the steady progress of gigantic glaciers

Main attractions
KETCHIKAN CREEK
BOLD ISLAND
RUDYERD ISLAND
NEW EDDYSTONE ROCK
RUDYERD BAY
PUNCHBOWL COVE
NOOYA CREEK

BELOW: New Eddystone Rock.

isty Fiords was designated by the US Congress as a national wilderness as well as a national monument, and within the 3,570 sq miles (9,240 sq km) of its largely untouched coast and backcountry lie three major rivers, hundreds of small streams and creeks, icefields, glaciers, old-growth rain forest, snowcapped mountains, and mountain-top lakes.

Glacial scenery

Eons ago, great glaciers thousands of feet deep filled what are now South-east Alaska bays and valleys. Slowly but relentlessly they ground their way seaward from mountain-top heights. In the process they carved and scoured great steep-walled cliffs that now plunge from mountain summits to considerable depths below sea level. The effect of this carving and scouring has never been more beautifully evident than it is in **Misty Fiords National Monument ②**.

It is the southernmost of Alaska's four national monuments and one of two in the Tongass National Forest (the other is Admiralty Island). Visitors to this 2.2-million-acre (890,000-hectare) wilderness experience every major ecosystem of Southeast Alaska, from the ocean swells on the outer coast to the high alpine lakes and icefields. There are tiny coves, great bays, and forest groves so thick you can barely see daylight through them.

Misty Fiords wildlife includes brown and black bears, Sitka black-tail deer, wolves, mountain goats, beavers, mink, marten, foxes, and river otters. But it is not only a place of scenery and wildlife on a grand scale: it also has tremendous commercial value. Some of Alaska's most productive fish-rearing streams are located here.

There are very few marks of human activity inside Misty Fiords. The area's first human inhabitants, the Native Tlingits and Haidas, are believed to have settled here many thousands of years ago, after crossing the land bridge from Siberia, but there is very little evidence of their passing.

Touring Misty Fiords

No roads lead to Misty Fiords, and visitors can reach the monument only by water or by air. Some travelers opt for a combination cruise/fly tour – going in by water and out by air, or vice versa. Some cruise ships visit the monument as part of an Inside Passage experience (*see page 87*). You can fly there with one of several Ketchikan air charter companies; you can cruise there by charter boat; or you can sign on with an outfit called Alaska Cruises (tel: 225-6045 or 800-228-1905; www.goldbelttours.com), and take one of the yacht tours which run daily in the summer time.

These excursions, aboard one of the company's 90-passenger vessels, can either be a round trip or one way, with one part of the journey – either coming or going – done by air. Round-trip cruises last about 6½ hours, while combination cruise-flightseeing trips are 4½ hours long.

On a typical cruise/fly tour, the boat will depart from near downtown Ketchikan in early to mid-morning, but coffee is always ready on the galley stove and donuts are on the serving table for passengers who arrive on the ship early. These boats are wide, beamy, comfortable cruisers with plenty of walking-around room, big view windows, and table seating for 32. When the weather is good, you can go onto an open-air deck above the cabin.

Salmon route

The sightseeing begins as soon as the boat's lines are cast off and the vessel begins its southeasterly path toward the lower end of Revillagigedo Island (the locals abbreviate it to Revilla Island), on which Ketchikan is located. Passing dockside fish processors, supply houses and the town's main business district, the vessel soon cruises past the entrance to **Ketchikan Creek**. Late in the summer, thousands of salmon assemble at this spot before

ascending the creek – and formidable waterfalls – to spawn in the upstream shallows and then die.

Shortly after Creek Street (Ketchikan's former red-light district), the boat goes past **Saxman** (*see page 112*), a Native village containing one of the largest collections of totems in the state.

Next is **Bold Island**, where passengers line the port (left-hand) rails and windows of the vessel in the hope of seeing bald eagles perched in the island spruce trees. For Southeast Alaskans, such sightings are commonplace, though they never become dull. For visitors, the sight of America's national bird is a highlight of the trip.

No permit is needed for camping in Misty Fiords, but visitors are advised to discuss plans with rangers before arriving. For details, contact the US Forest Service, tel: 907-225-2148.

BELOW: Punchbowl Lake, Misty Fiords National Monument.

Orca whales hunting for porpoises.

BELOW RIGHT:
a Sitka black-tail
deer crosses a
hiking trail.

At one point or another during the morning's cruise, most passengers will crowd into the yacht's little wheelhouse and talk to the skipper. Sometimes that's Dale Pihlman, former owner of the Alaska Cruises excursion firm. He generally welcomes the intrusion, as he is never reluctant to talk about the monument.

Pihlman, a former commercial fisherman, was one of the committed people who traveled to Washington in the late 1970s to lobby for the bill that created Misty Fiords National Monument in the first place. The provisions of the bill do protect most of the monument – and all of the wilderness – from any destructive exploitation.

Porpoise companions

As the boat cruises toward the fjords, the on-board guide and naturalist may announce that there are porpoises both fore and aft of the vessel, and the passengers – half going in each direction in order to keep an even kilter – scramble for a view of the small marine mammals. The porpoises swimming behind the yacht are too far away for a

close look – they are visible only as leaping, playing creatures 300 feet or more astern. But the ones in front are only a few feet away, clearly visible, and just as clearly having a wonderful time pacing the boat. It's obvious they could easily outdistance the vessel, but they prefer to stay and play.

By noon the vessel is in the monument and the skipper guides it through a narrow channel into an exquisite tree-shrouded cove on **Rudyerd Island**. Here you can see the steep granite rock formations on the shore and the occasional jet black vertical streaks, a few inches to a couple of feet or more wide, that appear among the brown granite walls. These were formed 60 million years ago when earthquakes cracked the granite, and hot molten magma came up from below the earth's surface to fill the cracks. The black streaks that you see are the magma.

Shapely rock

A little later, **New Eddystone Rock** *(see photograph on page 114)* comes into view. Depending upon the time of day when you see it and the angle from

Dressing Sensibly for the Southeast

The temperate rainforest of Southeast Alaska features a mild, wet, maritime climate. Average winter temperatures range from 29° to 39°F (–2° to 4°C)in Ketchikan (southernmost city) to 18° to 31° (–8° to –1°C) in Yakutat (northernmost community). Summers average 51° to 65°F (11° to 18°C) and 47° to 60°F (8° to 16°C) respectively.

The entire Panhandle experiences heavy precipitation (13½ft/4.1 meters per year average in Ketchikan; 11ft/3.3 meters in Yakutat), which creates the ideal environment for the unique flora and fauna of the area.

These conditions also create the need for summertime visitors to bring along excellent protection from wind and rain. Plan to dress in layers (to allow for warmth and comfort in a variable climate), and make sure the outer-most layer is waterproof. A quality-constructed, hooded rain jacket (with a drawstring to pull the hood close to your face), a lightweight, knitted hat, gloves, waterproof pants, and comfortable, waterproof footwear are ideal. Umbrellas, on the other hand, are difficult to manage, block your view and turn inside out in a sudden gust of wind… but this provides amusement for the locals.

Wintertime travelers should add winter-weight hooded coats, warm knit hats, mittens, and insulated boots to their clothing list.

which you approach it, the rock can resemble several things: sometimes it looks like a man-made building, at others, a ship under sail, or it can look exactly what it is – a high-rising volcano "plug" from millennia past. It was called Eddystone Rock by the British navigator Captain George Vancouver (1758–98), after whom the Canadian city is named, because he thought it looked very much like Eddystone Lighthouse off the shore of his native Plymouth, in England.

Overnight campers and kayakers who want to go into the fjords often travel with the day visitors on Alaska Cruises trips, and now leave the ship to paddle the waters off Winstanley Island. There's a US Forest Service cabin there, one of relatively few located on saltwater sites in Southeast Alaska.

The comfortable, weather-tight shelter is popular with campers who paddle around **Rudyerd Bay** during the day. On entering the bay, the cruiser often meets a welcoming committee of at least 20 seals, which lie basking on the rocks of an island to port. Minutes later, within the bay, the boat approaches the towering vertical walls of **Punchbowl Cove**. And it is here that you really begin to feel the magical, mystical effect of the place.

Punchbowl Cove

It can be truly eerie hereabouts, especially when – as the monument's name suggests – there is mist or cloud or fog in the air. Steep, stark granite walls descend from heights hidden in clouds. Waterfalls, which range from torrents to trickles, plunge from unseen sources just as high. Trees cling tenaciously to many of the cliff-sides, on surfaces that don't seem to have enough soil to support a house plant.

The waters around and beneath the boat are a cold, slate gray, and they descend to depths of 750ft (230 meters) or more. There have, as yet, been no sightings of sea monster reported in these waters – but it's exactly the right kind of place for them.

On board, thoughts turn to more practical matters: it is time for a lunch of seafood chowder, rolls and tossed green salad. After lunch, the vessel leaves Punchbowl Cove and cruises

TIP

Pronouncing certain place names in the Southeast can be tricky. Here's a guide:
Tlingit: *KLINK–it*
Haida: *HY–duh*
Tsimshian: *SIM–shee–an*
Revillagigedo: *ruh–vee–uh–ga–GAY–doh*
Metlakatla: *met–la–KAT–la*
Klawock: *kla–WOCK*
Gustavus: *gus–TA–vus*
Dyea: *die-ee*
Yakutat: *YAK–a–tat*

BELOW:
Walker Cove seen from a skiff.

Humpback whales are one of the area's great sights.

BELOW: up-close view of a waterfall in Rudyerd Bay.

toward the head of Rudyerd Bay. Along the shoreline that now replaces the steep cliffs, you may look out for bears, wolves or other wild creatures.

Creeks and waterfalls

The boat stops again an hour later, this time at **Nooya Creek** where, in season, 1,000 or more pink salmon descend to salt water each year from Nooya Lake in the high country. Here a trail leads to the uplands – although it is not as steep as the one which takes off, and up, from the Punchbowl Cove area. Camping and trout-fishing opportunities at the ends of the trails are outstanding.

Then, if you are lucky, it might be time for yet another memorable expe-rience. On some trips the skipper will edge his boat right up to the bottom of a large plummeting waterfall, and passengers are given paper cups which they can fill with the icy water. By mid-afternoon, it is time for those who fly back to Ketchikan to disembark and board the floatplane which taxis gently up to the boarding platform.

From the air

Fifteen minutes later, goodbyes are yelled to those remaining and the pilot drifts his plane away from the vessel. He then gives the aircraft full throttle, and within a minute it is airborne. Within three or four minutes more the airborne passengers may well be spot-ting white, furry mountain goats, usu-ally nannies and their youngsters, negotiating seemingly impossible cliff faces to the right of the plane. It is a dramatic flight back through the fjords, and the wildlife is only part of the excitement as the dark granite walls seem to be just inches away from the plane's wing tips – a bit too close for comfort, some may think, but passen-gers are in very safe hands. ❑

National Forests

Alaska is home to the nation's two largest national forests, the Tongass and the Chugach, in the Southeast and Southcentral regions.

At nearly 17 million acres (6.9 million hectares), the **Tongass National Forest** (tel: 225-3101; www.fs.fed.us/r10/tongass) is by far America's biggest. Stretching the entire length of Alaska's Inside Passage, it encompasses three-fourths of the Panhandle. The Tongass was created in 1907 by President Roosevelt to protect the region's timber resources, wildlife, and fisheries; its name is taken from the Tlingit Indian tribe's Tongass clan.

Within the Tongass boundaries are huge expanses of old-growth coastal rain forest – about 32 percent of the total acreage. Over the years, a little more than 6 percent of this old-growth forest area has been harvested, mostly by clearcut methods. The remaining expanse, comprising approximately 97 percent of the total old-growth area, remains today as it was 100 years ago, providing critical habitat for all sorts of animals, from brown and black bears to Sitka black-tail deer, moose, mink, river otters, beavers, and five species of Pacific salmon. Birds range from eagles and owls to loons and songbirds.

One of the forest's prime wildlife areas is Admiralty Island, near Juneau, with one of the world's densest populations of brown bears; some 1,500 to 1,700 inhabit Admiralty, or about one per square mile. It is also has one of the world's largest concentrations of nesting bald eagles; biologists have identified more than 800 nests along Admiralty's 700 miles (1,100km) of coastline. To protect its wildlife habitat, more than 90 percent of the island is protected as wilderness within Admiralty Island National Monument.

A second national monument within the Tongass National Forest is Misty Fiords National Monument, with more than 2 million acres (800,000 hectares) of coastal fjords, old-growth forest, mountains, rivers, lakes, and glaciers.

Besides its famed coastal forest, the Tongass includes a wide range of habitat, from coastal waters to high alpine tundra and huge icefields that feed hundreds of glaciers. Forest lands and waters are used for all sorts of recreation, from fishing to wildlife viewing.

The Chugach

Alaska's second vast forest, the **Chugach National Forest**, includes nearly 6 million acres (2.4 million hectares) within its borders. Centered around Southcentral Alaska's coastal area, it reaches across three geographic regions: the northeastern Kenai Peninsula; Prince William Sound; and the Copper River Delta. Within its borders are Kayak Island, where Europeans first stepped foot on Alaskan soil; Columbia Glacier, one of the world's largest tidewater glaciers; and the Copper River Delta's rich wetlands, which serve as a critical staging and breeding area for North American waterfowl and shorebirds during their yearly migrations.

The Chugach encompasses many types of habitat, from lush forests and rugged coastline to high mountains, jagged ridges, ice fields and glaciers. It is a playground for all types of outdoor enthusiasts. One of the Chugach's most popular destinations is the Begich-Boggs Center (tel: 783-2326) near Portage Glacier, less than an hour's drive south of Anchorage. Additional information on Chugach National Forest is available from the US Forest Service in Anchorage (tel: 743-9500; www.fs.fed.us/r10/chugach).   ❏

RIGHT: Tongass is an old-growth forest.

WRANGELL

Alaska
Anchorage
Wrangell

This was the only town in Alaska to fly the Russian, British, and American flags. Today it is known for sports fishing and petroglyph spotting

BELOW: Wrangell.

W hen you visit the heavily for-ested island community of Wrangell ❸, located 89 miles (143km) north of Ketchikan on Wrangell Island, what you see is pretty much what you get. There won't be any semi-submersible or zip-line tours like in Ketchikan; no streets lined with restored (or, as in Skagway, re-created), gold rush-styled false-front saloons or dance halls to amaze and amuse.

What you can look forward to is an authentic, working town of about 2,000 people, many of whom, for gen-erations, have fed their families by log-ging in the Tongass, working in local sawmills or commercial fishing. National forest management policies, responding to environmental con-cerns, have curtailed much of the Ton-gass logging, and Wrangell's lumberjacks have done what their grandfathers and great-grandfathers before them did: adapt. Their city is changing to a broader-based economy that includes seafood processing, value-added timber products and tourism.

Wrangell is one of the oldest settle-ments in Alaska. It has the distinction of having been ruled by four nations: Tlingit, Russia, England and the USA.

Tlingit heritage

Ancient Tlingit stories tell of a migra-tion to the area through "the hole in the ice", a possible reference to a river (flowing beneath the glacier ice) that led from interior Canada through the Stikine River corridor to the lush, coastal forests. The milder climate, pro-tected coastal waterway and rich resources of the Stikine River delta must have seemed like paradise to the Tlingits, and they fiercely defended their newfound home against the Haida and Tsimshian who arrived later. These same Tlingit warriors were also skilled traders, and their area of com-merce extended into interior Canada, up the Copper River and beyond.

Russian fur trade with the Stikine Tlingit began as early as 1811. Wrang-

ell Island was named in honor of the manager of the Russian American Company, Ferdinand von Wrangel, around 1830. In 1834, the Russians built a stockade, Redoubt St Dionysius, in the same general location as today's community of Wrangell. Recognizing the benefit of Russian protection and trade, Chief Shakes decided to relocate the nearby Tlingit village to a small island in the harbor near the stockade. In 1840, the British Hudson's Bay Company leased the stockade from the Russians, and the name was changed to Fort Stikine.

The Tlingit, while protesting the Hudson's Bay Company's use of their traditional trade routes, were already facing a new, more deadly battle. Two outbreaks of smallpox, in 1836 and 1840, resulted in the deaths of half of their population. By 1849, the over-zealous fur trade had dwindled, and both Russian and British interest in the area began to wane. One year after the US purchase of Alaska in 1867, a military post, Fort Wrangell, was built.

In 1861, an employee of the Hudson's Bay Company, Buck Choquette, found gold on the Stikine River and started the first of three gold rushes that shaped much of Wrangell's (and the rest of Southeast's) history. The second rush was in 1872, when two prospectors, Thibert and McCullough, found gold at Dease Lake (in Canada's Cassiar country). When the Klondike gold was discovered in 1897, Wrangell's population surged again as thousands of prospectors – and the attendant dance halls, gambling establishments, and suppliers – flooded the small town. Miners gathered provisions and then journeyed up the Stikine River into the gold fields.

The noted naturalist John Muir frequented the area in the 1880s. It is also told that the infamous Soapy Smith *(see page 149)* would occasionally hide out in Wrangell when the situation in Skagway became too dicey.

Cannery city

Wrangell incorporated as a city in 1903. Not long afterward, the flourishing fishing industry built several canneries within Southeast Alaska. By the late 1920s, four canneries (for salmon,

Wrangell's harbor.

BELOW: Chief Shakes Tribal House.

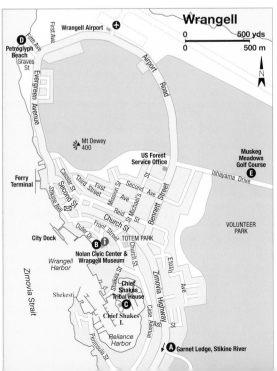

The legendary Wyatt Earp served as Wrangell's marshal for 10 days in 1897 as he and his wife were en route to the Klondike. During these gold rush days, false-front shops lined both sides of Front Street, which was then built on pilings over the water. Two tragic fires, in 1906 and in 1952, destroyed most of these historic buildings.

BELOW: children chisel the rocks at Garnet Ledge and sell the stones to tourists.

shrimp and crab) were operating in Wrangell. Chinese workers, who were willing to work long hours for low wages, were brought to Southeast Alaska to man the canneries. **Deadman's Island**, next to the Wrangell airport, is said to be where the Chinese preserved their dead in salt-brine barrels until they could be sent home for burial.

Due to the narrow channels surrounding the island, Wrangell is off the beaten path of large cruise ships, but the community welcomes smaller cruise ships, and the business of many sport fishers, birders, and water enthusiasts headed for the Stikine River. Perhaps because the city has not experienced waves of passengers from multiple large cruise ships docking just offshore on the same day, Wrangell is less altered by tourism than many other Southeast towns.

There are many sights unique to this delightful, laid-back town, so grab your quality rain gear and explore. On your way past the **city dock** area, you will likely see young merchants selling garnets dug from **Wrangell's Garnet Ledge A** *(see box below)*.

A good place to gather Wrangell information is the **James and Elsie Nolan Center B** (296 Campbell Drive; tel: 874-3699; www.wrangellalaska. org). The center houses both the city's **visitor center** and the **Wrangell Museum** (May–Sept Mon–Sat 10am–5pm, Oct–Apr Tue–Sat 1–5pm). The museum has a Tlingit spruce canoe and exhibits on gold, timber, fishing, and trapping.

The visitor center's staff will connect you with the tour operators who will take you around by foot, helicopter, kayak, boat, bus, or plane.

Totems and petroglyphs

Take a stroll out to **Chief Shakes Island**, accessible year-round by a walkway into Wrangell harbor. The island has intricately carved Tlingit totems and **Chief Shakes Tribal House C** (open by appointment), listed as an historic monument.

Also worth a visit is **Petroglyph Beach D** (1 mile from the ferry terminal), a State Historic Park which has the Southeast's largest concentration of ancient rock carvings. The origin of

Garnet Ledge

The ledge, a few miles from town at the mouth of the Stikine River, was well known to prospectors during the 1860 gold rush. It was also the setting of a unique, all-women mining company in the early 1900s. Ownership eventually transferred to Mr Fred G. Hanford, the former mayor of Wrangell. The site was given to the Southeastern Alaska Area Council of Boy Scouts of America (in 1962) for scouting purposes and to allow the children of Wrangell to continue collecting and selling the stones. Today, many Wrangell families make the 9-mile (14km) boat trip to the ledge each spring, allowing their entrepreneurial children to continue the tradition of chiseling, shoveling, and prying garnets from the rock ledge, and then returning home to sell them to summer visitors.

the petroglyphs remains a mystery. Visitors are encouraged to search the beach, where more than 40 known carvings are located. Visitors are free to take photographs, but rubbings should be made of replicas only, which are located on the observation deck overlooking the beach.

Wrangell also owns the distinction of having a USGA-rated, 9-hole golf course, **Muskeg Meadows** ❺ (tel: 874-4654; www.wrangellalaskagolf.com).

Bird-spotting

The nearby **Stikine River** delta is a fabulous area for birders, hosting over 120 species of migrating birds in spring and fall. In April, as many as 1,600 eagles swoop down to feast on the local hooligan run, and thousands of snow geese stop over on their northerly trek. Other wildlife includes sea lions, otters, bears, and moose.

For the more adventurous, a jet boat tour on the Stikine is a breathtaking opportunity for a rare glimpse of wild Alaska, or you could choose to soar over the area in a floatplane for a bird's-eye view. For a quieter and perhaps less

adrenaline-soaked experience, canoes, kayaks, and rafts are locally available.

Bear viewing

A trip by boat or floatplane to the **Anan Bear and Wildlife Observatory** (located 30 miles/48km southeast of Wrangell, near the mouth of the Bradfield Canal) provides an opportunity to see brown and black bears (plus bald eagles and sea lions) feasting on one of the largest pink salmon runs in the Southeast. Bears are viewed from a covered platform overlooking a waterfall. The US Forest Service has developed the Observatory (Wrangell Ranger District, 525 Bennett Street; tel: 907-874-2323).

Picknicking in the Stikine River delta, a great spot for birdwatching in the spring and fall.

BELOW LEFT: ancient rock carvings on Petroglyph Beach.

RESTAURANTS

Diamond C Café
223 Front Street
Tel: 874-3677
www.diamondchotel.com **$**
The third-generation owners of this clean, diner-style restaurant serve up breakfasts (early, during summer) and lunches only. A favorite gathering spot for locals, who heartily recommend the shrimp salad and the razor clams.

J & W's Fast Foods
120 Front Street
Tel: 874-2120 **$**
Serving classic American fast food

from burgers and fries to fish sandwiches and milkshakes every day for lunch and dinner.

Stikine Inn Restaurant
107 Stikine Avenue
Tel: 888-874-3388 or 874-3388 **$–$$$**
This family-style restaurant, affording beautiful views of the water and mountains, is open daily for breakfast, lunch, and dinner in the summer. The menu features fresh Alaska seafood, including a highly-touted seafood

chowder. Beer and wine served.

Zak's Café
316 Front Street
Tel: 874-3355 **$–$$$**
Considered by many to be the best spot in town for lunch (salads, homemade soups, wraps, sandwiches, and burgers) or dinner (steak, seafood, chicken, and pasta).

> Price is for dinner excluding tax, tip, and beverages:
> **$** = under $15
> **$$** = $15–20
> **$$$** = $20–30
> **$$$$** = over $30

PETERSBURG

The large cruise ships can't navigate the Wrangell Narrows to get here, which has helped Petersburg retain its small-town charm and the atmosphere of a bustling fishing village

Alaska has always been home to a diverse population, and the communities within the state reflect that diversity. The picturesque fishing hamlet of **Petersburg ❹**, on the northwest end of Mitkof Island, serves to illustrate that point. "Little Norway," as it is often called, is home to 3,100 residents. They offer warm, Scandinavian-style Alaskan hospitality to visitors of their charming city, which, like Wrangell, is not a port of call for large cruise ship traffic. Transportation to the city is provided by daily Alaska Airlines flights, air taxis, and the Alaska Marine Highway System ferries.

Humpback whales

Petersburg claims to be "blessed by geography," and so it is. This spic-and-span island community nestled in the heart of the Tongass, perches at the intersecting waterways of Wrangell Narrows and **Frederick Sound** – the latter being one of the best places in the world to observe the feeding behavior of humpback whales (*see margin note, page 126*). The area waters are also home to Steller sea lions, harbor seals, Dall's porpoise, and orcas (killer whales).

Other wildlife common to Petersburg includes wolves, black bears, deer, moose, eagles, Canada geese, trumpeter swans, and Marbled Murrelets. Just across the Frederick Sound are the towering peaks and glaciers of the Coast Mountains.

The mighty **LeConte Glacier ❺**, the southernmost active tidewater glacier in the northern hemisphere, is a mere 20-minute boat ride away from Petersburg and is a good spot for seal watching (*see box, page 126*).

As is the case throughout most of the Southeast Alaska communities, the Tlingits were the first ones on the scene, using the north end of Mitkof Island as a summer fish camp. In the late 1890s, Peter Buschmann, a Norwegian immigrant, established a cannery, a sawmill, and by 1900, a dock on the

Main attractions
FREDERICK SOUND
LECONTE GLACIER
HAMMER SLOUGH
SONS OF NORWAY HALL
CLAUSEN MEMORIAL MUSEUM
EAGLE ROOST PARK
SANDY BEACH RECREATION AREA
OUTLOOK PARK

LEFT: local transportation.
BELOW: Fourth of July parade, Petersburg.

Humpback Whales
The waters of Frederick Sound and Stephen's Passage are uniquely rich in plankton, fish, and marine mammals. The area is also the prime summer feeding grounds for hundreds of humpback whales each year. These endangered giants come to feed and play in Alaska waters prior to their fall return to Hawaii to give birth to their young. Whale watching tours are popular activities for many visitors to the Petersburg area.

BELOW: houses on stilts, Petersburg.

island. The Buschmann family's homesteads eventually grew into a community known for its strong Scandinavian influence. Today's Petersburg successfully maintains both its Tlingit and its Scandinavian flavors. Primarily a fishing town, the city also serves as a supply center for area logging camps.

Expert information

The **Visitor Information Center** Ⓐ (First and Fram streets; tel: 772-4636; www.petersburg.org; summer Mon–Sat 9am–5pm, Sun noon–4pm, winter Mon–Fri 10am–2pm) provides information on lodging and myriad guided boat, floatplane, helicopter, kayak, glacier-viewing, whale-watching, and fishing tours lasting from a few hours to a week or more. For those preferring unguided tours, boat, kayak, and equipment rentals are locally available, as are remote drop-off and pick-up flights. The center also has natural history information and trail guides.

The **Petersburg Ranger District Office** Ⓑ (12 North Nordic Drive; tel: 772-3871; www.fs.fed.us/r10/tongass/districts/petersburg/index.shtml) offers

maps, as well as information on current conditions, area trails, and remote US Forest Service cabin rentals (advance reservations essential in summer).

Downtown and harbor

The city of Petersburg centers on its harbor area, and nearly all the city's attractions are within easy walking distance. Take a stroll around the town and be sure to bring a camera. Petersburg is known for its natural beauty and unique public art displays, including interesting concrete stamps along the sidewalks and the colorful Rosemaling (Norwegian tole painting) on the homes and storefronts. You'll enjoy a variety of murals, totems, and sculptures by local artisans displayed throughout the area.

The boardwalk streets of **Hammer Slough** Ⓒ, the tidal area of a creek emptying into the waterfront, lead to an opportunity to photograph old, beautifully weathered boathouses reflecting in the slough's still water. The nearby **Sons of Norway Hall** Ⓓ, recognizable by the Viking ship in front, offers summer visitors a buffet

Seals of LeConte Glacier

The glacier, part of the Stikine Ice Field 20 miles (32km) east of Petersburg, is the southernmost, active, tidewater glacier in the northern hemisphere. Not only do giant hunks of ice crack off the head of the glacier and crash into the sea, but because of the deep (810ft/247-meter) waters of LeConte Bay, the glacier also calves from underwater. Huge slabs of icy missiles shoot up into the air, and then splash back into the sea. These "shooters" can reach out hundreds of yards from the face of the glacier. The sparkling, often deep-blue icebergs clog a spectacular 10-mile (16km) long fjord. Seals nonchalantly lounge on, or swim around the floating bergs. In June, visitors to the glacier from Wrangell or Petersburg tours are often treated to the sight of new seal pups on the ice floes.

that includes Norwegian pastries, fish cakes, and pickled herring (times coincide with cruise-ship arrivals).

You may also be treated to local storytelling and a performance of the **Leikerring Dance Group** (Petersburg children dressed in colorful Norwegian bunad costumes). It's worth stopping at the **Bojer Wikan Fisherman's Memorial** (next door), a memorial to those who lost their lives at sea.

History of fishing

The small but tasteful **Clausen Memorial Museum** E (Second and Fram streets; tel: 772-3598; www.clausenmuseum.net; May–Sept Mon–Sat 10am–5pm, Oct–Dec Tue–Sat 10am–2pm; charge) offers an insight into the history and art of fishing, life in Petersburg and Tlingit culture.

Eagle Roost Park F, on North Nordic Drive, near the town's edge, provides a platform for viewing eagles roosting in trees. It also has picnic tables, and a pathway to the beach to explore tidal pools. As in Wrangell, there are ancient petroglyphs (rock carvings) that can be seen at low tide 3 miles (5km) down

Sandy Beach Road at the **Sandy Beach Recreation Area** G. Along with the petroglyphs are 2,000-year-old Tlingit stone or wooden fish traps, supposedly found only in the 40-mile (64km) area around Petersburg.

On the way to Sandy Beach, the small **Outlook Park** contains a covered timber-framed shelter built by a local shipwright in the style of a Norwegian stave church. You can use the binoculars provided to scan Frederick Sound for marine life. ❏

Viking costumes are donned for the Little Norway Festival, held every May in Petersburg since 1958 to celebrate its Norwegian heritage.

Petersburg

0 ___ 200 yds
0 ___ 200 m

Hungry Point
EAGLE ROOST PARK F
Wrangell Avenue
3rd St
Balder St
1st Street
2nd Street
Charles West Street
Wrangell Narrows
Petersburg Fisheries Cannery
Nordic Drive (Main Street)
Dolphin Street
North Boat Harbor
Excel Street
Harbormaster
Harbor Way
Visitor Information Center A i
1st Street
2nd Street
Clausen Memorial Museum E
4th Street
Fram Street
3rd Street
Gjoa St
Gjoa Street
Petersburg Ranger District Office B
Sandy Beach Recreation Area G
Middle Boat Harbor
Library
Haugen Drive
Bojer Wikan Fisherman's Memorial
Sing Lee Alley
Hammer Slough
Birch Street
Sons of Norway Hall D
Ira Street

SITKA

Although Alaska's fourth city in terms of population, Sitka is the biggest in the United States in terms of the area that falls within this borough by the Pacific

Main attractions
HARRIGAN CENTENNIAL HALL
ISABEL MILLER MUSEUM
NEW ARCHANGEL DANCERS
ALASKA RAPTOR CENTER
SHELDON JACKSON MUSEUM
RUSSIAN BISHOP'S HOUSE
ST MICHAEL'S CATHEDRAL
TRIBAL COMMUNITY HOUSE
ST LAZARIA NATIONAL
     WILDLIFE REFUGE

BELOW: a cruise ship visits Sitka.

The historic city of Sitka ❻, population 8,900, sits on the western coast of Baranof Island in Southeast Alaska, backed by the Tongass National Forest and facing Sitka Sound and the open water of the Gulf of Alaska. Tlingit Indians lived in the area for many centuries before the island was discovered by Russian explorer, Vitus Bering, in 1741.

In 1799, Russian fur traders arrived. Alexander Baranov, of the Russian-American Company, built a fort and trading post, St Michael's Redoubt, a few miles to the north of Sitka's present-day location. Local Tlingits, fearing Russian domination and fur-trade enslavement, attacked the fort in 1802 killing most of the settlers. Baranov retaliated two years later by bringing a Russian warship into the harbor and bombarding the village.

The Tlingits fought bravely but after six days were driven from the area in what became known as the Battle of Sitka. The Russians then re-established the settlement and renamed it "New Archangel."

In 1808, Sitka became the capital of Russian America, and by the mid-1800s, the major port of the north Pacific Coast. Fur shipments to Europe and Asia were the primary commodity, though salmon, lumber and ice were also shipped to various locations along the western coasts of North and Central America.

America takes over

Eventually, as the lucrative fur trade declined, Russian interest in Alaska followed suit and, in 1867, Alaska was sold to the United States. The transfer ceremony was held in Sitka on October 18 (now a state holiday, "Alaska Day") and is re-enacted each year at the city's Castle Hill. Sitka remained the territorial capital of Alaska until 1906, when the seat of government was transferred to Juneau. Throughout the early 1900s, gold mines were an engine of growth.

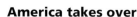

During World War II, the US Navy built an air base on nearby Japonski Island, which housed an astonishing 30,000 military personnel plus more than 7,000 civilians. Following the end of the war, the Bureau of Indian Affairs converted some of the former military buildings into a boarding school for Alaska Natives, Mount Edgecumbe High School, which is still operational today, educating more than 400 students from over 100 Alaska communities. The island is also the location for a US Coast Guard Air Station and Boat Station, the Sitka campus of the University of Alaska Southeast, the Mount Edgecumbe Hospital and Sitka's Rocky Gutierrez Airport. The O'Connell Bridge, built in 1972, connects Japonski Island to Sitka.

Cruising port of call

Sitka's broad-based economy is fueled by various industries including fishing, fish processing, retail and healthcare services, government, transportation, and tourism. Alaska Airlines offers daily flights to the community (as do various local air taxi services), and the

Alaska Marine Highway System provides both regular and high-speed ferry options. The city is a popular port for the cruise-ship industry, and for good reason. There are many interesting things to see and do within easy walking distance of the harbor (remember to bring adequate rain gear).

A convenient and profitable first stop is in the waterfront district at the **Harrigan Centennial Hall Ⓐ** (330 Harbor Drive; tel: 747-3225; www.cityof sitka.com/dept/cent/index), housing both the **Visitor's Center** and the **Isabel Miller Museum** (tel: 747-6455; www. sitkahistory.org; early May–late Sept "most days" 8am–5pm, winter Tue–Sat 10am– 4pm; charge). Check the schedule for

The New Archangel Dancers were formed in 1969 to keep alive Sitka's Russian heritage through dance. Although the members of the troupe are not professional dancers and are not descended from Russians, they have performed throughout the US and in Russia.

Sitka Music Festival
Held for three weeks
each June, this
renowned concert
series features out-
standing chamber
musicians from
around the world. A
giant, panoramic
window creates a
stunning backdrop
for the local concert
hall stage, beckoning
the audience's gaze
beyond the musicians
and out to the pictur-
esque Sitka Sound
(tel: 277-4852, 747-
6774 during June;
www.sitkamusic
festival.org).

BELOW: the Russian
Bishop's House.

performances of Russian folk songs and dances by the **New Archangel Dancers** (tel: 747-5516; www.newarchangeldancers.com; charge).

The **Convention and Visitors Bureau** ❸ (303 Lincoln Street, Suite 4; tel: 747-5940; www.sitka.org), while a bit tricky to find, is another helpful resource for visitors. Either location will provide you with the contacts for various tour operators wanting to show you the sights in and around Sitka via semi-submersible vessel, all-terrain vehicle (ATV), bike, bus, or on foot.

Additional exploration options include wildlife cruises, diving and snorkeling, flightseeing, and kayaking.

Birds of prey

If a self-guided walking tour is what you have in mind, you can make an east-to-west sweep of the city by heading, first of all, to the **Alaska Raptor Center** ❸ (1000 Raptor Way; tel: 800-643-9425; www.alaskaraptor.org; May–Sept daily 8am–4pm; charge). This small but fascinating facility's mission is to educate the public concerning raptors and their environment, to pro-

vide medical treatment for injured bald eagles (and other birds), and to conduct bald eagle research. Visitors have an opportunity for close-up raptor observation.

Native culture

When leaving the Raptor Center, take a delightful stroll across Indian River and through an old-growth rainforest as you head downhill (toward the Sound) to the **Sitka National Historical Park Visitors Center** ❸ (located at the east end of Lincoln Street; tel: 747-0110; www.nps.gov/sitka; May–Sept daily 8am–5pm, Oct–April Mon–Sat 8am–5pm, closed on Federal holidays during winter; charge). Within the 100-acre (40-hectare) park are beautiful Tlingit totem poles, the remains of historic Tlingit and Russian structures, and the 1804 battleground. Inside the cultural center is a museum featuring Indian history, art and Native artist demonstrations.

On leaving the Park, head west and stop at the **Sheldon Jackson Museum** ❸ (104 College Drive; tel: 747-8981; www.museums.state.ak.us/sheldon_jackson/sjhome.html; mid-May–mid-Sept daily 9am–5pm, winter Tue–Sat 10am–4pm, closed holidays; charge). The oldest museum in Alaska, it features one of the largest collections, gathered between 1888–1898, of Native cultural artifacts.

Russian Bishop's House

Continuing your westerly ramble, stop by the **Russian Bishop's House** ❺ (103 Monastery Street; tel: 747-0110; www.nps.gov/sitk; daily mid-May–Sept 9am–5pm, Oct–mid May by appointment only; charge). A National Historic Landmark, this 1842 example of restored Russian colonial architecture, complete with original furniture, appliances, and articles of clothing, gives you a glimpse of Sitka life during the Russian-America period.

Leaving the Bishop's House, head west again and visit **St Michael's Cathedral** ❼ (240 Lincoln Street; tel: 747-8120; summer Mon–Fri 9am–4pm,

call for Sat–Sun and winter hours; donation requested). The reconstructed Orthodox cathedral replaces what was Alaska's oldest church structure from the Russian era. The earlier building was destroyed by fire in 1966, but nearly all the icons were rescued. The church was later rebuilt, strictly following the original plans.

You'll probably regret it if you don't have a look at the **Russian Block House ❻**, located behind the Pioneers' Home. It is a replica of one of the three original structures that once separated the Russian and Tlingit segments of town following the Natives' return to Sitka around 1824.

Close by is the **Tribal Community House ❶** (200 Katlian Street; tel: 888-270-8687, 747-7290; www.sitkatribe.org; call for performance times; charge), which offers colorful Native dance performances, storytelling and other cultural events. A small gift shop features Native artwork.

Castle Hill, on the National List of Historic Places, is just south, across Lincoln Street. In addition to being the site of the 1867 Russian/US transfer ceremony, it is the former location of Baranof's Castle, built in 1837 and destroyed by fire in 1898.

Outdoor activities

To take in the sights outside Sitka, consider a wildlife cruise to see humpback whales, sea otters, sea lions, and eagles. Birders would enjoy a trip to **St Lazaria National Wildlife Refuge** at the mouth of Sitka Sound, where you'll see thousands of seabirds, including tufted puffins, murres, and auklets.

You could also take to the skies in a floatplane, scanning the forested landscape for brown bears or Sitka blacktail deer; or take a flight to peer into the volcanic crater of nearby, dormant Mt Edgecumbe or view the frigid expanse of the Baranof Icefields.

Sport fishers are not likely to be disappointed with local charter options. Kayak enthusiasts have a variety of paddling opportunities in area water, some locations calm and serene, others more challenging. For tours involving any of these activities (and many more), contact Sitka's Convention and Visitors Bureau (*see page 130*). ❑

Sunday services at St Michael's Cathedral are still performed in Church Slavonic, as well as in English, Tlingit, Aleut, and Yupik.

RESTAURANTS

The Backdoor
104 Barracks Street
Tel: 747-8856 **$**
Literally the backdoor of a popular independent bookstore in the heart of downtown, this local favorite features sandwiches, pastries, and expertly made espresso in its warm, cheerful interior.

Little Tokyo
315 Lincoln Street
Tel: 747-5699
$$–$$$
Offering excellent sushi and teriyaki, this is a popular Sitka staple for lunch and dinner. Free delivery as well as hot espresso available.

Ludvig's Bistro
256 Katlian Drive
Tel: 966-3663
www.ludvigsbistro.com
$$$–$$$$
Mediterranean fine dining in Sitka! This cozy, upscale restaurant is open for dinner year round, offering fresh, locally caught Alaska seafood, steaks, tapas, fresh bread, soups, salads, and desserts. Serves coffee, tea, beer, and wine.

Nugget Restaurant and Bakery
600 Airport Drive (located inside the airport)
Tel: 966-2480 **$–$$**
Famous among frequent flyers along the Southeast Alaska route for their

delicious pies, this full service restaurant offers breakfast (throughout the day), lunch, and dinner. Varied menu includes sandwiches, soups, fresh Alaska seafood, and prime rib. Poor weather means that flights are often re-routed to (and delayed at) Sitka airport, giving passengers a chance to fill up on something here; the banana cream pie is a favorite. There's a bar too, serving wine and beer.

Pizza Express
1321 Sawmill Creek
Tel: 966-2428 **$–$$$**
Open daily for lunch and dinner, this is the place to go in Sitka for Mexican

dishes as well as pizza. Consistently good food and reasonably priced.

Van Winkle and Sons
205 Harbor Drive
Tel: 747-7652
$$$–$$$$
A local favorite, the highlight of this restaurant is the ultra-fresh seafood, presented with an elaborate twist. The full bar provides excellent views of Sitka's harbor.

Price is for dinner excluding tax, tip, and beverages:
$ = under $15
$$ = $15–20
$$$ = $20–30
$$$$ = over $30

JUNEAU

Juneau is a small but busy capital, with narrow streets and alleys leading to museums, galleries, and bars downtown, and a variety of hiking trails to nearby glaciers and icefields

The delightful city of **Juneau ➐** today is a far cry from the wilderness site where gold was discovered by Joe Juneau and Richard Harris in 1880. About 31,000 Alaskans – whites, Native Tlingits, and other ethnic groups – call the community home. Most work for the government (state, federal or local) or provide services for those that do, or are employed in the tourism industry.

The town is as modern as the state-of-the-art computer center in the State Office Building and as old-fashioned as the plantation-style Governor's Mansion a few blocks away. It's as sophisticated as its symphony orchestra and as earthy as the notorious Red Dog Saloon or the equally frontierish Alaskan Hotel bar nearby; as urban as its high-rise office buildings and high-comfort hotels, and as rugged as the northern wilderness of thick, lush forests, glacial ice and salt water which surrounds it. The wilderness begins literally where the houses stop.

Gold fever

The town was first named Harrisburg – some say because Harris, unlike his partner Juneau, was able to write and recorded it that way. But the name didn't stick: after news of the gold strike spread to Sitka and elsewhere, nearly 300 prospectors swarmed to the scene, and decided to rename the place Rockwell. Shortly thereafter it became Juneau. By whatever name, the camp

was bustling with gold fever and, soon, gold production. It didn't take long for simple gold pans, pickaxes, and human labor to be replaced by miles-long flumes and ditches, carrying water to massive hydraulic earth-moving and sluicing operations. Within a decade of the Juneau/Harris discovery, wagon roads penetrated the valleys behind the camp-turned-town – roads you can still hike on.

Juneau is, of course, on the North American mainland. Across Gastineau Channel, on **Douglas Island**, even

Main attractions
ALASKA STATE MUSEUM
MARINE PARK
RED DOG SALOON
ST NICHOLAS RUSSIAN
  ORTHODOX CHURCH
STATE CAPITOL
JUNEAU-DOUGLAS MUSEUM
GOVERNOR'S MANSION
MENDENHALL GLACIER

LEFT: the Red Dog Saloon.
BELOW: Juneau seen from Mount Roberts.

The State Capitol in Juneau; inside, clay murals from the 1930s celebrate Alaska's rich coastal waters and native hunting traditions.

the Douglas community remains distinct to this day, much in the way that Alaska is part of, but somehow set apart from, the rest of the United States.

Early on, politics assumed considerable importance in Juneau. The future state's first political convention was held here in the summer of 1881. The camp became a first-class municipality under the law in 1900, and in 1906 the district government of Alaska transferred there from Sitka.

Frontier law

In 1913, Alaska's first territorial legislature convened, in what is now the Elks Hall on Seward Street. Nearly life-size photo murals of that distinguished group can be seen today on the first floor of the State Capitol Building.

more furiously paced development took place. By 1882 the world-famous Treadwell Mine was operational and expanding.

Near it, the proud community of **Douglas** grew up, and indeed rivaled Juneau in population, industry and miners' baseball for a good number of years. Eventually, more than 50 years later, the two towns would merge, but

As the city grew and prospered, enterprises such as fishing, saw-milling, and trading became important. But gold powered Juneau. Miners labored daily in miles and miles of tunnels that honeycombed the mountains both on the mainland and on Douglas Island. For recreation on days off they scoured the wild country beyond the urban

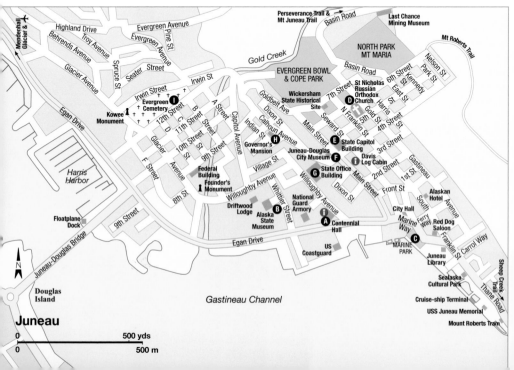

centers, digging, panning, hoping against hope that they, too, might strike it rich like Juneau and Harris. Yet these two early prospectors never realized much from their discoveries. Juneau died penniless in the Canadian Yukon and a collection had to be taken up to send his body home for burial in the city he co-founded.

Wartime boom

As the years passed there were ups and downs (definitely down when, in 1917, major portions of the Treadwell tunnels beneath the waters of Gastineau Channel caved in and flooded), but gold remained Juneau's, and Alaska's, mainstay, until relatively recent times. During World War II, the government ended an era when it closed down the massive Alaska-Juneau gold mine and milling operation for reasons of manpower and conservation.

But even with the mine closure, things didn't go too badly. By the time the 1944 shutdown came about, the city was experiencing something of a war boom, and with war's end there came a gradual but continuous rise in territorial government activity and employment.

By 1959, when Alaska became state number 49, government had all but filled the economic void left by mining's demise. And Juneau has since grown from a waterfront community hovering beneath the skeletal remains of the old Alaska-Juneau millsites, to a gregarious, outreaching city spreading for miles to the north and south.

The city's size was established in the mid-1960s when Juneau and Douglas and the Greater Juneau Borough were unified by a democratic vote into the City and Borough of Juneau.

Juneau is a small town in terms of population, but in square miles it is the biggest town in North America and second biggest in the world. Its 3,108 sq miles (8,050 sq km) are exceeded only by the city of Kiruna in Sweden, which has 5,458 sq miles (14,136 sq km) within its borders.

Touring the capital

It's a good idea to start your tour of Juneau with a visit to the **Centennial Hall Visitor Information Center** Ⓐ (101 Egan Drive; tel: 888-581-2201; www.traveljuneau.com; May–Sept daily 8am–5pm, winter Mon–Fri 8am–5pm), Year-round visitor information is also available at the Juneau International Airport and the Alaska Marine Highway System Ferry Terminal. Summertime information sources also include the cruise-ship terminal and the visitor information kiosk located at Marine Park. You can get a city map at any of these locations, plus information about Juneau's many points of interest and tour operators.

One of its biggest attractions, the **Alaska State Museum** Ⓑ (395 Whittier Street; tel: 465-2901; www.museums.state.ak.us; summer daily 8.30am–5.30pm, winter Tue–Sat 10am–4pm; charge) is within walking distance of downtown hotels and shopping. Inuit culture is represented here in the form of small, intricate ivory carvings and a huge 40ft (12-meter) *umiak*, or skin boat, of the type that were used for whale- and

An isolated capital Juneau is the only state capital in the USA that is not accessible by road. Some locals feel this keeps tourism in check. Others say it is an argument for moving the seat of government to Anchorage.

BELOW: Juneau's winter temperature seldom falls below 20°F (–6°C) and it is seldom hotter than 65°F (18°C) in summer.

Juneau's Trails

Few capital cities in the world can offer such a variety of hiking trails, suitable for the fit and the not so fit, right on its doorstep.

Juneau is a city for the outdoor type, offering a rich variety of hiking trails that can be reached easily from the city center. All of the starting points are clearly marked and you can get information about routes and the degree of skill and stamina needed from the US Forest Service volunteers at 8510 Mendenhall Loop Road (tel: 586-8800; www.fs.fed.us/r10/tongass; office hours Mon–Fri).

Among the best-known trails are Mount Roberts, Perseverance, and Mount Juneau. **Mount Roberts** takes off from a trailhead at the north end of Sixth Street. It's a steep climb, but a good one, with alpine ground cover above the treeline, and splendid views. You can cheat by hopping on the Mount Roberts Tram, which takes you from South Franklin Street, near the dockside, up to the treeline, where you can begin your hike, browse in the visitor center or watch a documentary in the theater.

The starting point for the more gentle and most popular trail, the **Perseverance Mine Trail**, is only

a few blocks further north, on Basin Road. Before setting off, pop into the Last Chance Mining Museum, near the trailhead (daily in summer; tel: 586-5338; charge) to get an idea of what life used to be like when the mines were functioning. On the Perseverance Mine Trail you have the chance to see and explore the ruins of some of the early mining sites, including the Silver Bowl Basin Mine and the Glory Hole. Or you can continue along the Granite Creek Trail, and hike as far as the creek basin.

The experienced and thoroughly fit hiker can link up with the steep **Mount Juneau Trail**, which provides the best view that can be had with two feet on the ground. Mainland Juneau and Douglas Island are laid out 3,500ft (1,100 meters) below the mountain summit, and the twisting, glistening Gastineau Channel seems to go on and on forever. This trail will bring you back full circle to join Perseverance near Ebner Falls. The less fit, or those with less time, can miss this loop, by retracing their steps from the Granite Creek Basin.

The **Sheep Creek Trail**, which starts in the southeast of the city, at Thane Road, takes you through the beautiful valley south of Mount Roberts, then up to Sheep Mountain and back on the Mount Roberts Trail.

Trails starting from Douglas

Several interesting trails start from Douglas, on the other side of the Gastineau Channel. The **Treadwell Ditch Trail**, which begins at D Street, is a 12-mile (20km) hike to Eagle Crest, but it can become a much easier walk by going only as far as the Dan Moller Trail, then returning on the road. Only the really experienced should try the **Mount Bradley Trail**, which sets off from Fifth Street in Douglas. Mount Bradley is 3,400ft (1,040 meters) high and the going can be tough, although the scenic rewards are great. An easier walk is 2-mile (3.5km) **Cropley Lake Trail**, which starts at Fish Creek Road.

The non-profit Trail Mix has a complete listing of Juneau's trails, their level of difficulty and current condition; tel: 790-6406; www.juneautrails.org. ❑

ABOVE: the Last Chance Mining Museum.
LEFT: the glistening Gastineau Channel.

walrus-hunting along the ice floes of the Arctic Ocean.

Southeast Alaska's ancient Native way of life is reflected in the re-creation of a community house, complete with totemic carvings, and the Athabascan Natives, from the Interior, are represented with displays of a birch bark canoe, weapons, and bead-decorated moosehide garments.

There is also gold-rush memorabilia, and natural history displays. And from the pre-gold rush Russian era are Orthodox religious exhibits including precious coins, priests' raiments, and the first American flag to be flown at Sitka when Russian America became American territory on October 18, 1867.

Most notable of all the museum's exhibits is the "eagle tree," just inside the front entrance. There, a model of a towering spruce tree rises from ground level almost to the ceiling of the second floor. In a fork of the branches is a nest holding a very authentic-looking young bald eagle, with its magnificent 5ft (1.2-meter) wings outstretched.

Marine Park

Most of Juneau's other attractions can be seen in a walking tour along the docks and among its meandering, frequently narrow, streets and alleys. Go east along Egan Drive to **Marine Park** **C** overlooking the city's dock and wharf area. It's a small, but pleasurable place of benches and shady trees situated near the ramp where cruise-ship passengers land after being lightered from ships at anchor offshore. This is where half of Juneau seem to eat lunch, especially on sunny summer days. Street vendors in the vicinity offer food ranging from fried halibut to hot dogs, from tacos to Vietnamese spring rolls.

The Red Dog Saloon

Cross Ferry Way to South Franklin Street, where you will find art galleries and stores that entice you with displays of Alaskan ivory, jade, totemic wood carvings, and leatherwork. Also on South Franklin (turn right from Ferry Way) is the best-known bar in the city, the fun but touristy **Red Dog Saloon**. Further up the street is the **Alaskan Hotel Bar**, which retains its gold-rush era decor and is well worth a visit.

Juneau's visitor information office, a re-creation of the town's first log school called Davis Log Cabin, is on Seward Street, on the way to the tiny **St Nicholas Russian Orthodox Church** **D** (summer Mon–Fri 9am–noon 1–5pm, Sat–Sun 10am–2pm; donation requested), one of the most picturesque houses of worship in Alaska. The onion-domed, octagon-shaped church, located on Fifth Street, was constructed in 1894 at the specific request of Ishkhanalykh, the then principal chief of the Tlingits of Juneau. It is the oldest original Orthodox church in Southeast Alaska and one of the senior parishes of the entire state.

State Capitol

Downhill on Fourth Street is the **State Capitol Building** **E** (daily 8.30am–4.30pm, tours running every half hour in summer). Built in the 1930s, many of its halls and offices have recently been

Patsy Ann
A statue of a bull terrier, Patsy Ann (1929–42) sits on the wharf to greet disembarking cruise-ship passengers. In 1934 she was dubbed "Official Greeter of Juneau, Alaska" by the mayor in recognition of her uncanny ability (especially as she was stone deaf) to anticipate the arrival of every ship.

BELOW: South Franklin Street.

Eating out by the harbor in summer.

BELOW: tourists visit Mendenhall Glacier by helicopter.

refurbished to reflect that era. You can see where the Alaska House and Senate meet during sessions; it's worth a stop.

On the corner of Fourth and Main streets is the **Juneau-Douglas City Museum** ❻ (tel: 586-3572; www.juneau. org/parksrec/museum; summer Mon–Fri 9am–5pm, Sat–Sun 10am–5pm, winter Tue–Sat 10am–4pm; summer charge, free in winter). It has interesting displays on the town's fishing and gold-mining history, and provides a free map of Juneau's nationally registered historic buildings and totem poles.

Across the road is the **State Office Building** ❼ on Fourth Street, where you can stroll through the skylighted great hall. And on Fridays, visitors can enjoy a special treat: a giant old Kimball theater organ – a magnificent relic of Juneau's silent movie days – has been relocated in the atrium of the building; visiting organists and local musicians celebrate the coming weekend by playing its pipes from noon to 1pm.

Two blocks beyond, on Calhoun Avenue, is the **Governor's Mansion** ❽, which cost $2 million to restore to the glory of its 1913 opening. You can photograph the exterior, but you are not allowed to go in.

Beyond the Governor's Mansion and across **Gold Creek** – where Joe Juneau and Dick Harris panned their first gold in the area – you come to the **Evergreen Cemetery** ❾ where the two prospectors are buried. The two founders' burial monuments are not overly impressive, but the partially wooded cemetery is a popular place for visitors and dog-walkers.

Mendenhall Glacier

From Juneau, a number of impressive glaciers can be reached by car or by trail, or viewed from the air. The best known is the **Mendenhall Glacier**, which can be seen from a US Forest Service information center about 13 miles (21km) north of town. The center sits on the edge of a frigid lake into which Mendenhall Glacier calves icebergs large and small. The face of the glacier is about 1 mile (2km) from the visitor center, while its 1,500 sq miles (3,885 sq km) of ice and snow is called the **Juneau Icefield**.

Perhaps the most exciting way to savor the glacier and its originating icefield is to take one of the flightseeing trips organized by one of several Juneau-based air charter companies, or to try one of the helicopter carriers that offer 45 minutes or so flying over the great white deserts of snow, and a landing on the surface of the icefield. Some companies supply a guide and equipment – boots, crampons, ice axes and so forth – for a two-hour trek and even a little ice climbing.   ❑

RESTAURANTS AND BARS

Price is for dinner excluding tax, tip, and beverages:
$ = under $15
$$ = $15–20
$$$ = $20–30
$$$$ = over $30

Breakwater Restaurant & Lounge
1711 Glacier Avenue
Tel: 586-6303
www.breakwaterinn.com/ restaurant/index.htm **$–$$$**
An upmarket place offering a lovely, waterfront view, fresh Alaskan seafood, steaks, and prime rib. Also serves breakfast and lunch. Lounge has wines, spirits, microbrew beers.

Chan's Thai Kitchen
11820 Glacier Highway
Tel: 789-9777 **$$**
This small restaurant, 20 minutes from downtown at the Auke Bay boat harbor, is popular with locals. Serving dinner Tuesday through Sunday, it opens at 4.30pm. Favorites include chicken cashew, spring rolls, and other delicious Thai dishes.

Douglas Café
916 Third Street
Tel: 907-364-3307 **$–$$$**
A favorite with locals, serving hearty breakfasts (weekends only), delicious lunches (the burgers are legendary), and more sophisticated dinners. Locally brewed beer on tap.

The Goldroom
In the Baranof Hotel,
127 N. Franklin Street
Tel: 586-2660 **$–$$$$**

Fine downtown dining featuring contemporary Northwest cuisine. Full bar.

The Island Pub
1102 Second Street, Douglas
Tel: 364-1595
www.theislandpub.com
$–$$
Across the bridge from Juneau on Douglas Island, this restaurant features delicious pizzas baked in a firebrick oven. Also serves sandwiches, salads, and an outstanding steak wrap. Enjoy a wonderful view of water and of downtown Juneau. Open for lunch and dinner. The full bar offers a wide selection of beer and "malternatives."

Olivia's de Mexico
222 Seward Street
Tel: 586-6870 **$–$$**
This Mexican restaurant has been operated by the same family, in the same spot for 30 years. Open for lunch and dinner, the menu includes favorites like halibut enchiladas and tacos, reasonably priced. Beer and wine served.

Rainbow Foods
224 Fourth Street
Tel: 586-6476 **$**
www.rainbow-foods.org
Housed in an old church, this natural foods grocery store has a strong feeling of community and is a great place to collect snacks and lunches for hikes in Juneau's backcountry. Soups, salads, baked goods, pizzas, and hot entrées are freshly made daily.

Silverbow Bakery
120 Second Street
Tel: 800-586-4146 **$**
The historic Silverbow building has housed a bakery since 1890. Now serving fresh bagels, artisan breads, and sandwiches, it is favorite spot for breakfast and lunch.

El Sombrero
157 S. Franklin Street
Tel: 586-6770 **$–$$**
Mexican cuisine includes menu items with Alaskan flair: halibut and salmon fajitas. Open for dinner only, casual. Serves beer and wine.

Thane Ore House Salmon Bake
4400 Thane Road
Tel: 586-3442
www.thaneorehouse.com
$–$$$
Located 4 miles (6km) south of downtown Juneau at the site of the historic Alaska Gastineau mine, this casual, rustic eatery offers indoor and outdoor seating daily (in summer) for lunch and dinner. Offers "all you can eat" helpings of delicious local wild salmon, halibut, barbecued beef ribs, burgers, and all the trimmings.

Twisted Fish Co. Alaskan Grill
550 S. Franklin Street
Tel: 907-463-5033 **$–$$$$**
Open May–Oct, this busy seafood hot spot is on the waterfront near the cruiseship dock. Features fresh Alaska seafood, pizza, burgers, and desserts.

Bars
The Alaskan Hotel & Bar
167 S. Franklin Street
Tel: 586-1000
This two-story Victorian barroom, built in the early 1900s, is loaded with frontier atmosphere, historic memorabilia, and local patrons.

Red Dog Saloon
278 S. Franklin Street
Tel: 463-3658
www.reddogsaloon.com
Near the waterfront, this raucous bar, complete with swinging doors, sawdust floors, and frontier memorabilia, is a much-hyped tourist favorite.

Triangle Club Bar
251 Front Street
Tel: 586-3140
Where the locals head for a hot dog (and other light snacks) and beer, wine, or spirits.

RIGHT: classic Alaska – crab claws and ice-cold beer.

GLACIER BAY NATIONAL PARK

The glaciers of the bay have retreated dramatically during the past two hundred years – a process which the visitors on large cruise ships can see is continuing today

BELOW: a sparkling ice cave.

Glacier Bay National Park and Preserve ❽ encompasses 3.3 million acres (1.3 million hectares). Located at the northern end of Alaska's Panhandle, the park's center lies approximately 90 miles (145km) northwest of Juneau and 600 miles (965km) southeast of Anchorage.

Most visitors arrive at Glacier Bay on large cruise ships or package tours, but you can reach **Gustavus** by air and boat charters from Juneau. This village of 500 year-round residents has an attractive beach and the 9-hole **Mount** Fairweather Golf Course (www.gustavus.com/activities/golf.html), which golfers in early summer share with flocks of Canada geese.

In a land comprising three climatic zones – marine to arctic – seven different ecosystems support a wide variety of plant and animal life. From the endangered humpback whale and Arctic peregrine falcon to the common harbor seal, black and brown bears, mountain goats, marmots, eagles, and ptarmigans, Glacier Bay provides a rich overview of Alaska's wildlife.

Glacier Bay's physical environment is as diverse as any found in Alaska. Sixteen massive tidewater glaciers flowing from the snow-capped mountain peaks of the **Fairweather Range** (reaching 15,300ft/4,663 meters) plunge into the icy waters of the fjords. Besides the jagged icebergs, the ice-scoured walls of rock lining the waterways, the salt-water beaches, and protected coves, numerous fresh-water lakes and thick forests of western hemlock and Sitka spruce are also found in the area.

History and exploration

Evidence of human habitation in the Glacier Bay region dates back 10,000 years. Researchers have outlined seasonal patterns of hunting, fishing, and gathering from semi-permanent villages. Native Tlingit folklore includes tales of periodic village destruction from earthquakes, tsunamis, and other natural forces.

European exploration of the area began in July 1741, when Russian ships sailed the outer coast. French explorer Jean François de la Perouse arrived 45 years later, and in 1797 he published his detailed observations and map of Lituya Bay, with its five surrounding glaciers.

Other explorers followed, such as Captain George Vancouver, who charted the waters of the Inside Passage in the 1790s. But it was the widespread publicity soon after naturalist John Muir's first reconnaissance of the area in 1879 that stimulated extensive scientific investigations and early tourism. Where early explorers had found only a massive wall of ice, Muir paddled in waters newly released from glacial ice, which had begun to retreat up the fjords it had carved.

Today's visitors see views very different from those which were observed in Muir's day, as glaciers – and their steady retreat – have further changed the landscape in the past century. In Muir's time, the network of fjords had not yet been established; a huge glacier extended into areas which are now open water. Early steamship excursions during the 1880s carried up to 230 passengers. But the flock of curious scientists and tourists halted abruptly when, in 1899, a violent earthquake struck, causing huge amounts of ice from the Muir Glacier to calve, falling into the sea. An unbroken jam of floating ice choked the waterway and extended more than 10 miles (16km) from the glacier's terminus.

When ships could no longer sail closer than about 6 miles (10km) to the Muir Glacier, excursions to the area ceased. Touring slowly developed again after 1925, when the Glacier Bay National Monument was established.

The glaciers retreat

These glaciers have, over time, retreated and advanced due to severe climatic fluctuations. De la Perouse and Vancouver both observed glacier ice at the mouth of the bay in 1786 and 1794. During Muir's trip to Glacier Bay in 1879, however, the ice had retreated 32 miles (51km) to a point near what is now the mouth of Muir Inlet. Ninety years later, the Muir Glacier had

Whales at risk
Commercial whaling in the 20th century reduced the world population of humpback whales from an estimated 125,000 to just 5,000. Today the population is something like 20,000. Princess Cruise Lines paid a $200,000 fine and $550,000 to the National Park Foundation after one of its ships hit and killed a humpback whale in Glacier Bay.

BELOW: examining a glacier at close quarters.

Getting close to a humpback whale.

BELOW: a good vantage point for spotting Glacier Bay's abundant marine life.

from the release of thousands of air bubbles that became trapped in the ice from high pressure during its formation. From the air, the sound cannot be heard above the drone of an aircraft engine, but the perspective of shimmering ice flowing from mountain top to sea is a dramatic one.

Plant and animal life

Two hundred years ago, when a glacier filled what is now a network of inlets in Glacier Bay, only a small number of plant and animal species inhabited the region. Since the retreat of the ice, life has flourished. Today, the nutrient-rich waters of the fjords are important feeding grounds for large marine mammals, and even the windswept, insect-free upper slopes of the glaciers provide welcome refuge for mountain goats and other animals.

receded another 24 miles (39km). Today the bay is more than 65 miles (105km) long.

Glacier Bay visitors can often watch entire sections of glacier ice calve from 150ft (46-meter) walls. The cracking ice produces a thundering roar, easily heard by those on the water. Huge bergs are set adrift, and waves sweep across sandbars outward from the glacier's tidewater base.

Kayakers are warned to keep a safe distance from the glacier faces. Those on the water, close to ice chunks slowly melting in the salty bay, may hear a crackling sound similar to breakfast cereal or champagne, which comes

The four land and three marine ecosystems in Glacier Bay support life forms adapted to the environment. Near Gustavus, an ecosystem of sandy grassland, thick coniferous forests and damp marshes provides habitat for sandhill cranes, river otters, wolves,

bears, coyotes, and moose. **Bartlett Cove**, the park's only area of development, lies within a region dominated by coastal western hemlock and Sitka spruce; watch for bald eagles flying overhead.

In the magnificent backcountry, you may climb to elevations of 2,500ft (760 meters), or much higher if you're an experienced mountaineer. Here, in the alpine tundra ecosystem, the thick vegetation of lower elevations is replaced by shrubby plants – alpine grasses and dwarf blueberry. Delicate flowering plants and lichens should be respected, for regeneration in this environment is extremely slow; glacial history can be computed by studying the steady rate of lichen growth.

Although few visitors venture onto the higher snowfields and glaciers, life in this seemingly barren, mountainous environment does exist. The ice worm, the only earthworm known to live on snow and ice, feeds on a red-pigmented green algae and organic debris swept onto the frozen surface. The glacier flea, a vegetarian insect, also lives above the treeline.

Possibly the most threatened species here is the humpback whale. Wintering near Hawaii or Mexico, humpbacks feed in the icy waters of southeastern Alaska and Glacier Bay in the summer. Killer and minke whales are sometimes spotted in the bay as well. Environmentalists fear that excessive numbers of cruise ships may drive out the whales. Besides small intertidal creatures, Glacier Bay is also home to many varieties of fish and shorebirds. Sea lions and otters, harbor seals and porpoises are frequently sighted.

Park attractions

A small, free campground in Bartlett Cove fills to capacity only two or three times a season. **Sandy Cove**, approximately 20 miles (32km) north, offers a good anchorage and attractive scenery for those traveling by boat.

The National Park Service (tel: 907-697-2230; www.nps.gov/glba) provides guided nature and walking tours on two well-maintained trails, starting from Bartlett Cove, and a floating ranger station in **Blue Mouse Cove** is open during the summer.   ❏

Well equipped in the Fairweather Range.

BELOW: dwarf fireweed and Indian paintbrush in front of the Brabazon Range, St Elias Mountains.

HAINES

This quirky seaside town is hemmed in by glacier-laden mountains and is under the watchful eyes of thousands of bald eagles

Main attractions
FORT WILLIAM H. SEWARD
ALASKA INDIAN ARTS
    CENTER
TOTEM VILLAGE TRIBAL
    HOUSE
SHELDON MUSEUM AND
    CULTURAL CENTER
HAMMER MUSEUM
AMERICAN BALD EAGLE
    FOUNDATION
CHILKAT BALD EAGLE
    PRESERVE

BELOW: Haines is bypassed by the major cruise lines.

Most motorists traveling through Haines ❾ are anxiously looking forward to only one of two things. If southbound, the main focus is *not missing the ferry*. They're intent on getting in line at the Alaska Marine Highway terminal, driving their car onboard, grabbing a bite to eat at the ship's cafeteria and then finally making their way to a recliner (or, better yet, a comfortable stateroom) to recover from a marathon drive.

If they're headed north, they're consumed with making it 40 miles (65km) beyond Haines to the Canadian border (appropriate paperwork in hand) *during the hours of operation*, then getting on with their all-day or all-night drive to Interior Alaska or Canada. Haines is a town most Alaskans have traveled *through*, but seldom *to*. And that's a shame, because this little city, in many ways, exemplifies the very best that Alaska has to offer.

Like Wrangell and Petersburg, most major cruise lines bypass Haines, choosing to dock at Skagway instead. The townspeople are divided over whether this fact constitutes a slight or a blessing. It certainly makes for less summertime congestion as the 1,800 local residents go about earning their living, primarily through commercial fishing, government, tourism and transportation. There is no major, commercial airline service to Haines.

The road connection

The city is one of only three Southeast cities (Haines, Skagway and Hyder) connected to the state's (or Canada's) road system. Air taxi service from Anchorage and various Southeast cities is available, and the Alaska Marine Highway Service provides regular ferry transports throughout the year.

For visitors who are clever enough to actually plan a trip *to* Haines, the opportunity to experience a genuine, small, quirky seaside Alaska town, hemmed in by glacier-laden mountains and under the constant, watchful

eyes of literally thousands of bald eagles, is its own great reward.

Ancient trade route

Like most of Southeast Alaska, the first inhabitants of the Haines area were two tribes of Tlingit Indians, the Chilkat and the Chilkoot. The Natives called their home "Dei-Shu" or "End of the Trail." The ancient Tlingit trade route, up the Chilkat Valley into interior Canada, later became the Dalton Trail used by prospectors to access distant gold fields. Today, parts of this long-used trail have become the Haines Highway, connecting Haines to the Canadian and Alaska road systems.

The noted naturalist John Muir visited Haines in 1879. Muir's traveling companion and friend, S. Hall Young, was the first missionary to arrive in the area. Muir and Young successfully petitioned the Chilkat for permission, and the Presbyterian Women's Executive Society of Home Missions for funds, to build the Willard Mission and School.

The name of the mission was later changed to Haines in honor of the Society's secretary, Mrs F.E. Haines, who raised the necessary building funds for the project. As the gold rush frenzy accelerated in the late 1890s, the area became a mining supply center. The fishing industry was also booming at that time, and by the turn of the century four canneries were in full operation.

Military fort

In 1904, responding to border issues with Canada, the first US government military post in Alaska (and the only one prior to World War II) was built just south of Haines and named **Fort William H. Seward** Ⓐ. The fort, in rather stark contrast to Haines' rustic frontier motif, was a collection of stately, white clapboard buildings surrounding the central parade grounds. The fort was decommissioned in 1947, and listed as an Historic Landmark in 1972. Today, these same white buildings serve as private homes, accommodation establishments, art galleries, and restaurants. A Tlingit clan house in the center of the Parade Field makes Haines' housing juxtaposition complete.

A walking tour brochure for Fort Seward is available at the **Haines**

Threatened tribe
Having been denied any claim to land in the 1971 Alaska Native Claims Settlement Act, the Chilkoot Tlingit were in danger of seeing their culture die out. In 1990 the tribe, half of whose 480 members live in Haines, formed the Chilkoot Indian Association, which has rebuilt the tribal identity and plays a full role in the town's affairs and culture.

BELOW: open year-round for breakfast, lunch, and dinner.

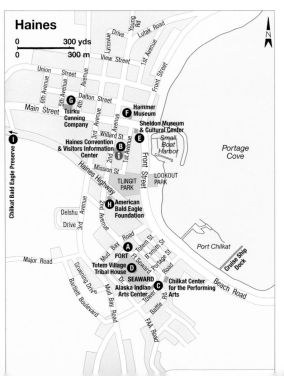

TIP

Hiking Haines

With five state parks surrounding the small city, there are plenty of places to retreat into the wilderness. Try visiting the untouched Chilkat Islands State Marine Park, or follow Mount Riley Trail to its stunning apex, high above the Chilkat Inlet. For more information visit Alaska State Parks at http://dnr.alaska.gov/parks/units/haines.htm or call 907-465-4563.

BELOW RIGHT: a totem carver at work in the Alaska Indian Arts Center.

Convention and Visitors Bureau Visitor Information Center **B** (122 Second Avenue; tel: 800-458-3579, 766-2234; www.haines.ak.us; summer Mon–Fri 8am–6pm, Sat–Sun 9am–5pm, winter Mon–Fri 8am–5pm).

The staff will also connect you with local tour operators eager to show you the sights (in and around Haines) in a number of creative ways: kayak or bike rentals, rafting trips, day cruises, flightseeing, landings on glaciers (and dogsledding), Native cultural tours, fishing charters, and birding or photography treks. The center also offers a bearviewing guide, a birding checklist, area tide books, a list of ten nearby totem pole locations, plus maps and lots of helpful advice.

Regardless of whether you opt for a tour or take off on your own, you'll want to stroll over to Fort Seward and check out the **Alaska Indian Arts Center C** (located in the old fort hospital building on the south side of parade grounds; tel: 766-2160; Mon–Fri 9am–5pm), where you can watch local carvers, silversmiths, and other artisans at work. The **Totem Village**

Tribal House D (the one located in the middle of the parade grounds) offers performances of the **Chilkat Dancers Storytelling Theater** every weekday afternoon in summer (tel: 766-2540; charge).

Pioneer museums

In the Small Boat Harbor area, visit the **Sheldon Museum and Cultural Center E** (11 Main Street; tel: 766-2366; www.sheldonmuseum.org; summer Mon–Fri 10am–5pm, Sat–Sun 1–4pm, winter Mon–Sat 1–4pm; charge). The museum has Haines' pioneer history exhibits as well as those of early Native Tlingit culture.

For an even more unique collection, check out the one-of-a-kind **Hammer Museum F** (108 Main Street; tel: 766-2374; www.hammermuseum.org; summer Mon–Fri 10am–5pm; charge). In this interesting, though admittedly oddball museum you'll find exhibits of over 1,500 historic (and new) hammers used throughout the world for a dizzying array of purposes.

Continuing along Main Street, another interesting museum is the

Alaska Bald Eagle Festival

Haines is famous for hosting the largest concentrated gathering of bald eagles (over 3,000) in the world. In celebration of this distinction, the town holds the Bald Eagle Festival in mid-November. Despite the winter rain/snow, winds, and cold, birders, photographers, artists, and nature lovers of all ages and stages have been congregating here each year since 1994.

Powerfully drawn by the lure of these extraordinary birds and perversely undaunted by the bitter weather, they don their polypropylene long underwear and channel their enthusiasm into guided eagle-viewing treks, photography workshops, and expert lectures. A highlight is the releasing of a rehabilitated eagle back into the wild and participants can even bid for the privilege of personally releasing the bird. For further details, visit the festival website: www.baldeaglefestival.org.

Tsirku Canning Co. ⓖ (located at Fifth Avenue and Main Street; tel: 766-3474; www.cannerytour.com; mid-May–mid-Sept, hours vary, call for schedule; charge). This perfectly restored, working line of 1920s-era cannery equipment gives visitors an opportunity to watch the entire canning process while learning about the history of canneries in Alaska.

Eagle enterprises

To view interesting wildlife display, visit the **American Bald Eagle Foundation** ⓗ (located at Second Avenue and Haines Highway; tel: 766-3094; www.baldeagles.org; May–Oct Mon–Fri 9am–6pm, Sat–Sun 1–4pm). This natural history museum features more than 180 dioramas of mounted bald eagles and other wildlife common to the area. The center is a non-profit educational foundation dedicated to the protection and preservation of bald eagle habitat.

If you travel 18 miles (29km) out the Haines Highway, you will find roadside pullouts for eagle viewing in the **Chilkat Bald Eagle Preserve** ⓘ, created in 1982 by the State of Alaska, and

probably the best spot in the world to view bald eagles. This is especially true from early October until January each year, when over 3,000 eagles congregate in the Chilkat Valley in order to feed on the late run of salmon spawning in the Chilkat River. The preserve also provides interpretive displays, trails and shelters. The prime viewing areas are from mile 18 to 21, but the eagles often disregard those boundaries and can be seen, sometimes a dozen or more to a single cottonwood tree, maintaining a constant, watchful eye on salmon swimming upstream. ❑

Chilkat dancers perform in Haines. The highly stylized blankets, depicting clan symbols and animals in abstract geometric patterns, could take a year to weave and were very valuable, selling for $30 (a huge sum) in the mid-19th century. A few weavers keep the tradition alive.

RESTAURANTS

33-Mile Road House
Mile 33 Haines Highway
Tel: 767-5510
www.33mileroadhouse.com
$–$$
Locals head here for a change-of-pace restaurant, or to take relatives when they visit. Authentic roadhouse decor, historic memorabilia, consistently good food. Beer and wine served.

Bamboo Room Restaurant and Pioneer Bar
Second Avenue and Main Street
Tel: 766-2800 **$–$$**
Despite its name, this is your classic Alaska dinner/bar. Complete with red vinyl booths and housed in a gold-rush era building, the Bamboo Room is the place

to come for fish and chips and a game of pool. Breakfast, lunch, and dinner served daily. Full bar.

Blacksmith Road
Historic Building 37
Tel: 766-3838 **$$**
Located in the fort area of Haines, this bistro offers pizza, calzones, soup, salad, pasta, and other light Italian dishes. Outdoor seating is available, as are all local beers on tap. Serves dinner Tuesday through Saturday. Lunch in the summer only.

Chilkat Restaurant and Bakery
Fifth Avenue and Dalton Street
Tel: 766-3653 **$–$$**

The bakery side of this establishment is where neighbors congregate for coffee, donuts, and gossip. The restaurant side offers daily breakfast and lunch. Open for dinner, weekends only, featuring Thai dishes.

Commander's Room
in Hotel Halsingland,
13 Fort Seward Drive
Tel: 766-2000 **$$$**
Excellent seafood but creative meat dishes too. The chef has his own herb garden. Open for breakfast and dinner.

Fogcutter Bar
Main Street, between First and Second avenues

Tel: 766-2555 **$**
Conveniently situated near the harbor, and open year round. Light snacks, pool tables, big-screen TV and a dance floor.

Lighthouse Restaurant (and Harbor Bar)
101 Front Street
Tel: 766-2442 **$$–$$$**
Breakfast, lunch, and dinner. Casual but good dining, with a view of the waterfront.

Price is for dinner excluding tax, tip, and beverages:
$ = under $15
$$ = $15–20
$$$ = $20–30
$$$$ = over $30

SKAGWAY

The town was founded on gold and dreams, and its brief period of glory is recreated – in a suitably sanitized way, of course – for the enjoyment of today's cruise-ship tourists

BELOW: Skagway's architecture recalls the gold rush era.

Familiar sounds resonate in **Skagway** 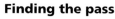, where the rollicking past has been preserved. On a calm midsummer night when the sun has just skipped behind the last peak, you can't help but hear them coming from behind those false fronts as you walk up the boardwalk on Broadway Street. They are the sounds of a not-too-distant era: ragtime pianos, whooping cancan girls, ringing cash registers, songs, and raucous laughter; the happy sounds of gold fever run rampant at the start of the trail. Recreated for the tourist mar-

ket, they give visitors a taste of the past and boost the local economy.

There's no town in Alaska quite like Skagway when it comes to blending history with natural beauty. Situated at the northern end of Southeast Alaska's Inside Passage, Skagway is the natural jumping-off point for anyone taking the shortcut over the coastal mountains into Canada's Yukon. In 1897–8, stampeders took to the trail, and a town of 10,000 to 20,000 people sprouted. Today, many of the old buildings still stand and the town's 800 or so residents cater to the crowds of tourists.

Finding the pass

When you approach Skagway from the south – by Alaska Ferry, cruise ship or air taxi – you see a tiny town at the base of a river valley surrounded by mountains ranging from 5,000 to 7,000ft (1,500 to 2,100 meters) above sea level, rising almost straight out of the saltwater fjord. You would not expect to find a pass to the closed-in valley, but there is one – the White Pass.

The first white man to discover it was Captain William Moore, a member of an 1887 Canadian survey party, a 65-year-old dreamer who had captained steamboats on rivers all over the western hemisphere. The big strike in the Yukon did not occur until August 1896, and by October 1897 Skagway's first newspaper reported 15 general stores, 19 restaurants, four meat mar-

kets, three wharves, 11 saloons, six lumber yards, eight pack trains, and nine hotels. Three other newspapers were established within a year.

Skagway was not alone in its quest to become the "Metropolis of the North." **Dyea**, a city on the bay 10 miles (16km) to the west, sprang up as well. It sat at the foot of the Chilkoot Trail, an established Native route that was shorter but steeper than the White Pass Trail.

The White Pass Trail, nicknamed "Dead Horse Trail" because of the 3,000 pack animals that perished in the canyon, was used by fewer prospectors, but Skagway won the battle for survival. The White Pass and Yukon Route Railroad laid its first tracks up the middle of Broadway Street on May 28, 1898, and by 1900 the narrow-gauge line was completed, 100 miles (160km) to Whitehorse, future capital of the Yukon Territory. By providing an easy route to the gold fields, it turned Dyea into a ghost town. Today, its sparse remains can be seen at the start of the Chilkoot Trail *(see margin note, page 152)*.

The White Pass and Yukon Route Railroad was Alaska's first railroad and still has an international reputation as a first-class feat of engineering. It is to this day something to marvel at.

The Klondike Rush had subsided by 1900, but Skagway was set up for life as the port for the Yukon. Its population has fluctuated between 400 and 3,000 in the years since, due to a continuous boom-and-bust cycle. Food, fuel, war supplies, minerals and tourists have all been hauled by the railroad in various volumes and numbers. In the early 1980s the railroad went through a bad patch and closed down, but was re-opened in 1988.

Riding the railroad

Riding the narrow-gauge train over the White Pass is the best way to get a feel of what the gold rush was like. You travel in turn-of-the-20th-century parlor cars, pulled by steam or diesel engines, which seem to cling to the small cut in the mountainside. Hundreds of feet below are the still visible remains of the old trails. Excursions are available to White Pass Summit (2,890ft/880 meters) or passengers may book a one-way ticket from Skagway to

"Soapy" Smith
Jefferson Randolph "Soapy" Smith, who had been chased out of Colorado, set up his gang in Skagway in 1897. For nine months, under the guise of a civic leader, he won the allegiance not only of prostitutes and gamblers, but also of bankers, editors, and church builders. But when one of his men robbed a miner, Soapy refused to bow to vigilantes and return the gold. He died in a shootout while trying to break up the lynch mob.

BELOW: many of the old Victorian buildings were originally brothels.

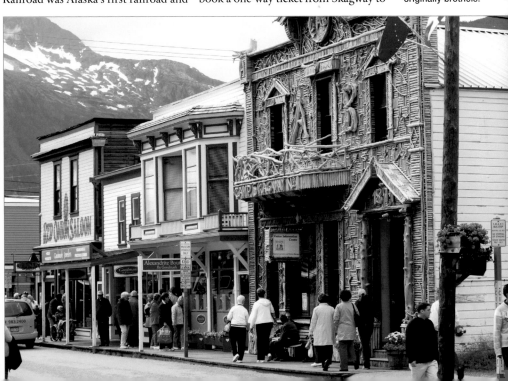

BELOW: the White Pass and Yukon Route Railway.

Fraser, British Columbia, where they continue to Whitehorse by bus. Visitors can also drive the Klondike Highway, which climbs the opposite side of the canyon from the railroad. The 3-hour drive gives you much the same splendid scenery as is seen from the railroad: Skagway River Gorge, Pitchfork Falls, White Pass Summit, and the beautiful lake country of British Columbia and the Yukon.

The gold rush recalled

The center of activity in Skagway is along Broadway Street, which starts at the dock and ferry terminal, where more than 60 gold-rush era buildings still stand. The **Klondike Gold Rush National Historic Park ⓫**, created in 1977, took over ownership of many of these buildings and has since spent millions of dollars on their restoration. Private restoration has also taken place. Restaurants, saloons, hotels, art galleries, ice-cream parlors, and other businesses, are here, many of them staffed by people in gold-rush period dress.

Start a tour of the town with a visit to the **Klondike Gold Rush National**

Historic Park Visitor Center Ⓐ (tel: 983-2921; www.nps.gov/klgo; daily, May–Sept 8am–6pm, Oct–Apr 8am–5pm) on the corner of Second Avenue and Broadway Street. The center contains a small museum, offers informative talks, shows an atmospheric movie about the gold rush days, and conducts free walking tours of the district three or four times a day.

Nearby, on the corner of Third Avenue and Broadway Street, and also under the egis of the National Historic Park, is the **Mascot Saloon Ⓑ**. Built in 1898, when it was one of many barrooms designed to slake the miners' thirst, it has some well-displayed exhibits which conjure up the rough, tough atmosphere of the saloon's heyday.

The **Arctic Brotherhood Hall Ⓒ** is just across the street. Its exterior covered with thousands of pieces of driftwood, it is now the home of Skagway's **Convention and Visitors Bureau** (tel: 983-2854; www.skagway.com).

Walk up Broadway Street and turn right on Fifth Avenue to **Moore's Cabin Ⓓ**, built by the city's neglected founder and his son in 1887 and trans-

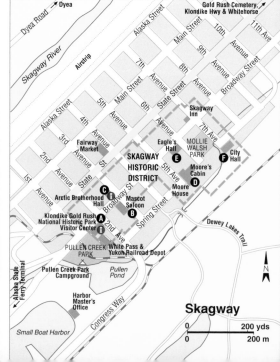

Skagway

ferred to this spot when stampeders trampled over their land. This, too, has been renovated by the National Historic Park Service.

On the corner of Broadway Street and Sixth is **Eagle's Hall** ⓔ, where the "Skagway in the Days of '98" show re-creates the Soapy Smith story *(see margin on page 149)* nightly. This one-hour melodrama follows an hour of live rag-time music and gambling. The dealers are cast members, the money is phoney, and some of the tables date back to the gold rush. The show's popularity has kept it going since 1925.

At the end of Seventh Avenue (turn right off Broadway Street just past the post office) is the **City Hall** ⓕ, a century-old building that has been both a place of learning (the McCabe College, which is why it is often known locally as the "McCabe Building") and a courthouse. Outside, you will find a display of historic rail cars.

Gold Rush Cemetery

Running parallel with Broadway Street is State Street; follow this northeast for just over 2 miles (3km) and you will come to the **Gold Rush Cemetery**, where Soapy Smith and Frank Reid were laid to rest after reaching their violent mutual end.

Fun and festivities

Skagway has the reputation for being a party town, above all in summer: ask any Yukoner who bolts for the coast on weekends. There are two saloons which are usually hopping, especially on days when the cruise ships are in town.

Jazz musicians working on the cruise vessels sometimes jump ship in Skagway for a few hours to attend jamming sessions, because, they say, it's the only day that they don't have to play "old folks' music." If business is good, the bars will stay open right through until 5am, the official closing time.

Visitors are welcome to join locals in the town-wide parties. The Summer Solstice Party, held on June 21 – the longest day of the year – is a rollicking event, with bands performing in city parks throughout the night.

A traditional gold-rush style Independence Day is celebrated on July 4, complete with parades, races, and jovial

A one-armed bandit carries on the town's gambling traditions.

BELOW: a local mural celebrates the railway tradition.

contests of all kinds. Four days later, on July 8, is Soapy Smith's Wake, a party and a champagne toast to Skagway's notorious con-man, which is held at the Eagle's Hall.

The Klondike Trail of '98 Road Relay is held on the second weekend of September. About 100 10-person teams run a distance of 110 miles (176km) from Skagway to Whitehorse, ending, naturally enough, with a party.

The last two weeks of June see the Dyea to Dawson race, in which competitors recreate the 19th-century gold-rush trek over the Chilkoot Trail to Lake Bennett, then take to canoes for the final leg: Dawson City in the Yukon.

The Chilkoot Trail

Around Skagway, there is much to be seen. If you're reasonably fit and own a backpack, hiking the **Chilkoot Trail**, also part of the Klondike Gold Rush National Historic Park, is the most adventurous option for tracing the route of the gold seekers. The trail extends nearly 35 miles (53km) from old Dyea to Lake Bennett, British Columbia.

Most hikers allow three to five days to capture the scenery and explore the thousands of gold-rush relics left behind during the stampede. A limited number of permits (about 50; fee charged) are available daily to cross the pass.

Contact the National Park Service (tel: 907-983-2921; www.nps.gov/klgo) or Parks Canada (tel: 800-661-0486; www.pc.gc.ca/lhn-nhs/yt/chilkoot).

As you approach the base of the Chilkoot Pass and look up at the steps carved in the snow by the day's hikers, you can't help but visualize the scenes of more than a century ago, when men went out, full of high hopes, to seek their fortunes, and so many returned empty-handed. Fortunately for us, it was captured in photographs and in print.

Edwin Tappan Adney recorded the scene for *Harper's Weekly* in September 1897: "Look more closely. The eye catches movement. There is a continuous moving train; they are perceptible only by their movement, just as ants are. The moving train is zigzagging across the towering face of the precipice, up, up into the sky, even at the

TIP

Dyea ghost town Old Dyea, which was killed off by the coming of the railroad in 1900, can be reached by driving 9 miles (14km) along the twisting Dyea Road. There's little left of the town, apart from a few ruined cabins, but on the way the **Skagway Overlook** viewing platform provides a great view of Skagway and its surrounding peaks.

BELOW: pioneer families tramped over the Chilkoot Pass.

very top. See! they are going against the sky! They are human beings, but never did men look so small."

Other hiking trails

There are several other trails, most described in a booklet obtainable from the National Park Service Visitor Center on the corner of Broadway Street and Second Avenue (daily). The center will also advise on campsites and cabins.

The **Dewey Lake Trail System** comprises various trails, the shortest (about half an hour each way) being to Lower Dewey Lake, where pink and silver salmon run in August and September, and which has picnic spots and camp spaces. From here you can continue up to the Upper Dewey Lake and the Devil's Punchbowl. For a tougher hike, try the **Skyline Trail**, officially called the AB Mountain Trail, which starts on Dyea Road, just over 1 mile (2km) out of town, and takes a whole day from start to finish. The **Denver Glacier Trail** is another option. It takes you up the Skagway River to the Denver Glacier, but it's tough going and not for the faint-hearted.

The best weather for exploring the area is in spring. Skies are clear, the sun is hot, and the snow is still deep on White Pass until mid-May. Cross-country skiers and snow-mobilers drive to the top of the highway, and go all day. Later in the summer, after the snow has melted, hundreds of small ponds form on the moon-like terrain.

Heading for the Interior

Since the opening of the **Klondike Highway** out of Skagway, more and more travelers drive the 360-mile (580km) "Golden Circle" route to include both Skagway and Haines on their way to or from the Interior.

Driving up the Alaska Highway from the south, you can cut off to Skagway, put your car on the ferry for the short ride to Haines, and then proceed north along the Chilkoot River on the Haines Cut-Off till you meet the Alaska Highway again at Haines Junction. This is the most direct road route to Alaska's interior from the Panhandle. ❏

The White Pass and Yukon Route Railroad is still admired as a first-class feat of engineering.

RESTAURANTS

Lemon Rose Bakery
330 Third Avenue
Tel: 983-3558 **$**
Making everything from scratch, this bakery has a taste of home with plentiful cookies, apple turnovers, and sticky cinnamon buns.

Olivia's Restaurant at the Skagway Inn
Seventh Avenue and Broadway Street
Tel: 983-2289
www.skagwayinn.com **$$$$**
Housed in a former brothel, this high-end restaurant serves tapas, revolving around fresh Alaska seafood and local fresh produce picked from an organic garden next to the inn. Full bar and select wines available.

Reservations required. Closed in winter.

Red Onion Saloon
205 Broadway Street
Tel: 983-2222 **$**
Decked out as a gold rush saloon, with life-size replicas of 19th-century prostitutes. Cocktails, beer, and pub fare can all be found here, while occasional live music adds to the atmosphere.

Skagway Brewing Company
Seventh Avenue and Broadway Street
Tel: 983-2739
www.skagwaybrewing.com **$–$$$**
Opened since 1897, this pub easily mixes locals with tour-

ists along the long, brass accented oak bar. Serving pub fare including bratwurst, macaroni cheese, and fresh crab cakes, it has something for everyone, including plenty of local beers. Patio seating available.

Skagway Fish Company
210 Congress Way
Tel: 983-3474 **$$–$$$**
Adjacent to the small boat harbor and right off the railway line and cruise-ship dock, this is a great place to enjoy local seafood over checkered tablecloths. Fish and chips are a particular favorite, known for their crisp exterior and tender, juicy interior. Open for lunch and dinner.

The Stowaway Café
205 Congress Way
Tel: 983-3463 **$$–$$$**
Grilled salmon and halibut are the specialty at this charming little house a short distance from the historic sites. Open only in summer, this waterfront restaurant also offers a variety of beef and pasta dishes. Small dining room (reservations recommended) and a walk-up window for lunchtime carry-out meals. Beer and wine.

Price is for dinner excluding tax, tip, and beverages:
$ = under $15
$$ = $15–20
$$$ = $20–30
$$$$ = over $30

THE GREAT KLONDIKE GOLD RUSH

Gold was discovered in the Klondike in a period of economic depression, attracting the penniless, the adventurous, and the unscrupulous

During 1897–8, 100,000 people poured into Dawson in the Klondike in search of gold. Although Dawson is in Canada, the best way to reach it was by ship, 600 miles (960km) from Seattle to Skagway, then overland, across one of two treacherous passes – the White Pass from Skagway or the Chilkoot from Dyea. The former was believed to be slightly easier, but it was controlled by "Soapy" Smith – a villain who virtually ran Skagway during the gold boom (*see margin note, page 149*) – and stories of men being robbed and murdered were rife.

On the Chilkoot Pass it was the elements that were the killers, particularly avalanches and winter's extreme cold. The journey was made more difficult by the fact that, after some of the early prospectors died of starvation, the Canadian government insisted that each man should take a year's supplies – which weighed roughly a ton.

Dreams and desolation

While some people became rich, and others found just enough to give them security, many of the so-called stampeders, having sunk everything they owned into the enterprise, were ruined. It's estimated that fewer than 100 of the gold rushers retained or built on their wealth in the long term.

BELOW: prospectors eye the scales and weigh the gold that has been gleaned during a long winter's work. By 1900, more than $250 million of gold had been found.

ABOVE: prospectors crossing the Chilkoot and White passes to Dawson, during the coldest winter in living memory, set up makeshift encampments en route. On Palm Sunday, 1898 spring sunshine began to melt the snow and an avalanche engulfed a Chilkoot Trail camp, killing 70 people.

DISHING THE DIRT IN DAWSON

Mining was a laborious business and those who went to the gold fields thinking the precious metal was there for the taking were soon disillusioned. The early prospectors had been lucky, striking gold near the surface, but by the time the great influx of hopefuls reached Dawson they were digging for gold which could be some 50ft (15 meters) beneath the surface. To reach it, they had to force their way through permafrost, burning fires to soften the land, then sinking shafts which might, or might not, hit the right spot.

Once the "paydirt" – the mixture of earth and gold – had been extracted it had to be separated and cleaned, and this was done in a primitive sluice. When the streams began to thaw in spring, water channeled through the sluice separated the precious dust from the dirt. The more sophisticated hydraulic sluicing methods introduced in Silver Bow could not be used in Dawson because of the difficulty of getting equipment across the passes.

The sluice pictured above is "Long Tom" in Nome, where gold was discovered in late 1899.

LEFT: services sprang up in the towns and along the route. This laundry, set up in Dawson, was a welcome sight to people who had spent months on the trail.

: those who could afford it loaded their provisions and equipment to pack horses, but many of the animals failed to survive the trip, ice the nickname given to the White Pass – Dead Horse Trail.

OVE: gold was discovered in Silver Bow Basin in the 1880s, most two decades before the Klondike strike, and was a lot easier each. Gold pans and pick axes were soon replaced by hydraulic th-moving and sluicing operations, and the camp eventually came the town of Juneau.

GHT: Mary's Hotel in Bonanza Creek was one of many roadhouses ich sprang up along the Klondike creeks for the mutual benefit of owners and the gold diggers. These hostelries provided a few me comforts, and gave the lucky ones somewhere to spend their ney, distributing the rewards of the gold fields.

YAKUTAT

The tiny, superlative-laden community of Yakutat is far off the beaten path of, well, just about everybody. It is the northernmost town of Southeast Alaska, located on Monti Bay, the only sheltered, deep-water port in the Gulf of Alaska

Main attractions
MALASPINA GLACIER
HUBBARD GLACIER
SITUK RIVER

BELOW: fireweed brightens Harlequin Lake, to the southeast of Yakutat.

The majestic 18,008ft (5,489-meter) spire of Mount St Elias, the second-tallest mountain in North America, dominates the northwestern skyline of **Yakutat** 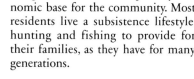 (about 620 residents). Providing a formidable backup is the rest of the St Elias Mountain Range, the highest coastal range in the world (exceeding the Himalayas in vertical relief). The area also boasts the greatest number of glaciers in North America – giant ones – surrounding the town on three sides. In fact, the 45-mile (72-km) -wide **Malaspina Glacier**, a few miles west of Yakutat, is North America's largest piedmont glacier and covers more area than the state of Rhode Island.

The **Hubbard Glacier**, to the north, is the longest tidewater glacier in Alaska. Twice in recent history (in 1986 and again in 2002), this galloping glacier has built suspense among the world's glaciologists (and among *everyone* in Yakutat) by surging forward, damming the mouth of Russell Fjord, and creating an ominous, rapidly rising freshwater lake. In both instances the ice dam eventually gave way, allowing the water to flow into Yakutat Bay, the trapped marine mammals to escape to the sea, and the residents of Yakutat to breathe a sigh of relief.

Commercial fishing, fish processing and government form the primary economic base for the community. Most residents live a subsistence lifestyle, hunting and fishing to provide for their families, as they have for many generations.

The first settlers

Eyak-speaking people, driven from the Copper River area by Tlingit warriors, were probably the first settlers of Yakutat (the name meaning "the place where the canoes rest"). Throughout the 18th and 19th centuries, explorers from Russia, Spain, France and England made their way to the area's protected harbor. In 1805, the Russian-American Company built a

fort in Yakutat to advance the sea otter trade. Tlingit warriors, having been denied access to their traditional fishing grounds by the Russians, eventually attacked and destroyed the fort. Gold was mined from the black-sand beaches of the area in 1886. The Swedish Free Mission Church built a sawmill and school in Yakutat in 1889, and by the early 1900s a railroad, store and cannery were constructed nearby. Like much of Alaska, Yakutat gained a sudden surge of military population during World War II, and a paved runway that is still in use today.

In fact, another local superlative involves that very runway: Yakutat is one of the smallest communities in the country to enjoy daily jet service (from Seattle and from Anchorage). Other options for travel include air taxis and floatplane services. In summer, the Alaska Marine Highway provides a scheduled ferry service, but only two or three times a month.

Popular activities include beachcombing, birding, and kayaking. In recent years, big waves have attracted surfers from all over. If the idea of catching a glassy wave beneath Mount Elias appeals to you, visit Icy Waves Surf Shop (635 Haida Street; tel: 784-3226; www.icywaves.com) where the owner will get you outfitted or at least chat with you about the day's break.

But Yakutat is probably best known for its world-class sport fishing. The **Situk River**, 11 miles (17km) from town, has the largest run of steelheads in the state. All five species of Pacific salmon may be found in the area. Other species include halibut, rainbow and cutthroat trout, and northern pike.

Outdoor activities

Local lodges offer fishing packages, glacier and wildlife viewing, hunting trips, kayak or river-running support, boat rentals, and a host of other services. The office of the **Yakutat Ranger District** (712 Ocean Cape Road; tel: 784-3359; www.fs.fed.us/r10/tongass/districts/yakutat/index) is a good source of information, as is the **Greater Yakutat Chamber of Commerce** (tel: 784-3933; www.yakutatalaska.com) or the **City and Borough of Yakutat** (tel: 784-3323; www.yakutatak.govoffice2.com). ❏

BELOW LEFT: surfing's popularity justifies a specialist surf shop in town.

RESTAURANTS

Glacier Bear Lodge Restaurant
812 Glacier Bear Highway
Tel: 784-3202
www.glacierbearlodge.com
$–$$$$
Located between Yakutat airport and downtown, this popular lodge serves continental breakfasts, as well as full lunch and dinner, to locals and visitors alike. In the airy restaurant, the friendly staff serve ferry burgers, salads, seafood, and pasta to hungry diners. Homemade soups, breads, and desserts are also on the menu.

Glass Door Bar and Liquor Store
550 Mallott Ave
Tel: 784-3331 **$**
This local watering hole has a wide range of domestic beers and mixed drinks. Bar snacks keep the patrons satisfied and in case you are ready to move on, but want to take something for the road, the bar sells bottles to go.

Yakutat Lodge
111 Airport Road
Tel: 784-3232
www.yakutatlodge.com **$–$$$$**
Adjacent to the Alaska Airlines terminal, this quaint log cabin lodge offers a full-service restaurant. With dishes including steaks, seafood and other Italian fare, it is a favorite with fishermen and hearty eaters. Full bar and liquor store.

Price is for dinner excluding tax, tip, and beverages:
$ = under $15
$$ = $15–20
$$$ = $20–30
$$$$ = over $30

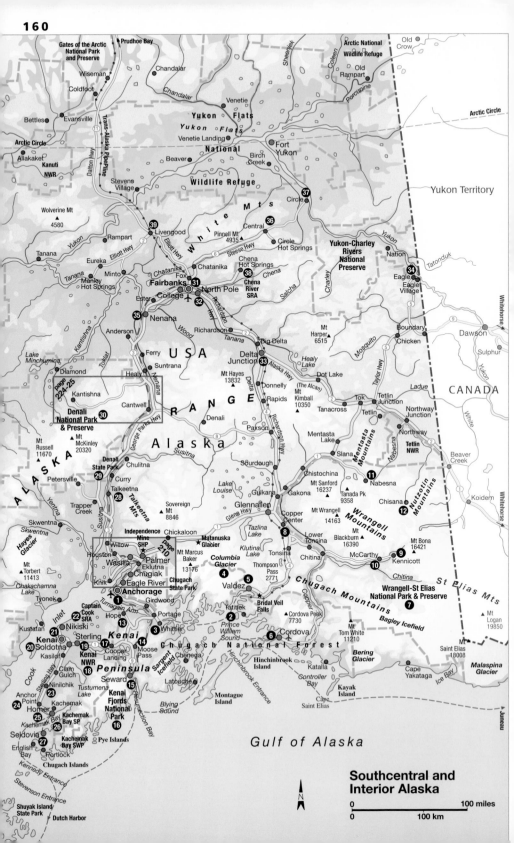

Southcentral and Interior Alaska

0 ——————— 100 miles

0 ——————— 100 km

SOUTHCENTRAL ALASKA

This vast expanse of awe-inspiring countryside
includes Anchorage, Matanuska-Susitna Valley,
Prince William Sound, Copper River Valley,
and the Kenai Peninsula

Southcentral Alaska extends from the coastal fjords, glaciers and forests of the Kenai Peninsula and Prince William Sound areas, northeast through the remote Copper River Valley, or northwest through Anchorage (Alaska's largest city, in terms of population), then past the picturesque farmlands and sobering mountain ranges of the Matanuska-Susitna Valley, and finally to the wild, southern boundary of the alluring Denali National Park and Preserve.

The history of the various communities of Southcentral is as diverse as the land itself. Athabascans were the first inhabitants of much of the area, though Alutiiq and Eyak peoples populated the area now called Cordova. Intrepid explorers from Russia traveled to the mainland of Alaska beginning in 1741, and were soon followed by other adventurers from Britain, Spain, and America.

The discovery of valuable minerals, primarily copper and gold, drew boatloads of prospectors to the area, prompted the construction of two railroad systems in the early 1900s, and spawned many of the communities of both the Copper River Valley and Prince William Sound, as well as Seward, Anchorage, Palmer/Wasilla, and Talkeetna. From 1939 to 1957, US military construction created new roads, airports and harbors throughout the region.

Accessible adventures

Because of the mind-boggling size and scope of the state, today's visitors to Alaska are faced with a difficult choice: which area should one explore during the typical two-week vacation? In many ways, it could be argued that Southcentral Alaska, because of the climate, location, availability of goods and services, road system and transportation options, may well provide the greatest number (and variety) of accessible adventure options.

Anchorage is not Alaska's capital, but has many of the attributes of a capital city. Approximately 42 percent of Alaska's total population lives here. Most visitors to Southcentral arrive via commercial airlines into Anchorage, by cruise ship (through Whittier or Seward), or by Alaska

PRECEDING PAGES: a hiker surveys Anchorage's skyline from the Chugach Mountains. **ABOVE:** wild camping; Native art in Anchorage Museum.

Marine Highway System ferry (through Whittier). Southcentral is largely connected by road and easily accessible by car, RV or bus.

Flightseeing opportunities

Every town in Alaska, regardless of size, has some sort of airport, ranging from the modern Ted Stevens Anchorage International Airport, to unpaved strips in the bush. Pilots also land on beaches, gravel bars, and lakes where no constructed facilities exist. Air taxis can be chartered in most communities to take you to outlying villages, on day trips for dramatic flightseeing opportunities, or they will drop you off in remote areas for a backcountry experience, and return to pick you up at a pre-arranged time and location.

In addition to traveling to and within Southcentral by air, sea or road, there is also the delightful and scenic option of "riding the rails." While no US nor Canadian rail system provides rail service to Alaska, the Alaska Railroad (www.akrr.com) provides excellent (though not inexpensive) opportunities to see Southcentral Alaska during the summer months, from Kenai Peninsula city of Seward, north through Anchorage, Wasilla, Talkeetna and on into the interior city of Fairbanks (*see page 237*).

The climate

Summer temperatures in Southcentral Alaska are generally pleasant. Anchorage's July temperatures average from 51° to 65°F (10–18°C), and average yearly precipitation is 15ins (38cm) – compared to 162ins (411cm) in Ketchikan, and 5ins (13cm) in Barrow.

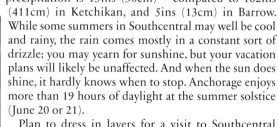

While some summers in Southcentral may well be cool and rainy, the rain comes mostly in a constant sort of drizzle; you may yearn for sunshine, but your vacation plans will likely be unaffected. And when the sun does shine, it hardly knows when to stop. Anchorage enjoys more than 19 hours of daylight at the summer solstice (June 20 or 21).

Plan to dress in layers for a visit to Southcentral Alaska. Long pants (although the locals, especially the younger ones, will likely be wearing shorts), short-sleeved T-shirts, a light, rain and wind resistant, hooded jacket, and comfortable, casual walking shoes would be perfect for a summer visit. Add a fleece jacket, a warm, knit hat, and gloves if you plan to go out on the water for a day cruise. If it's overcast or rainy, with even a slight wind, you'll be glad for the extra warmth.

Don't forget to bring sunscreen along, and mosquito repellent can be your best friend if you plan to camp or hike anywhere in Alaska. For wintertime visits, add a warm, winter-weight jacket, heavier hat and gloves, snow pants, and warm, insulated boots to your ensemble. You may feel a bit bulky, but rest assured, you'll fit right in. ❏

ABOVE: a well-equipped fisherwoman; a fisherman and his floatplane.
RIGHT: unusually strong fall colors on the Seward Highway.

ANCHORAGE

Anchorage is a good jumping-off point for many parts of the state, but it has a lot more to offer, from interesting museums to lively nightlife, and ski slopes right on the doorstep

Imagine you're a passenger aboard one of the many domestic and international air carriers serving **Anchorage ❶** daily. About three hours out of Seattle, the pilot announces you'll be landing in Anchorage in a few minutes – but, as you peer out of the window, you can see few signs of civilization.

Just as you're beginning to wonder if the pilot has lost his way, you spot Anchorage. Sitting on a roughly triangular piece of land that sticks out into Cook Inlet, with Turnagain Arm bordering the southwest shore and Knik Arm the northwest one, the city sprawls out over a 10-mile (16km) length, seeming to spread over most of the available land between the inlet and the Chugach Mountains to the east.

Commercial center

With over a quarter of a million residents and 42 percent of Alaska's population, Anchorage is the state's largest metropolis and its commercial center. This port city didn't get a good purchase on life until 1915, but in the decades since has developed from a railroad tent camp to a city of high-rise offices, ethnic restaurants, and world-class trail systems for biking, hiking, and skiing.

Captain James Cook, the British explorer, sailed into Cook Inlet in 1778, while looking for a Northwest Passage

to the Atlantic. Trading furs and fish with the Dena'ina Natives, he noticed that they carried iron and copper weapons, the first evidence of trade with the Russians who had set up trading posts in lower Cook Inlet and at Kodiak.

Russian influences can still be seen today at Eklutna, a Dena'ina village inside the northern boundary of the municipality of Anchorage.

When Cook found no way out of the arm of Cook Inlet to the south of Anchorage, he ordered his ships, the *Resolution* and the *Discovery*, to turn

Main attractions
SHIP CREEK
ANCHORAGE MUSEUM OF HISTORY AND ART
ALASKA CENTER FOR THE PERFORMING ARTS
IMAGINARIUM
OSCAR ANDERSON HOUSE MUSEUM
ALASKA NATIVE HERITAGE CENTER
EARTHQUAKE PARK
ALASKA ZOO
H2OASIS INDOOR WATERPARK
EAGLE RIVER NATURE CENTER
ANCHORAGE COASTAL WILDLIFE REFUGE
GIRDWOOD
EKLUTNA VILLAGE HISTORICAL PARK
ALYESKA RESORT AND SKI AREA

LEFT: downtown Anchorage by night.
RIGHT: statue of Captain James Cook.

Snow sculpture in Anchorage.

around, hence the name "Turnagain." Knik Arm gets its name from the Eskimo word for fire, knik, which was used in reference to the Dena'ina people and their villages.

The gold rush

After Alaska was purchased from the Russians in 1867, gold seekers worked the land along Turnagain Arm and at Crow Creek and Girdwood, which is now the southern boundary of the municipality. The gold rush rapidly spread north and across Knik Arm. The old mining supply center of Knik is located across the inlet from downtown Anchorage.

During its short history, Anchorage has reverberated with the sounds of several major construction booms: laying track for the Alaska Railroad, building two adjacent military bases during World War II, the discovery and development of the Cook Inlet and Kenai Peninsula oil fields, and, in the 1970s, the construction of the 800-mile (1,285km) trans-Alaska oil pipeline from Prudhoe Bay to Valdez. The most recent boom has been of the retail variety: several national chains have opened stores in Anchorage in the past 15 years.

Rugged individualism

The Good Friday earthquake of 1964, measuring 9.2 on the Richter scale, was the most powerful earthquake ever recorded in North America, and it brought Alaskans together to work for a common cause. While the quake devastated many homes and businesses in Anchorage and in other communities, the reconstruction generated a mini-boom and Anchorage emerged a new city. Quakes still shake Anchorage and Southcentral Alaska occasionally, including a 7.9 tremor in 2002.

During the past decade Anchorage has striven to overcome the consequences of its boom-and-bust economy – unemployment, out-migration, poverty, to name a few. While the record high fuel prices of 2008 kept Alaska's economy relatively strong through the begining of the most recent economic downturn, its growing reliance on tourist dollars keeps the majority of Alaskans working in the service sector on edge.

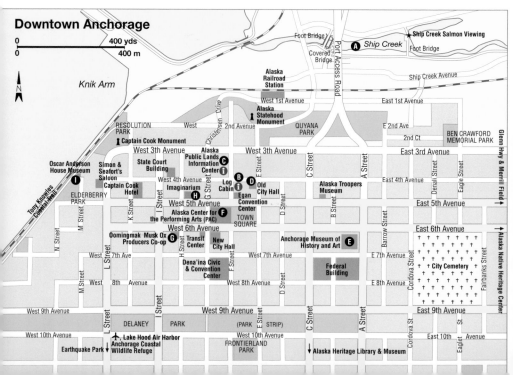

Downtown Anchorage

Backyard wilderness

Some people move to Anchorage from other parts of the USA because they are attracted by the adventure of living at the "last frontier." This is a city where one needs only to walk out of the back door to see – and, in some cases, step into – the wilderness.

Although some residents take off at weekends to pursue various outdoor activities, many others find no need to get away. Not surprising, perhaps, when it is quite common to see a moose outside the living room window, or a bald eagle flying overhead, and when you can share city parks with lynx, owls, and bears. Even wolf packs sometimes prowl the city's edges. Wildlife is so ubiquitous that no one who lives here blinks when they see a moose along the Glenn Highway. An estimated 2,000 moose, 200 black bears and 60 brown bears live in the metropolitan Anchorage area and nearby foothills.

Fishing enthusiasts have to go no further than **Ship Creek Ⓐ**, on the north side of downtown, to have the chance of catching a 40lb (18kg) salmon. The king salmon run lasts from early June to mid-July, and the silver salmon run from late July until later October. For regulations, check www.adfg.state.ak.us.

Discovering the city

Anchorage is an air crossroads, with several major airlines offering direct flights, primarily from Seattle, but also from other US cities, Tokyo and the Russian Far East. It is as close to London or Tokyo as it is to Houston. More than 200 flights arrive daily at the Anchorage International Airport.

If you are staying downtown, you can easily explore this section of the city on foot. Start at the **Visitor Information Center Log Cabin Ⓑ** (tel: 274-3531; daily June–Aug 7.30am–7pm, May and Sept 8am–6pm, Oct–Apr 9am–4pm) on the corner of Fourth Avenue and F Street. Built in 1954, the log cabin is surrounded by flowering foliage in the summer. Note the 5,145lb (2,333kg) block of solid jade, the state's official gemstone, outside the cabin. Here you can pick up maps and brochures, including a booklet outlining a suggested walking tour; or you could

BELOW: Ship Creek, famous for urban combat fishing downtown.

*The Visitor
Information Center
Log Cabin.*

BELOW RIGHT: the
Anchorage Museum
of History and Art.

walk a block down the street and take one of the local trolley tours.

From here, you can cross the road diagonally to reach the **Alaska Public Lands Information Center** ❸ (tel: 644-3661; www.nps.gov/aplic; summer daily 9am–5pm, winter Mon–Fri 10am–5pm). You can see wildlife exhibits, watch DVDs on the regions and activities available, and generally pick up all the information you'll need.

Armed with this information, you can then continue your urban tour. First go back to the **Old City Hall** ❹, a classic 1930s construction next door to the Log Cabin, where the lobby holds a display of photographs and other exhibits that trace the city's history.

Continue your walking tour by heading east along Fourth Avenue. You will pass many T-shirt shops and stores offering Native art, including carved walrus ivory, soapstone, and baskets. Genuine Native crafts are identified by a tag, either showing a silver hand or stating "Authentic Native Handicraft."

Three blocks past the mall (and the main post office), turn right down A Street to the recently expanded

Anchorage Museum of History and Art at Rasmuson Center ❺ (tel: 343-4326; www.anchoragemuseum.org; summer daily 9am–6pm, winter Tue–Sat 10am–6pm, Sun noon–6pm; charge). Among the museum's permanent collections are the Alaska Gallery, with historical exhibits, and a fine selection of Native art and works by travelers, explorers and early residents, displayed in skylit galleries.

Arts center

A few blocks west is the **Alaska Center for the Performing Arts** ❻ (tel: 263-2787; www.alaskapac.org). Some view this building (locally referred to as "the PAC") as a monstrosity, while others consider it to be architecturally innovative, but its lush flower garden beds certainly add to the beauty of the downtown area.

Alaskan artists have designed much of the interior, including the carpets and upholstery, and the center is decorated with numerous Native masks. Tours are available, but by appointment only. There is no set charge, but a donation is appreciated.

What to Do After Dark

The Crow's Nest at the top of the Captain Cook Hotel (on the corner of Fifth Avenue and K Street) has gourmet cuisine and a formal atmosphere, together with great views. But if you fancy a taste of nightlife in the last frontier, complete with sawdust on the floor, you won't do much better than Chilkoot Charlie's on Spenard Road. Don't bother with a coat and tie; this is where Alaskans go in their boots and jeans to dance, drink and be entertained.

The Bear Tooth Theaterpub and Grill, just off Spenard Road, offers second-run movies on a big-screen, tasty food and draft beer or wine. Humpy's, across from the PAC (Performing Arts Center), serves good beers, food and hosts live music performances. Anchorage also has a number of cinemas and theaters, as well as the events which take place at the PAC. See the local press for listings.

One popular and multiple-award-winning theater in the downtown area is Cyrano's (413 D Street to find out schedule and fee information visit www.cyranos.org or call tel: 274-2599). This theater/coffeehouse/book store entertains locals and visitors alike with live theater (including classics, Alaska originals and contemporary works), comedy improvisation, poetry readings and more. Customers may enjoy beer and wine along with a selection of appetizers and desserts.

Also, while you're there, those who long to see a display of the Northern Lights may do so, virtually speaking, via a 40-minute digital show set to music. Twenty-five years worth of nature's light shows may be seen within the PAC, at the Sidney Laurence Theater (tel: 263-2993; www.thealaska collection.com; end May–early Sept, call for schedule; charge). The PAC is also a hub of activities for the arts. Check local newspapers, especially the Anchorage Daily News, and visitors' guides for events.

One block further west, on the corner of Sixth Avenue and H Street, you will find the **Oomingmak Musk Ox Producers' Co-op G** (tel: 272-9225; www.qiviut.com) where you can buy, or just admire, distinctive garments made of musk ox wool, called qiviut (pronounced *kee-vee-ute*). These are made in Inuit villages.

From the Co-op, turn up H Street again to Fifth Avenue, where you will find the **Imaginarium H** (tel: 276-3179; www.imaginarium.org; Mon–Sat 10am–6pm, Sun noon–5pm; charge). While aimed primarily at children, this award-winning science museum has a wealth of exhibits and hands-on experiences that are also popular with adults. If you want to know more about marine life, wetlands and the solar system, this is a good place to find out.

Continue west a few blocks along Fifth Avenue to M Street, to the **Oscar Anderson House Museum I** (tel: 274-2336; summer Mon–Fri noon–5pm, closed in winter; charge), set in the attractive little Elderberry Park. Listed on the National Register of Historic Places, this is Anchorage's first wood-frame house, built by Swedish immigrant Anderson in 1915.

Leaving downtown behind

Outside the downtown area, but worth seeing, is the **Alaska Heritage Library and Museum J** (tel: 265-2834; summer Mon–Fri noon–5pm, winter Mon–Fri noon–4pm; free), in the lobby of the Wells Fargo Building on Northern Lights Boulevard and C Street. There is a large selection of Native art and artifacts and a number of works by Sydney Laurence (1865–1940), known as "the painter of the north."

The Oscar Anderson House Museum

BELOW: memories of yesteryear's transportation.

Musk oxen can be seen at Alaska Zoo.

Continue as far west as you can go along Northern Lights and you'll reach **Earthquake Park**, founded on the spot where, during the 1964 earthquake, 130 acres (52 hectares) of land fell into the inlet and 75 houses were destroyed. A walking trail and interpretive signs make it worth the stop, and there are good views of the city and Mount McKinley.

To the east, travel the Glenn Highway to the Muldoon Road Exit to reach the **Alaska Native Heritage Center** (tel: 330-8000; www.alaskanative.net; summer daily 9am–5pm, winter Sat 10am–5pm; charge), a gathering place for all of Alaska's Native cultures where you can learn about traditional customs and see master Native artists at work.

Alaska Zoo

Visitors unable to see a bear in the wild can see several (polar, brown and black) at the **Alaska Zoo** (4731 O'Malley Road; tel: 346-2133; daily, summer 9am–6pm, winter 10am–4.30pm; charge). It's a 20-minute drive to the southeast of the city, and a shuttle bus operates from the Hilton, Captain Cook and Sheraton hotels. There's a two-hour tour in the early afternoon.

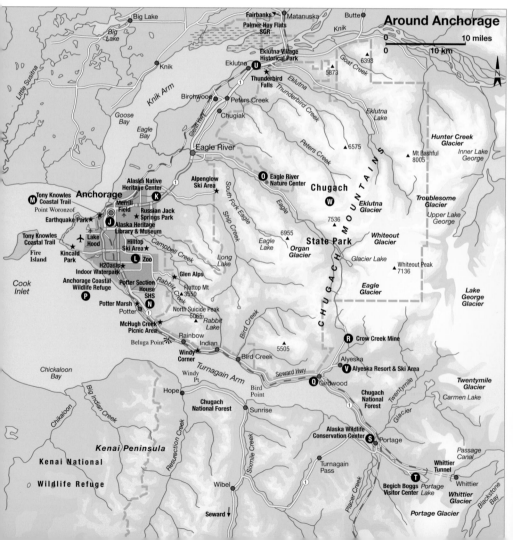

The 25-acre (62-hectare) zoo houses just under 100 birds and mammals, including natives such as moose, musk oxen, and caribou, seals and otters, but also such non-natives as alpacas, Amur tigers, and a Bactrian camel. Its most famous resident, Maggie, a Zimbabwean elephant who has been trained to play the harmonica, caught the attention of international animal rights activists, who argued that a lone tropical elephant could not be happy in a climate which confined her indoors most of the year. The zoo responded in 2006 by installing a $100,000 treadmill for Maggie's exclusive use, but in 2007 agreed that she should transfer to a zoo in the Lower 48.

The zoo had its genesis in 1966 when a local grocer, Jack Snyder, won a contest offering as a prize $3,000 or a baby Asian elephant, Annabelle. He chose the elephant and the idea of a zoo took shape.

Also in this area is **H2Oasis Indoor Waterpark** (1520 O'Malley Road; tel: 522-4420; summer daily 10am–9pm, winter Mon, Wed, Fri 3–9pm, Sat–Sun 10am–9pm; charge). It has wave pools, body slides, hot tubs, a children's pirate ship play area, and a water coaster. It's a warm sanctuary for locals in winter.

Getting about by bike

Anchorage is a great place for cyclists, with more than 120 miles (190km) of paved paths, and plenty of bikes for rent (ask at the Visitor Information Center log cabin).

The Tony Knowles Coastal Trail.

The best-known and most scenic route is the **Tony Knowles Coastal Trail** , which starts near Elderberry Park on Second Avenue. The trail – which bicyclists share with walkers, joggers, rollerbladers, and stroller-pushing parents and the occasional moose – is 11 miles (19km) long and parallels Cook Inlet, continuing past Westchester Lagoon and Point Woronzof, and ending at Kincaid Park. In winter, the path becomes a cross-country ski trail. There are other bike routes in town: trail maps are also available from the Parks and Recreation department, as well as at the Visitor Information Center. Bicycling is an ideal way

BELOW: café society.

Dall sheep can be seen in spring and summer from the Seward Highway.

to get around, and offers great views of the city and the waters of the inlet, where migrating beluga whales are sometimes seen on the surface.

Around Anchorage

If you want to experience the Alaska outdoor life, try a flightseeing trip. Excursions can easily be arranged by flight operators at Lake Hood or at Merrill Field. Not far from downtown near the international airport is **Lake Hood Air Harbor**, the busiest seaplane base in the world. On summer days when the skies are clear, there are 600 or more take-offs and landings. Channels on Lake Hood and Lake Spenard provide the runways for these seaplanes. Merrill Field (800 Merrill Field Drive), located one mile east of downtown Anchorage just off the Glenn Highway, was the first real airport in Anchorage and still today serves as a commercial service airport for the general aviation community. Alaskans fly into the bush

for fishing, hunting, hiking and myriad other activities. If you want to experience the Alaska outdoor life, try a flightseeing trip. Flight operators at Lake Hood or at Merrill Field can easily arrange excursions.

At Anchorage's back door to the east is **Chugach State Park** *(see page 180);* the park headquarters are located across from Potter Marsh in the **Potter Section House State Historic Site** ◐ (tel: 345-5014; www.alaskastateparks.org; Mon–Fri 8am–4pm). Here you will find a railroad museum and an old rotary snow plow on the track behind the house. Chugach State Park covers 495,000 acres (200,500 hectares) and offers visitors a wide variety of opportunities to experience the Alaska outdoors without being too far away from civilization.

Eagle River Nature Center

The **Eagle River Nature Center** ◐ (tel: 694-2108; www.ernc.org) is north on the Glenn Highway from Anchorage. Only a 20-minute drive (14 miles/23km) from downtown Anchorage, Eagle River is a pleasant area. The nature

Fur Rondy

Fur Rendezvous ("Fur Rondy") is a 10-day celebration (late Feb–early March) featuring more than 150 events, ranging from sled dog races to the annual snowshoe softball tournament between 9th and 10th avenues on the Delaney Park Strip. Competitions are held for the best snow sculpture (which draws competitors from as far away as Japan) and the fastest canoe in the Downhill Canoe Race. Other events include the traditional Eskimo blanket toss and the largest outdoor public fur auction in the United States. The highlight of the carnival is the World Championship Sled Dog Race. For three days competitors run heats totaling 75 miles (120km). Participants start on 4th Avenue and continue on the city streets to the outskirts of town where they circle back. Dog mushing is the official state sport.

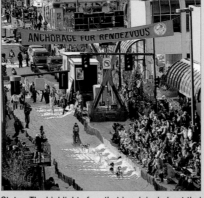

On the last Saturday of Fur Rondy (usually in early March), the Miners' and Trappers' Ball is held. This is not a black-tie affair and everyone in the city is invited, although tickets must be purchased in advance. It is held in a huge warehouse and people arrive in every conceivable attire, some hoping to win the contest for the most unusual costume. Fur Rondy is a great time to experience Alaskans letting their hair down and celebrating all that is original about their state. It is a time of camaraderie among the local people and visitors are welcome.

As the event is becoming more popular, it is best to book well in advance. Greater Anchorage Inc can be contacted for the exact dates of the festival and travel deals (tel: 274-1177; www.furrondy.net).

center is another 15 to 20 minutes from downtown Eagle River, at the end of 12-mile-long (19km) Eagle River Road. The drive through the lake-dotted valley is worth the trip in itself, and once at the center there are displays, nature videos, and several hiking trails, from easy to rigorous. During August the berries are plentiful, and cross-country skiing is a popular winter activity.

Heading south

With only two roads leading in and out of Anchorage, selecting a day trip is easy: you go north or south. Heading south on Seward Highway, visit Girdwood, Crow Creek Mine and Portage Glacier. The drive parallels the Turnagain Arm, an extension of Cook Inlet, and offers breathtaking views and wildlife viewing opportunities. For those with sturdy legs and time to spare, there is a bike trail flanking the highway all the way down to Portage.

Beginning at the southern edge of town, you can see a variety of waterfowl at **Potter Marsh**, part of the **Anchorage Coastal Wildlife Refuge** ℗. This 2,300-acre (920-hectare) wetland area is the nesting ground for migratory birds during the summer. Bald eagles, Arctic terns, trumpeter swans, sandhill cranes, shorebirds, and many species of geese and ducks are commonly spotted; Canada geese and mallards raise their young here. From the boardwalk that borders Potter Marsh's western edge, salmon are visible from mid-July to September as they return to spawn in nearby Rabbit Creek.

Not far from Potter Marsh, down the Seward Highway, visitors have a chance to see larger wildlife. During spring and summer it is common to see Dall sheep peering over the rocks of the adjacent cliffs at passing motorists; the best viewing is at **Windy Corner**, about Mile 107. Several spots on this road allow visitors to watch the waters for belugas, the small white whales that chase salmon up the Turnagain Arm. Stop at Beluga Point Interpretive Site in spring and fall, where you will find spotting 'scopes, benches and information about the area.

If you just want to contemplate the beauty and mammoth size of Alaska, you can grab a take-out lunch in town

TIP

If you are itching to experience the excitement of riding in a dog sled, tours are available year round. In the summer, an expensive helicopter trip will take you to a dog camp on a glacier, while in the winter, tours run a section of the Iditarod Trail or cruise the area around Girdwood. For more information contact the Alaska Visitors Center; www. alaskavisitorscenter. com/images/ dogsledtours.html; tel: 929-2822.

BELOW: cross-country skiing is popular in winter.

Viewing Portage Glacier, which has been in retreat since the early 1800s but is now melting more rapidly than ever.

BELOW: road from Whittier overlooking the Begich Boggs Visitor Center.

and picnic at nearby **McHugh Creek Picnic Area**, just a few miles down the road from Potter Marsh. Here you can see miles down the inlet, look at the majestic mountains on the other shore, and take a short hike along the 9½-mile (15km) long Turnagain Arm Trail.

At Mile 90, the Alyeska Highway, will take you into the forested town of **Girdwood Q**. A quaint community, it sees an influx of tourists in the summer and skiers in the winter. A ride on the Alyeska Ski Resort tram on a clear day provides an incredible view of the surrounding mountains and the inlet.

Outside Girdwood, 3 miles (5km) up Crow Creek Road, is **Crow Creek Mine R**. The placer mine and its eight original buildings, listed on the National Register of Historic Sites, represent the first non-Native settlement in the area. Visitors can pan for gold in this scenic setting, and for the robust, nearby **Crow Pass Trail** climbs through beautiful mountain valleys.

Continuing down the Seward Highway, at **Twentymile River**, visitors may often see Arctic terns, bald eagles, mew gulls, and moose from the observation platform. Plaques on the platform have information on the various species.

Just beyond is the **Alaska Wildlife Conservation Center S** (Mile 79, Seward Highway; tel: 783-2025; www.alaskawildlife.org; charge), a 140-acre/57-hectare, drive-through animal park that is dedicated to the rehabilitation of orphaned and injured animals. Get a close-up look at Alaska's wildlife, and starting in May, their young.

Mile 78.9 is the turn-off for **Portage Glacier**. Following your turn, look on the right-hand side of the road to see Explorer Glacier (there's an excellent photography vantage point). Stop at the bridge over Williwaw Creek to see salmon spawning from late July to mid-September. Sadly, Portage Glacier is rapidly retreating, and with it the once dramatic view of Portage Lake with its huge blue icebergs.

At the end of the road is the **Begich Boggs Visitor Center** ☎ (tel: 783-2326; www.fs.fed.us/r10/chugach; summer daily 9am–6pm). The center's state-of-the-art displays cover the natural history of Chugach National Forest. Don't miss an award-winning documentary film, *Voices from the Ice*, shown hourly during the summer (charge).

Black bear territory

There are several impressive glaciers in Portage Valley with a number of trails where visitors can view glacial features, including a profusion of wildflowers and plant life. Take the short walk to **Byron Glacier**. Signs near Portage Glacier Lodge mark the road to the trailhead. Black bears, smaller cousins of the grizzly, are commonly seen in this area. Portage Glacier is the turn-around point for this trip to the south. From the visitor center there is a new road that will take you to the toll road and tunnel leading to the Prince William Sound community of Whittier *(see page 184)*. Call 1-877-611-2586 for further details and road and tunnel opening information.

Heading north

Traveling on the Glenn Highway north of Anchorage on a day trip, visitors have an opportunity to observe the cultural remnants of Alaska's past and to enjoy several scenic areas in the fertile Matanuska-Susitna Valley.

In Eagle River, stop at the **Eagle River Nature Center** *(see page 181)*, 14 miles (20km) out of town in Chugach State Park. Continuing on the Glenn Highway, you will see beautiful **Mirror Lake** wayside area on the right. Here, if you're brave, you can swim in the icy water on a warm day, or ice fish in the winter. A mile further takes you to the entrance of **Thunderbird Falls Trailhead**, also in Chugach State Park. This is a pleasant 1-mile (2km) walk to the rushing falls.

Eklutna Lake is Anchorage's largest lake. There is a state park campground and a wide, multi-use trail to **Eklutna Glacier**, whose waters feed the lake, good wildlife viewing and berry picking.

The Anchorage area's oldest building may well be the **St Nicholas Russian Orthodox Church**, which is part of **Eklutna Village Historical Park** ⓤ

Girdwood's origins
Originally known as Glacier City, Girdwood began life as a supply camp for miners working the local creeks. It was renamed in recognition of Colonel James Girdwood, a Belfast-born entrepreneur and linen merchant who staked the first gold claims along Crow Creek in 1896.

BELOW: Crow Creek Mine.

Taking a rest on the slopes.

BELOW: on the move at Alyeska, near Girdwood.

(summer Mon–Sat 10am–4pm; services held Thur 6pm, Sat 5pm, Sun 9am) on the Eklutna turn-off, off the Glenn Highway. It was constructed with hand-hewn logs, and the surrounding spirit houses represent the interaction between the Natives and the Russians.

This was the site of the first Dena'ina Indian settlement east of the Knik Arm, in around 1650. The "spirit" houses show how Native beliefs were mixed with Russian orthodoxy. Spirit houses were placed over traditional graves and contained personal items thought to help the spirit in the afterlife. A three-bar Orthodox cross was placed at the foot of the grave.

Small spirit houses indicate the resting place of a child and a large house with a smaller one inside means a mother and child were buried together. A picket fence around a spirit house means that the deceased was not a Dena'ina.

Winter activities

Winters are long in Alaska, but Alaskans have found ways of coping with the season, from competitions to festivals. During Thanksgiving week, the University of Alaska Anchorage, located on several acres of wooded land in the city, hosts the **Great Alaska Shoot-Out**, an invitational college basketball tournament. Seven Division I college basketball teams from across the United States come to Anchorage to compete in a tournament, which has gained national prominence and is televised via satellite.

After the Christmas holiday season, Anchorage residents prepare for their own 10-day carnival in February – **Fur Rendezvous** *(see panel on page 172).*

The best skiing

Downhill and cross-country skiing in Anchorage can be found in **Russian Jack Springs Park,** with gentle slopes and rope tows for beginners. The **Hilltop Ski Area** has a chairlift and is an excellent facility for novice skiers. It also has night skiing and is accessible by public bus. For advanced skiers, **Alpenglow at Arctic Valley Ski Area** offers slightly more challenging slopes. Two chairlifts, a T-bar and three rope tows service the area, which has a

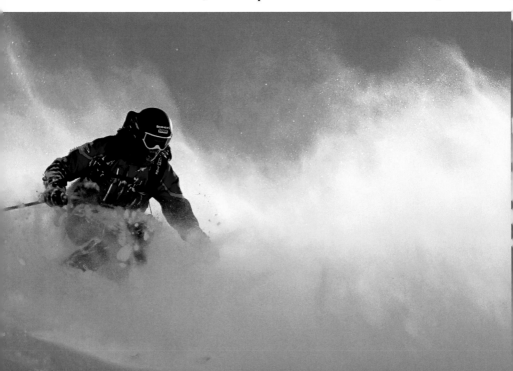

1,000ft (300-meter) drop. Runs can be very steep and maintenance is sometimes questionable.

Alaska's largest and most popular ski area – **Alyeska Resort and Ski Area**  is 40 miles (64km) southeast of Anchorage in Girdwood. With a vertical drop of 2,500ft (760 meters), it caters to all levels of skiers and is a full-service resort with both day and night skiing. The area has six lifts, including a quad chairlift and four doubles, and a high-speed gondola, which operates in the summer months, taking visitors to a restaurant on the mountain top.

Cross-country skiing

Anchorage offers more than 140 miles (225km) of cross-country trails. **Kincaid Park** on Raspberry Road has 34 miles (55km) of Nordic ski trails, nine of them illuminated. Near Service High School and Hilltop Ski Area, another trail is lit for skiers. In Chugach State Park, just east of the city, there are dozens of hiking trails, which in winter are frequently used by cross-country skiers. The **Glen Alps** area at the top of Upper Huffman Road offers breathtaking views of the city and is manageable for skiers of any level. To get to it, take the Seward Highway to the O'Malley turn-off going east, continue toward the mountains, turning on to Hillside Drive, and making a left on Upper Huffman, then follow signs to the trailhead.

An hour's drive north of Anchorage is an excellent cross-country ski area with an historical flavor. **Hatcher Pass** is at the heart of the majestic Talkeetna Mountains off the Glenn Highway on Fishhook Road. At the turn of the 20th century Independence Mine was a hub of gold-mining activity. Today it is a state historic park and its abandoned buildings and machinery have become landmarks of the past *(see page 214)*.

The area has miles of groomed ski trails that pass through treeless alpine bowls and on a clear day you can see all the way down the valley to the city of **Palmer** (20 miles/32km). Accommodations are available at a lodge that has individual cabins for guests (Hatcher Pass Lodge; tel: 745-5897; www.hatcherpasslodge.com). ❑

TIP

Weather warning
When exploring areas such as Crow Pass Trail, be sure to have some basic hiking gear, including water and extra food and clothing, before attempting any hike into the mountains. Weather in Alaska can change quickly and dramatically, and hikers should always be prepared.

BELOW: sleigh ride in Matanuska Valley.

RESTAURANTS AND BARS

Price is for dinner excluding tax, tip, and beverages:
$ = under $15
$$ = $15–20
$$$ = $20–30
$$$$ = over $30

Aladdin's
4240 Old Seward Highway
Tel: 561-2373
www.aladdinsak.com $–$$
This friendly family-owned and operated restaurant has attracted a sizable and loyal clientele by consistently serving up excellent Mediterranean dishes, including falafel and mousaka. Be sure to try the homemade lemon ice-cream. Open Wednesday through Saturday for dinner only. Beer and wine are served.

The Bake Shop
Alyeska Resort, Olympic Circle, Girdwood
Tel: 783-2831
www.thebakeshop.com $
This small bakery and sandwich shop is a year-round favorite with skiers and non-skiers alike. Famous for its delicious, daily (bottomless) homemade soups, fresh-baked breads, potato plates, sourdough pancakes, sandwiches, pizzas, and especially its giant, warm sweet rolls. The dining is casual, the food simply terrific, and the staff efficient and kind.

Club Paris
417 W. Fifth Avenue
Tel: 277-6332
www.clubparisrestaurant.
com $$$–$$$$

The bar up front is dark, smoky and full of character – and a favorite haunt of long-time Alaskans and visitors in the know; the steaks and prime rib served in the back are big, tender, and flavorful. Full bar.

Crow's Nest
939 W. Fifth Avenue
Tel: 276-6000
www.captaincook.com/
restaurants.php
$$$$
Located atop tower 3 of the Hotel Captain Cook, this multiple-award-winning restaurant offers fine dining and the best view in town of Anchorage, Cook Inlet, and the Chugach mountains. Full bar.

Double Musky
Mile 0.3 Crow Creek Road, Girdwood
Tel: 783-2822
$$$$
Another award-winning restaurant, this one excelling in Cajun-style Alaska seafood and steak cuisine. No reservations are accepted, but most people don't mind the wait. Busy, crowded, noisy, and delicious.

Glacier Brewhouse
737 W. Fifth Avenue, Suite 110
Tel: 274-2739
www.glacierbrewhouse.com
$$–$$$
Popular downtown restaurant known for fresh Alaska seafood, rotisserie-grilled meats, wood-fired pizzas, and hand-crafted ales. Open daily for lunch and dinner.

Gwennie's Old Alaska Restaurant
4333 Spenard Road
Tel: 243-2090
www.gwenniesrestaurant.
com
$$–$$$
An Alaska-themed (look for the totems) family-friendly restaurant known for its large portions. Open for breakfast, lunch, and dinner.

Indian House Restaurant
Mile 103.5 Seward Highway, Indian
Tel: 653-7313
$$
This place is 100 percent pure Alaskan: stunning scenery outside, and crusty sourdough inside. The full bar is friendly and full of locals, often serving bowls of chilli to hungry drinkers.

Kaladi Brothers Coffee
1340 W. Northern Lights Boulevard, Ste 409
Tel: 277-5177
www.kaladi.com $
Anchorage's answer to Starbucks, the chain of Kaladi Brothers coffee shops can be found throughout the city, reliably serving locally roasted Fairtrade and Certified Organic coffee and espresso. This location is next to the largest independent bookstore in Alaska: Title Wave.

Kaze Restaurant
930 W. Fifth Avenue
Tel: 276-2215
$$–$$$
Serving some of the best sushi in the city, this unassuming cave-like

restaurant is locally owned and features delicate sushi rolls, fresh sashimi, and crisp-bottomed pot stickers.

Marx Brothers' Café
627 W. Third Avenue
Tel: 278-2133
www.marxcafe.com **$$$$**
Innovative fine dining and an extensive wine list can be found at this little frame house on a downtown bluff. Built in 1916, it has been renovated by the restaurant's owners. The 12-table café was opened in 1979 and has earned a reputation as one of Anchorage's finest restaurants, worthy of a special occasion.

Moose's Tooth Pub and Pizzeria
3300 Old Seward Highway
Tel: 258-2537
www.moosestooth.net
$–$$$
This brewpub and pizzeria offers handcrafted ales and gourmet pizzas with a great range of toppings, such as artichoke hearts, feta cheese, and spinach.

Orso Ristorante
737 W. Fifth Avenue
Tel: 222-3232
www.orsoalaska.com
$$$–$$$$
Creative Italian cuisine assembled with fresh-made pastas and Alaskan seafoods, served in a bustling, cozy restaurant. Extensive wine list. Modern art on the walls adds to the Mediterranean ambiance.

Sack's Café
328 G Street
Tel: 274-4022
www.sackscafe.com
$$$–$$$$

This popular urban café offers interesting combinations of ingredients all carefully prepared on main dishes such as chicken and scallops, free-range chicken, and salmon or halibut. Especially popular at lunchtime and also for dinner before the theater or for a long and lazy Saturday or Sunday brunch.

Seven Glaciers Restaurant
Alyeska Resort,
1000 Arlberg Road,
Girdwood
Tel: 754-2237
www.alyeskaresort.com/
page.asp?intNodeID=10903
$$$$
Ride the Alyeska Ski Resort aerial tram up to this mountaintop restaurant (elevation 2,300ft) for fine dining and extraordinary views of Turnagain Arm, the Chugach Mountain Range, and seven "hanging" glaciers. Specializes in fresh Alaska seafood, beef, and free-range chicken entrées. Full bar.

Simon and Seafort's
420 L Street
Tel: 274-3502
www.r-u-i.com/sim
$$$–$$$$
Fine dining and bar with an outstanding view of Cook Inlet. Open for lunch and dinner with broad menu selections. Full bar.

Snow City Café
1034 W. Fourth Avenue
Tel: 272-2489
www.snowcitycafe.com **$**
Famous for delicious breakfasts, served all day in this popular restaurant. Sandwiches and vegetarian choices also available.

Snow Goose Restaurant and Brewery
717 W. Third Avenue
Tel: 277-7727
www.alaskabeers.com
$–$$$
One of the original brewpubs in Anchorage, this restaurant features sunny (in summer...), outdoor decks overlooking Ship Creek and Cook Inlet. Great local beers, pizza, burgers, beer-battered halibut, and ribs.

Taproot Café
1330 Huffman Road
Tel: 345-0282 **$**
Serving espresso, as well as beer and wine, this tiny café at the south end of town also hosts musical acts in the evenings and serves soup and sandwiches made from largely local ingredients throughout the day.

White Spot Café
109 W. Fourth Avenue
Tel: 279-3954 **$**

A true Alaska classic, the White Spot serves up crisp fries (everything comes with fries, and don't argue!), deep fried halibut sandwiches and no-nonsense. The cook/owner also takes the orders and tolerates few questions. Keeping everything in her head, she is a local favorite.

Yak and Yeti Himalayan Restaurant
3301 Spenard Road
Tel: 743-8078 **$**
www.yakandyetialaska.com
Surrounded by Anchorage's snow-capped peaks, find a taste of the Himalayas. Open for lunch Monday through Friday, and dinner Thursday through Saturday, this small restaurant offers a mix of Tibetan, Indian, and Nepalese food that includes curries, naan, Tibetan hot buns, and spicy stir-fried pork. Affordably priced with beer or wine available.

LEFT: Alaskan smoked salmon. **RIGHT:** fresh produce at Anchorage's Saturday market.

CHUGACH STATE PARK

Established in 1970, Anchorage's "backyard wilderness" offers all sorts of recreational opportunities for residents and visitors within a short distance of Alaska's urban center

Main attractions
MOUNT BASHFUL
FLATTOP MOUNTAIN
EAGLE RIVER NATURE
  CENTER
WINDY CORNER
TURNAGAIN ARM

BELOW: Matanuska Peak in the Chugach Mountains.

Just to the east of Anchorage is a rugged chain of peaks, the **Chugach Mountains**. Stretching 300 miles (480km) across Alaska's Southcentral region, the range arcs from Cook Inlet almost to the Canadian border. The westernmost portion, touching the edges of Alaska's largest city, is encompassed by **Chugach State Park** Ⓦ, a 495,000-acre (200,000-hectare) piece of land that many locals have long considered their "backyard wilderness."

Among the oldest and largest of Alaska's state parks, Chugach was estab-lished in 1970, thanks to the deter-mined efforts of a few Anchorage residents who wanted to protect the neighboring alpine wilderness. Their passion ignited a grass-roots movement of the sort rarely seen in Alaska, before or since.

Various recreational groups – hunt-ers, horseback riders, skiers, hikers – had tried to get the western Chugach Range preserved as parkland since the 1950s, to no avail. Then, in 1969, the state announced it would open two of the range's forested valleys to commer-cial logging. One of those valleys, known as Indian, was especially popu-lar with community groups, ranging from the Boy Scouts and Girl Scouts to hikers and mountaineers. Appalled by the plans, four Anchorage residents – Sharon Cissna, Art Davidson, Ted Schultz, and Skip Matthews – filed a lawsuit and forced the state to cancel the sale.

Creating a jewel

Though satisfying, the court victory left the foursome wanting more. In August 1969, a group of about 20 activ-ists began a campaign to establish a wilderness park, nearly a half-million acres (200,000 hectares) in size. Within a few months, they gained the support of nearly all of Anchorage's recrea-tional organizations. They also gar-nered the backing of local politicians, who pushed a bill in the Alaska Legis-lature to establish a new park. Legisla-

:ion to create Chugach State Park
passed both the state senate and house
n May 1970 and Governor Keith
Miller signed it into law in August of
:hat year. Cissna, now a state represent-
tive herself and known in some quar-
:ers as the "mother of Chugach State
Park," still marvels at the speed and
:ase of the effort, more than 30 years
ater. "I think it was meant to happen,"
he says. "It was a moment in time
when the right people and the right
dea came together at exactly the right
:ime. And so we created a jewel."

The lure of Flattop

Though it is little known outside
Alaska, Chugach is a wild and pristine
wilderness on a par with many of
America's national parklands. Within
ts boundaries are more than 150 peaks,
dozens of glaciers, beautiful alpine val-
eys that in summer are brightened by
dozens of wildflower species, and crystalline mountain streams. The moun-
ains within Chugach park are modest
by Alaska standards; the highest,
Mount Bashful, rises only to 8,005ft
2,440 meters). Yet many are steep, jag-

ged peaks with substantial vertical
relief, as they rise thousands of feet
from sea level.

Still, the most popular of the Chugach's mountains is Flattop, a humble
hill that looks as if its top has been
sliced off. Standing only 3,550ft (1,082
meters) above Cook Inlet at its summit, **Flattop Mountain** has a special
pull on locals. Less than 15 miles
(24km) from downtown Anchorage,
Flattop is visible throughout the city.
And city roads approach to within a
mile or so of its base. Easy to find and
easy to reach, Flattop is also easy to
climb: from the main trailhead, the
mountain's summit is only half a mile
and 1,350 vertical ft away (412
meters).

When winter's snows have melted
away, the ascent is more of a strenuous
hike than a climb, though some rock
scrambling is necessary near the top.
(That's not to say the mountain can't
pose dangers: over the years, a handful
of people have died on its slopes.) Most
people can be up and back to the trailhead within two or three hours. All
sorts take the trail to Flattop's summit,

What Visitors to Chugach Need to Know

The park is easy to reach from
Anchorage. Several of its most
popular trailheads can be reached
from city streets, while other trails
and park facilities are accessible
from either the Seward or Glenn
highways.

Maps showing trail routes and
campgrounds are available from
Chugach State Park headquarters,
located at Mile 115 of the Seward
Highway in the **Potter Section
House** (HC52, Box 8999, Indian, AK 99540; tel: 345-5014;
www.alaskastateparks.org) or the Alaska Public Lands Information Center in downtown Anchorage (tel: 644-3661; www.
nps.gov/aplic). Some three dozen trails criss-cross the park,
totaling nearly 200 miles (320km). Many have parking lots,
information displays, and latrines at their trailheads.

One of the park's most popular facilities is the **Eagle
River Nature Center**, at the end of Eagle River Road (30–45

minutes' drive from downtown
Anchorage; tel: 694-2108; www.
ernc.org). Among its attractions
are natural history displays, Dall
sheep-spotting scopes, nearby
trails, and year-round naturalist
activities for adults and children;
they range from guided hikes to
bear-awareness talks, a winter
astronomy program, plant and
mushroom identification, and but-
terfly identification.

The prime visitor season is June–Sept, but locals frequent the park year-round. Summers tend to be cool, with
overcast skies and frequent rain, often as drizzle. Summer
daytime temperatures normally range from the 50s into
the 60s Fahrenheit (12°–18°C), though temperatures
occasionally rise above 70°F (21°C) or sink below freezing
at night. Snowstorms may occur throughout the year at
higher elevations.

Biking near Flattop Mountain.

from preschoolers to senior citizens, and hill runners to curious tourists.

Flattop is easily the most climbed peak in all of Alaska. Shuttle service to Flattop is available from downtown Anchorage at the Downtown Bicycle Rental shop (tel: 279-5293; www.alaska-bike-rentals.com).

For those who are more experienced and ambitious, there are dozens of peaks within a few hours of Chugach park's many trailheads. Hikers headed to Flattop may share the trail with dozens, but go a few miles beyond, and you can have an entire mountain or alpine basin to yourself.

The million or so people who enter the park each year are mostly locals. It is estimated that three-fifths of Alaska's population lives within 40 miles (64km) of Chugach Park.

Abundant wildlife

Though it's on the perimeter of Alaska's urban center, Chugach is rich in wildlife. The park's alpine tundra, forested valley bottoms, and coastal waters are inhabited by nearly 50 species of mammals – from orca and beluga whales to little brown bats and porcupines – 100 species of birds, 9 species of fish, and 1 amphibian, the wood frog. An estimated 2,000 Dall sheep live here, as well as some 500 mountain goats, 400 black bears, two-dozen grizzlies, and at least two wolf packs.

Some of the best Dall sheep-viewing in Alaska occurs along Chugach's southern edge, at a place called **Windy Corner** (*see page 173*). From April through August, ewes and lambs and young rams inhabit steep cliffs and grassy meadows above the Seward Highway and **Turnagain Arm**, between mileposts 106 and 107.

Peak viewing occurs in June and July, after the ewes have given birth. Only rarely are the older, full-curl rams seen; they prefer backcountry solitude, away from the highway crowds.

Moose are also seen along the park's fringes, though they prefer wooded habitat to alpine terrain. Black bears, too, are encountered in forested areas, along with squirrels and porcupines and more rarely, lynx. Eagles may be seen soaring overhead, and there are many songbirds. ❑

State Parks

Alaska is famous for its national parks. But the wild gems protected by the Division of Parks and Outdoor Recreation are less well known.

Established in 1970 by the Alaska Legislature, the Alaska State Parks system has become the nation's largest and grandest; its 130 or so units encompass 3.2 million acres (1.3 million hectares), while stretching more than 1,100 miles (1,770km) across Alaska. Their numbers include recreation sites and areas, historic sites and parks, marine parks, wilderness parks, state trails, and a world-famous preserve: the Alaska Chilkat Bald Eagle Preserve, which each winter attracts between 1,000 and 4,000 eagles.

While many are small and located along the road system, a handful rank among America's premier wilderness parks: Chugach, Kachemak Bay, Wood-Tikchik, Shuyak Island, and Denali.

Unspoiled wilderness

Three of those parklands – Denali, Kachemak Bay, and Wood-Tikchik – include lands and waters once proposed for national park status. Within their boundaries are rugged mountains, glaciers fed by large ice-fields, centuries-old coastal forests, high alpine meadows that grow bright with wildflowers in summer. Here too there are salmon-rich streams, enormous river-and-lake systems, and all manner of northern wildlife, from grizzlies and wolves, to Dall sheep, wolverines, little brown bats, whales, bald and golden eagles, loons and owls, and scores of songbird, shorebird, and seabird species.

Though these parks protect large expanses of unspoiled wilderness, they are, by Alaska standards,

surprisingly easy to reach – and in most cases, easy to explore. Even the wildest, remotest state parks are within 325 miles (520km) of Anchorage. Chugach and Denali state parks are connected to Alaska's road system, while Kachemak Bay is a short boat ride from Homer, an end-of-the-road tourist town 220 highway miles (350km) south of Anchorage. None of the three requires air service to reach the backcountry. While Wood-Tikchik's wilderness is most easily reached by plane, the park's lowermost lake is only 20 road miles (32km) from Dillingham, the largest city in the Bristol Bay region. The remotest wilderness park, Shuyak, is less than 100 air miles (160km) from Homer.

By contrast, wilderness within Alaska's national parks in many cases is remote and expensive to reach. Two-thirds of the national units are more than 300 miles (480km) from Anchorage, and a third are within the state's Arctic region. Backcountry trips in most national parks require the use of air taxis.

Most parks are user-friendly, with campgrounds, public-use cabins, and trail systems. They also permit many activities, from hiking to sport hunting, skiing to snowmobiling, paddling to power-boating.

For more details, contact Alaska's Department of Natural Resources Public Information Center, 550 W. 7th Avenue, Suite 1260, Anchorage, AK 99501-3557 (tel: 907-269-8400; www.alaskastateparks.org). ❑

ABOVE: wildlife is abundant in many parks.
RIGHT: Eagle River, Chugach State Park.

PRINCE WILLIAM SOUND

Glaciers, birds and marine life are the highlights of this wild country southeast of Anchorage, yet its towns – Whittier, Valdez and Cordova – are reminders that nature has its harsher side

Main attractions
WHITTIER
COLUMBIA GLACIER
MONTAGUE ISLAND
VALDEZ
CORDOVA
COPPER RIVER DELTA

BELOW: gazing over the Sound.

Few slide shows or promotional clips present pictures of rain in **Prince William Sound ❷**. Usually, it's sunshine flickering on water cascading from the flukes of a breaching humpback whale. Or kayakers wearing T-shirts silhouetted in front of a brilliant blue-white glacier. Or sea otters munching on crab plucked from the ocean floor. All such images are taken on the Sound's few clear days.

Each year those photographs, along with the stories told by the travelers who took them, draw more people to see the Sound's wonderful natural displays of flora and fauna, ice, forests, and mountains. Few are disappointed, yet it is wise to remember that, as in much of coastal Alaska, it rains a lot here. Often it pours.

Getting there

You can savor the atmosphere of Prince William Sound simply by crossing it on a ferry or tour boat (*see page 345* for details of the Alaska Marine Highway ferry). **Whittier ❸** (population 117) is where many people begin a tour of the Sound. It is easily reached by road from Anchorage through tunnels in the Chugach Mountains. A road connecting Whittier to the Seward Highway opened in 2000. Historically, the site where Whittier stands was a resting place for Native and Russian traders carrying their wares between the Sound and Cook Inlet. Later, gold miners and mail carriers crossed Portage Pass to reach the Iditarod Trail, which led to Alaska's far-northwest gold fields (now better known for Alaska's biggest sled dog race). But Whittier didn't really develop until World War II, when the army used its ice-free harbor for a strategic fuel dump and the town became an important military port. Troops blasted two tunnels through the Chugach Mountains to connect Whittier with the Alaska Railroad depot at Portage.

In the 1964 earthquake (*see page 52*), Whittier was hit by three successive

tidal waves, one of which crested at 104ft (32 meters), and a huge amount of damage was done to the town and its harbor. There's not a lot to see in Whittier, a town of two tall concrete apartment blocks built by the military, in which all the residents live, but if you have some time to spare, the helpful **Visitor Center** staff near the Small Boat Harbor will give you information about the hiking trails around town. It's also a great place for sea kayaking, but it's best to organize this in Anchorage in advance.

Columbia Glacier

Passengers traveling by boat between Whittier and Valdez sometimes see bears and, occasionally, goats balanced on cliffs above them. Humpback and killer whales frequent the route, and Dall porpoises surf the bow wake. Sea lions haul out on rocks, and harbor seals rest on chunks of ice that drift with the wind and tide away from the glaciers. There are dozens of glaciers in the Sound, and some calve huge chunks of ice into the ocean in spectacular explosions of spray. **Columbia**

Glacier ❹ is the largest among the many that drop down from the Chugach Mountains into the northerly fjords of Prince William Sound.

Fed each year by enough snow to bury a five-story building, Columbia Glacier covers an area the size of Los Angeles. It flows more than 40 miles (64km) from the mountains to Columbia Bay, where its 4-mile (7km) wide face daily drops hundreds of thousands of tons of pristine ice into the sound.

The glacier's output of ice increased in 1983, when it began a rapid retreat. Now, glaciologists estimate that 50 cubic miles (210 cubic km) of icebergs could possibly be released during the next half century. So much ice has filled the bay in recent years that boats can't approach the glacier as closely as they could in the past, when passengers were provided with a close-up view of massive flakes peeling from the 300ft (90-meter) wall. When the flakes come down, the harbor seals resting on bergs in the bay are rocked by the resulting swells. They don't even look up.

Meanwhile, gulls and other birds swarm around the glacier face; the

TIP

Weather watch
Often enough, the clouds seem as durable as concrete, apparently anchored in place by gray, rocky peaks and black, green, and gray forests of Sitka spruce and western hemlock. Horizons close in, and newcomers camping in this cloud-shrouded funereal world can feel depressed. Frequent visitors aren't particularly bothered by the weather, though: they recognize that rain accounts for much of the Sound's mystique and abundant life.

BELOW: a cruise ship calls at Whittier.

Keystone Canyon, near Valdez, provides some of Alaska's best whitewater rafting.

plunging ice stirs the seafood-rich water, bringing shrimp and other delicacies to the surface for their consumption. Thus, the glaciers are an intrinsic part of the life cycle of Prince William Sound.

Quakes and tidal waves

BELOW: harbor seals at the Columbia Glacier.

Forces other than slow-moving glaciers also shape the land. Earthquakes cause sudden, dramatic changes in the lay of the country. On March 27, 1964 – Good Friday – bedrock shifted just west of Columbia Glacier. The shock waves, believed to have registered 9.2

on the Richter scale, were the most intense ever recorded in North America. In just a few minutes, extensive new beach lines emerged as the land rose in some areas; in other places the ground sank, killing large stands of trees. The most dramatic geological adjustment occurred at the southern end of **Montague Island**, which tilted upward 38ft (11.5 meters).

But tsunamis did the most damage. Whittier suffered badly, but among the worst human disasters was that at **Chenega**, a village of 82 on an island south of Whittier near the western edge of the sound. A wave enveloped all the buildings but the school and one house, and swept away 23 residents. The village was rebuilt on another site 25 years later.

Many hard rock and placer claims lie under rockslides and fast-growing alder and hemlock. In a few places, like the Beatson Mine on **La Touche Island**, piles of tailings stand out, along with a few unstable old buildings, rust-red lengths of steel pipe and pumps, and stripped trucks whose tires have been eaten by porcupines.

Valdez

Valdez ❺, the next port of call for ferry and tour boats after Whittier and situated to the east of the earthquake epicenter, was completely destroyed, and had to be rebuilt on a different site. The tsunami that wiped out the waterfront also killed 32 people. Consequently there are no buildings of historic interest in Valdez, but it's a lively town of 3,700 residents, which grew to prosperity as the terminus of the trans-Alaska pipeline. Its setting, between the Sound and the Chugach Mountains, is splendid.

Drop in at the **Valdez Convention and Visitors Bureau** on Chenega Street (tel: 835-4636; www.valdezalaska. org; summer daily 8am–8pm, winter Mon–Fri 8am–5pm) for information, and to see their film about the 1964 earthquake.

The **Valdez Museum and Historical Archive** (tel: 835-2764; www.valdez museum.org; summer daily 9am–6pm, winter Mon–Fri 1–5pm, Sat noon–4pm; charge) on Egan Drive is worth a visit to see a variety of exhibits, including one on the *Exxon Valdez* oil spill.

Valdez can also be reached by air from Anchorage (there are numerous daily flights) or by the Alaska Marine Highway System's fast ferry out of Whittier (www.dot.state.ak.us/amhs; www. akferry.com). You can also rent a car here and drive along the **Richardson Highway** through the scenic Copper River Valley toward **Glennallen** and the Wrangell-St Elias National Park *(see page 190)*. It's a beautiful stretch of road. Leaving Valdez, you pass the site of the original, pre-1964 town, although there's not much to see except a commemorative plaque.

Some 12 miles (20km) further on, you come to the **Keystone Canyon** and the lovely **Bridal Veil Falls**. Drive on for another 7 miles (11km) or so and the trans-Alaska pipeline comes into view. Nearby is an attractive camping spot with good trout fishing.

Now you carry on up to **Thompson Pass**, perhaps Alaska's most spectacular mountain road. Passing the Edgerton Highway junction (82 miles/132km from Valdez), you will reach **Copper Center**, a village that was an early mining camp and is well worth a stop

TIP

The Copper River Delta Shorebird Festival

Every May, bird lovers flock to the tidal flats of the Prince William Sound community of Cordova for the Copper River Delta Shorebird Festival. It provides exciting opportunities to observe millions of migrating shorebirds as they rest and feed in the rich delta area. The festival includes workshops, community events, and other related activities. For more details, contact the Cordova Chamber of Commerce (tel: 424-7260; www.cordova chamber.com).

Cordova, a pretty community of wood-framed houses.

BELOW RIGHT:
Cordova's harbor.

(accommodation is available) before visiting the national park.

Cordova

Cordova ❻ became a transportation center in the early 20th century. The important mineral was copper, and the deposit, the richest in the world, was at **Kennicott**, 200 miles (320km) up the Copper and Chitina rivers *(see page 190)*. Cordova, an attractive community of wood-framed houses, was born a railroad town with the arrival of a shipload of men and equipment on April 1, 1906. The railroad was the brainchild of Michael J. Heney, an engineer who had also pushed the White Pass & Yukon Route Railroad through the White Pass from Skagway to Whitehorse in Southeast Alaska in 1900.

Engineering achievement

For the next five years, Cordova was the operations center for the Copper River & Northwestern Railroad construction project. Along with the oil pipeline, this ranks among history's greatest engineering achievements. Heney had to contend with temperatures of −60°F (−50°C), a ferocious wind that knocked boxcars off the tracks, and drifting snow that buried his locomotives.

The ore transported was almost pure copper, and it added to the fortunes of the railroad backers, a syndicate led by J.P. Morgan. But by the mid-1930s the price of copper had fallen and all the high-grade ores had been mined; in 1938 the railroad was abandoned.

Cordova today is a pretty little fishing town where not much happens. You can't reach it by road. Whittier–Valdez ferries stop here, and a new dock has brought some of the cruise ship operators to town. Otherwise, it is reached by a short flight from Anchorage, and airport buses run you into town. The **Chamber of Commerce** on First Street will fill you in on current activities.

The **Small Boat Harbor** is a lively spot and there's the **Cordova Historical Museum** (tel: 424-6665; www.cordovamuseum.org; summer Mon–Sat 10am–6pm, Sun 2–4pm, winter Tue–Fri 10am–5pm, Sat 1–5pm; $1 donation recommended) on First Street with historical and marine exhibits

How to See the Sights of Prince William Sound

Various tour companies offer day trips into the many fjords surrounding Whittier. Tidewater glaciers thrill visitors and seasoned boat captains alike with their sudden, percussive, cracking sounds followed by thunderous roars as massive chunks of ice break loose and crash down into the sea. Larger companies, like Prince William Sound Cruises and Tours (tel: 877-777-2805 or 907-777-2800; www.princewilliam sound.com), will arrange transportation from Anchorage via motorcoach or train, and a day cruise into western Prince William Sound.

Exciting glacier tours operate out of Valdez as well. Stan Stevens Cruises (tel: 866-867-1297; www.stanstephenscruises.com), for example, offers comfortable 6½- and 9½-hour tours to visit the magnificent Columbia Glacier (the largest tidewater glacier in Southcentral Alaska), or a 9½-hour cruise to witness the active calving of Meares Glacier in the eastern area of the Sound.

The surrounding coastal areas provide rich habitat for whales, seal lions, puffins, seals, sea otters, bears, goats, and eagles (and much more), and multiple sightings are common. For a complete listing of tour options for both Whittier and Valdez, contact the Whittier Visitor Center (tel: 472-2327; www.whittieralaskachamber.org) or the Valdez Convention and Visitors Bureau (tel: 835-2984; www.valdezalaska.org).

including many evocative old photographs; and there's a marvelous view of the town and the Sound from the **Mount Eyak Ski** area.

But the main attractions of the area are out on the 50-mile (80km) Copper River Highway, which traces the railroad line across the biologically rich **Copper River Delta** to Child's Glacier. The delta is a birdwatcher's paradise, home to the world's entire nesting population of dusky Canada geese and swarms of migrating waterfowl.

Industries in flux

The Sound is still rich in copper and gold, molybdenum, tungsten, and silver, but low mineral prices mean those resources will be left in the ground for the immediate future. The timber industry has also been doing poorly, and fur harvesting has long been abandoned.

The long-term ecological consequences of these industries, including the disastrous oil spill in 1989, are unknown. Still, the sound continues to heal, and wildlife officials have reported seeing animals return to the area. Commercial fishing remains a major source of income for the 7,500 people who live along the Sound. In the mid-1990s, a record 14 million pink salmon returned to the port of Valdez, but runs have been erratic in recent years and the fishing industry is suffering from increased competition in other parts of the world together with lower prices.

The most promising resources in the Sound are its wilderness and its wildlife. After author Rex Beach documented the construction of the Copper River & Northwestern Railroad in his 1913 bestseller *The Iron Trail: An Alaskan Romance*, Cordova and its nearby glaciers became one of the state's greatest attractions. Kayakers and others often pitch tents on beaches. The increase in requests for cabin-use permits is one sign of a growing number of visitors to the Sound. ❏

Ecotourists dig for clams in Prince William Sound.

RESTAURANTS

Cordova

Cordova Ambrosia Restaurant
410 First Street
Tel: 424-7185
$–$$$
Open for lunch and dinner March through October. Seafood and pizza, along with other Italian dishes are served in a family-friendly atmosphere. Beer and wine are available.

Killer Whale Café
504 First Street
Tel: 424-7733
$
This café is open for breakfast, lunch, and dinner, offering soups, sandwiches made with freshly baked breads, and daily specials.

Valdez

Alaska's Bistro
102 N. Harbor Drive
Tel: 835-5688
www.alaskasbistro.com
$$–$$$
Mediterranean cuisine featuring local seafood and pizza in an elegant setting. Large windows overlook the harbor. Full bar.

The Pipeline Club
112 Egan Drive
Tel: 835-4444
$$$–$$$$
This establishment offers fine dining, evenings only, from a menu that specializes in steak and fresh Alaskan seafood. You can also play a round of pool or indoor golf. Bar.

Totem Inn
144 East Eagan Drive
Tel: 835-4443 or
888-808-4431
www.toteminn.com
$–$$
Locally owned and operated since 1972, this restaurant is a local favourite. Serving breakfast, lunch, and dinner, the food is traditional American fare with lots of hamburgers, seafood, and fries.

Whittier

Lazy Otter Café
Located next to east boat ramp
Tel: 472-OTTR/6887
$
Cozy café offers delicious chowders, bagels, sandwiches, soft-serve ice cream, and espressos.

Varly's Swiftwater Seafood Café
Located "on the triangle"
Tel: 472-2550
www.swiftwaterseafoodcafe. com **$**
When possible, dishes are made from local rockfish, shrimp, or halibut. Menu includes fish and chips (or shrimp and chips), homemade chowders, and rhubarb crisp. Beautiful view. Beer and wine. Open seasonally.

Price is for dinner excluding tax, tip, and beverages:
$ = under $15
$$ = $15–20
$$$ = $20–30
$$$$ = over $30

WRANGELL-ST ELIAS NATIONAL PARK

America's largest national park has emerged from obscurity to become a magnet for those seeking backcountry adventure

BELOW: a glacial rock in the park.

U ntil the mid-1980s, **Wrangell-St Elias National Park and Preserve** ❼ was an overlooked and undervalued mountain wilderness. Created in 1980, America's largest park – at 13.2 million acres (5.3 million hectares), the size of six Yellowstones – was also one of its least known and least visited. But some time in the late 1980s, Wrangell-St Elias was "discovered." And, though it hasn't yet become "the next Denali" as some in the tourism industry had predicted, the park's use has grown significantly in the past 10 to 15 years. Before visiting the park, stop off at the headquarters and visitor center at **Copper Center** ❽ on the Richardson Highway 6, some 200 road miles (320km) east of Anchorage, for maps, publications, and advice.

A potted history

At the turn of the 20th century, a couple of prospectors named Jack Smith and Clarence Warner spotted a large green spot in the Wrangell Mountains, on the ridge between the Kennicott Glacier and McCarthy Creek which proved to be mineral staining from a fantastically rich copper deposit.

Mining engineer Stephen Birch bought the copper claims and won the backing of the Guggenheimer brothers and J.P. Morgan. Known collectively as the Alaska Syndicate, the investors formed the (misspelled) Kennecott Mines Co., which later became the Kennecott Copper Corp.

The copper discovery sparked the construction of the 200-mile (320km) Copper River & Northwestern Railroad, connecting the mining camp to the coastal town of Cordova. When the mine closed in 1938 it had produced over 4½ million tons of ore, worth $200 million. At its peak, around 600 people lived at **Kennicott** ❾. The main settlement included all the operations needed to mill the ore, as well as houses, offices and stores, a school, hospital, post office, dairy and recreation hall. Just down the road, a second com-

munity, eventually named McCarthy, sprang up around 1908.

In a perfect complement to staid, regimented Kennicott, **McCarthy** ⑩ played the role of sin city. Among its most successful businesses were several saloons, pool halls, gambling rooms, and back-alley brothels. In its heyday, 100 to 150 people lived in McCarthy. But after the mine shut down, only a few people stayed on.

For decades after the mine's closure, McCarthy–Kennicott served as the quintessential haven for Alaska recluses. But more recently the region has become a major tourist draw, complete with lodges, a hotel, bed-and-breakfast inns, ice-cream parlor, air-taxi operators, wilderness guide operations, museum, and even an espresso bar – impressive for a community whose year-round "hard core" population numbers a couple of dozen people.

Access to the park

The northern entry to the park is the 45-mile (72km) Nabesna Road, which connects the state's highway system with the tiny mining community of Nabesna ⑪ (population about 25). The road's first 5 miles (8km) are paved; the remainder is gravel. Four-wheel drive vehicles are recommended for the final 5 miles, which cross several creeks and are not regularly maintained by the state.

Motorists should check for updated road conditions before making the drive, as sections of it are occasionally washed out during summer rainstorms; call ahead to park headquarters and check in at the ranger station, at Mile 0.2. Planned improvements include more passing places and wayside natural history exhibits.

Although some gold, silver, copper, iron, and molybdenum were discovered in the Nabesna area early in the 20th century, a much bigger attraction now is the wildlife. Caribou, moose, and even grizzlies may be spotted in the open countryside bordering Nabesna Road, and large populations of Dall sheep are found in the hills surrounding the 9,360ft (2,850-meter) Tanada Peak, about 15 miles (24km) southwest of the road's end. (Trophy hunting for sheep and other species is

TIP

When to visit
The park is open year-round, but peak visits occur in August. Wildflowers and mosquitoes peak in June and July. The prime mountaineering season is from mid-March to early June. Snow is possible at any season in the high country.

BELOW: the abandoned Kennicott Mine.

BELOW: the interior
of McCarthy Lodge.

allowed in the preserve, which encompasses about 37 percent of the unit's total area.)

The principal avenue into Wrangell-St Elias is **McCarthy Road**; 60 miles (95km) long and unpaved, it stretches from Chitina, at the park's western boundary (where it connects with the Edgerton Highway) to the "gateway" community of **McCarthy**, located deep within one of America's most spectacular wildlands. At its doorstep are rugged peaks that rise above raging rivers, fed by massive glaciers.

The number of people funneled down McCarthy Road has grown dramatically, from about 5,000 in 1988 to more than 20,000 visitors currently. Overall park visitation has increased at a slower pace, but still jumped nearly fourfold in 25 years (from 14,000 to 50,000 visits).

Only a small percentage of those who drive the McCarthy Road actually visit the park's awesome backcountry. Most are content to hang out in McCarthy, take hikes to the nearby **Kennicott Glacier** and **Root Glacier**, or travel some 4 miles (7km) to the abandoned Kennecott copper mining camp (the original company misspelled the name). Until 1997 visitors could reach McCarthy-Kennicott only by crossing the glacially fed Kennicott River on hand-pulled trams. These historic trams have been replaced by a foot bridge that makes the crossing considerably easier. Local residents remain opposed to any sort of vehicular bridge, however, fearing it might open up their community to large-scale "industrial" tourism, so visitors still have to leave their cars, trucks and RVs behind.

Treasures beyond the road

The park's real treasures lie in a wild and magnificent alpine world that wilderness guides call "North America's mountain kingdom." It's a kingdom that includes four major mountain ranges – the St Elias, Chugach, Alaska, and Wrangells – and six of the continent's 10 highest peaks, including 18,008ft (5,490-meter) **Mount St Elias**, fourth-highest in North America.

Here, too, is North America's largest subpolar icefield, the **Bagley**, which feeds a system of gigantic glaciers; one

of those, the Malaspina Glacier, covers an area of more than 1,500 sq miles (4,075 sq km) – larger than Rhode Island. Hubbard Glacier, which flows out of the St Elias Mountains into Disenchantment Bay, is one of the continent's most active glaciers; in 1986, Hubbard was nicknamed the "Galloping Glacier" when it surged more than a mile and sealed off Russell Fjord. The ice dam later broke and the glacier retreated, but it advanced again in 2002 to create yet another temporary ice dam and scientists say it's only a matter of time before the Hubbard closes off the fjord permanently.

The glaciers have carved dozens of canyons; some, like the Chitistone and Nizina, are bordered by rock walls thousands of feet high. Rugged, remote coastline is bounded by tidewater glaciers and jagged peaks. The park's alpine superlatives, along with those of neighboring Kluane National Park in Canada, have prompted their combined designation as a Unesco World Heritage Site.

Much of what's been "discovered" in Wrangell-St Elias by modern-day explorers was known to local residents centuries ago. This is especially true of the **Skolai Creek-Chitistone River** area, the most popular of the park's backcountry destinations.

More recently, both the Chitistone and Skolai Pass routes were used by stampeders traveling from McCarthy to **Chisana** ⓬, the site of Alaska's last major gold rush. Chisana's boom times lasted only a few years, from 1913 to 1915. But during that short period, as many as 10,000 people may have traveled through the mountains. Fewer than 10 people now live year-round in Chisana, located within the northeast corner of Wrangell-St Elias.

Modern explorers

Nine decades later, people attracted by wilderness values rather than gold are retracing the footsteps of the Chisana stampeders. This newest rush into the Wrangell-St Elias backcountry is, so far, much smaller and more benign. Most modern explorers lured into this vast mountain landscape are curious adventurers, and they bring a minimum-impact ethic and leave little or no trace of

BELOW: an ice cave on Root Glacier.

Sunset in the Chitina River Valley. Overnight lodging is available at McCarthy and Kennicott and a "wilderness lodge" is located in the backcountry, but park facilities are intentionally minimal.

BELOW: lichen-covered rock, Wrangell-St Elias National Park.

their visit. Still, there's no question that they are having a cumulative effect.

In the first four years that he explored the Skolai–Chitistone area, wilderness guide Bob Jacobs saw only one set of footprints not made by his own parties. A quarter-century later, it's difficult to go more than a day or two without seeing signs of other backpackers, or at least hearing aircraft traffic. The increased use has taken a toll; there's been some trampling of vegetation, littering, crowding, and a growing potential problem with bears that have learned to associate humans with food.

It was only natural that the Skolai–Chitistone area became Wrangell-St Elias' heaviest-used backcountry area. It is one of the park's premier wilderness

spots, ruggedly spectacular country in the heart of the mountains. Yet despite its vast, primeval richness, the area is easily accessible by plane, located less than 30 miles (48km) from McCarthy – a short hop by Alaska bush pilot standards.

This is "big country" in the truest sense of the word. The scale of things is immense. In every direction are stark, jagged, ice-carved peaks, most of them unnamed and unclimbed. Here, too, are massive, near-vertical rock faces thousands of feet high, hanging glaciers and waterfalls by the dozen.

Yet for all the rock and snow and ice, this is not a barren or alien world. In the valley bottoms are alder groves and tundra meadows brightened with legions of rainbow-hued flowers: blue forget-me-nots, lupin and Jacob's ladder, purple monkshood, yellow paint brush, white mountain avens, tall pink fireweed, and wintergreen. Ptarmigan hide in the alder, clucking in the early morning like roosters. Bands of Dall sheep inhabit high rocky places, while occasional moose, wolves and brown bears prowl valleys and hillsides. The

Coping with Mosquitoes

Jokingly referred to as the "Alaska State Bird," mosquitoes fare extraordinarily well in Alaska's climate and are especially prevalent between mid-June and the end of July. While there are reported to be from 25 to 40 different species common to the state, there have been no reported cases of West Nile Virus and the two mosquito species that transmit it in the Lower 48 don't live in Alaska.

Visitors are encouraged to wear long sleeves and long pants made of tightly-woven, light material – mosquitoes are supposedly attracted to darker colors – while hiking in the backcountry. Mosquito repellant is helpful and can be bought in almost any store. In remote areas the use of mosquito headnets is advised. And – not that it's any consolation – the caribou are attacked just as much as humans.

valleys are also home to pikas, ground squirrels, shorebirds, and robins. And overhead, eagles soar.

Preserving the wilderness

All these variables have dramatically boosted recreational visits to Skolai and Chitistone valleys, and park officials are keen to protect them. Their biggest concern isn't the traditional wilderness traveler, but the novice explorer. Visitor education is one solution. Another has been to spread the use to other beautiful but neglected areas – for instance, to **Tebay Lakes**, which are similar to California's High Sierras, with beautiful granite peaks, excellent fishing and hiking.

Other areas that haven't been used as heavily include **Goat Creek**, which offers good hiking, and the wide-open, wildlife-rich upper Chitina Valley.

Commercial facilities

Many of Wrangell-St Elias' natural wonders are inaccessible to those who remain along the road system. Only in recent years have a small number of trails have been established to parts of the backcountry. From Nabesna Road, the **Skookum Volcanic Trail** leads to a tundra area with interesting volcanic dikes and basalt flows and is ideal for day hikers.

Two other trails begin along the McCarthy Road; one leads to the Crystalline Hills, which offer superb views of the surrounding mountains and the Chitina River valley. A longer, more challenging backcountry route, the **Dixie Pass Trail**, follows a path used by prospectors and miners.

Air-taxi services provide transportation into the park and several guide outfits offer river-rafting, climbing, and trekking opportunities. Increasingly popular are "flightseeing tours," out of McCarthy, Chitina, Gulkana, and Nabesna.

There's a fairly primitive campground along the McCarthy Road and several public-use cabins (built by miners, hunters or trappers) in the backcountry, available on a first-come first-served basis. A list of facilities and services is available from park HQ (PO Box 439, Copper Center, AK 99573, or visit www.nps.gov/wrst). ❏

BELOW: trees provide shelter for Wrangell's wildlife.

KENAI PENINSULA

This is Alaska in a nutshell: glaciers, salmon fishing, hiking trails, stunning scenery, and friendly towns, all within easy reach of Anchorage

It's often said that Alaska is too big to see in a single lifetime, let alone a single vacation. But there is one place where tourists can sample most of the best of Alaska, and do so within a few weeks: the Kenai Peninsula.

The entire peninsula is within easy driving distance of Anchorage, and people in the city like to refer to the Kenai as their backyard. But please, don't use that line on the peninsula. On a map of the state, the Kenai Peninsula looks deceptively small. It's worth remembering that the peninsula covers 9,050 sq miles (23,000 sq km), making it larger than the combined areas of Rhode Island, Connecticut and Delaware. It is bordered by Prince William Sound and the Gulf of Alaska on the east and Cook Inlet on the west, and attached to the mainland of Southcentral Alaska by a narrow mountainous neck of land at the north.

Artistic center

The peninsula is home to one of Alaska's more artistically inclined cities, Homer. The population is also very socially aware, and for every development-minded resident, you'll find another who belongs to an environmental group. Some apparently belong to both camps, which is partly what makes Homer such a lively place.

Touring the peninsula

Driving out from Anchorage, you will cross into the peninsula just south of Portage, a town that formerly sat at the eastern end of Turnagain Arm, the thin finger of Cook Inlet that separates the peninsula from the Anchorage Bowl. Portage was completely destroyed by the 1964 earthquake, and only a few ruins remain. About 5 miles (8km) after passing the wreckage of Portage, you begin to climb through the Kenai Mountains, with a maximum elevation of about 3,500ft (1,050 meters).

Mileage along the Seward and Sterling highways is measured from Seward. At about Mile 70 is the summit of

Main attractions
HOPE
MOOSE PASS
SEWARD
COOPER LANDING
STERLING
SOLDOTNA
KENAI
NINILCHIK
HOMER
SELDOVIA

LEFT: camping by Kenai Lake.
BELOW: an inviting Seward eatery.

Resurrection Bay, outside Seward.

Turnagain Pass, elevation 988ft (296 meters). It's popular in winter for cross-country skiing and snow-machining.

The pass and much of the area along the highway are part of the **Chugach National Forest** (tel: 743-9500; www.fs.fed.us/r10/chugach). Creeks, lakes and campgrounds are scattered through this area. The camps are generally open from Memorial Day through Labor Day (the last Monday in May to the first Monday in September).

Fees are charged for camp use. Facilities often include tables, fire grates, tent pads, and some type of water and sanitary facilities. While fires are usually allowed in these sites, it's a good idea to carry a small camp stove with you.

Hope

The first town you encounter on the peninsula is **Hope** ⓭, a mining community of about 150, founded in the late 1890s. A trip to Hope requires a 16-mile (25km) detour onto the Hope Cutoff, Mile 56 of the Seward Highway, but it's worth it. The town is the site of the oldest schoolhouse in Alaska – a red, one-room school still in use. Other

attractions include the one-room Hope–Sunrise Historical & Mining Museum on Old Hope Road (tel: 782-3740; Memorial Day–Labor Day daily noon–4pm; free), a store, a couple of cafés, a bar, and a lodge.

An ideal site for pink salmon fishing, moose, caribou and black bear hunting, Hope also is the head of the **Resurrection Pass Trail**, one of the most popular hiking areas on the peninsula. The trailhead is located at Mile 3.5 of the Resurrection Creek Road. The entire trail is 38 miles (60km) long, and hikers emerge at **Schooner Bend**, Mile 52 on the Sterling Highway.

One option is to turn off the Resurrection Trail at Mile 20 and take the 10-mile (16km) **Devil's Pass Trail**, which emerges at Mile 39 of the Seward Highway. The Resurrection Pass Trail connects with the Resurrection River Trail to form the 72-mile (116km) Resurrection Trail from Hope to Seward.

The Forest Service operates some cabins along the Resurrection Trail; most have bunk space for six, and

Athabascans, Alutiiqs and Russians

The Kenai Peninsula was originally home to Dena'ina Indians, a branch of the Athabascan family, and to Alutiiqs, whose linguistic group extends as far west as Eastern Russia. Their descendants still live here, mostly in small, remote villages, but they now account for something less than 10 percent of the population. Modern ways have long since replaced those of the Natives; they speak and dress very much like their white neighbors, and have a lifestyle which melds traditional and mainstream American ways.

The Russians were the first whites to establish permanent communities on the peninsula. From their base on Kodiak Island, they sent out missionaries to found churches all along the eastern shore of Cook Inlet. The town of Kenai began when a Russian settlement was established in the center of a Dena'ina village in 1791.

Other Russian-founded communities include Seldovia, which also dates to the 18th century, and Ninilchik, founded in the early 1800s. Seward didn't then exist as a town, but the area around Resurrection Bay was used as a shipbuilding site for the Russian-American Company. Early Russian influence is still to be seen in the onion-domed churches, and heard in the names of places and people in some peninsula communities.

wood stoves. If a cabin is on a lake, it usually has a row boat and oars. Campers must bring their own food, utensils, and sleeping bags. Because of the route's popularity, it is wise to make cabin reservations well ahead; they can be made up to six months in advance (tel: 877-444-6777; www.reserveusa.com).

The Resurrection Pass Trail can take between two and six days to cover, while the entire route may take a week or more. Trout fishing is possible in several lakes. The trail also provides spectacular scenery for the photographer.

The Seward Highway

On leaving Hope and rejoining the Seward Highway, the first decision is whether to go west or head south at the Seward Junction at Mile 40. To the south lie Moose Pass and Seward; to the west lie Cooper Landing, Kenai, Soldotna, Anchor Point, Ninilchik, Homer, and Seldovia, which can be reached only by taking a ferry. There are several smaller towns as well, including Clam Gulch and Kasilof.

Heading south, the first community is **Moose Pass** ⓮. This is a quiet town of less than 200 people. Residents enjoy hiking, fishing and biking – the town has one of Alaska's relatively few bike trails. One of the highlights of the year is the annual Summer Festival, held to celebrate the solstice. The exact date of the festival changes from year to year, but is always held on the June weekend with the most total hours of sunlight. Activities include a barbecue, carnival, softball games, and an auction.

Continuing south on the highway you come to **Seward** ⓯, an attractive city of about 2,600 residents. Founded in 1903, it was for years the leading port city of Alaska. It was eventually eclipsed in that role by Anchorage, and the 1964 earthquake devastated the economy. Twenty years later, it began to regain its financial legs and now is once again a thriving port. The Chamber of Commerce (2001 Seward Highway; tel: 224-8051; www.seward.com) is at the entrance to town, on the highway.

In the heart of town, on Third Avenue, is the **Seward Historical Museum** (tel: 224-3902; summer daily 10am–5pm, winter hours vary; charge). The town library, on Fifth Avenue, features photographs and a film on the effects of the 1964 earthquake on Seward.

One of the main attractions of the area is **Resurrection Bay**. Charter boats for sailing or power excursions on the bay are available at the city harbor, as are kayak rentals. Boats can also be hired for sightseeing or fishing trips. The state ferry system also has a dock in Seward, offering trips to Kodiak and the Prince William Sound areas.

Seward is the northern terminus for a number of cruise ships crossing the Gulf of Alaska. These ships bring thousands of visitors through Seward on their way to or from Southcentral Alaska.

Another major attraction is the **Alaska SeaLife Center**, built on a 7-acre (3-hectare) site next to the Marine Education Center on the shores of Resurrection Bay (301 Railway Avenue; tel: 224-6300 or 800-224-2525; www.alaskasealife.org; daily, summer

Drivers brave snowy conditions on the Seward Highway.

BELOW: Kasilof's Tustemena Lodge displays 24,000 hats – and a painting of Elvis.

BELOW: cycling by Kenai Lake.

8am–7pm, winter 10am–5pm; charge). This marine science enterprise combines research on saving marine species and aiding recovery from industrial damage, with the rehabilitation of maimed or stranded birds and mammals. It also aims to provide education and entertainment for the thousands of visitors to the center each year.

Kenai Fjords National Park

Seward is also the gateway to **Kenai Fjords National Park** ⑯ (tel: 224-7500; www.nps.gov/kefj), declared a national monument in 1978 and designated a national park two years later. As well as the rugged coastal fjords for which it is named, and the glaciers which, for many, are its chief attraction, the park is home to porpoises, sea otters, sea lions, humpback and orca whales, puffins, bald eagles, and other animals. Several local tour operators offer frequent wildlife cruises into the park, starting from Seward's Small Boat Harbor.

Most of the park is only accessible by boat: the only vehicle access is to the northwest of Seward, at Exit Gla-

cier Road. Exit Glacier is the most easily accessible point of the **Harding Icefield**, a remnant of the Ice Age that caps a section of the Kenai Mountains 50 miles (80km) long and 30 miles (48km) wide. The glacier itself lies less than a mile (1km) past the car parking area at the end of the road; you simply head up the trail, passing a visitor cabin along the way.

It's an easy walk to the face – but visitors are warned to not get too close, because of the danger of falling ice. There are ranger-led hikes but you can go it alone, taking care not to go beyond the warning signs. A challenging hike rises along the side of the glacier to the icefield above. For further information on this and all aspects of the park, contact the Park Service Information Center on Fourth Avenue by the Small Boat Harbor in Seward (tel: 224-2125; summer only).

After leaving the park and initially driving north, it's time to head west on the Sterling Highway. Turn left at the junction; the road is marked as Alaska Route 1. Out toward **Cooper Landing** ⑰, you enter an area that's been closed

to Dall sheep hunting. As a result, it's often a good area to spot them. But looking for sheep while driving can be dangerous, so pull off at one of many designated stops before peering up to look for the white specks high on the peaks.

Cooper Landing is a community of about 350 people, spread out along the headwaters of the Kenai River. Here the river is a beautiful turquoise color, and in winter the open stretches of water are a prime feeding ground for majestic bald eagles. Sport fishing (particularly for salmon and rainbow trout), hunting, and tourism, are the area's main industries, although the town began as a mining area.

At nearby **Kenai Lake**, you can fish for Dolly Varden, lake trout, rainbow trout and whitefish. The Kenai River has trout and four species of salmon. Trophy rainbow trout, some weighing as much as 20lbs (9kg), are caught here by spin- and fly-fishing enthusiasts, and catch-and-release fishing is widely practiced. Rafting is another popular activity on the river, and several local businesses offer fishing and float trips.

Continuing west, just outside of the Cooper Landing area at the confluence of the Kenai and Russian rivers, is the turn-off to the **Russian River Campground**. The site is easy to spot in the summer, as it's usually busy. The 20-mile (32km) **Russian Lakes Trail** is a delightful and not over-demanding hike, with cabins en route. Reservations are needed (tel: 877-444-6777; www.reserveusa.com). The Russian River is the largest freshwater fishery in Alaska, and draws more than 30,000 fishermen each year, all hoping to catch a red salmon.

Kenai National Wildlife Refuge

Heading west on the Sterling Highway, you leave the Chugach National Forest and enter the **Kenai National Wildlife Refuge ⓲**. Refuge regulations, as well as trail maps and information about things to do in the refuge, are available from the unit's Soldotna headquarters (tel: 262-7021; http://alaska.fws.gov/nwr/kenai/index.htm), up Ski Hill Road from the Sterling Highway south of the Kenai River Bridge. The refuge,

Puffins inhabit the Kenai Fjords National Park.

BELOW: the small boat harbor at Seward.

which was established by President Franklin D. Roosevelt as a wildlife range to preserve the moose population, then later expanded, is also the habitat of coyotes, grizzlies, caribou, and wolves. It comprises the western slopes of the Kenai Mountains, and spruce and birch forested lowlands bordering Cook Inlet.

Among the major recreational areas in the refuge is the 20-mile (32km) **Skilak Lake Loop**, which intersects the Sterling Highway near the Visitor Center. This road takes you to **Skilak Lake**, and also provides access to several other smaller lakes, streams and some 200 miles (320km) of trails in the area. The most arduous trail is the Skilak Lookout Trail, which takes you up some 1,450ft (440 meters) and provides stunning views. The Visitor Center provides details on the Swanson River Canoe Trail.

Skilak Lake itself has a surface area of some 24,000 acres (57,600 hectares). It is prone to sudden and violent storms – warning signs should be taken very seriously. The lake offers fishing for salmon, trout and Dolly Varden.

Sterling

To the west from Cooper Landing along the highway you come to **Sterling** ⑲, a community of about 5,000, based at the confluence of the Kenai and Moose rivers. It's a very popular salmon-fishing area, and is the main access point to the Swanson River oil field and an endless string of lakes that are excellent for canoeing. Another attraction of the area is the **Izaak Walton Recreation Site**. It is believed the area was an Eskimo village more than 2,000 years ago and several depressions mark the sites of ancient houses.

Sterling is also the site of the popular Moose River Raft Race, an annual event that is held on the weekend after the 4th of July. Area businesses construct rafts in a variety of categories, then race down the Moose River to the Kenai River.

Soldotna

Heading on past Sterling, you come to the city of **Soldotna** ⑳, seat of the borough government and home of about 3,900 people. With its central location at the intersection of the roads to Kenai

Fishing Fever

The name "Kenai" is synonymous with the term "fishing," especially during salmon season – and on the Kenai River, that's pretty much all summer long. When word spreads that the salmon are "in," (meaning huge numbers of salmon have suddenly decided to fight their way upstream to spawn) fishers from throughout Southcentral impatiently wait until the workday is over, then jump into cars and drive three hours (or more) south to the Kenai River. There they stand, shoulder-to-shoulder along the banks of the river, casting their lines in a mostly-friendly synchrony called "combat fishing."

When someone actually hooks a fish and yells out "fish on," a time-honored code of conduct demands that all other fishers reel in their empty lines to give that angler the best chance of landing his prize. Then it all starts over again. As everyone "limits out" or becomes exhausted with

the effort (usually in the wee morning hours), they load themselves and their fish into their cars for the long drive back home. Often there's just enough time for a quick shower and to head back to work. There's no known cure for this type of "fishing fever." It has to run its normal course, usually lingering from early June through mid-September.

Should you feel yourself susceptible to this particular recurrent "malady," Alaska State law requires both resident and non-resident anglers, 16 years of age or older, to have a valid sport-fishing license in their possession while fishing. Nearly every grocery, sporting goods, or general merchandise store sells sport-fishing licenses, or you can purchase them by mail or online.

For details, contact the Alaska Department of Fish and Game, PO Box 115525, Juneau 99811-5525; tel: 465-2376; or www.admin. adfg.state.ak.us/license.

and Homer, Soldotna has become the hub of the central peninsula. It is a popular spot to meet up with professional fishing guides, most of whom specialize in helping their clients find king salmon.

The amount of traffic on the Kenai River has become the subject of statewide controversy. Twenty-five years ago, only a handful of locals fished for king, sockeye, and silver salmon on the river. Now the Kenai River system is the most popular sport-fishing area in the state, and has been designated a Special Management Area to protect its natural resources and manage the recreational use of the river.

The most up-to-date information on river use is available from the **Visitor Center**, at the corner of the Sterling Highway and Kalifornsky Beach Road, which also houses the offices for the local Chamber of Commerce (tel: 262-9814; www.soldotnachamber.com).

Soldotna's festivals include Progress Days, held on the last weekend in July, a winter sports festival and the sled dog racing championships, which take place in late February. Because of its location near the coast, Soldotna often doesn't receive enough snow to cover the sled dog course. For that reason, the city usually stockpiles snow scraped off the city streets, to spread over the course a few days before the races.

Kenai

Heading west from Soldotna on either the Kenai Spur Highway or Kalifornsky Beach Road, you come to **Kenai** ㉑, the largest city on the peninsula with a population of about 6,900, and also the oldest permanent settlement, founded (in the center of a Dena'ina village) by Russian fur traders and Orthodox priests during the late 18th century.

Kenai is home port to a good share of the peninsula's drift-net fishing fleet. In summer a parade of boats can be seen coming in and out of the mouth of the river in a quest for red salmon. During the spring, the flats along the mouth of the river are temporary nesting ground for thousands of snow geese. They stay in the area for about two weeks and are a popular subject for early-season photographers.

Sunset over the Kenai Mountains.

BELOW LEFT: wood-carving shop in Soldotna.
BELOW: fishing on the Kenai River.

In the saddle at Kachemak Bay.

BELOW: aurora over Ninilchik's Russian Orthodox Church.

Kenai is also home to the peninsula's largest airport and has the most regularly scheduled flights. Airlines also fly in and out of Anchorage, Soldotna, Seward, and Homer, and charter flights can take you almost anywhere else.

Diverse culture

One of Kenai's main attractions is the **Kenai Visitors' and Cultural Center** on the corner of Main Street and Kenai Spur Highway (tel: 283-1991; www.visit kenai.com; summer daily; free). The center features exhibits and displays of Kenai's rich and diverse culture, from its Native and Russian history through the industries that currently fuel the area: oil and commercial fishing.

Head down Overland Avenue, where you will find Fort Kenay, although the present one is only a replica of the original 19th-century fortification. On the other side of Mission Street is the **Holy Assumption Russian Orthodox Church**, the oldest Orthodox place of worship in Alaska.

If you follow Mission Street to Riverview Avenue you will come to the **Beluga Whale Lookout** where, in early summer, you can watch for white whales feeding on salmon in the river.

Special events include the 4th of July parade and the "Christmas Comes to Kenai" celebration on the weekend following Thanksgiving; the fête includes a fireworks display at about 4pm. Since the peninsula has very long days during the summer, the people of Kenai hold off on fireworks until November, when they can easily be seen against the dark late-afternoon sky.

Continuing north of Kenai on the Spur Highway, you come to the Nikiski industrial area, with a large chemical plant, two oil refineries and a natural gas liquification plant. The plants aren't open to the public.

The area north of Kenai has several names. Some call it simply "North Kenai," while others say "Nikishka," "Nikiska," or "**Nikiski**." The last name won a popularity vote in the area, but stick to what the locals say when talking to them.

North of the refineries is the **Captain Cook State Recreation Area ㉒**, a popular spot for hiking, camping, fishing, and snow-machining. There are a couple of good campsites and great views across the Cook Inlet. Much of what you see across the inlet is part of the **Lake Clark National Park** (tel: 781-2218; www.nps.gov/lacl; *see pages 320–5 for a detailed description*). Charter flights to the park can be arranged in Kenai – ask at the Visitor Center there for details.

From the recreation area, drive along the Bridge Access Road and connect with Kalifornsky Beach Road to return to the Sterling Highway. Farther south, the highway begins to parallel Cook Inlet and runs past some fine clamming areas in the appropriately named Clam Gulch. Digging for clams requires patience, practice, a shovel and pail, a fishing license, and a current tide book. But for those who like to eat the mollusks – particularly the razor clams, said to be the best of all – a day in Clam Gulch could well be one of the highlights of their visit. You could stay at the

local lodge, which serves very good clam chowder in its restaurant.

At Mile 135 on the highway is **Ninilchik ㉓**, a fishing village founded by the Russians more than 100 years ago. Fishing is still popular here today, with many visitors coming in search of halibut or salmon. The town's 800 residents mostly live in recently constructed homes along the highway. The original village, which can be visited, is an attractive spot, sitting on the inlet at the mouth of the Ninilchik River.

On a hill above the old village is the town's Russian Orthodox Church, not open for tours but still used by the parish. The modern community of Ninilchik hosts the Kenai Peninsula State Fair on the third weekend in August. Ninilchik is another good spot for clam digging.

Continuing south, you come to **Anchor Point ㉔**, the most westerly point in North America that is accessible by continuous road system. The 1,800-member community hosts a king salmon derby from Memorial Day weekend through the third weekend in June. In addition to kings, the area is a popular fishing spot for silvers, steelhead, halibut, and trout.

Homer

Still farther south is **Homer ㉕**, the southern terminus of the Sterling Highway. Homer sits on the shore of **Kachemak Bay**, which is known for the variety of its marine life. Homer itself, a pleasant little town in a picturesque setting between mountains and sea, is best known for the Homer Spit, which extends 5 miles (8km) out into the bay.

Major attractions around here include boat tours and halibut-fishing trips, but call into the **Homer Visitor and Information Center** at 201 Sterling Highway (tel: 235-7740; www. homeralaska.org; summer daily) to find out what else is offered to visitors.

Be sure to stop at the **Alaska Islands and Ocean Visitor Center** (95 Sterling Highway; tel: 235-6961; www.islandsand ocean.org; summer daily 9am–6pm, contact for winter hours; free). Operated as a partnership between the Alaska Maritime National Wildlife Refuge and the Kachemak Bay Research Reserve, the center offers

The graveyard at Ninilchik's Russian Orthodox Church.

BELOW: carved figures at Kachemak Bay.

BELOW: a good day's catch in Homer.

guided walks that include exploration of the slough, tide pools, and the marine discovery lab.

You will also discover the **Pratt Museum** on Bartlett Street (tel: 235-8635; www.prattmuseum.org; summer daily 10am–6pm, winter Tue–Sun noon–5pm; charge), a natural history museum that focuses on marine life in Kachemak Bay. It also has an award-winning exhibit on the effects of the Exxon Valdez oil spill.

Homer has quite a reputation as a local arts center. On Pioneer Avenue, which joins the highway, galleries display pottery, jewelry, and paintings. In downtown Homer there are also several good restaurants and souvenir shops, and there are productions year-round by an amateur theater company.

The town is also the jumping-off point for trips to the other side of the bay, which is dominated by **Kachemak Bay State Park** ㉖ (tel: 262-7024 or 262-5581; www.alaskastateparks.org), with the **Grewingk Glacier**, rugged mountains, coastal rain forest, steep-walled fjords, and alpine tundra. Also across the bay are **Halibut Cove** – where there

are more artists and galleries – and the pleasing little town of Seldovia. The state ferry service links Homer to Seldovia, Kodiak, and Whittier in summer.

Seldovia

Seldovia ㉗ (tel: 234-7612; www.seldovia.com) is accessible only by air and water. You can bring a vehicle on the state ferry, but it isn't necessary; the town is within easy walking distance. It is home to yet another of the peninsula's still active Russian Orthodox churches. Seldovia's Russian history predates the church, however. It was the site of one of the earliest coal mines, first worked in the late 18th century. By the 1890s, the mine had been exhausted and Seldovia had become a fishing and shipping center.

Much of the town's boardwalk area was destroyed in the 1964 earthquake. Seldovia also has a winter carnival, which brightens up the peaceful, quiet months. With most visitors gone and with nearby trails for hiking and cross-country skiing, winter is one of the nicest times to venture over to the southern shore of Kachemak Bay. ❏

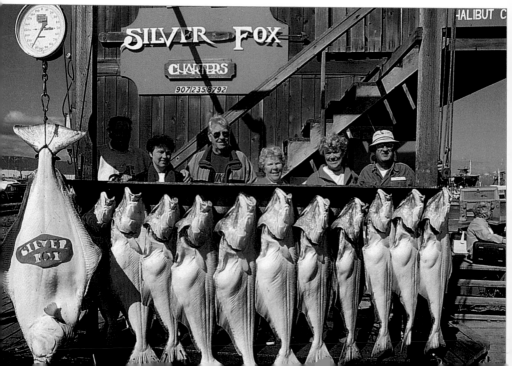

RESTAURANTS AND BARS

Price is for dinner excluding tax, tip, and beverages:
$ = under $15
$$ = $15–20
$$$ = $20–30
$$$$ = over $30

Apollo Restaurant
229 Fourth Avenue
Tel: 224-3092 **$$–$$$**
Stroll two blocks north of the Alaska Sealife Center and have lunch or dinner here. Serves Greek and Italian cuisine, steaks, pizza, and classic Alaskan seafood, Mediterranean style. Beer and wine available.

Peking Restaurant
338 Fourth Avenue
Tel: 224-5444 **$–$$**
Take a break from Alaskan food and try this well-prepared Chinese fare, pleasantly served.

Ranting Raven Bakery & Gifts
228 Fourth Avenue
Tel: 224-2228 **$**
Serves espresso along side housemade bread, pastries, soup, and sandwiches in an earthy, local atmosphere. Part of the space is devoted to selling Alaska gifts and handicrafts by local artists.

Ray's Waterfront
1316 Fourth Avenue
Tel: 224-5606 **$$–$$$$**
Large windows overlook Seward's small boat harbor in this popular local restaurant. Lunch and dinner offered daily. Deliciously prepared seafood and chowder. Box lunches

can be made up to take along on your fishing charter. Full bar.

Resurrection Roadhouse
At the Seward Windsong Lodge
31772 Herman Leirer Road, or Mile 0.5 Exit Glacier Road
Tel: 224-7116 **$$–$$$$**
Located on the Seward Windsong Lodge property in the beautiful Resurrection River Valley. Open seasonally. Fresh Alaska seafood and steak entrées. Full bar.

Soldotna

Mykel's
35041 Kenai Spur Highway
Tel: 262-4305 **$$–$$$$**
Located in the Soldotna Inn. Serves breakfast, lunch and dinner. Menu includes fresh Alaskan seafood, steaks, poultry, and pasta dishes. Bar.

Sal's Klondike Diner
44619 Sterling Highway
Tel: 262-2220 **$**
Where the locals head when they want burgers, sandwiches, halibut fish and chips, and more served in an efficient, friendly manner. Children's menu.

Homer

Café Cups
162 W. Pioneer Avenue
Tel: 235-8330 **$$$**
Locals and visitors alike crowd into this cozy dining room for lunches and dinners that feature fresh pasta, local seafood, and an eclectic, but reasonably priced, wine selection.

Fresh Sourdough Express Bakery & Café
1316 Ocean Drive
Tel: 235-7571
www.freshsourdough express.com **$**
The first certified "green" restaurant in Alaska, this bakery and café serves breakfast, lunch, and dinner made largely from locally grown ingredients served along with bread baked with grain they grind daily. Boxed lunches also available.

Homestead Restaurant
Mile 8.2, East End Road
Tel: 235-8723
www.homesteadrestaurant. net **$$$–$$$$**
This former log roadhouse 8 miles (13km) from downtown Homer specializes in steak,

prime rib, and seasonal seafood creatively prepared with garlic, citrus fruits, macadamia nuts, or spicy ethnic sauces. Closed in winter. Beer and wine.

Saltry in Halibut Cove
Tel: 296-2223 or 800-235-0435 (Central Charters) for reservations
www.halibut-cove-alaska. com/saltry.htm **$$–$$$$**
Across Kachemak Bay in Halibut Cove. Serves lunch and dinner and highlights local seafood in nearly every dish. A wide selection of imported beers. Take the Danny J ferry from the Homer Spit boardwalk through Central Charters. Reservations are necessary. Closed mid-Sept–late May.

RIGHT: king crab caught at Homer.

MATANUSKA-SUSITNA VALLEY

Alaska

Anchorage

"Yahoo! Mat-Su!" is the slogan for this area, referred to locally as "the Mat-Su," or simply "the Valley." The phrase captures the spirit of cowboy enthusiasm common to those who live, farm, hike, fish, hunt, dog mush, mud bog, and snow-machine here

Main attractions
PALMER
WASILLA
MATANUSKA GLACIER
LAKE LOUISE
INDEPENDENCE MINE
WILLOW
TALKEETNA
DENALI STATE PARK

BELOW: a caribou bull crosses the river.

The stunningly beautiful and diverse Mat-Su area encompasses the Matanuska-Susitna River Drainages, over 23,000 sq miles (6 million hectares), beginning north of Anchorage on the Glenn Highway, north along the Parks Highway to the southern border of Denali National Park and Preserve, and east along the Denali Highway as far as Lake Louise, near Glennallen.

Wildlife sightings in the area likely include moose, bear (brown and black), birds (bald eagles, hawks, owls, swans, and loons), and on the far northern and eastern edges of the Mat-Su, impressive caribou herds. Historically the agricultural breadbasket of Alaska, today the Mat-Su is one of the state's fastest growing residential and commercial regions.

A host of new housing developments, springing up on former farmland, are filled with people who commute daily to Anchorage, at least an hour's drive (under ideal weather and traffic conditions) south along the Glenn Highway.

The making of the Mat-Su

The Mat-Su Valley has an interesting history, beginning in 1935 when President Franklin D. Roosevelt – in response to the crushing economic depression and widespread drought of the times – invited 203 families from the hardest-hit states of Minnesota, Wisconsin and Michigan to journey to Alaska for a new start with the Matanuska Colony Project. The name of each family was drawn from a box, and 40 acres (16 hectares) of farmland per family were parceled out.

The community of **Palmer**, established in 1916 as a stop along the Alaska Railroad's track to the Chickaloon coalmines, was selected to be the base of operations for this "New Deal" project. Housing options for the colonists were few, and barns were non-existent. Following plans drawn up by a government architect, the colonists began constructing homes and the

area's distinctive 32ft square, gambrel-roofed barns, many of which are still standing today.

The members of Matanuska Colony faced many of the same problems common to the Valley's current-day farmers: short growing season, high freight and labor costs, and great distances to relatively small markets. Within five years, more than half of the original 203 families had given up and left the area; by 1965, fewer than 20 of the original colonists were still farming.

Driving north from Anchorage along the Glenn Highway, just before reaching the city of Palmer, you'll come upon a broad expanse of flat, marshy grasslands of the **Palmer Hay Flats State Game Refuge Ⓐ**. The 45 sq miles (116 sq km) of the refuge provides nesting and feeding grounds for tens of thousands of various duck and geese species en route to and from northern breeding grounds. Trumpeter and tundra swans also frequent the marshlands during spring and fall. Sandhill cranes may be found in the drier, more isolated regions. The area is a major calving and wintering ground

for the Matanuska Valley moose population. The streams, wetlands, lakes and tide flats of the refuge are also popular recreation areas for local salmon fishers and waterfowl hunters.

An excellent place to begin your exploration of the Mat-Su is at the **Visitor Information Headquarters Ⓑ** (Parks Highway to Trunk Road Exit, 7744 E. Visitors View Court; tel: 746-5000; www.alaskavisit.com; mid-May–mid-Sept daily 8.30am–6.30pm). The friendly folks inside the log cabin can give you information on tours, attractions and lodging options in the area, and also have a pay phone, free wi-fi internet access and a gift shop.

Palmer

After leaving the Mat-Su Visitor Information Headquarters, head a few miles farther north along the Glenn Highway to **Palmer Ⓒ**, a small farming town of 5,500 residents happily situated in a majestic rural setting, and conforming to the image many visitors expect of Alaska. The city offers a variety of modest lodging and restaurant options, as well as an 18-hole golf

Pick your own
An important stop along the Pacific Flyway, the Knik Arm Estuary, within the Palmer Hay Flats, is a great place to spot huge flocks of snow and Canadian geese, sandhill cranes, and trumpeter swans. The Anchorage Audubon Society frequently guides birding trips here. For more information, call 338-2473, or visit www. anchorageaudubon. org.

BELOW: fly fishing on Rabbit Creek, Palmer Hay Flats State Game Refuge.

A rider takes a tumble at the Alaska State Fair.

course with distracting views of the surrounding mountain and glacier grandeur.

Stop in at the **Palmer Museum of History and Art ⓓ** (723 S. Valley Way; tel: 745-2880; May–Sept daily 9am–6pm, Oct–Apr Tue–Fri 9am–1.30pm; donations welcome) to chat with those who know the town best. The museum displays colony-era household relics, farm implements, and woodworking tools, in addition to providing up-to-date information on points of interest throughout the greater Palmer area. Many local artists have their works displayed here as well, and just outside the building you can stroll through an interesting garden area featuring various local flowers and vegetables.

A short walk from the museum is the **Colony House Museum ⓔ** (316 E. Elmwood Avenue; tel: 745-1935; summer Tue–Sat 10am–4pm, winter by appointment only; charge), a restored Colony home (*c.*1935), where you'll likely hear a direct descendant of

an original pioneer family describe what life was like during the Matanuska Colony Project.

Palmer is best known for being the site (in late August) of the **Alaska State Fair ⓕ** (tel: 745-4827; www.alaskastatefair.org), which features the famous valley produce. Grown to gigantic proportions due to proper seed selection, careful tending and 19 hours of sunlight during the growing season, the largest cabbage wins the blue ribbon – and it must weigh at least 75lbs (34kg) before it is even eligible to enter the competition. Displays also include farm animals and hand-made local items. There is a colorful carnival and a host of food stalls. The 11-day event, which ends on Labor Day, attracts more than 250,000 people a year and shouldn't be missed.

Wasilla

Palmer's significantly less-quaint sister city is **Wasilla ⓖ** (*wa sill uh*). North along the (George) Parks Highway, it is dominated by mile after mile of strip mall-styled commercial development and known as the "Home of the Idi-

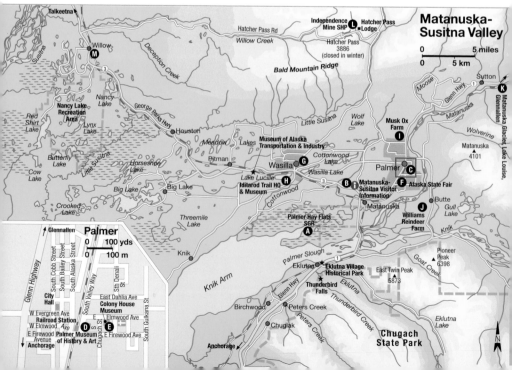

tarod", the land "among the lakes", and, most recently, the town where Sarah Palin began her political career. After two terms as mayor (1996–2002), Palin won the Govenor's Mansion and later joined John McCain on the Republican ticket in an unsuccessful run against Barak Obama in 2008 *(see also margin, page 212)*.

Today, Wasilla (population 6,775) is the site of many of the large, new residential developments in the Valley. Housing and land prices are generally more reasonable here than in Anchorage; the trade-off is that most residents must then make the daily one hour (plus) commute each way – in all kinds of weather – to their Anchorage jobs. That's OK, though. In Wasilla, the folks tend to be hard drivers, hard workers and hard players; just watch out for heavy commute traffic in the early morning and late afternoon.

Like many of the other cities and towns in Southcentral, the community of Wasilla arrived by rail. The original Dena'ina Indian residents called this area Benteh, or "among the lakes", sandwiched as it is between Lake Lucille

and Wasilla Lake. The name "Wasilla" came from the highly-respected local Dena'ina Indian, Chief Wasilla. Depending on whom you ask, the name means either "breath of air," or else it's simply a derivative of the Russian name, "William."

The first non-Native settlers of the region lived in the nearby town of Knik, a "boom town" of about 500 people in 1915, providing supplies and services to the gold miners at Cache Creek and Willow Creek. In 1917, Wasilla was founded following the construction of the Alaska Railroad.

The Northern Lights illuminate a barn near Palmer.

BELOW: giant cabbages at the Alaska State Fair.

The residents of Knik, realizing the advantages of living near a rail service, simply packed up and moved there. Some actually dragged their houses along behind them, leaving Knik to become a ghost town. The construction of the Parks Highway in early 1970 opened up road access to the area, and made it possible to become a bedroom community for Anchorage.

The Iditarod's HQ

Wasilla is the home of the world famous Iditarod Trail Sled Dog Race *(see pages 302–3)*. The **Iditarod Trail Headquarters and Museum** ❼ (Mile 2.2 Knik Road; tel: 376-5155; www.iditarod.com; summer daily 8am–7pm, winter Mon–Fri 8am–5pm) is well worth a visit. Aside from the very interesting exhibits depicting the history of the Iditarod, there's a unique gift shop and, during the summer, you can go for a dogsled ride (daily 9am–5pm).

There are two other museum options in Wasilla. The **Dorothy Page Museum** (323 N. Main Street; tel: 373-5973; Apr–Sept Mon–Sat 9am–5pm, Oct–Mar Wed–Fri 9am–5pm; charge), was

named in honor of Dorothy G. Page who joined with Joe Reddington, Sr. in 1967 to organize the first Iditarod Trail Race, a 50-mile race (run in two 25-mile heats) to commemorate the 100th anniversary of US purchase of Alaska from Russia. The museum, housed in a 1931 structure, offers exhibits and lectures on the history of gold mining and dog mushing (among other things) in Wasilla. You can also visit the historic buildings of the **Old Wasilla Townsite Park** while you're there.

The **Museum of Alaska Transportation and Industry** (3800 W. Museum Drive, off Mile 47 Parks Highway; tel: 376-1211; summer daily 10am–5pm; charge) displays interesting examples of old planes, trains, tools, vehicles and farm equipment.

Reindeer and musk ox

Just north of Palmer is the **Palmer Musk Ox Farm** ❶ (Mile 50, Glenn Highway; tel: 745-4151; www.musko farm.org; summer daily 10am–6pm, winter by appointment; charge), with the world's only domesticated musk oxen. In the summer, visitors can watch

Mat-Su Bounty

Although Alaska imports nearly 98 percent of its food, the Mat-Su Valley remains Alaska's rural heartland. Most farms have given way to housing developments, but in recent years there has been an interest in reviving its agricultural heritage. Farmers' markets are blossoming, and Mat-Su farmers have been adding vegetables to their standard load of alfalfa and grains. Others are raising poultry, and milking cows to make milk and cheese. Organic farms are also sprouting up, adding apples, corn, and tomatoes to the mix. Still, what you'll find at the majority of markets and roadside farm stands are Alaska's staple crops like carrots, peas, cabbage, and potatoes. Even if you prefer a peach to a carrot, be sure to stop by a local market and take a bite out of an Alaskan carrot; it will be the sweetest you ever tasted.

the newborns romping with their parents in the pasture. The coats of these shaggy animals produce a rare type of wool known as qiviut, which is used by Alaska Natives to create hand-knitted hats, mittens, gloves, and scarves in traditional patterns. The Oomingmak Musk Ox Producers' Co-op in downtown Anchorage *(see page 169)* sells a range of these products.

The **Williams Reindeer Farm** ⓳ (5561 Bodenburg Loop Road, in the Butte area off the Old Glenn Highway; tel: 745-4500; www.reindeerfarm.com; summer daily 10am–6pm; charge) offers a rare chance to get a close look at the smallish creatures that are Santa's seemingly unlikely choice for worldwide air cargo transport.

Matanuska Glacier

Continuing your road trip east along the Glenn Highway, you will pass the small communities of Sutton, Chickaloon and Eureka. At Mile 102, the **Matanuska Glacier** ⓴ (tel: 745-2534; www.matanuskaglacier.com; daily Mar–Oct, winter by appointment only; charge) is visible on the south side of the road. At 27 miles (43km) long and 4 miles (9km) wide, it is the largest glacier accessible by car in the state. For the more adventurous, camping, hiking, and ice climbing (including gear and instructions) are available.

To visit Lake Louise, a popular spot among locals for trout fishing, **turn left at** Mile 159.9 and travel 19 miles (30km) down the road. The surrounding areas afford views of Tazlina Glacier, private lodges, campgrounds, and, in winter, snow-machining and cross-country skiing opportunities. The Nelchina caribou herd can be seen passing through this region during spring and fall migrations, while cormorants, trumpeter swans, and ptarmigans, as well as wolves, bears, wolverine, foxes, and moose are common sightings. The Copper River Valley community of Glennallen *(see page 187)* sits just another 27 miles (43km) on the Glenn Highway.

The Iditarod Trail Sled Dog Race is run from Wasilla.

BELOW: campfire at dusk by the Matanuska River.

Planes, trucks and tractors at the Museum of Alaska Transportation and Industry (see page 212).

BELOW: sharing the news in Talkeetna.

Independence Mine

One of the highlights of any trip to the Mat-Su is a visit to Hatcher Pass and the **Independence Mine State Historical Park ⓛ** (tel: 745-2827; http://dnr. alaska.gov/parks/units/ind mine.htm; visitor center summer daily 11am–6pm; charge for parking and guided tours). Accessed just north of Palmer at Mile 49.5 Glenn Highway, turn left onto Palmer-Fishhook Road (which becomes Hatcher Pass Road), and make the scenic drive on the well-maintained, paved roadway through pleasant woodlands. The Little Susitna River runs alongside the road as you begin to climb and gradually wind your way to an elevation of 3,886ft (1,184 meters) at Hatcher Pass.

The **Hatcher Pass Lodge** is located 17 miles (27km) from the Glenn Highway turnoff. This rustic establishment, open year round, offers good food, reasonable prices, cabin rentals, and spectacular views of the Talkeetna Mountains

and alpine foothills that will have you looking around for Heidi and her grandfather. The area is a popular year-round recreational destination for hiking, picnicking, berry picking, camping, and, in winter, skiing, snowboarding and snowmachining (*see also page 177*).

A mile or so beyond the lodge is the gravel parking area for Independence Mine State Historical Park. You can ramble on your own (or take a guided tour) through abandoned buildings of this 1930s gold mine operation, at that time one of the largest producers in Alaska, employing more than 200.

Hatcher Pass Road continues along, now as an old-time, un-maintained, real Alaska gravel road. During the summer you can complete the 50-mile (80km) drive (from the Glenn Highway turnoff) to **Willow Ⓜ** (located on the Parks Highway), a community of nearly 2,000 residents, many of whom are competitive mushers. The scenery of this stretch is nothing short of spectacular, but the road is steep, narrow, often rough, and switch-backed. It is not a good option for large RVs.

Talkeetna

If you're driving north of Wasilla on the Parks Highway towards the Interior, don't pass up the opportunity to spend a few hours in **Talkeetna** ㉘ (pronounced *tal* **keet** *nuh*; turn north at Mile 98.7, then travel 14 miles/22km along the Talkeetna Spur Road), the staging area for climbers planning to summit Mount McKinley.

The Talkeetna Lodge (on the right, about a mile before Talkeetna), owned by the Cook Inlet Region, Inc. (CIRI) Native corporation, is a clean, modern, beautifully "rustic" post-and-beam style hotel nestled in a quiet, wooded area of Talkeetna. On clear days, a fine view of Mt McKinley awaits you on the observation deck in front of the hotel.

In Talkeetna's "downtown" area, renovated, rustic miners' cabins have been spruced up and converted into gift shops, lodgings, and restaurants. The town is famous for its annual Moose Dropping Festival (held in July), which includes quirky events like the Mountain Mother Contest (where mothers compete in diaper changing, wood chopping, water hauling, and pie mak-

ing for the coveted "Crown of the Mountain Mama") or the Moose Drop Dropping (where shellacked and numbered moose nuggets are dropped from the air onto a target).

Talkeetna also offers fishing charters, river rafting adventures, and flightseeing tours to Mt McKinley. Contact the Talkeetna Chamber for more details (PO Box 334, Talkeetna 99676; tel: 733-2330; www.talkeetnachamber.org).

Denali State Park

An often-overlooked option for those wanting to see Mt McKinley during their Alaska vacation is to visit **Denali State Park** ㉙, where outstanding views of the mountain are possible from a less-crowded vantage point. One of the best roadside views, weather permitting, may be enjoyed from the southern viewpoint (Mile 135.2).

You can also take a day hike to **Kesugi Ridge**, or if you're interested in backpacking adventures, a trek into the **Peters Hills** (in the western end of the park). Both options offer stunning, panoramic views of Mt McKinley – if the weather cooperates.

TIP

Safety in Denali

Because the state park is essentially a wilderness, hiking trails are not always clearly marked and good USGS topographic maps are essential since whiteout conditions can occur in any season. Maps can be found at the Visitor Contact Station at the Alaska Veterans Memorial, Mile 147.1, Parks Highway.

BELOW: view of Hatcher Pass from Independence Mine.

From Talkeetna by Train

The Alaska Railroad offers flag-stop service for a 55-mile (88km) wilderness run from Talkeetna to Hurricane and back. The train leaves Talkeetna, usually Thursday through Sunday only, at 11.45am and returns in time for dinner. It threads its way along the Susitna River and through the Indian River Canyon.

Passengers can get off the Hurricane Turn train for a fishing or river-rafting adventure along the way, and then board the train again on its return trip (or else camp overnight and flag down the next day's train). Since 1923 locals have been using this route, one of the last flag-stop services in the country, for accessing remote cabins in the area.

Tickets may be purchased on board (cash only), or reserved in advance by calling 800-544-0552 or 265-2494.

Hatcher Pass.

Other recreation opportunities include camping, and kayaking or canoeing at the **Byers Lake Campground**. Wildlife common to the park includes moose, grizzly and black bears, wolves, lynx, coyotes, red fox, and land otters.

The area is also rich in birds, as more than 130 species use the park for breeding or during migration. Additional information is available at the visitor contact station, Mile 147.1, or contact the Denali Ranger (Alaska State Parks, Mat-Su/CB Area, HC 32, Box 6706, Wasilla 99654-9719; tel: 745-3974; http://dnr.alaska.gov/parks/units/denali1.htm).

For full coverage of Denali National Park (not to be confused with the state park), *see pages 223–33*.

Mat-Su Backcountry

Conveniently accessible from Anchorage, the backcountry opportunities of the Mat-Su are plentiful and varied.

The area has the largest trail system in the Alaska State Parks network, offering over 2,000 miles (3,200km) of trails for all abilities. Prime examples include a nature walk through Denali State Park, where you can – when the weather conditions smile upon you – catch rare and glorious glimpses of Mount McKinley and the Tokositna Glacier.

In addition to Hatcher Pass *(see page 214)*, another excellent option is to explore some of the many trails in the **Talkeetna Mountains** – leading to alpine valleys, tundra vistas, and mountain streams.

The **Nancy Lake Recreation Area** (Mile 67.2 Parks Highway, near Willow) offers water enthusiasts a total of 130 interconnected lakes for their paddling pleasure – also canoe and kayak rentals, remote cabin rentals, campgrounds, and superb fishing for rainbow trout, Arctic, char and northern pike.

Guided rafting adventures (white-water or leisure floats) are available on the **Matanuska or Knik Rivers**. For details on these (and other) adventures to be experienced in the Mat-Su region, go to www.alaskavisit.com. ❏

RESTAURANTS AND BARS

Price is for dinner excluding tax, tip, and beverages:
$ = under $15
$$ = $15–20
$$$ = $20–30
$$$$ = over $30

Palmer

Hatcher Pass Lodge Restaurant
17 miles from the Glenn Highway intersection on the Hatcher Pass Rd, PO Box 763
Tel: 745-5897
www.hatcherpasslodge.com
$–$$
This lodge-style restaurant, in an unpretentious A-frame building at Hatcher Pass, offers an amazingly varied menu of simple-but-tasty beef, chicken, and seafood dishes, as well as salads and a choice of sandwiches. The service is surprisingly fast, the portions generous, the company of fellow-diners eclectic, and the view spectacular. Bar.

Turkey Red
550 S. Alaska Street
Tel: 746-5544
http://turkeyredak.com $$$
Serving Mediterranean-inspired dishes from largely local ingredients, this warm bistro style restaurant is a Palmer favorite. Expect to find lots of locals nibbling on Alaskan wild red salmon salad or the tasty moussaka, a layered Greek dish.

Vagabond Blues
642 S. Alaska Street
Tel: 745-2233 $

Located in the center of downtown Palmer, this trendy café offers delicious vegetarian soups, salads, sandwiches and wraps, and locally roasted coffee. Casual environment, patrons generally bus their own tables before leaving. Frequent live performances by local musicians add to the atmosphere.

The Valley Hotel Restaurant
606 S. Alaska Street
Tel: 745-3330 $–$$
The place local residents congregate for basic small-town restaurant fare. Nothing fancy, but you can count on generous portions, friendly staff, clean dining area, large and varied menu, consistently good food. Bar.

Wasilla

Alpine Garden Grille
Mile 45.2 Parks Highway, 259 South McCallister Drive
Tel: 357-6313
www.alpinegardengrille.com
$$$–$$$$
This restaurant's stated goal of fine dining in a setting of casual elegance is being well received by local Wasilla diners. The menu is described as international with Italian and French influence. Specialties include a baked brie with roasted garlic appetizer, oven-roasted leg of lamb, and hazelnut-stuffed chicken roulade. Desserts made fresh daily. More than 100 wines are available.

Shoreline Restaurant
Best Western Lake Lucille Inn, 1300 W. Lake Lucille Drive
Tel: 373-1776 $$–$$$$
Within one of the area's better hotels, this restaurant offers a quiet, pleasant place to go for that special night out in Wasilla. Windows afford lovely view of the lake and mountains beyond. Open breakfast, lunch, and dinner. Dinner menu primarily features beef, chicken, and seafood entrées. Bar.

Talkeetna

Talkeetna Alaskan Lodge
23601 S. Talkeetna Spur Road
Tel: 907-733-9500 or 888-959-9590
www.talkeetnalodge.com
$$–$$$$

Offering everything from casual bistro fare, beer and pub food, to high-end fine dining, this sprawling Alaskan lodge has it all, including views of Mt McKinley. Featuring Alaskan specialities and a full bar, it is only open during the summer.

Talkeetna Roadhouse
Main and C Street
Tel: 907-733-1351
www.talkeetnaroadhouse.com $$
Originally built in 1917 as a staging house for gold miners' supplies, today the roadhouse offers lodging as well as a bakery and café. Hearty breakfasts and lunches served daily in summer, limited hours in winter. A popular spot for Mt McKinley climbers.

RIGHT: eating out at Talkeetna.

THE INTERIOR

You can follow in the footsteps of the 19th-century gold prospectors and discover the beauties, and the hardships, of Alaska's Interior. The area includes Denali National Park and Preserve, Fairbanks, outlying areas, and the Alcan highway

The cry of "Gold!" has lured men and women to the Interior for more than a century. That initial, passionate hunger for a handful of valuable nuggets – spawning the first of Alaska's many "rushes" – is history now, but the spirit of the Interior still summons the adventurer.

The extraordinary wildlife-viewing, photography, and back-country opportunities of Denali National Park and Preserve *(see pages 223–33)*, the many historic sights and sounds of the heartland city of Fairbanks (the second-largest population base of Alaska; *see pages 237–49)*, and the scattered, outlying communities, hunkered down in the wilderness along mighty rivers, still sing out their siren call. And those who answer that call board planes, catch trains (from South-central Alaska), or simply pack up their cars (or RVs) and head north *(see The Alcan, pages 234–5)*.

There *is* gold in the Interior, gilding every aspen leaf in the autumn explosion of color, glancing off the wingtips of geese, shimmering in the river current as it flows into a blazing sunset. It splashes across the midnight sky as the aurora and dances as moonlight over the hulking white shoulders of mountain peaks. Many who visit the Interior also find that the people have what can only be called hearts of gold. There is a long-standing tradition of caring, generosity and warm-heartedness that welcomes the traveler back again and again to the edge of the frontier.

Stark contrasts

The Interior of Alaska, that one-third of the state north of the Alaska Range, south of the Brooks Range and east of Alaska's western coastal areas, is an area of stark contrasts. Mount McKinley, 20,320ft (6,195 meters) and snowcapped year-round, towers above the temperate Tanana and Yukon valleys. The Alaska Range is girdled with miles and miles of glaciers, while in the valleys, forests of white spruce, birch, and aspen fold into straggly stands of black spruce, tangles of willow, and muskeg.

If you are visiting the Interior in summer, as most people do, try conjuring up an image of what it would be like in winter, with low light reflecting blue off the snow-covered riverbed, and temperatures plummeting to –40°F (–40°C) or below. Summer weather is glorious, with nearly around-the-

clock daylight and temperatures as high as 96°F (36°C). Travelers often find it hard to sleep because of all the light. The most practical advice is: don't even try to sleep until you're really tired, but enjoy the late evening light – this is the season that makes the cold dark winter worth enduring.

You will also find that the later evening is a fine time for photography. Light of this quality is experienced at lower latitudes for only a few

moments around sunrise and sunset. In Alaska's Interior, the special glow hovers for hours, casting gigantic shadows and ethereal reflections.

Exploring the rivers and woods

Outdoor adventure is the glue that binds people to the land in the Interior. The mountains, rivers and valleys offer unparalleled opportunities for hiking, canoeing, hunting, and fishing. The best source of outdoors information is the **Alaska Public Lands Information Center** at 101 Dunkel Street, Fairbanks (tel: 459-3730; www.nps.gov/aplic). This multi-agency information center and museum sells maps and answers questions about all categories of land.

The usually blue skies of summer coupled with hundreds of miles of wild and scenic rivers make water travel a natural pastime. Canoeing offers an idyllic opportunity to observe game animals undisturbed as the boat slips silently past. With the entire Interior river system at your paddle tip, deciding where to explore depends on ability and time. The Chena and Chatanika rivers offer a multitude of easily accessible possibilities for day trips or longer expeditions. For experienced wilderness canoeists, the more challenging clear waters of the Birch Creek can be accessed at Mile 94 Steese Highway, or consider a 5-day sojourn on the broad sweep of the **Tanana River** from Delta to Fairbanks. These rivers are all conveniently accessible by road.

Legendary fishing

The Interior is a fisherman's promised land, and the Arctic grayling is its manna. The flash of the strike and the fight of the silver streak on light tackle is a treasured memory for many. The Clearwater, Salcha, Chatanika and Chena rivers are superior grayling producers and are accessible by road. In fact, all clear-flowing creeks and rivers in the Interior are well stocked with grayling. Northern pike, burbot, and lake trout abound in the clear, cold waters throughout the Interior.

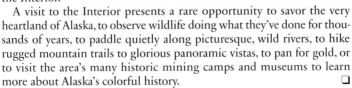

A visit to the Interior presents a rare opportunity to savor the very heartland of Alaska, to observe wildlife doing what they've done for thousands of years, to paddle quietly along picturesque, wild rivers, to hike rugged mountain trails to glorious panoramic vistas, to pan for gold, or to visit the area's many historic mining camps and museums to learn more about Alaska's colorful history. ❏

PRECEDING PAGES: a bull moose amidst the fall colors of Denali National Park. **LEFT:** panning for gold; playing a sealskin drum. **ABOVE:** train at El Dorado mine, Fairbanks; fishermen are lured to the Interior.

DENALI NATIONAL PARK AND PRESERVE

Dominated by the magnificent Mount McKinley, Denali, one of the world's greatest wildlife sanctuaries, is the most visited of all Alaska's national parks

laska's Athabascan Indians called the mountain by several names, but they all meant essentially the same thing: "The Great One." Denali was the most common of those names and it's the one preferred by many Alaskans today, though the peak's official name remains **Mount McKinley**. Whether Denali or McKinley, North America's highest peak (20,320ft/6,195 meters) is also among the continent's most spectacular. In one sense it is among the highest mountains in the world: the north face of Denali rises almost 18,000ft (5,500 meters) above its base, an elevation gain which surpasses even Mount Everest.

The mountain is surrounded by one of the world's greatest wildlife sanctuaries, **Denali National Park and Preserve ⑳**. A one-day trip through the park will almost certainly allow you to see grizzly bears, caribou, Dall sheep, moose and perhaps a wolf. Denali Park is, for many, the ultimate Alaskan adventure.

Geology and history

Denali is part of the **Alaska Range**, a 600-mile (960km) arc of mountains stretching across the state from the Alaska Peninsula almost to the Canadian border. The oldest parts of the range are made up of slate, shale, marble, and other sedimentary deposits formed under an ancient ocean. Approximately 60 million years ago, the collision and subsequent overlap-

ping of two tectonic plates produced such intense heat that sections of the earth's crust began to melt. A gigantic mass of molten rock deposited beneath the current location of Denali eventually solidified into granite.

The overlapping of the plates caused the whole region to rise. Granite and sedimentary rock were forced upward to form the mountain range. As the uplift petered out, the process of erosion slowly wore down the range. As Denali is chiefly composed of erosion-resistant granite, it wore down at a

Main attractions
VISITOR ACCESS CENTER
SAVAGE RIVER
PRIMROSE RIDGE
SABLE PASS
POLYCHROME PASS
STONY HILL OVERLOOK
EIELSON VISITOR CENTER
WONDER LAKE
KANTISHNA

LEFT: the Alaska Railroad provides access to the park.
BELOW: Mount McKinley.

An Arctic ground squirrel in Denali.

slower rate than surrounding sedimentary rock. A later period of tectonic plate collision and uplift began two million years ago and continues to this day. This ongoing uplift is responsible for the towering height of Denali.

The first humans came on seasonal hunting trips to what is now Denali Park about 12,000 years ago. Later, the Athabascans followed suit, but built their villages in lower, warmer, sheltered locations, next to lakes or rivers that offered dependable fishing. However, the lack of large salmon runs limited Native habitation.

The Athabascans of the Yukon and Tanana rivers gave Denali its name; one story refers to it as "the home of the sun." During the longest days of summer, the sun makes an almost complete circle in the local sky and drops below the horizon for only a few hours. From certain angles, it appears that the sun rises and sets from behind Denali.

The first recorded sighting of Denali by a white man occurred in 1794. While sailing in Cook Inlet, the English Captain George Vancouver sighted "distant stupendous mountains covered with snow." Undoubtedly this was the Alaska Range. Other explorers, surveyors and adventurers in later decades commented on the mountain's great size and estimated its height.

The naming process

Denali became known as Mount McKinley through a strange set of circumstances in 1896 when William Dickey went on a gold-prospecting expedition in the area just south of Denali. While camped within sight of the mountain, he met other miners and they argued at length whether gold or silver should back US currency. (The miners were against the gold standard while Dickey was for it.) When Dickey later returned to the Lower 48, he wrote an article about his Alaskan adventures, and proposed that the highest mountain in the Alaskan Range be named after the Republican presidential candidate William McKinley, the champion of the gold standard. McKinley won the 1896 election and the name stuck.

One of the first white men to explore the Denali region was a naturalist and

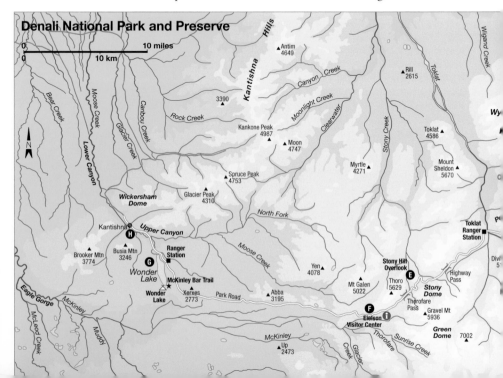

Denali National Park and Preserve

hunter, Charles Sheldon, who proposed that it be set aside as a national park and wildlife preserve. Sheldon made two extensive trips through the area in 1906 and 1907–8, and thought that the opportunity to see and study wildlife was the most impressive feature of the region.

After leaving Denali, Sheldon used his considerable influence to gather support for the proposed Denali National Park. Largely due to Sheldon's efforts, the park became a reality in 1917. To his disappointment, Congress chose to call it Mount McKinley National Park.

The Sourdough Expedition

While Sheldon was campaigning for the park, others were endeavoring to make the first ascent of Denali. In late 1909, four miners (Billy Taylor, Pete Anderson, Charley McGonagall and Tom Lloyd), not intimidated by the fact that they had never climbed a mountain before, decided to scale

Denali. They figured if they had survived the Alaskan winters they could do anything.

The so-called Sourdough Expedition set off from Fairbanks. ("Sourdough" was the nickname given to prospectors because of the yeasty mixture they brought with them to make bread) in December 1909 and spent much of the next few months establishing a series of camps. The group reached Denali's Muldrow Glacier in March. And on the morning of April 3, 1910, McGonagall, Taylor and Anderson set out for the summit from their camp at 11,000ft (3,300 meters), carrying a spruce pole that they hoped would be visible from mining camps at Kantishna, and evidence of their ascent. McGonagall

Spring comes to Wonder Lake, near Mount McKinley.

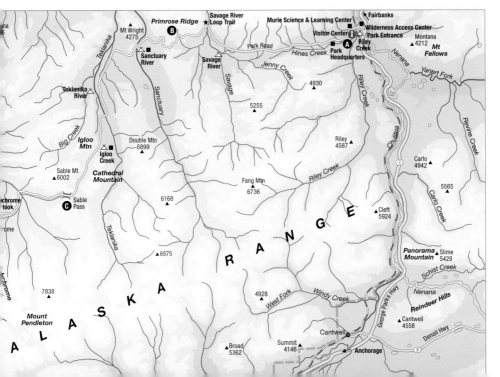

stopped part way up, but by mid-afternoon Taylor and Anderson stood atop Denali's North Peak: they had achieved their goal despite their total lack of experience. Unfortunately for them, the North Peak is 850ft (260 meters) lower than the South Peak, Denali's true summit. Taylor and Anderson were never credited with being first to the continent's top.

In 1913 Hudson Stuck and a party of three climbers mounted the first Denali expedition to actually reach the mountain's summit. Using route descriptions made by earlier parties, they ascended the Muldrow Glacier, which flows down the northeast side of Denali.

After a difficult climb, they reached Denali Pass, the saddle between the North and South Peaks, only 2,100ft (640 meters) below the summit. The high elevation, low oxygen and extreme cold made those last few hundred feet the hardest part of their climb. Walter Harper, a young Athabascan employed by Stuck and the strongest member of the team, was the first to stand on the summit of Mount Denali.

TIP

Camping permits
A backcountry use permit, required for overnight camping, must be obtained in person at the Backcountry Information Center (adjacent to the Wilderness Access Center) in summer and at park headquarters in winter. A quota system is enforced.

BELOW: relaxing at a camp in Kantishna.

Recent changes

From 1917 to the early 1970s, few people visited Mount McKinley National Park. The park's remoteness and lack of direct access by vehicle combined to limit tourism. In the five years prior to 1972, the average annual number of visitors was about 15,000. In 1972, the Anchorage–Fairbanks Highway was completed and it suddenly became much easier for tourists and Alaskan residents to get here. In a short time, the numbers jumped to more than 140,000 a year, almost a ten-fold increase over the previous figures.

National Park Service rangers were concerned about the effect this dramatic rise would have on the park and the quality of visitors' experiences. One major problem was that the single dirt road that bisects the park was too narrow to handle the increased traffic. Another concern was the park's wildlife, which in the past had always been readily visible from the road. The extra traffic and noise created by a ten-fold increase in numbers was likely to drive the animals out of sight; and huge influxes of people could result in more encounters with the park's dangerous animals, grizzly bears, and moose.

The creative solution to these problems was the initiation of a shuttle and tour bus system: private vehicles must be parked in the entrance area and visitors board buses that run throughout the day, causing little disturbance to wildlife. However, visitors are allowed to drive their own vehicles as far as the Savage River bridge, about 15 miles (24km) from the park entrance. That first stretch of road is paved, while the 75 miles (120km) or so beyond are gravel. The park road is closed beyond Mile 3 in winter, but a campground loop is plowed for campers.

In 1980, with the passing of the Alaska National Interest Lands Conservation Act (ANILCA), the park was expanded by 4 million acres (1.6 million hectares) and renamed the Denali National Park and Preserve, recognizing the longstanding Alaskan use of the

name Denali even though the mountain is still officially Mount McKinley.

Arriving in the park

The entrance to Denali Park is along the **George Parks Highway**, 240 miles (385km) north of Anchorage and 120 miles (193km) south of Fairbanks. Access to the park is also provided by the Alaska Railroad, which has a daily summer service from Anchorage and Fairbanks. The train depot, the **Visitor Center** Ⓐ (tel: 683-2294; summer only), a bookstore and grill, the Wilderness Access Center, the Murie Science and Learning Center, the Riley Creek Campground, a post office, and a general store are all within walking distance of each other. Shuttle buses provide a free service between them every half hour.

Campground and backcountry camping registration also takes place at the **Wilderness Access Center**. Denali Park has seven public roadside campgrounds containing a total of 215 sites. A couple of them, Igloo Creek and Sanctuary River, are very small and have no water. One is for backpackers only. Some advance reservations are accepted by campgrounds by phone or fax (tel: 800-622-7275, fax: 602-331-5258; reservation forms can also be downloaded from www.nps.gov/dena) and the rest are available on a first-come, first-served basis.

During the peak summer season (late May–early Sept), all sites are often occupied by mid-morning. Should you arrive to find all campgrounds within the park full, you might check with the private campgrounds (located outside the boundary) that cater, primarily, to RV campers.

Dogsled demonstrations

While in the park entrance area visit the sled dog kennel, located behind the park headquarters building at Mile 3 of the Park Road. Since the 1920s, park rangers have used sled dogs as a means of patroling the park, as they are the most practical means of getting around Denali in the winter months. The dogs have become so popular with visitors that rangers put on several dogsledding demonstrations every day during the summer season.

A guard on the McKinley Explorer.

BELOW: shops on the George Parks Highway.

TIP

Blueberries: The Mosquito's Gift

By the end of July much of Denali's tundra, particularly in Kantishna, is a blanket of plump blueberries. A hiker's delight, the berries are a splendid reward for the taxing tundra trekking. While indulging, remember to thank the mosquito: It is the sole pollinator of Alaska's blueberries and is responsible for the bounty every summer.

BELOW: glacier walking at Ruth Glacier.

The shuttle bus system

The adventure of experiencing Denali National Park by road really begins when you step on a shuttle bus for an all-day trip into the park. There are several different bus trips, which all start at the **Wilderness Access Center**. The rangers can give you a bus schedule, and will explain how the system works. (*See page 369 for more information on making shuttle or tour bus reservations.*)

The green "camper" bus trips, which go the whole 85 miles (136km) to Wonder Lake, do not provide a formal guided-tour program, although drivers will answer questions and help spot wildlife. Passengers can get on and off anywhere along the road, space permitting. The buses get very full in summer and should be booked well in advance, or at the Wilderness Access Center two days ahead.

The Denali History Tour bus goes to Primrose Ridge, about 17 road miles (27km) into the park, and the Tundra Wildlife Tour to the Toklat River (Mile 53) or, if Denali is "out", to the Stony Hill Overlook (Mile 62). Snacks are included in the tour bus ticket price and there are rest stops, but passengers must re-board the same bus.

Your chances of seeing wildlife, as well as Denali itself, are increased by taking as early a bus as possible. The first few depart at 6am. During the rest of the morning they leave every half-hour. The early buses are often in high demand. No food or drinks are available along the bus route, so be sure to take with you what you'll need for the day. Always be prepared for cool temperatures and rain regardless of what the early morning weather might be like.

The first leg of the bus route is the 14-mile (22km) stretch between the entrance and the **Savage River**. The first glimpses of Denali hove into view in this area. This section of the Park Road goes through prime moose habitat; any time a moose or other animal is spotted, the bus will stop to allow passengers to watch and photograph the wildlife.

Moose are the biggest animals in the park – mature bulls can weigh as much as 1,500lbs (680kg). During the spring, watch for calves in this area. Cow

National Parks from the Air

If you're trying to spread limited financial resources across a very large state, here's a sound piece of free advice: go ahead and splurge by taking a flightseeing trip. No other mode of exploration will give as good an overview of all that makes this land so extraordinary.

Soar over mountain peaks, swoop low over glacier-laden fjords, land on a glacier, peer down into deep, icy crevasses and get a bird's-eye-view of wildlife, rivers, forests and scenic alpine meadows you'll otherwise only see in travel brochures. For more information, see page 346 or check with the Convention and Visitors Bureau in the city nearest your destination. In Denali, both Talkeetna Air Taxi (tel: 800-533-2219 or 733-2218) and Kantishna Air (tel: 683-1223) offer spectacular tours of Mt McKinley.

moose usually have one or two calves each year. At birth, a calf weighs about 30lbs (14kg). Moose calves are one of the fastest-growing animals in the world. By their first birthday, they often weigh over 600lbs (270kg).

Each September and October this section of Denali Park becomes a rutting ground for moose. The huge bulls challenge each other over harems of cows, and they are deadly serious. A bull can kill his opponent with his sharp antler points. Rutting bulls and cow moose with calves should always be considered extremely dangerous and given a wide berth. If they are approached too closely, both cows and bulls will charge a human. If you should surprise a moose, run from the animal immediately; unlike bears, they will not chase you down once you leave their "personal space."

Primrose Ridge

As your bus continues beyond the Savage River, you will pass a mountain to the north known as **Primrose Ridge** ❸. Dall sheep are often seen on the higher slopes of Primrose. They have pure white wool – perfect winter camouflage – but in summer, they readily stand out against the green tundra or dark rock formations. Like all wild sheep, Dall are generally found on or near steep cliffs, which are their security, as no predator can match their climbing speed or agility. Wolves and grizzlies can usually only catch weak or injured sheep, or those that have wandered too far from the crags.

The Dall ewes utilize the steepest cliffs in this area as lambing grounds. With luck, you may be able to spot young lambs on the higher slopes. Within a few days of birth, the lambs can match their mother's climbing ability. The lambs spend hours each day playing games of tag, king of the mountain and head-butting, which helps them develop their strength, agility and coordination.

Bands of rams may also be seen in the Primrose Ridge region. Rams are very concerned with the issue of domi-

Dall lambs seem to be born with the ability to climb.

BELOW: two moose exchange views.

nance. A band will establish a pecking order based on the size of their horns, which are their most important status symbol. The older rams have horns of such size that they can easily intimidate the younger ones. Head-butting contests determine which of the mature animals will be dominant. The reward comes during the fall rutting season when the top rams are the ones who get to do most of the mating.

The grizzlies of Sable Pass

By the time you reach **Sable Pass C** at Mile 39 you are surrounded by tundra, which is any area of plant growth above the treeline. Sable Pass has an elevation of 3,900ft (1,188 meters), well above the average local treeline of 2,400ft (730 meters). The cool temperatures and strong winds at these altitudes are too severe for trees. The low-growing tundra vegetation survives by taking advantage of the slightly warmer and less windy micro-environment at ground level.

Sable Pass is prime grizzly country. So many bears use this area that the Park Service has prohibited all off-road

hiking here. Denali Park's total grizzly population is estimated at 200–300 bears. Grizzlies are omnivores: like humans, they eat both meat and vegetation. They would prefer to eat large animals such as moose, caribou, and Dall sheep but they are not often successful as hunters. The tundra vegetation in places like Sable Pass offers a dependable, easily obtainable source of nutrition, while Arctic ground squirrels, nicknamed "bear burritos" by some park naturalists, make up much of the difference. Visitors are frequently treated to an amusing show as grizzlies scramble to capture these rodents.

Grizzly cubs are born in January or February in the mother's hibernation den. The sow gives birth to between one and four cubs – the average is two – weighing about 1lb (200gm) each. Sable Pass is one of the best places in the world for viewing grizzly families. You may see the cubs being nursed, or racing across the tundra, play-fighting with each other. The sow usually drives off her young when they are 2½ years old, when they may weigh 100–150lbs (45–67kg). She then breeds

BELOW: hiker above the Toklat River, Polychrome Pass.

again and gives birth to another litter the following winter.

When it feels threatened, the grizzly is among the most dangerous animals in North America. No visitors have been killed by a grizzly since the park's creation in 1917, and only a few people have been injured in bear attacks here, but these are large, powerful animals that can threaten your life if they are agitated or alarmed by your behavior. Visitors should do everything possible to avoid provoking a bear. Most will steer clear of humans if given the opportunity. The few attacks by bears on people in Denali have almost always been provoked, for instance mothers protecting their cubs from people who approached too closely. Park rangers can give you information on avoiding problems with grizzlies.

Your bus will stop for a rest break at **Polychrome Pass** ❷ at Mile 45. The visually stunning, brightly colored Polychrome cliffs are volcanic rocks formed around 50 million years ago. The spectacular view to the south includes part of the Alaska Range, as well as a vast area of tundra.

Wolf observation

Polychrome Pass is a good place to watch for wolves. A local pack sometimes uses these flats as its hunting grounds, especially in spring when caribou are in migration. The Denali wolves range from white to black but most are gray. They may be traveling alone or in small groups. If a pack is sighted, look for a wolf with its tail in the air. This will be the alpha wolf, the leader of the pack, although he may well be bringing up the rear. The alpha male often delegates the lead position to the beta wolf, his second in command.

In a wolf pack, the only members who normally breed are the alpha male and the alpha female. Their litter is born in the spring and all other members of the pack help to feed the young pups. Feeding a litter of five to 10 pups is a difficult job, even for the entire pack. If all its members tried to breed, the territory could not support the number of offspring. The pack is better served by limiting breeding to the dominant pair, who have proved themselves to be the fittest animals.

Tundra flowers.

BELOW: observing a gray wolf in Denali National Park.

TIP

Picture hints

A walk around the tundra ponds between Eielson and Wonder Lake will turn up many great photo compositions. Lighting on Mount McKinley is best in the early morning or late evening, when it is most likely to be cloud-free.

BELOW: photo opportunity for a moose at Wonder Lake.

Much of what is now known about wolves was discovered by Adolph Murie, a biologist who was assigned to the park in the 1930s: he was the first scientist to extensively study wolf behavior in the field. Much of his observation took place in the Polychrome area (his cabin is located at Mile 43). In 1944, Murie published *The Wolves of Mt McKinley*, one of the great classics of animal behavior. He concluded that wolves, which were preying primarily on the sick and weak Dall sheep, caribou and moose, were a necessary part of the Denali ecosystem because they ultimately helped to keep their prey species in a strong and healthy state.

Caribou country

Caribou, the most social of the large Denali animals, are commonly seen in the Highway Pass area at Mile 58. In the spring, herds of several hundred pass through this area, heading toward their calving grounds to the east. Later in the season, they migrate back, moving toward their wintering grounds in the western and northern sections of the park. The herds are constantly on the move. Even as they feed, they rarely browse for more than a few moments at a time. If they spent too long in one area, they would kill off the fragile tundra vegetation.

Caribou, like moose, have antlers rather than horns. Antlers are formed of bone and are shed every year, while sheep horns consist of keratin, the same material as our fingernails, and are never shed. The caribou bulls' antlers are fully developed by September and are used to fight for harems. These matches usually occur between Highway Pass and Wonder Lake. After their rutting season is over, the antlers drop off; without their massive weight the caribou have a better chance of surviving the winter, a stressful time.

Denali Park is a paradise for watching and photographing wildlife. Binoculars and a telephoto lens will allow you to enjoy the animals from a safe distance and in a way that won't disturb them, or threaten you.

As your bus approaches **Stony Hill Overlook** Ⓔ, Mile 61, be prepared for a spectacular view of Denali. From the

overlook, it is 37 miles (60km) to the summit. On a cloudless day, the crystal-clear Alaskan air makes the mountain appear much closer. After a stop at Stony Hill, the bus will continue 4 miles (6km) to the recently remodeled **Eielson Visitor Center ⑤**. Park rangers here can answer your questions and suggest good hiking routes in the local area. Restrooms, drinking water, maps, and books are available too.

If you are on a shuttle bus that continues on to **Wonder Lake ⑥**, an additional 20 miles (32km) beyond Eielson, this will add about two hours to your day. If the weather is clear, it's well worth the time, particularly in the fall when the color is brightened by reds, oranges, and yellows, and caribou frequent the area. Denali remains in full view along the entire route. On the way, many species of waterfowl are seen in tundra ponds, and in the evening, you can see beavers swimming across.

The park road ends in **Kantishna ⑦**, five miles beyond the turn out for the Wonder Lake campground. Once a thriving mining community, Kantishna's hills are dotted with abandoned mines, cabins, and roads that lead nowhere. Today, there are four independent backcountry lodges that were incorporated into the park when it extended its boundaries in 1980. At the Roadhouse, non-guests are welcome to sidle up to the bar and drink in the pioneer flavor.

Walks and hikes

Most of Denali National Park is a true wilderness, and the best way to experience the park is by getting off the road, even if you go only a quarter mile or so. There are few official trails and these are mainly in the entrance area. Elsewhere, you are on your own. Despite the vast size of the Denali wilderness, route-making is not difficult for those who are experienced with maps. Since most of the park is open tundra, it is easy to choose a destination visually and hike straight to it,

though often the distance is farther than you might expect and the terrain more rugged. You may leave the shuttle bus wherever you choose, hike for a few hours and then catch a later bus anywhere along the road.

Good areas for day hikes include the Savage River, Primrose Ridge, Polychrome and Highway Passes, the Eielson area and Wonder Lake. Before you begin a day-hike, talk to a ranger at one of the visitor centers about safety tips, and ask for a map. Permits are required for overnight trips into the park's backcountry.

National park rangers offer a wide variety of information to help you appreciate the area. Schedules of activities are posted at the Denali Visitor Center and at other locations throughout the park. The award-winning, high-definition film *Heartbeats of Denali* is shown in the Denali Visitor Center's Karstens Theater, and guided walks and half-day hikes are given each day in different sections of the park. ❑

Moose antlers on display in Denali National Park.

RESTAURANTS

229 Parks Restaurant & Tavern
Mile 229.7 Parks Highway
Tel: 683-2567
www.229parks.com
$–$$$$
Housed in an airy timber frame cabin, this casual, yet sophisticated, eatery serves locally grown food with unique creativity and culinary skill. Rabbit stew, seared scallops and rack of elk share the menu with Caesar salad, blue cheese burger, and flat bread pizza. Beer and wine available. Coffee

shop fare served in the morning.

Black Bear Coffee House & Cyber Café
Mile 238.5 Parks Highway
Tel: 683-1656 **$**
Situated on the boardwalk in "Glitter Gulch" just north of the park entrance, this little café offers espresso, beer, wine, sandwiches, and snacks. Internet also available.

McKinley Creekside Café
Mile 224 Parks Highway

Tel: 683-2277
www.mckinleycabins.com **$–$$$**
Open 6am to 10pm daily, this is a great place to stop for an espresso, halibut sandwich, or a hearty dinner of steak or grilled salmon. Enjoy a beer or a glass of wine on the luxurious outside deck.

Price is for dinner excluding tax, tip, and beverages:
$ = under $15
$$ = $15–20
$$$ = $20–30
$$$$ = over $30

THE ALCAN

They said it couldn't be built. But the Alaska–Canada Highway, conceived as a military route in World War II, now runs all the way from Seattle to Delta Junction

Main attractions
DELTA JUNCTION
WHITEHORSE
THE YUKON
BRITISH COLUMBIA

BELOW: more than 18,000 men helped build the highway.

In 1942, while the world was at war, thousands of American soldiers drove bulldozers instead of tanks, as they spent eight months building a 1,500-mile (2,400km) highway from Dawson Creek, British Columbia, to Delta Junction, Alaska, just south of Fairbanks.

Construction of the Alaska–Canada Military Highway (the Alcan) was approved by President Franklin D. Roosevelt after the bombing of Pearl Harbor in 1941. The road linked the contiguous United States to Alaska, then still a territory, and a part of the US that many feared would be the next target. (In a propaganda broadcast, the Japanese forces thanked workers for opening a way for their own troops.)

Construction began in March 1942 and was completed by October. Soldiers battled the untracked wilderness of western Canada and eastern Alaska, along with spring mud, mosquitoes and, in fall, subfreezing temperatures. Rather than following the most direct route, the road linked existing airfields at Canada's Fort St John, Fort Nelson, Watson Lake, and Whitehorse. At the project's peak, more than 11,000 military troops and 7,000 civilians were at work on the highway.

Wildlife viewing

Today, the former military road provides a leisurely and scenic way for visitors to reach Alaska year-round. The Alaska Highway still more or less follows its original path, wiggling its way north-west through British Columbia and the Yukon into Alaska's Interior. But what was once a wilderness adventure road is now a paved highway. The scenery is still breathtaking and the chances of seeing wildlife are good, but continual road improvements have eased many of the dangers that once made driving north to Alaska an ordeal.

Which is not to say the road is a Sunday drive. It's only two lanes wide, often without a center line, and although the entire length is asphalt-

surfaced, sections have to be repaved continually. Drivers should watch for wildlife and construction workers on the road as well as potholes, gravel breaks, and deteriorating shoulders. On the northern section of the highway, frost heaves – the result of the freezing and thawing of the ground – cause the pavement to ripple.

It's a long drive. Towns dot the map along the highway, but stretches of wilderness threaten drivers with tiredness or boredom. And the "towns" are often no more than a collection of houses clustered around a store/gas station/hotel. When accidents occur, particularly in winter, it can be a long time before someone happens along to rescue a stranded or injured driver.

"I survived"

Despite the rigors of the road, more than 100,000 people make the trip every year. In Alaska, you'll often see cars sporting bumper stickers that proclaim "I survived the Alcan Highway." Most make the journey during the summer months – June, July, and August, when the days are long and the weather

poses fewer hazards. From Seattle it's about 2,300 miles (3,700km; including the route along Interstate 5 to Trans-Canada Highway 1 and BC Highway 97 to Dawson Creek) and it takes most people about a week. An excellent guide is the Alaska *Milepost*, a 770-page map book (updated yearly) that documents the Alcan, plus almost every mile of every major highway in the state. ❑

It's a long way to New York... or London...

BELOW: bull moose are a traffic hazard.

FAIRBANKS

Beneath its workaday exterior, Fairbanks is a lively place with a friendly population. It offers the clearest view of the Northern Lights, and the museum at the University of Alaska Fairbanks is one of the best anywhere in the state

On August 26 1901, E.T. Barnette had just been dropped on a high wooded bank along the Chena River, along with 130 tons of equipment. How did this riverboat captain, dog musher and aspiring entrepreneur become marooned in the middle of the Alaska wilderness? The answer has all the ingredients of a true Alaskan adventure tale.

The birth of Fairbanks

Barnette journeyed to the Klondike in 1897, taking what was considered the rich man's route. He sailed from Seattle to St Michael (a coastal community on an island at the mouth of the Yukon River), where he was supposed to catch a sternwheeler to Dawson.

But when he arrived in St Michael, the boat had already departed. Undaunted, Barnette and several others bought a dilapidated sternwheeler, and set off for Dawson. Barnette piloted the craft to Circle and finally arrived in Dawson via dogsled, after freeze-up. He prospered that winter selling much-needed supplies to men in the gold fields, but the Klondike was too tame for the likes of this man.

During the winter of 1901, Barnette returned south to Seattle, and arranged a deal that, he speculated, would make him a rich man. He and a partner purchased $20,000 worth of equipment to outfit a trading post, not in the Klondike but at the half-way point of the trail connecting Valdez, on the coast, with

Eagle, on the Yukon River. Barnette considered this to be a strategically sound location to build what he hoped would become the "Chicago of the North," the industrial hub of the territory. It was at this point that the Valdez-to-Eagle Trail crossed the Tanana River, and he planned to accommodate both overland and river traffic.

Barnette shipped the equipment to St Michael and departed for Circle to purchase a sternwheeler. He arrived in St Michael without incident, but there the sternwheeler struck a submerged

Main attractions
IMMACULATE CONCEPTION CHURCH
ST MATTHEW'S EPISCOPAL CHURCH
OLD FEDERAL COURTHOUSE
EMPRESS THEATER
PIONEER PARK
STERNWHEELER NENANA
MUSEUM OF THE NORTH
UNIVERSITY OF ALASKA FAIRBANKS
GEOPHYSICAL INSTITUTE
CREAMERS FIELD
ESTER
GOLD DREDGE NO. 8

LEFT: prepared for winter. **BELOW:** a global outlook.

The bridge across the Chena.

rock, and the bottom was torn from the boat. At this point, Barnette was more than 1,000 miles (1,600km) from his destination with 260,000lbs (120,000kg) of equipment, including a horse, a quantity of food, no ready cash, and a worthless sternwheeler. It was time for another partner. He convinced the customs agent in St Michael to co-sign notes and made him a full partner.

Barnette struck a deal with the captain of the sternwheeler *Lavelle Young* to take him to Tanacross (Tanana Crossing). The fine print on the contract stated that if the *Lavelle Young* went beyond the point where the Chena joined the Tanana River and could go no farther, Captain E.T. Barnette would then disembark with his entire load of supplies, no matter where they were.

As destiny would have it, the *Lavelle Young* could not float through the Tanana shallows, called Bates Rapids, so the captain steamed up the Chena River, convinced by the increasingly desperate Barnette that it would join up again with the Tanana River. It did not. Captain Barnette had no choice

but to offload his massive pile of gear on a high bank with a good stand of trees. It seemed that his string of bad luck could get no worse.

The new gold rush

Two down-and-out prospectors watched the sternwheeler's progress up the Chena from a hillside, now called Pedro Dome, about 20 miles (32km) north of where Fairbanks is now located. The miners had found some "color" but no major strike, and were faced with the frustration of a 330-mile (530km) round-trip hike back to Circle City to replenish much-needed supplies. The prospectors, Felix Pedro, an Italian immigrant, and Tom Gilmore, eagerly set off for the stranded boat, hoping to purchase necessities.

Barnette was surprised to see the prospectors but pleased to sell them anything they needed. Still possessed by his wild scheme to establish a trading post at Tanacross, Barnette sent to Montana for Frank Cleary, his brother-in-law. Cleary would guard the cache of supplies while Barnette and his wife returned to Seattle to obtain a boat

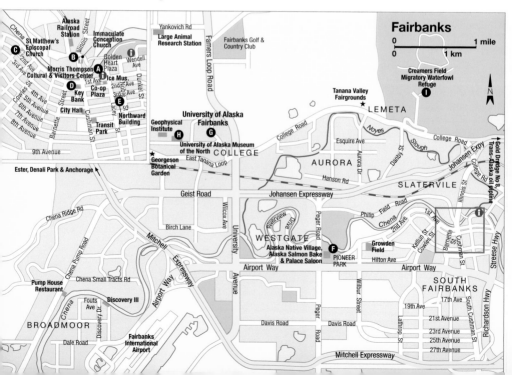

capable of traveling the remaining 200 miles (320km) up the Tanana River to Tanacross. Braving the –40°F (–40°C) temperature, the Barnettes then departed for Valdez and points south in March 1903.

In their absence Cleary decided to outfit Felix Pedro again, on credit this time because Pedro had no collateral. Although this broke Barnette's rule, Cleary's decision proved wise and shaped the future of the Interior. Just three months later, in July 1902, Pedro quietly announced to Cleary that he had struck paydirt.

Learning of the strike upon their return to the Chena camp later that summer, the Barnettes immediately abandoned all thoughts of moving to Tanacross. They had two shiploads of supplies in hand and were on the brink of the next gold rush. Clearly, there was money to be made.

Hundreds of gold-hungry prospectors swarmed out of Circle City, Dawson and Nome, and stampeded to the newest gold fields in the north. By the time they arrived, much of the promising land was already staked, most of it

by "pencil miners" like Barnette who secured the claims only for the purpose of selling them later.

These clever businessmen staked as many as 100 claims of 20 acres (8 hectares) each, thus controlling vast amounts of potentially rich ground. And still the stampede continued.

On the return trip from Seattle, Barnette had spoken with Judge Wickersham about naming his little settlement. The judge offered his support to Barnette if he would use the name "Fairbanks," for Senator Charles Fairbanks of Indiana, who later became Vice President under Teddy Roosevelt; Fairbanks it was.

The community of Fairbanks in 1903 consisted of Barnette's trading post, numerous tents, a few log houses, and wooden sidewalks where the mud was particularly deep. What a fine tribute to the senator from Indiana.

Fairbanks today

Unless you have driven up the Alaska and Richardson or Parks highways, you'll arrive in **Fairbanks** ❸ at the airport. You will have to handle your own

Long and short days
The maximum daylight on June 21 (summer solstice) in Fairbanks is 21 hours, 49 minutes. The sun rises at 1.59am, and sets at 11.48pm. On December 21, the sun rises at 10.59am and sets – just 3 hours and 42 minutes later – at 2.41pm.

BELOW: panning for gold in Fairbanks, tourist-style.

The Immaculate Conception Church.

luggage as there are no porter services. Many hotels offer guests free transport and will send a vehicle if called, and taxis are usually plentiful.

While 31,000 people call Fairbanks home, few people visit the town in winter, unless they absolutely have to; the city's short days and frigid temperatures are hardly a draw; on the winter solstice, Fairbanks gets just three hours and 42 minutes of sunlight. Temperatures plummet to –40°F (–40°C) or even lower for days or weeks at a time, with the average December temperature registering –14°F (–26°C) in the city. A rather unpleasant side effect of temperatures below –20°F (–29°C) is ice fog, which hangs in the still air. The fog results from a temperature inversion trapping ice crystals, smoke and exhaust fumes in a blanket of cold air.

Orientation

To begin your Fairbanks adventure, visit the riverside park, **Golden Heart Plaza**. There you'll find the bronze statue, *The Unknown First Family*, and the attractive new **Morris Thompson Cultural and Visitors' Center** Ⓐ (101

luggage as there are no porter services. Dunkel Street; tel: 459-3700; daily, summer 8am–9pm, winter 8am–5pm). In addition to showing films and hosting art exhibits, the center is home to the Alaska Public Lands Information Center (tel: 459-3730), and the Fairbanks Convention and Visitors Bureau (tel: 456-5774 or 800-327-5774; www.explorefairbanks.com). As well as a comprehensive guide to the Interior and a brochure for a self-guided tour of the town, it offers a useful visitor information line (456-INFO).

A stroll through town

The monument to E.T. Barnette, located near First Avenue and Lacey Street marks the spot where the town was born and is a good starting place for modern-day explorers. Here, too, is the obelisk that marks **Milepost 1,523** of the Alaska Highway. The milepost is hidden behind posing tourists most of the summer. Even with the completion of the Dalton Highway to Prudhoe Bay, Fairbanks has, since World War II, been touted as the end of the highway. Residents like to say this is where the road ends and the wilderness begins.

Ice Sculpting

Competitors in the World Ice Art Championships, held in Fairbanks in March, carve their masterpieces from mammoth blocks of ice cut from ponds. Freezing together blocks, lifted into position by fork-lift trucks, can enable sculptures up to 24ft high (7 meters) high. These can survive for three or four weeks in a park by the Chena River, depending on the weather. *(See also page 251.)*

From May to September, you can view ice carvings at **Fairbanks Ice Museum** (500 Second Avenue; tel: 451-8222; www.icemuseum.com; May–Sept daily 10am–7pm; charge). Located in Lacey Street Theater, built in 1936, the museum features a film chronicling the championships. You can also have your picture taken sitting in an ice chair, and a 20ft (6-meter) ice slide provides a brief thrill.

Turn right across the Cushman Street Bridge pausing for a look at the Chena River. The **Immaculate Conception Church**  stands across the river from the Visitors' Center. The church originally stood on the opposite side of the river at the corner of First and Dunkle. In 1911, Father Francis Monroe decided it should be closer to the hospital on the north side of the Chena. Many Catholics pitched in to move the building across the frozen river. Visitors are welcome to come inside and admire the stained-glass windows and the pressed-tin ceiling paneling.

Half a block north on the opposite side of the street is the ***Fairbanks Daily News Miner*** building at 200 N. Cushman Street. The *News Miner* publishes seven days a week, carrying on a long tradition. Judge Wickersham (the man who originally suggested to Barnette that the town should be called Fairbanks) published the first paper, the *Fairbanks Miner*, on May 9, 1903. All seven copies sold for $5 each, making the first edition one of the most expensive in the world. He used the money to help finance his 1903 expedition to climb Denali (Mount McKinley) – the first group to ever make such an attempt. Wickersham's pioneering group reached an elevation of about 11,000ft (3,350 meters) before being turned back by near-vertical walls and tremendous avalanches.

Recross the Chena River to **St Matthew's Episcopal Church**  at 1029 First Avenue. The altar of St Matthew's was carved from a single piece of wood, but no one is quite sure of the origin of the huge chunk. The stained-glass windows are of special interest; they portray images of Jesus, Mary, and Joseph with Alaskan Native features.

Near the church, at the corner of First and Cushman, is the **Key Bank** , which was started as a First National Bank on that very site in June 1905. "Square Sam" Bonnifield and his brother John founded the bank, now the oldest national bank in Alaska. "Square Sam" was given his nickname because he had been an honest gambler in Circle City, and miners could turn their backs while he was weighing a poke of gold.

Winter and summer
A winter draw is the aurora borealis; Japanese tourists, in particular, have been coming to Fairbanks to watch the spectacular Northern Lights ripple and wave in winter skies. But then there's summer, with the sun lingering for up to 22 hours each day. In July, the average temperature in Fairbanks can be more than 61°F (6°C).

BELOW: winter, when Fairbanks is left to the Alaskans.

Downtown

Head south down Cushman Street, the heart of downtown Fairbanks – although not exactly a fast-throbbing one. The **Old Federal Courthouse** stands near the intersection of Second Avenue and Cushman. When Judge Wickersham officially moved the Federal Court here in 1903, he built the courthouse on this piece of real estate, donated by Barnette, securing the future of the young settlement. The original wooden structure burned down, and the present building was completed in 1934. It included the first elevator in the Interior. Federal offices soon required more space and were relocated, leaving the building open for remodeling into offices and shops.

The next stop is **Co-op Plaza** at 535 Second Avenue. Of 1927 vintage, this building was Captain Lathrop's gift to the people of Fairbanks. Before then, the buildings in Fairbanks were constructed of wood because, it was believed, no other material could withstand the test of a −60°F (−51°C) winter. This concrete affair was originally the **Empress Theater**, with 670 seats and the first pipe organ in the Interior. Locals tend to use "the Co-op" as a meeting place.

During the mid-1970s, while the trans-Alaska oil pipeline was under construction, Second Avenue was the scene of incessant activity, with bars packed at all hours. Workers flew to town during rest periods from remote construction camps, only to spend most of their time (and money) along Second Avenue.

If you carry on down Cushman, you will come to the area known as **The Line**, the block of Fourth Avenue to your right, as far as Barnette Street. The boulevard was lined with small log cabins housing prostitutes, and to ensure that no one unwittingly wandered into this sinful area, the booming city of Fairbanks erected Victorian wooden gates at both ends. The Line is gone now, replaced by less colorful downtown businesses and parking lots.

The Ice Palace

Cross Cushman Street again and continue on Fourth Avenue past Lacey Street. On the next block, bounded by

BELOW: a tribute to the pioneers, *The Unknown First Family*.

Lacey and Noble streets and Third and Fourth avenues, towers the "**Ice Palace**." Officially the **Northward Building** E, it was the first steel-girded skyscraper built in the Interior, and became the inspiration for Edna Ferber's 1958 novel *Ice Palace*. The "palace" in the novel is a modern skyscraper built by a ruthless millionaire named Czar Kennedy. Fairbanks' locals recognized in Czar Kennedy the reflection of a prominent businessman, developer and politician, Captain Austin E. Lathrop.

City shopping

Fairbanks offers a cornucopia of gifts for the traveler. Gold-nugget jewelry, always a favorite, is priced by the pennyweight (dwt) with 20 dwt equal to one troy ounce (1 dwt = 1.555 grams). Remember that nuggets used in jewelry command a premium price, which is higher than that for raw gold.

Native handicrafts from the Interior are also treasured souvenirs. The Authentic Native Handicraft Symbol assures visitors that they are buying the genuine article. Be careful, as counterfeits abound. Favorite items include beaded slippers, beaded mittens and gloves, birch bark baskets, porcupine quill jewelry, and dolls made with fur.

Pioneer Park

Pioneer Park G, a 44-acre (18-hectare) city park at the corner of Airport Way and Peger Road, to the south of the downtown area, is filled with a number of attractions offering a snapshot of life in the "golden heart of Alaska" (tel: 459-1087; www.co.fairbanks.ak.us/Parksand Recreation/PioneerPark; summer daily noon–8pm; free). You can get a shuttle bus to the park from the Visitors' Bureau and from many of the main hotels in town.

The "**Mining Valley**" on the west end of the park exhibits many machines used to extract gold. Sluice boxes, dredge buckets, a stamp mill, and other equipment lend an air of authenticity to the display.

Take a stroll through the **Mining Town** section of the complex, which includes an assortment of original structures rescued from the boomtown period. Every building is a piece of history, including Judge Wicker-

TIP

The fur trade
The Alaskan Interior produces some of the finest lynx, marten, wolverine, fox, and wolf fur in the world. Many people disapprove of buying furs; if you want them, Fairbanks is the place to purchase raw or tanned furs and fur coats, jackets and hats – although you should be aware of customs regulations if you are taking such items out of the United States.

BELOW: barbecue at Pioneer Park.

TIP

Bird's-eye view
A memorable way of
seeing those parts of
Interior Alaska close to
Fairbanks is by taking a
flightseeing trip in an air
taxi, helicopter or hot-air
balloon. Operators
change, but the Fair-
banks Convention and
Visitor Bureau has up-
to-date details of repu-
table firms (www.
explorefairbanks.com).

sham's home, the first frame house in Fairbanks, which was built by the judge in 1904 as a surprise for his wife. It is a rather melancholy reminder of life in early Fairbanks: the bedridden Mrs Wickersham spent most of that summer sleeping in a tent as fresh air was thought to help cure tuberculosis.

Within the park you'll also find the **Alaska Native Village**, with artifacts and demonstrations of crafts still carried out in remote parts of the Interior. Nearby, the **Sternwheeler Nenana** is listed in the National Register of Historic Places because so few of these vessels remain. It is a classic paddlewheeler with a colorful history on the waterways of the Interior. Imagine leaning back in the captain's chair, the stack belching sparks, and the crew scurrying about the deck as you maneuver the craft through the Yukon River.

Even the building that now houses the **Park Office** had a spicy past as a brothel, and the **Gold Rush Town** is packed with small shops containing an interesting array of crafts.

If you get hungry, follow your nose to the **Alaska Salmon Bake** – great value for a tasty Alaskan meal; king salmon, halibut, and ribs are grilled over an open alder fire to give them a very special flavor. After dinner, you could saunter over to the **Palace Saloon** and enjoy a drink while cancan girls entertain you.

University pursuits

The **University of Alaska Fairbanks** ❻ (UAF) is located on a bluff overlooking Fairbanks and the Tanana Valley (take a Red or Blue Line bus from the town center). Established in 1917 as the Alaska Agricultural College and School of Mines, UAF is the main campus for a system that operates four-year satellites in Anchorage and Juneau. An emphasis on high latitude and Alaska research has earned UAF an excellent reputation.

The 2,500-acre (1,000-hectare) campus is a town unto itself, with its own post office, radio and TV stations, a fire department, and the traditional college facilities. A trip to the UAF campus is well worthwhile, and it's also a good opportunity to relax en route at the turnout on Yukon Drive and absorb the view of the Alaska Range. The large marker, with mountain silhouettes and elevations, helps you identify the splendid peaks fringing the southern horizon. It's the best Fairbanks view you'll get of Mount McKinley. Free guided walking tours of the university are offered most days during the summer (tel: 474-7211; www.uaf.edu).

The **University of Alaska Museum of the North** ❽ on the UAF campus is a great idea for visitors to the Interior (907 Yukon Drive; tel: 474-7505; www.uaf.edu/museum; summer daily 9am–9pm, winter Mon–Sat 9am–5pm; charge). The museum is one of the best in the state, combining cultural artifacts, scientific equipment, and displays such as prehistoric objects extricated from the permanently frozen ground. A huge, 36,000-year-old bison carcass found near Fairbanks, preserved in the permafrost, is displayed, complete with skin and flesh.

BELOW: flowers adorn an historic cabin at Pioneer Park.

The Native Cultures displays are an educational introduction to the Athabascan, Eskimo, Aleut and Tlingit cultures. The collections date back to 1926, when the president of the school assigned Otto William Geist the task of amassing Eskimo artifacts. In the summer, there are daily shows on the aurora and Native culture.

Tours are also provided at the **Geophysical Institute** (tel: 474-7558 for tour information or check www.gi.alaska.edu), a world center for arctic and aurora research, during which a spectacular film of the aurora borealis is shown. A free UAF off-campus tour is offered on Yankovich Road about 1 mile (2km) from Ballaine Road at the **Large Animal Research Station** (tel: 474-7207), formerly known as the Musk Ox Farm. These woolly prehistoric creatures graze in research pastures together with moose, reindeer, and caribou.

A wildlife trail

Save a little shoe leather for a very special wildlife trail situated within the city limits of Fairbanks. **Creamers Field ❶** (tel: 459-7307; www.creamers field.org) at 1300 College Road was originally Charles Creamers' dairy farm, started in 1920. The 250 acres (100 hectares) remained in active production until the land was purchased by the state and was set aside as a waterfowl refuge in 1967.

While hiking the nature trails you can see many species of animals, including diving ducks, shorebirds, cranes, foxes, or even a moose. The real show, however, takes place in late April to early May and again in August and September when the sandhill cranes, Canadian honkers, and ducks congregate in the field – it really is something to see. Take a Red Line bus to the trailhead, where the Department of Fish and Game office will provide you with a trail guide.

Wheel into the past

Riverboats have never been far removed from the history of Fairbanks, since E.T. Barnette's load of supplies was put ashore. In 1950 the late Jim and Mary Binkley continued the tradition with river tours aboard a boat made in the

It's safe to approach this grizzly, on display at the University of Alaska Museum.

BELOW: the University of Alaska Fairbanks.

Moose matters
Like caribou, moose
have antlers instead
on horns. They shed
their "racks" following
the fall mating
season, and begin
to re-grow them
in the spring. During
the month of June,
the points on moose
antlers grow over
one-third of an inch
(1cm) – and gain as
much as one pound
(450 grams) in
weight – per day.

BELOW: Discovery
III on the Chena.

Binkley's backyard. Today, the company remains in family hands operating the 700-passenger *Discovery III* for excursions on the Chena and Tanana rivers. The Binkleys' narration brings history to life along the river banks.

The sternwheeler's port of departure is at the end of Discovery Drive, just off Airport Way. Reservations are recommended (1975 Discovery Drive; tel: 479-6673 or 866-479-6673; www.riverboat discovery.com).

Take note of the **Pump House Restaurant**, where you can enjoy grilled Alaskan halibut and a glass of wine after your river tour *(see page 249)*.

Special events in Fairbanks

The winter festival spirit has been revived in Fairbanks and is now called the **Winter Carnival**, celebrated during the second and third weeks of March. Fairbanks has traditionally hosted the **North American Open Sled Dog Championship** at this time. The North American, as locals refer to it, was first run in 1946 and is not to be missed. The sprint race is run on three consecutive days (20 miles/32km the first two days and a tough 30 miles/48km the third day), with the start and finish line in downtown Fairbanks on Second Avenue. It attracts the finest sprint dog mushers, racing teams of up to 20 dogs.

Another sled dog race, not a sprint, is the **Yukon-Quest**, a grueling 1,000-mile (1,600km) race between Whitehorse, Yukon Territory, Canada, and Fairbanks, following the old Gold Rush and mail delivery routes. Held in February, the race, first run in 1984, ends in Fairbanks in odd-numbered years and runs in the opposite direction in even-numbered years. The fastest recorded time, in 2007, was 10 days, 2 hours and 37 minutes.

A full slate of events continues throughout the festival including ice carving. The **Festival of Native Arts** takes place in February at the university's main campus, along with Native-style potlatches.

The Olympics

For those in Fairbanks during July, the **World Eskimo-Indian Olympics** is recommended. The list of games

includes some surprises as well as the expected: the blanket toss competition is fun to watch, as is the Native Baby Contest; the Knuckle Hop, Ear Pulling, and Ear Weight competitions are exactly what they say, and seem excruciatingly painful; and the muktuk-eating contest (muktuk is whale blubber), fish-cutting and seal-skinning competitions are opportunities to learn more about the Native cultures. It is also a rare opportunity for travelers to buy arts and crafts directly from Native artisans – beadwork, baskets, skin garments, masks, and carvings. (*For more, see pages 250–1.*)

Although officially called the **Alaska State Fair** on even years and the **Tanana Valley Fair** on odd years, almost everyone uses the latter name every year. The fair, held at the College Road fairgrounds during the second or third week of August, has grown to be the most popular event in the Interior, with attendances of more than 100,000 people. The prime attraction for travelers is the Harvest Hall filled with colossal vegetables. Here you will see what the long hours of summer daylight can produce in the Interior, including huge radishes and 70lb (32kg) cabbages.

Then there is nature's own special event, the Northern Lights (aurora borealis), which are seen frequently and vividly in and around Fairbanks from late August through early April (when skies are darkest). In winter this extraordinary show can last for hours; in mid-summer the sky is too light for it to be visible.

The fringe

To enjoy a trip back in time, head for the settlement of **Ester**, 7 miles (11km) from Fairbanks off the Parks Highway. To the outsider, Ester is just another faded mining community, but during the summer, the **Malemute Saloon** swings open its doors to vaudeville shows and evening readings of Robert Service. The latter usually silences even those lively *cheechakos* (newcomers to the north) who hang around near the door. The sawdust floor and sourdough bartenders pushing beer across the bar mingle in a frozen moment, and past and present become one as the deep-voiced rendition of Service's *The Shoot-*

TIP

Take to the river
You can get a relaxed view of Fairbanks by hiring a canoe and spending the day paddling around the Chena River. Canoes can be hired for $37–52 a day from Alaska Outdoor Rentals & Guides (Pioneer Park; tel: 457-2453) or 7 Bridges Boats & Bikes (4312 Birch Lane; tel: 479-0751).

Spot the Difference in Golden Days

Felix Pedro, the prospector who hit gold back in 1903, sported a beard, and so does most of the male population during the third week of July when Fairbanks celebrates Golden Days. One event is a Felix Pedro Look-Alike Contest *(pictured right)*, and there is a re-enactment of Pedro's ride into town after he discovered gold in 1902.

His ride is part of the festival's biggest attraction, a parade through downtown Fairbanks complete with antique cars, clowns, and marching bands. Innocents need to be aware of the roving jail, because those not wearing a fund-raising button are liable to be incarcerated for as long as it takes them to bribe the jailkeeper.

Other party events include an E.T. Barnette Look-Alike Contest and a Hairy Legs, Chest, Beard and Mustache Contest. A Rubber Duckie Race offers prizes worth more than $20,000. Spectators buy numbered tickets, after which the Golden Days executive committee drops about 6,000 yellow ducks, each carrying a number, from the Wendell Street Bridge into the Chena River. The numbered ducks float downstream to the finish line at the Golden Heart Plaza.

Golden Days has been described as a politically incorrect blend of Mardi Gras, Halloween and Founders' Day – with a decidedly Alaskan twist.

Hard hats for sale on Steese Highway.

BELOW: gold dredge on Steese Highway.

ing of Dan McGrew rings out. The neighbouring **Ester Gold Camp Restaurant** serves a gourmet camp-style buffet, while Firehouse Theater has daily summertime showings of "The Crown of Light", a Northern Lights slide show put to music.

The gold dredges in the vicinity of Fairbanks, mute since 1966, stand like aging, silent dinosaurs, with necks outstretched, waiting. The dredges, like so many pieces of local history, are strewn about the hills waiting for some new purpose.

The easiest of the dredges to visit from town is **Gold Dredge No. 8**, rusting at Mile 9 Old Steese Highway. The five-deck ship, over 250ft (76 meters) long, displaced 1,065 tons as it plied the gold pay dirt of Goldstream and Engineer creeks. Tours of the dredge are available daily during the summer (tel: 457-6058; www.golddredgeno8.com). The admission fee of $25 includes a chance to try your hand at gold pan-

ning, and for $10 more you are treated to a hearty stew lunch in the historic dining hall. The dredge is only 600ft from the **trans-Alaska oil pipeline** (at Mile 8.4), which parallels the highway above the permafrost-rich ground.

The big ditch

Large-scale mining demands lots of water. J.M. Davidson proposed building an 80-mile (130km) water system to bring water from the Chatanika River to the diggings on Fox, Cleary and Goldstream creeks. A 5,000-kilowatt power plant was erected, as well as six or seven dredges, and shops and camps to maintain the equipment and house the crews.

During construction of the **Davidson Ditch**, sections of the Steese Highway were built to facilitate access. The Ditch was completed in 1930 and was capable of carrying 56,000 gallons (254,500 liters) of water a minute. After the dredges were put to rest, this system continued to generate electricity until the flood of 1967 destroyed it. Remnants of the Ditch are visible in several places along the Steese Highway. ❑

RESTAURANTS AND BARS

Price is for dinner excluding tax, tip, and beverages:
$ = under $15
$$ = $15–20
$$$ = $20–30
$$$$ = over $30

Bakery Restaurant
69 College Road
Tel: 456-8600 **$–$$**
Home-style meals and freshly baked desserts are available in this family-friendly restaurant. Open for breakfast, lunch, and dinner.

Chowder House
206 Eagle Avenue
Tel: 452-2882 **$**
This small eatery is home to some of Fairbanks' most beloved chowder, halibut sandwiches, and delicious milkshakes. Expect a wait at lunch, but as locals will tell you, it is well worth it.

Gambardella's Pasta Bella
706 Second Avenue
Tel: 457-4992
www.gambardellas.com
$–$$$
Southern Italian cuisine, including its famous lasagne, is served indoors on white table-cloths or, in summer, out-side on a garden terrace. Beer and wine.

Lavelle's Bistro
575 First Avenue
Tel: 450-0555
www.lavellesbistro.com
$$$–$$$$
Wine is king here in this sophisticated upscale eatery, but with a full bar, the cocktail crowd will not

go away disappointed. Using produce grown locally, the menu is eclec-tic and includes such popular dishes as filet mignon, bacon wrapped halibut, Chinese potstick-ers, and coconut shrimp. Dinner only; reservations recommended.

Lemon Grass Thai Cuisine
388 Old Chena Pump Road, Ste K
Tel: 456-2200 **$$–$$$**
A local favorite, this res-taurant on the edge of town serves up excellent Thai food made from ingredients grown at nearby farms.

Pike's Landing
4438 Airport Way
Tel: 479-6500
www.pikeslodge.com
$–$$$$
A favorite local restaurant and bar located on the banks of the Chena River. Dine inside on linen-draped tables or out on the deck in the sunshine. Lunch and dinner.

The Pump House Restaurant and Saloon
796 Chena Pump Road
Tel: 479-8452
www.pumphouse.com
$$$–$$$$
Steak and seafood served in large dining rooms in an historic gold-mining building on the banks of the Chena River. Tables on a deck over the water are available, weather permitting. Beer and wine.

Second Story Café
3525 College Road
Tel: 474-9574
www.gullivers-books.com **$**
Upstairs in Fairbanks' largest independent bookstore, this small café, open roughly from 9am–6pm daily, serves soups, salads, and sand-wiches. Vegetarian options always available, as well as to go orders.

Soapy Smith's
543 Second Avenue
Tel: 451-8380 **$$**
Reliable burgers served in family-run café dressed up as pioneer saloon-bar. A Fairbanks classic.

The Turtle Club
Mile 10 Old Steese Highway
Tel: 457-3883
www.alaskanturtle.com
$$–$$$$

Known for delicious, generous servings of prime rib and seafood, fine wine, and friendly service. This busy restaurant, a favorite with locals and visitors, is 10 miles (14km) out of Fairbanks. Bar.

Two Rivers Lodge/ Tuscan Gardens
Mile 16 Chena Hot Springs Road
Tel: 488-6815
www.tworiverslodge.com
$$–$$$$
Located inside a rustic log roadhouse, this outstand-ing restaurant's menu includes steak and sea-food served in a relatively formal setting. Outside, on the deck over the duck pond, inexpensive, casual meals are cooked in a Tuscan brick oven. Bar.

RIGHT: Fairbanks eateries provide great variety.

THE WORLD ESKIMO-INDIAN OLYMPICS

The annual games in Fairbanks may seem pretty whacky, but there's a good reason why the participants are proud of their skills

To those unfamiliar with Alaska Native tradition and lifestyle, the athletic feats performed during the annual World Eskimo-Indian Olympics in Fairbanks each July may seem bizarre. What are those people doing hopping around on their toes and knuckles? And why are they playing tug-o-war with their ears? You won't see conventional events here, such as the pole vault or the 100-meter dash. Instead, be prepared for games of raw strength, endurance, agility, and concentration.

Games of survival

Survival has been the name of the game for Alaska's Native people for thousands of years. It was essential to be disciplined both mentally and physically, to be ready for the unexpected. It was also important to work together for the common good.

The four-man carry, for example, represents the strength needed to haul firewood or moose or caribou carcasses back home. During this game four men hang from a fifth, who walks as far as he can before collapsing. The one- and two-foot high kicks require contestants to jump off the floor and kick a suspended object before landing on the kicking foot. Other events include the blanket toss, fish-cutting competition, and seal-skinning contest.

The games, first held in 1961, bring to life a time when Native people would gather in villages for friendly competitions, storytelling, dancing, and games. The host village provided food and lodging and visitors brought news from the surrounding areas.

TOP: traditional dancing has always been an important aspect of the Eskimo-Indian Olympics, and contestants are lured onto the floor to join spectators during any breaks in the competition. There are also performances by various dance groups.

ABOVE: the ear pull, among the most painful of the games' events, is strictly a game of endurance. Elders say the ability to withstand great pain was necessary for survival. Contestants sit on the floor facing each other with a piece of twine looped over one of their ears. A tug of war begins. If the twine slips from a participant's ear the other contestant wins the round. The winner is the one who wins two out of three rounds. Then there's the toe kick, the Eskimo stick pull, the arm pull, the ear weight...

RIGHT: a woman competes in the one foot high-kick. Native women began participating in the annual games in the 1970s and in 1983 were allowed to enter the punishing "knuckle hop," in which competitors, adopting a push-up position, have to hop forward on their knuckles and toes.

SNOW SCULPTING: AN EPHEMERAL ART

Anchorage is a long way from Fairbanks and the Eskimo-Indian Olympics, but it has its own crowd-pulling event, the annual Fur Rendezvous. Snow sculpting is among its most popular attractions, and holds its own against zany games of snowshoe softball and sled dog races. The finished creations draw hundreds to the display site north of downtown.

Sculptors create their whimsical masterpieces from giant blocks of soft, clean, hard-packed snow. Each block stands 10ft (3 meters) tall and stretches 8ft (2.5 meters) across. Towering lights allow participants to work round the clock during the week preceding the festival. The rules are straightforward: no power tools, props, or extra snow; other than that, almost anything goes.

Unlike ice sculpting, which is more precise and requires greater skill, snow sculpting attracts a wide variety of participants, from scout troops and high-school students to corporate executives – anyone crazy enough to want to spend hours in the cold turning a block of show into a gold rush-era saloon, a trapper's cabin or a replica of The Three Bears.

LEFT: a village elder drums and sings during the games. The drums are made in the traditional style, using animal skin stretched tightly across a wooden frame.

BELOW: a young competitor concentrates hard as he tries to maintain his balance on the greasy pole, one of the events most popular with the games' onlookers.

BELOW RIGHT: a Native woman dances to the infectious beat of the drums during a pause between competitive events.

OVE: spectators often wear elaborate dance costumes, whose terial depends on which part of the state the wearer comes from. ny have intricate bead work.

BEYOND FAIRBANKS

Mining trails, dogsled tracks, and rivers
provided early transportation links connecting
Fairbanks to the surrounding communities,
and with the rest of Alaska

T rails, like the threads of a spider's web, spun into Fairbanks from every direction in the early 1900s. The more popular routes were eventually transformed from dogsled tracks to the roadways that now link the rest of Alaska to Fairbanks, the commercial hub of the Interior.

The first trail-cum-highway in all of Alaska, the **Richardson**, was originally a pack trail between the then-bustling mining settlements of Eagle and Valdez. Following the gold rush, the trail was extended to Fairbanks, linking the Interior to an ice-free port. Today, the Richardson joins with the Alaska Highway for the 98 miles (157km) between Fairbanks and Delta Junction.

North Pole

If you take the Richardson Highway, your first stop may well be 14 miles (22km) southeast of Fairbanks at **North Pole ㉜**, the home, children are delighted to learn, of Santa Claus. Urban renewal forced Santa to move closer to the highway, where he's situated today. He poses year-round for pictures at **Santaland** (tel: 907-488-9123; www.santalandrv.com), a thriving RV park on the Richardson Highway, and one that gives visitors an idea of the enterprising types who homesteaded this area during the 1930s and 1940s.

They were a new wave of pioneers who found Fairbanks too crowded and who didn't mind living in this low-lying basin where winter temperatures are

severe enough for the nickname "North Pole" to stick and become official.

Today, North Pole is home to more than 1,700 people and a surrounding population of 13,000. It has its own utilities, brand-new shopping malls and a large Williams petroleum refinery taking crude from the nearby trans-Alaska pipeline. It is best known as the town where it's Christmas all year, where the **Santa Claus House** (101 St Nicholas Drive) sells every kind of festive item you could dream of, and the post office is swamped with children's

Main attractions
NORTH POLE
EAGLE
NENANA
CENTRAL
CIRCLE
CHENA HOT SPRINGS
AURORA ICE MUSEUM
LIVENGOOD
MANLEY HOT SPRINGS

LEFT: the Northern Lights.
BELOW: Santa checks his mailbox at North Pole.

Beware of collisions.

BELOW RIGHT:
panning for gold in
the Yukon River.

letters in December; it will mail letters "from Santa" for $7.50 or $10.

As surely as there is gold in the hills, there are buffalo and barley in **Delta Junction ㉝**. The **Tanana Valley** is one of the state's largest agricultural areas, with most of the farming centered in the Delta area. Despite the typical Interior winter climate, the valley supports the Delta Barley Project, a state-sponsored attempt to introduce large-scale grain production to the Interior. Although beset by troubles, at 90,000 acres (36,500 hectares), this farming venture, begun in 1978, keeps alive the pioneering spirit.

But what about the buffalo? Although they could be the spirit watchers of the shaggy bison who ranged the Interior millennia ago, this herd was actually imported from Montana and introduced to the area specifically as a game animal. The original 23-member herd now numbers a few hundred. They have even been granted their own large farm but this in no way discourages them from haunting the barley patch. Although the buffalo are rarely seen from the road in summer,

pull over at Mile 241 on the Richardson Highway and scan the country across the Delta River for a glimpse.

Landing up at Eagle

After Delta Junction, the road forks: the southern extension being the Richardson Highway, while the Alaska Highway stretches east. Continue east some 110 miles (175km) to Tetlin Junction and take the rough gravel Taylor Highway for a further 160 miles (255km) and you will come to **Eagle ㉞**, where the road ends (the road closes in winter and snow isolates the community). This is a jumping-off place for Yukon River paddlers, as well as an official stop for river explorers floating from Dawson City. The first city on the American side of the Yukon, Eagle has a post office where river travelers check in with US customs.

Present-day Eagle had its beginnings in 1874 when the far-reaching and powerful Northern Commercial Company (NC) stretched its commercial fingers along the Yukon River and established a trading post near here. With the arrival of prospectors over-

A Town Called Chicken

The Interior town of Chicken, Alaska is located about 100 road miles southwest of Eagle, at Mile 66 of the Taylor Highway. The original inhabitants of the area were Han Kutchin Indians. Following the discovery of gold on (what is now) Upper Chicken Creek in 1886, a settlement was soon established as a hub for miners of the Fortymile Mining District. The residents wanted to name their new town "Ptarmigan," after the plump, ground-dwelling, game bird (now the state bird of Alaska) but were unsure of the spelling. They eventually settled on the more easily spelled "Chicken."

The author Robert Specht brought considerable notoriety to the area with the publication of *Tisha*, in 1984. Based on a true story, the book told of a 19-year-old schoolteacher, Anne Purdy, who traveled to Chicken in 1927, taught the children, married a local Indian man and remained in the community throughout much of her life. The dozen or so buildings of the original town site are listed on the National Register of Historic Places.

Today, the town's 22 residents enjoy lives of quiet isolation, home schooling their children and fur trapping during winters, and panning for gold or working in tourism in summer.

flowing from the 1898 Klondike gold rush at Dawson City, just upriver over the border in Canada, this quiet riverbank was transformed into a brazen mining town of 1,700 people.

Judge James Wickersham built a federal courthouse here in 1900, a major army fort was established, and the Valdez-to-Eagle telegraph line spun out an historic message in 1905 when Roald Amundsen, passing through after his successful expedition into the Northwest Passage, made his announcement to the world from Eagle. By 1910 the gold muckers had vanished, trekking after even richer dreams near Fairbanks. They left behind 178 people, about the same population as today. But the buildings still stand and Eagle has undertaken a program to restore many of its fine older structures.

The Eagle Historical Society (tel: 547-2325; www.eagleak.org) conducts a free walking tour that includes **Judge Wickersham's Courthouse**, built by fines he imposed on gamblers and prostitutes in the rowdy mining town. Inside are the judge's desk and an early map of the country constructed of papier-mâché and moose blood. Also open for inspection is US Army **Fort Egbert**, abandoned in 1911, and the only remaining frontier fort of its type left in the state.

Summer visitors will find the basic necessities – laundry, restaurant, lodging, groceries, gas station, airstrip, and mechanic shop. For those who want to go further "upriver," a daily commercial cruise motors between Eagle and Dawson City. Make reservations in advance with Gray Line of Alaska (tel: 888-452-1737; www.graylinealaska.com), which also offers a package tour of the area. For information on paddling through the Yukon-Charley Rivers National Preserve, contact the National Park Service Visitor Center, just off First Avenue across the airstrip from town (tel: 547-2233; www.nps.gov/yuch).

Railway town

Just over 60 miles (100km) south of Fairbanks, State Highway 3, the **George Parks Highway**, leads you to **Nenana** ㉟. Taken from the Athabascan word Nenashna, Nenana loosely translates as "a good place to camp between two

BELOW: historic boiler in Eagle.

Gold prospector Felix Pedro (left) and partner.

BELOW: the Alaska State Railroad Museum.

rivers," and it's appropriately situated at the confluence of the Tanana and Nenana rivers. Always one of the main river-freighting centers in Alaska, the town changed when the Alaska Railroad was completed in 1923.

The railroad made headlines in 1985 when it was purchased from the US government by the state of Alaska. Shortly after, the station was listed on the National Register of Historic Sites, and now incorporates the **Alaska State Railroad Museum** (tel: 832-5556 year-round, 832-5500 in summer; summer daily 9am–6pm; free). The train still chugs along at about 50mph (80kmh) but it doesn't make scheduled trips.

Nenana is also the terminus port for tug and barge fleets that still service the villages along the Tanana and Yukon rivers, loaded with supplies, fuel and tons of freight. For a closer inspection of an old tug, visit the refurbished *Taku Chief* behind the **Visitor Information Center** on the corner of A Street and Parks Highway.

Nenana is home to the **Nenana Ice Classic**, Alaska's coolest lottery. In an event that could only be held in the land of ice and cabin fever, cash prizes totaling $300,000 are awarded to those who guess the exact time – to the minute – of spring break-up on the Tanana. Break-up is that moment when suddenly there's more water than ice on the river, when massive blocks of ice surge and grind against one another in a spectacular release of winter energy. A tripod frozen into the river and attached by wire to a clock tips over when break-up occurs.

The Tanana River again becomes the focal point a month or so later with **River Daze**, celebrated during the first weekend in June. One event is the raft race down the Tanana from Fairbanks to Nenana, when participants create a variety of floating contraptions and enter them as rafts. Anything goes in this race, providing it floats and utilizes only "natural" power.

Off to the gold fields

To drive the **Steese Highway** northeast of Fairbanks is to travel with the spirits of the old gold prospectors. The road angles to the northeast for 162 miles (260km) before ending at the Yukon

River. Go past the Gold Dredge No. 8 and the viewing point for the trans-Alaska pipeline *(see page 248)*, and you will come first to the community of **Fox** at Mile 11, an early mining encampment which took its name from a nearby creek. The community is best known now for its excellent spring water. The symmetrical piles of gravel surrounding Fox are the dregs of the mighty earth-eating dredges.

Next stop is the **Monument to Felix Pedro** at Mile 17 (27km), a reminder of the Italian immigrant who was the first to strike it rich in these valleys in 1902 – a find that provoked a stampede. Gravel in the creek on the opposite side of the road has shown some "color," so you could practice panning here.

The subsequent 3 miles (5km) of road gradually ascend to **Cleary Summit**, offering a magnificent panoramic view of the Tanana Valley, the White Mountains and the Alaska Range. Back in 1905, the notorious "Blue Parka Bandit" found this encompassing lookout quite handy for his nefarious trade: Charles Hendrickson, engineer-turned-robber and terror of the trails, haunted these granite crags, pinching the pokes of unsuspecting gold miners.

Pioneer camps

Anyone interested in Alaskan gold-rush lore will not want to miss **Fairbanks Creek Road**. Leave the Steese Highway and Cleary Summit and travel south along the ridgeline for 8 miles (13km) to Alder Creek Camp. Beyond this, there's a 1-mile (1.5km) walk to **Meehan**, an abandoned machine-shop area where maintenance was done on mining equipment, and rusted equipment can still be found strewn along the trail.

Fairbanks Creek Camp is an additional 2 miles (3km) below Meehan. Tusks, teeth, and bones of Pleistocene mammals were uncovered here during stripping operations. One famous fossil is a well-preserved baby woolly mammoth found in 1949.

Central's summer influx

The old Circle District is not yet devoid of gold or the miners who search for it. Some of them live in **Central ㊱**, a small mining community strung out

Gamblers gained notoriety in the saloons of the boom-and-bust towns. One who went on to national fame was Tex Richard, 24 years old when he trekked into Circle City in 1895. He later built Madison Square Garden in New York City.

BELOW: the trans-Alaska pipeline.

Chena River State Recreation Area shelters one of the state's most visible moose populations. Other wildlife includes bears, caribou, wolves, wolverines, lynx, and river otters. Hikes of varying length, from one hour to three days, are possible on the park's trails.

along the Steese Highway, "three miles long and one block wide." An active winter population of less than 100 swells to nearly 1,000 during the summer when miners and vacationers return. Since the addition of a permanent school in 1981, more and more "summer people" have stayed on late into fall. Overnight accommodations, camping facilities, and general "pit-stop" services are available in town.

A worthwhile stop is at the **Circle District Historical Society Museum**, located on the highway (tel: 520-1893; summer daily noon–5pm; charge). The museum displays authentic pieces of mining equipment alongside gold nuggets, dogsleds, a period cabin containing genuine artifacts, and examples of some of the hardy alpine wildflowers that are found on Eagle Summit.

Circle

All roads end some place. For the Steese, it's all over at **Circle** ㊲, a tiny community 50 miles (80km) south of the Arctic Circle, poised along a bend in the Yukon River. In gold-rush days Circle had a population of 1,000; today that has dwindled down to about 100.

Once the largest gold-mining town on the Yukon, Circle was nearly abandoned after the gold strikes in the Klondike and Fairbanks areas and little now remains to be seen by visitors. Gone are Jack McQuesten's two-story log store, two dozen saloons, eight dance halls, theaters, and the music hall that earned Circle City the somewhat exaggerated title of the "Paris of the North." In their places reign a modern-day trading post with a motel, a café, a general store, a bar, and a gas station. Rudimentary tourist facilities are geared for summer visitors. Chartered flightseeing trips and boat tours are available, but it's wise to call ahead.

There's usually plenty of waterfront activity in this popular stopping-off place for canoeists and rafters traveling the Yukon River. One popular river trip begins in either Eagle or Circle and terminates at Fort Yukon or farther downstream under the Dalton Highway bridge.

Circle, so named because early miners thought they were camped at the Arctic Circle (although they actually had about another 50 miles/80km to go), still offers some activity. Fishwheels smack the water as they turn in the current, flat-bottomed boats zoom up and down the river, and barges still make their way to points upriver. River travelers could easily miss all of this; the "land" in front of Circle is actually an island concealing another channel of the mighty Yukon.

To get a real feel for the town, wander upriver to the Pioneer Cemetery and look at some of the weathered gravestones of the early settlers.

Chena Hot Springs Resort

Take a right turn at Mile 3 on the Steese Highway and you will go roller-coasting through some stunning countryside on Chena Hot Springs Road. This paved beauty, which is only 56 miles (90km) long, passes through the middle of the 254,000-acre (103,000-hectare) **Chena River State**

BELOW: a cabin at Chena Hot Springs.

Recreation Area *(see margin note, opposite)*, and terminates at the gates to the **Chena Hot Springs Resort** ⸰ (tel: 451-8104 or 800-478-4681; www.chena hotsprings.com).

The closest thermal resort to Fairbanks and the best developed with regard to the comfort of guests, the resort is commercially equipped with all the necessities for extended, year-round visits, and has winter ski trails. The **Aurora Ice Museum** (Dec–Mar, June–Sep 11am–9pm; Oct–Nov, Apr–May 11am–7pm), sculpted from 1,000 tons of ice and snow, has rooms with sleeping bags on ice beds covered with reindeer hide; the temperature averages 28°F (–2°C). Most alluring are the steaming hot-water pools of **Monument Creek Valley**, and the indoor swimming and indoor and outdoor soaking facilities.

Those interested in a cool chance to witness the spectacular Northern Lights may do so during a winter visit to the resort, while soaking in the 110°F (43°C) water of Rock Lake. Or you can hop on one of the resort's large track vehicles and rumble to the top of a nearby ridge for unobstructed views. There's even a yurt for your comfort, complete with tea, cider, and hot chocolate.

Blueberries and black gold

The last of the four major highways in the Interior extending out of Fairbanks (five if you count Chena Hot Springs Road) is the **Elliott Highway**, running northwest, and continuing on to the Dalton Highway. The Elliott branches off the Steese 11 miles (18km) north of Fairbanks and winds through 152 miles (245km) of gold-mining country trimmed with broad valleys, bubbling creeks, blueberries and poppies, homesteads, and mining camps.

The Dalton Highway

Livengood ⸰, near the junction of the Elliott and Dalton highways, once held the "end-of-the-road" position, but the isolated little community was transformed into a pipeline construction camp. Five months of intensive labor, and millions of tons of gravel created a 414-mile (666km) service road paralleling one of the most ambitious projects

An invigorating dip in the outdoor hot springs at Chena Hot Springs Resort.

BELOW: the Aurora Ice Bar serves up martinis in sculpted ice glasses.

ever undertaken in the North American Arctic – the trans-Alaska pipeline.

This service road-cum-state highway, officially called the **Dalton Highway** but often known as the "Haul Road," opened up thousands of acres of wilderness territory that can be explored from the comfort of a vehicle. The road is maintained from Livengood to Prudhoe Bay, and although privately owned vehicles used to be allowed only as far as **Disaster Creek** near Dietrich Camp, about 280 miles (450km) north of Fairbanks and 200 miles (322km) south of the Arctic Ocean, the whole length of the road is now open to the public.

A journey north on the Dalton Highway *(see page 279)*, above the Arctic Circle, through the land of sheep, bears, wolves, and foxes is a challenge. Several tour companies offer excursions to the Arctic Circle and Prudhoe Bay. But if you choose to do it alone, beware. Conditions are hazardous; the roadway is rough and dusty in summer and slippery in winter. Because this is primarily a service road, heavily loaded 18-wheelers rule the route. Automobile towing charges on the highway are expensive, and rental agencies do not allow their cars to be driven on it.

Service station facilities and emergency communications are available at only two locations, the Yukon River Crossing at Mile 56, where you will also find the Yukon Crossing Visitor Center; and Coldfoot at Mile 173.6, shortly before you get to Wiseman. For road conditions, tel: 511 in Alaska or check http://511.alaska.gov.

Manley Hot Springs

If you feel you can do without the extra challenge of driving the Dalton Highway, continue to the left on the Elliott Highway when you get to Livengood. This will take you to the Athabascan village of **Minto** on the Tolovana River, and to **Manley Hot Springs**, a good spot if you feel like pampering yourself.

The resort has now closed, but the hot springs are still open for use, a short walk from a public campground that the local community maintains. Beyond the resort is the little mining center of **Manley**, and this is where the road runs out. ❏

Easy riding.

BELOW: the Dalton Highway will take you beyond the Arctic Circle.

Yukon Villages

Labor-saving devices and the other benefits of modern technology could transform life in the remote Interior. Yet their impact has been slight.

What lies beyond Pedro Dome, Cleary Summit and the White Mountains? What is it that the Chena, the Chatanika and the Tanana rivers are all drawn toward? It is, of course, the Yukon River, flowing north of Fairbanks, and seemingly possessing a magnetic force of its own.

If Fairbanks is the heart of the Interior, the Yukon is a life-supporting artery. Not unlike the pioneers, today's visitors to Fairbanks often feel the urge to soar over the mountain peaks or float with the river current right to its mouth.

Centuries before European explorers spread out over the land, the Yukon River and its many tributaries were a common link in the survival of the nomadic Athabascan tribes living in the Interior. Ironically, the Yukon then provided access to intruders who came up-river in their sternwheelers from St Michael on the Bering Sea to reap the benefits of the fur country and the gold fields.

An unmerciful land

When explorers, missionaries, and fortune hunters penetrated this wilderness in the 19th century, the Athabascans were living as they had for generations, subsisting on salmon, moose or caribou, berries, and water birds. They were survivors in a harsh and unmerciful land, still living a semi-nomadic life, but with the arrival of outsiders, they congregated into small communities for better protection against whatever dangers might present themselves.

Scattered along the Yukon are the Athabascan river villages. Dozens of tiny settlements still exist in this inhospitable land. The historical perspective of each community varies, but, remarkably, they are part of 21st-century Alaska, while paying silent tributes to the Athabascans of the past.

It would be naive to believe that the villages are untouched by the modern world. Conversely, it would be presumptuous to assume that they continue to provide a viable existence due only to space-age technology. Generally, villagers main-

tain a traditional subsistence lifestyle, hunting, fishing, trapping, gardening, and gathering berries. Daily life embraces the rhythm of the seasons, and survival demands adjusting to weather conditions and unpredictable wildlife cycles, just as it has always done, only today, there is the persistent hum of diesel generators in the background. Satellite TV and the internet have arrived, while snowmachines and ATVs (jeep-like vehicles) compete with the traditional dogsled and canoe.

Elementary schools, many containing modern equipment and built in the 1980s when oil dollars began financing the state, are a part of every village, and many villages also offer high school education to their young people. Typical village teenagers, carrying the dreams of their ancestors, often find themselves at a crossroads, both personally and culturally.

The village elders, those keepers of the culture, go on dispensing wisdom. And, while many of the benefits of 21st-century life are enjoyed, village pride seems to have deepened in recent years, as outside influences have pressed into the core of Athabascan strongholds. Almost forgotten dialects now roll easily from the lips of youngsters. Ancient drumbeats and dances are as popular as the latest rock music. The village is a microcosm of contrast, evoking a strong sense of the past as it surges toward the future.   ❑

RIGHT: having fun in a Yukon village.

The Far North

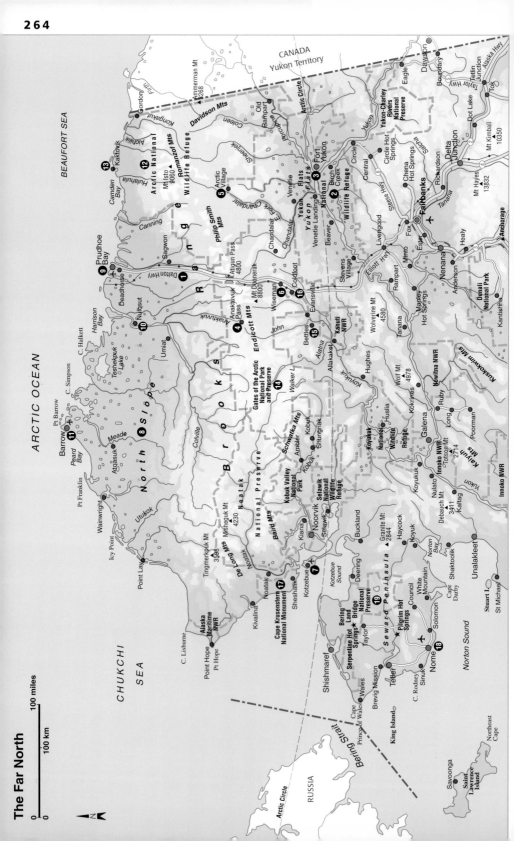

ARCTIC OCEAN

CHUKCHI SEA

BEAUFORT SEA

CANADA
Yukon Territory

RUSSIA

Bering Strait

Norton Sound

Kotzebue Sound

Arctic Circle

0   100 miles
0   100 km

THE FAR NORTH

This vast land of caribou migrations, oil fields, and protected wilderness consists of The Arctic, Gates of the Arctic, Arctic National Wildlife Refuge, Cape Krusenstern, and the Seward Peninsula

W hen people think of Alaska, they're usually not picturing the moss-laden, towering Sitka spruce of Southeast, nor picturesque fishing communities like Cordova or Dillingham, and certainly not the modern high-rise apartment buildings, satellite dishes or trendy shopping malls of Anchorage; they're envisioning vast, desolate stretches of windswept, treeless tundra, pack ice dotted with prowling polar bears, Eskimos venturing out on whale hunts in walrus-skin boats, or perhaps wooden racks perched on the banks of a remote river fish camp – loaded with colorful, dangling strips of drying salmon. They're thinking "land of the midnight sun" or perhaps of endless, dark frigid winters – all of which are accurate descriptions of Alaska's Far North.

But that's by no means a complete list. This northernmost part of the state is, indeed, a place of extremes. It's a land that evokes many strident opinions, yet few visitations. It's a wilderness where self-sufficiency will save your life, while carelessness will surely claim it. It's a treasure trove of scarce and invaluable natural resources for an increasingly needy world, located beneath an incredibly fragile arctic ecosystem that could easily and forever be destroyed.

Diverse regions

Alaska's Far North includes many diverse regions, each with distinct climates, peoples, wildlife, and other distinguishing characteristics, and the resultant lures and liabilities for travelers. The remote **Yukon Flats** area, for example, extends eastward from the Dalton Highway to the Canadian border. The Flats are situated in a marshy area near the Yukon River and its Porcupine and Chandalar river tributaries. The region, not surprisingly, is prime breeding grounds for more than 150 species of birds and important spawning grounds for fish, including

PRECEDING PAGES: planes bring food, parcels, and visitors to remote Arctic villages.
ABOVE: a helicopter hovers over a glacier; watching the ice break up.

three species of salmon. This area is also extremely isolated, expensive to visit, difficult to traverse and, in summer, swarming with thick clouds of mosquitoes.

The glorious and remote mountains of the Brooks Range extend east-west across the wide expanse of northern Alaska. And nestled right in the "heart" of the Range is the stunning **Gates of the Arctic National Park and Preserve**. It's important to note that this Preserve has no roads, no grocery stores, no amenities or services whatsoever – not even medical help.

Yet it is a wilderness historically inhabited by Native Inupiaq Eskimos and Athabascan Indians, and also by trappers and homesteaders, who together add up to a whopping 1 person per every 5,000 acres (2,000 hectares). The Preserve does offer 8 million acres (3.2 million hectares) of pristine wilderness for those who are adequately prepared, self-sufficient and in need of a prolonged ramble, river-run, or climb within a wild, unpeopled land.

Arctic National Wildlife Refuge

East of Gates of the Arctic, between the Dalton Highway and Canada, and north from the Brooks Range to the coastal tundra is much-discussed **Arctic National Wildlife Refuge** (ANWR). The Refuge encompasses traditional subsistence areas and homelands of both the coastal Inupiaq Eskimos and the interior Athabascan Indians. Its arc-

tic and subarctic ecosystems support the greatest variety of plant and animal life in any Park or Refuge in the circumpolar region. Probably the most noted mammals in ANWR are the nearly 200,000 caribou that make up the Porcupine and Central Arctic herds. These herds make yearly migrations from the boreal forests of Interior Alaska and Canada to summer calving grounds in ANWR's coastal plains – the same area thought by many to contain significant quantities of oil and gas. Of the 19 million total acres (7.7 million hectares) of the refuge, it is these 1½ million acres of coastal plains that have spawned national and even international debate on whether to allow oil and gas development in the Refuge, or to preserve it as a wilderness area for future generations.

Farther west along the northern coast of Alaska's Far North is the **North Slope** and the industrial oil facility called **Prudhoe Bay**. Transient oil workers regularly cycle in and out from their homes and families in the more populated areas of Fairbanks, Anchorage, the Kenai Peninsula, or even Texas to their two- or three-week stints on the North Slope. They eat, work, and sleep in the surreal environment of large indoor work stations and housing buildings, which may include a library, gymnasium, cafeteria, and satellite TV.

But the North Slope is considerably more than just Prudhoe Bay. Continued westerly travel along the coastline of the Arctic Ocean leads to the tiny Inupiat community of **Nuiqsut** (population 400) and then the lethally cold **Barrow** (population 4,000), which has the twin distinction of being the largest Eskimo settlement in the world and the northernmost community in North America.

In the western coastal area of the Far North, located just above the Arctic Circle on Kotzebue Sound is the City of **Kotzebue**. A major transportation and services hub for northwestern Alaska, this predominantly Eskimo community of 3,000 residents also serves as the jumping-off point for treks into **Noatak National Preserve**, **Kobuk Valley National Park**, **Bering Land Bridge National Preserve**, and **Cape Krusenstern National Monument**.

And finally, southwest of Kotzebue is the Seward Peninsula and, on the southwest corner of the Peninsula, the city of **Nome**. A resilient town that's endured countless boom-and-bust cycles, the 3,500 residents of Nome seem to just keep coming back for more. It's a frontier community with a colorful history of miners frantically panning the streams and turning over the beaches in search of gold. Visitors still today, in fact, are welcomed to try their hand at panning for gold on the sandy beaches of Nome.

Nome is also a blessed sight for the mushers and dog teams of the grueling 1,150-mile Iditarod Trail Sled Dog Race *(see pages 302–3)*, as the suddenly re-energized teams dash toward the finish line located under Nome's famous burl arch. The race, which takes place every year in March, commemorates a far more sober "race for life," when desperately-needed diphtheria serum was delivered to Nome by dogsled in 1925.

Wild and bewildering

Travelers considering a trip to Alaska's Far North – particularly to the most remote refuges, monuments and preserves – should give the idea the most careful consideration and thoughtful planning. While a regular scheduled airline service is available in the larger communities of Barrow, Kozebue, and Nome, far-flung destinations are generally accessible by floatplane or bush plane alone.

It's a place where all possible contingencies must be carefully planned out in advance. It is a wild, even bewildering locale, unlike any other, featuring polarized extremes of weather, temperatures, daylight, resources, geography, peoples, and even politics. It's the sort of place adventurers often dream of, but are only rarely gifted with the opportunity, skills and tenacity to experience. ❏

LEFT: checking out the trans-Alaska pipeline; whale bones at Barrow.
ABOVE: a brown bear catches his lunch.

THE ARCTIC

The lands north of the Arctic Circle can be grouped into four main areas: the Yukon Flats lowlands just south of the Brooks Range in eastern Alaska; the northwest coast; the Brooks Range; and the North Slope

Alaska
Anchorage

Stretching east-west from the Canadian border to the Bering Sea and north-south from the Arctic Ocean to the Arctic Circle, (66° 33' north latitude), Alaska's vast Arctic region comprises about a quarter of the state's mainland. It's a region characterized by extremes of light and temperature; rural communities of mostly Native inhabitants; vast stretches of wilderness; several of Alaska's wildest parklands and refuges; America's largest oil field – and its largest caribou herds.

Only a small percentage of travelers come this far north; but those who do will find wilderness on a scale unmatched anywhere else in Alaska or the other 49 states. Here too they will find a thriving Inupiat Eskimo culture that balances its centuries-old subsistence lifestyle – including the annual hunt for whales – with modern technology and western culture.

The majority of visitors to this region get here by plane, but each year a few thousand also drive the **Dalton Highway** ❶, the only road into the Arctic that connects with Alaska's statewide highway system (*see page 279*).

The Yukon Flats

Extending from the Canadian border to foothills just east of the Dalton Highway, this is a flat, marshy, lake-dotted area dominated by the northernmost segment of the **Yukon River** and several large tributaries, including the Porcupine and Chandalar rivers. Few visitors come here, both because it is remote and expensive to reach, and because it is difficult to get around; it is also a major mosquito-breeding ground in summer.

The primary recreational activities are boating and fishing, within the **Yukon Flats National Wildlife Refuge** ❷ (tel: 456-0440; http://yukonflats. fws.gov). Encompassing 8.6 million acres (3.5 million hectares) of lowland lakes, streams, and wetlands, the aptly named **Yukon Flats** is best known for

Main attractions
DALTON HIGHWAY
YUKON FLATS NATIONAL
   WILDLIFE REFUGE
FORT YUKON
ANAKTUVUK PASS
ARCTIC VILLAGE
WISEMAN
KOTZEBUE
NORTH SLOPE
PRUDHOE BAY
NUIQSUT
BARROW

LEFT: polar bears prey on seals.
BELOW: ice fishing in Kotzebue.

Athabascan crafts for sale.

BELOW: a remote lodge in the Brooks Range, reached most easily by floatplane.

its avian breeding habitat; the refuge is one of North America's premier waterfowl nesting grounds.

Ducks and geese come here from such varied wintering grounds as Costa Rica, Mexico, and Russia. By summer's end, some 2 million ducks and geese – including one-fifth of the continent's canvasback ducks and large numbers of Canada and white-fronted geese – will prepare to leave the refuge's 40,000 lakes and ponds on southbound migrations. Large numbers of common, Pacific, and red-throated loons are among the 150 species of birds to breed here each year.

Nearly all those birds leave in fall, though 13 species live here year-round, from boreal chickadees to great gray owls, spruce grouse, and ravens.

As might be expected the flats' many rivers are important spawning grounds for fish, including three species of salmon – chinook (or king), chum, and coho – that travel more than a thousand river miles to reach these waters.

The Yukon Flats has some of the continent's greatest annual temperature extremes. In deepest winter, temperatures may drop to –50°F (–45°C)

or even lower for weeks at a time. In such extreme cold, trees may crack and ice shatter, while sounds are carried for miles in the dense, dry air. In summer, by contract, temperatures of up to 100°F (38°C) have been recorded here – the highest temperatures ever noted north of the Arctic Circle.

The region is home to Athabascan Indians, but few communities are located here. The largest, **Fort Yukon ❸**, is located near the confluence of the Yukon and Porcupine rivers. Home to 600 people, mostly Athabascans, Fort Yukon is used as a jumping-off spot by visitors to the Yukon Flats and Arctic National wildlife refuges.

The Brooks Range

Extending east-west across the width of Alaska, the **Brooks Range** is Alaska's northernmost chain of mountains, the farthest-north extension of the Rocky Mountains. More than 700 miles long and up to 200 miles across (1,000 by 320km), the Brooks Range is considered by many to be Alaska's premier alpine wilderness. Within the chain are several distinct groups of peaks, from

the Baird and De Long Mountains in the west, to the Endicott and Schwatka mountains in the central Brooks and the Philip Smith, Romanzof, and Davidson mountains in the east. Here too are several of Alaska's premier conservation units, protecting much of the range's wild lands and wildlife.

Remote and expensive to reach – and therefore visited by few people – this range is relatively subdued by Alaskan standards; its tallest peak, **Mount Isto**, is only 9,060ft (2,761 meters) high and few others reach higher than 6,000ft (1,820 meters). But that is one of its beauties. Wave after wave of mountain ridges can be ascended by adventurers with little or no mountaineering experience. And once upon a ridgeline or mountain top, you can look across a mountain wilderness that seems to go on forever.

That's not to say these mountains are easy to climb; ascents of tundra and bare rock require stamina and good conditioning. And while many of the mountains are rounded domes or sedimentary rocks, several groups within the chain rise precipitously into the sky. The most notable of those are the **Arrigetch Peaks**, in the central Brooks Range. Taken from the Nunamiut Eskimo people, the name for this group of granite spires means "fingers of the hand, extended."

For a mountain chain, the Brooks Range gives a sense of wide-open spaces. In part this is because much of the range is north of the tree line, and ground-hugging tundra plants populate valley bottoms as well as high alpine meadows. But the openness is also accentuated by the broad glacially carved river valleys that cut through the mountains north and south.

Like other portions of the Arctic, the Brooks Range is a place of extremes. Winters are long, cold, and dark. The sun disappears for days to weeks at a time (the farther north you go, the longer the winter night lasts) and temperatures drop to –40°F (–40°C) or even colder for long stretches. Winter's

first snows may arrive in August and the landscape doesn't thaw and begin to "green up" until May or even sometimes June. Summer's short season is marked by weeks of light, low rainfall – much of the Brooks Range qualifies as a desert climate because of its low precipitation – and bursting life.

Summer wildlife

A surprising diversity of wildlife can be found here in summer. Dozens of bird species nest in lowlands and alpine meadows; most avoid the long, harsh winter by migrating long distances each spring and fall but a few – for instance, chickadees, ravens, and ptarmigan – somehow survive year-round. Mammals include the grizzly and black bear, moose, Dall sheep, wolves, foxes, wolverines, porcupines, and caribou. The caribou, as much as grizzlies and wolves, symbolize this northern mountain chain. Hundreds of thousands migrate through the Brooks Range each year on yearly migrations; after wintering on the range's southern fringes, they head north in late winter toward calving grounds on the North

Yukon River
The Yukon is Alaska's longest river, flowing about 2,000 miles (3,200km) from its headwaters near Atlin Lake in northern British Columbia to the Bering Sea. Its entire length was floated in 1883 by Lt. Frederick Schwatka, mostly on a log raft, the "Resolute."

BELOW: Arctic fox cubs.

Canoeing on the Yukon River.

BELOW: a gray wolf in the Noatak National Preserve.

Slope, then return south at summer's end.

Only a handful of human settlements are located here; most of those are along the mountain's fringes and number a few dozen people or less. Most of them are Native communities, of Athabascan or Eskimo origin. One village, **Anaktuvuk Pass ❹**, is deep within the Central Brooks range, at 2,300ft (700 meters) along the Arctic Divide. This is the only remaining settlement of Alaska's Nunamiut people, a tribe of inland Eskimos whose nomadic ancestors followed migratory herds of caribou across the western Arctic. The Nunamiut maintained a semi-nomadic lifestyle deep into the 20th century, following caribou and other game across the landscape in small groups. Not until 1949 did they permanently settle at Anaktuvuk Pass.

About 300 people now live in Anaktuvuk; all but a few are Nunamiut.

Nearly everyone depends on subsistence harvesting – hunting, fishing, trapping, berry picking – to some degree, with caribou at the center of it all. No longer do residents need caribou for tools and shelter, but the animals remain a chief source of food. Some still use caribou parts for clothing: boots, parkas, gloves, and hats.

Arctic Village

Much farther to the east is **Arctic Village ❺**, a community of about 150 people, mostly Athabascan Gwich'in. Like the Nunamiut, the Gwich'in were once a semi-nomadic people. They remain dependent on the Porcupine caribou herd, which numbers more than 130,000 animals and ranges through northeastern Alaska and northwestern Canada.

Both Arctic Village and Anaktuvuk Pass are located within preservation units (the Arctic National Wildlife Refuge and Gates of the Arctic National Park, respectively) and are sometimes visited by Brooks Range adventurers; however, both communities have limited visitor facilities.

The small town of **Wiseman**  represents a third culture: white gold miners. Prospectors were drawn to the area in the early 1900s, but that boom has long passed. Today the town's 20 or so residents are a mix of miners, trappers, and homesteaders who've found a niche along the Middle Fork of the Koyukuk, not far from the Dalton Highway *(see page 279)*.

Much of the Brooks Range wilderness is protected within a series of seldom-visited parks, preserves, and refuges that have few or no traveler facilities: from west to east, these include the **Noatak National Preserve** (tel: 442-3890; www.nps.gov/noat), **Kobuk Valley National Park** (tel: 442-3890; www.nps.gov/kova), **Gates of the Arctic National Park and Preserve** (tel: 694-494; www.nps.gov/gaar; *see pages 286–9 for a more detailed discussion)*, and the **Arctic National Wildlife Refuge** (tel: 456-0250; http://arctic.fws.gov; *see pages 280–5 for more details)*.

Northwest Alaska

At the Arctic's far western end, from lowland flats south of the Brooks Range then north along the mountain chain's western fringes, is an area inhabited by several Inupiat Eskimo communities, the majority of whom still depend on traditional subsistence lifestyles. Several small Inupiat villages are located along the **Kobuk River** just south of the Brooks Range: **Kobuk**, **Shungnak**, **Ambler**, and **Kiana**, to name a few. Other communities are along the coast, from Selawik in the south up to Kivalina and Point Hope.

The landscape is varied, ranging from the tundra-topped hills and mountains of the Brooks Range to lowland forests and wetlands south of the mountains, and coastal marshes and beaches where marine mammals such as walruses and seals haul out. Polar bears roam the offshore sea ice, occasionally coming onto land and whales migrate past the region on seasonal travels.

Crystal clear streams born in the mountains feed the region's largest waterway, the Kobuk River. Nearly 350 miles (560km) long, the Kobuk's headwaters are in the Schwatka Mountains; the river then flows south a short way before turning west, where it eventually empties into Kotzebue Sound. The Kobuk is critically important to the Inupiat, both for transportation and as a source of food: fish, birds, and the caribou that cross the river each year.

The cultural center of Northwest Alaska is **Kotzebue** , a large, predominantly Eskimo community that is served by daily jet service out of Anchorage and Fairbanks. Kotzebue is the headquarters for NANA, one of the regional Native corporations established in 1971 with the passage of the Alaska Native Claims Settlement Act. That act granted Alaskan Natives nearly $1 billion in cash and title to some 44 million acres (18 million hectares) of land. Thirteen Native corporations, formed to manage the sudden wealth, divided up the money and the ground. NANA's share was significant and it is now one of the more successful of the

Boys from Kotzebue.

BELOW: peeling birch bark from a tree, near Ambler.

corporations. Several other business ventures of a more contemporary nature round out NANA's holdings in industries, including mining, oil and tourism. The company is a significant economic force in northwestern Alaska.

In and around Kotzebue

In the heart of downtown Kotzebue, the Park Service's new **Northwest Arctic Heritage** (100 Shore Avenue; tel: 442-3890) will provide visitor services and information for those venturing out into surrounding national parks, monuments and wildlife preserves. The center, scheduled to open in 2010 at the location of the former **NANA Museum of the Arctic**, will also feature interpretive and artist exhibits and a bookstore, and will host Native craft exhibits and dance performances.

To get a little deeper into the Native Inupiat community, take a trip to **LaVonne's Fish Farm** (tel: 276-0976 in winter, 442-6013 in summer; www. fishcamp.org). At this compound of cabins just five miles (8km) from town, you can pick berries, set tradi-

tional Eskimo salmon nets, or observe a nearby reindeer herd. Birdwatching is plentiful, as are native stories, crafts, dancing, and games. LaVonne's offers a rare look into Eskimo life on the Chukchi coast.

Northeast of Kotzebue, NANA also helped develop the **Red Dog Mine**, a world-class zinc mine that provides hundreds of local jobs, transforming the economy of this sparsely populated area. Cominco, a Canadian-based mining concern, has helped to develop the roads and other infrastructure necessary to support the venture. Zinc deposits are expected to last for at least 20 years and recoverable quantities of silver, lead and other minerals are also being mined.

But Kotzebue is still traditional. Fishermen tend nets in Kotzebue Sound and nearby streams. Native walrus, seal, whale, and polar bear hunters still brave the elements in pursuit of their quarries. Kotzebue is a rare combination of the old and the new, and one of the few places where traditional and contemporary lifestyles are blending together in reasonable harmony.

Kotzebue Sound
The Sound took its name from Otto von Kotzebue, who explored the region for Russia in 1818. The city, which has a current population of over 3,000, had been a trading location for Natives for hundreds of years.

BELOW: the NANA Museum of the Arctic.

Parks in the Arctic

Kotzebue is also the jumping-off point for those seeking wilderness adventure in the Noatak National Preserve and the Kobuk Valley National Park *(see page 273 for contact information)*. Also accessible by charter aircraft from Kotzebue are **Cape Krusenstern National Monument** *(see page 290)* and the **Bering Land Bridge National Preserve**. These remote lands were all set aside as part of the 1980 Alaska National Interest Lands Conservation Act.

Charter flights

The distances involved means that there is no easy or inexpensive way to get to these remote parks and preserves. There are no roads. Charter airplanes from Kotzebue, with prices starting at about $200 an hour, are about the only means of access. Check carefully with the National Park Service office in Kotzebue (tel: 442-3890) before you set out: activities such as reindeer herding are allowed to take place on portions of these lands, and if you are planning a wilderness trip to seek peace and soli- tude you won't want to land in the middle of a commercial reindeer drive.

The North Slope

Bush pilots on Alaska's north coast have little use for aerial charts, because there are few usable landmarks that can be depicted on a map to aid a pilot in this world of myriad tiny lakes and meandering rivers. Pilots usually plot their positions by counting the number of rivers crossed from a known starting point. Rivers flow from south to north on the **North Slope** ❽, a vaguely defined but huge chunk of territory that includes everything north of the Brooks Range. Once a pilot locates a particular river by flying east or west, he turns inland toward terrain with more features, the treeless northern side of the mountains about 100 miles (160km) to the south.

There are no roads between communities and distances are great, so most people fly bush planes to get from one place to another; in winter many residents also depend on snowmobiles (and, to a lesser degree, sled dog teams). Fog is a year-round hazard: a 1,500ft

The traditional parka provides good protection against the climate.

BELOW: snow-machining through the sun fog on the North Slope.

TIP

Visiting Prudhoe Bay
Tour companies offer flights to the Prudhoe Bay oilfields, often with a return by bus over 500 miles (800km) of gravel road to Fairbanks. A fixed fee provides a bed for the two-night trip, meals at a North Slope dining facility, and the round-trip airfare. Four-hour tours of the oil-fields round out the arrangement. It is also possible to take a one-day package, flying both ways.

BELOW: oil worker, Prudhoe Bay.

(460-meter) thick cloud of mist blankets the north coast of Alaska for many days of the year. It often stretches inland for about 20 miles (32km), thus hiding the airports of North Slope villages, which are concentrated along the coast.

Stark, trackless beauty and the undisturbed miracles of nature surround you on the North Slope. Almost every stone or fossil is a clue to the varying layers of rock underlying the flat coastal plain, a clue that can lead – and has led – to the discovery of oil. Such clues are zealously guarded by the company that finds them, for finding and developing oil is the name of the game on the North Slope. Initial explorations by geologists are just the first move by the players.

For now Alaska's economy floats on an ocean of black gold, most of it pumped from beneath the tundra on the North Slope. Oil generates about 80 percent of the state government's income and provides a reasonable living for a large transient population of oil-industry workers who commute to and from the Arctic coast.

Prudhoe Bay

Prudhoe Bay ❾ is a working person's world, visited by only a handful of tourists. Several hundred people live and work at the industrial facility – there are no schools, no public roads and few entertainment facilities. The work-day is 12 hours long, seven days a week. The pace, though, is temporary. After two or three weeks on the job, workers fly to Anchorage, Fairbanks or even Dallas, Texas, for a week or sometimes two of vacation. It's not uncommon for a worker on the slope to make $75,000 a year for only 26 actual weeks on the job.

The larger oil companies house and feed their personnel, at no expense to employees. Living quarters may include a library, a gymnasium with an indoor track, weights room, game rooms, and satellite television, but they tend to be quiet places where the workers settle into a routine – and there is little time for more than working, sleeping, and eating.

Visitors to the Prudhoe Bay oilfields are usually impressed by the neatness of the facility and how little the buildings disturb the landscape. The silver slash of the trans-Alaska oil pipeline originates here, then winds south toward the Brooks Range. Seeing all this, you realize that here beats the heart that pumps black gold, the lifeblood of Alaska's contemporary economy.

North Slope Native life

West of Prudhoe Bay and east of Barrow, **Nuiqsut ❿** is geographically placed between oil and tradition. Unlike most northern communities, this Inupiat Eskimo village of 400 residents is several miles inland from the coast, at the apex of the Colville River delta, about 60 miles (100km) from Prudhoe. Inupiat men still hunt whales off the coast (although regulations now strictly limit the number of whales they may take each year), as well as polar bears and seals.

Although most continue to lead a traditional lifestyle of hunting and gathering, a few jobs are available, mostly in government-run organizations. But for those who still venture onto the frozen sea in search of animal food and skins, their safety is less in the hands of chance these days. If they are late returning to their modern frame houses in the village, one quick telephone call launches a helicopter to search the coastline near the delta's mouth.

Barrow

Located to the west and just south of Point Barrow, the northernmost tip of North America, **Barrow** ⓫ is Alaska's largest Eskimo settlement, with about 4,000 residents (most of those Inupiat). It is the headquarters of the Arctic Slope Regional Corporation, a Native corporation formed to manage the huge sums of money and vast tracts of land deeded to Alaska Native groups by the Alaska Native Claims Settlement Act of 1971. When the US Congress approved that legislation, Barrow and other key Native villages in Alaska instantly became corporate centers, modern enclaves of big business in a traditional land. Barrow today stands as the ultimate contrast between tradition and technology.

Skin whaling boats are still used for the spring hunt, while modern aluminum craft are used for the fall hunt, when sea ice is farther from shore, which means that whalers may have to travel greater distances to find whales. Whaling is now very strictly regulated, but captains teach their sons the secrets of harpooning and landing the bowhead whale, more as a means of keeping the culture alive than as a necessary tool of survival.

The opportunity to see an ancient culture and its traditions lure some visitors to Barrow; others come to see the midnight sun, which does not set here from mid-May to early August, and for a chance to stand momentarily on the continent's northern edge – for many visitors the most vivid memory of their Barrow trip.

For winter visitors, the Northern Lights are another attraction, but they are equally apparent in Fairbanks, which is a great deal more accessible than Barrow.

A Native elder in Barrow.

BELOW: a whaling team at Barrow prepares to launch an *umiaq*.

Alaskan Native Eskimo dancers, Kotzebue.

BELOW RIGHT: an Inupiat blanket toss, part of a festival celebrating a successful spring whaling season.

Most people come here as part of a package tour. Travel agencies offer overnight trips to Barrow from Anchorage and Fairbanks for a fee that covers a hotel room, a few local tours and the use of a parka. Contact Alaska Airlines (tel: 800-468-2248; www.alaskaair.com) for details.

The package tours and independent visitors alike stop at **Pepe's North of the Border Restaurant**, Barrow's most famous eatery, which serves typical American-Mexican food (*see listing below*). Others may squeamishly try a bite of muktuk (whale blubber), or perhaps a piece of seal meat. But these local delicacies are available only sporadically and visitors who like to live on the culinary edge may have to search for them.

Inupiat culture

It is unfortunate that most trips to Barrow are so brief. Inupiat culture is varied and ancient, but it is difficult and time-consuming for an outsider to

gain a detailed knowledge of it. And, although English is spoken by most Inupiats (except for the very old), traditional behavior may be confusing and interfere with communication.

For example, Inupiats are not being impolite when they fail to respond immediately to a question or acknowledge a statement. It is simply not their custom to do so, but outsiders may find their long pauses uncomfortable. Saying "thank you" is also not customary: traditionally, Inupiat people will simply return a favor – and expect no thanks from the recipient.

Perhaps the best advice for tourists to Barrow – or any part of the Arctic for that matter – is to assume a slower-paced style of speaking and behaving, a pace more attuned to traditional lifestyles, and to remember that the Inupiat people live not by the clock but by the change of seasons. Changing one's behavior takes a conscious effort, and may be hard at first, but a journey to the Arctic is an unparalleled opportunity to live, albeit briefly, in a different way and experience an unfamiliar culture. ❑

RESTAURANTS

Barrow
Arctic Pizza
125 Upper Apayauq
Street
Tel: 852-4222
$$$
Seafood, steaks and Mexican cuisine for lunch or dinner. Casual, family dining downstairs. Upstairs is a more formal atmosphere with a view of the Arctic Ocean.

Osaka
980 Stevenson Street
Tel: 852-4100
$$
Generous breakfasts and very good sushi are served here.

Pepe's North of the Border Restaurant
1204 Agvik Street
Tel: 852-8200 **$$$**
Popular restaurant serving breakfast, lunch and dinner. Ample portions of Mexican and American dishes.

Kotzebue
Bayside Restaurant
303 Shore Avenue
Tel: 442-3600 **$–$$$**
Open daily for breakfast, lunch, and dinner, this restaurant located in the Bayside Inn features Chinese, American

and Italian cuisine. No alcohol.

Empress Chinese Restaurant
301 Front Street
Tel: 442-4304 **$$**
Open Monday through Saturday for breakfast and lunch, this restaurant offers good value Chinese fare and friendly service. Takeout available.

Price is for dinner excluding tax, tip, and beverages:
$ = under $15
$$ = $15–20
$$$ = $20–30
$$$$ = over $30

The Dalton Highway

Once used solely by truckers serving the pipeline, this remote, unforgiving road is now being used by hunters and anglers.

The only road north of the Arctic Circle to connect with Alaska's highway system, the Dalton Highway – named after James Dalton, an Alaska-born engineer – ties Interior Alaska to the oilfields at Prudhoe Bay. Some 414 miles (666km) long, the Dalton was built in 1974, during the state's oil-boom days, so that trucks could haul supplies to Prudhoe and pipeline construction camps in Alaska's northern reaches. Hence the Dalton's other name: the Haul Road.

Thousands of 18-wheeler rigs still drive the Dalton each year, but they now share it with hunters, anglers, and sightseers. Parts were opened to the public in 1981, but the entire route didn't officially open until 1995. That summer, 6,000 people signed the Bureau of Land Management's (BLM) guest register, a large jump from previous years. Numbers have risen only slightly since then.

That doesn't mean the Dalton has suddenly become an easy drive. It's narrow as highways go, often winding, and has several steep grades where it passes through mountains. Sections may be heavily potholed or washboarded and its coarse gravel is easily kicked up into headlights and windshields by trucks that travel 65 or 70mph (105–112kmh) along some straight sections.

Food and fuel

Besides being tough on vehicles, the road has few visitor facilities. From its start at the Elliott Highway (84 road miles/135km northwest of Fairbanks) to its endpoint at Deadhorse (the small construction community that serves the Prudhoe Bay oilfield workers), there are only three places to get fuel, lodging and food — and two of those are within the first 60 miles/100km (Mile 56, at the Yukon River Crossing Visitor Contact Station and Mile 60.3, the Hot Spot Cafe); the third and last food-and-fuel stop before reaching the end of the road is at Coldfoot, Mile 175.

Drivers are therefore urged to take four-wheel-drive cars or trucks, loaded with extra provisions: reserve gas, spare tires, several engine belts, drinking water, enough clothing to survive an alpine snowstorm (which may occur at any time of year), and food and fuel for two weeks of camping. Because of the road hazards, car-rental companies normally prohibit their vehicles from being taken up the Haul Road.

The great majority of Dalton Highway adventurers travel no farther than the Arctic Circle, at Mile 115.3, most just to be able to say they've been there. A Bureau of Land Management wayside has picnic tables, grills, outhouses, and interpretive displays. There's also a nearby primitive campground. Other designated campgrounds are few and far between; a popular one is the BLM's Marion Creek Campground at Mile 179.7.

Beyond Coldfoot, road traffic diminishes greatly, as the road ascends gradually into the heart of the Brooks Range mountains. Though much of the highway's first 180 miles (290km) is bordered by monotonous lowland forest, here the landscape is grandly, ruggedly beautiful.

At Mile 244.7, the Haul Road tops out at 4,800ft (1,460-meter) Atigun Pass, along the Arctic Divide; it's the highest highway pass in Alaska and conditions may be wintry, even in mid-summer.

For an update on road conditions at any time of the year, telephone 511 (in Alaska) or 866-282-7577; http://511.Alaska.gov.   ❏

RIGHT: the dusty Dalton Highway, built in 1974.

ARCTIC NATIONAL WILDLIFE REFUGE

In Alaska's far northeast corner, the refuge is home to grizzlies, packs of wolves, and a thundering herd of caribou, but you can go days or weeks without seeing another person

Main attractions
BROOKS RANGE
AICHILIK RIVER VALLEY
HULAHULA
KAKTOVIK
FORT YUKON

BELOW: a Porcupine caribou herd migrates.

Drifting off to sleep his first night in the Aichilik River Valley, a backcountry explorer hears, or perhaps imagines, the distant howling of *Canis lupus*. Entering the visitor's dreams, wolves celebrate a successful hunt with wolf song. Several hours later the camper is awakened by the cries of *Homo sapiens*, singing the praises of a glorious Arctic morning. He quickly leaves his tent and joins the rest of his party for breakfast beneath a cloudless cerulean sky. Stirred by breezes that keep mosquitoes away, the

late-summer air is surprisingly warm. By mid-morning the group's thermometer registers 68°F (20°C) in the shade and in sunlight the air is 10–15°F (5.6–8.4°C) warmer.

The party of six – three Bostonians, two Alaskans, one Californian – have been flown into the remote and roadless **Arctic National Wildlife Refuge** ⑫ (tel: 456-0250; http://arctic.fws.gov), in extreme northeastern Alaska. The refuge was established in 1960 as an 8.9-million-acre (3.6 million-hectare) "wildlife range" whose primary intent was to preserve unique wildlife, wilderness, and recreational values. The range was expanded and upgraded to refuge status in 1980. Stretching from Alaska's Interior to the Arctic's North Slope and Beaufort Sea, it protects 19 million acres (7.7 million hectares), 42 percent of which is designated wilderness.

It is home to a remarkable assemblage of birds and mammals, including some of North America's most charismatic animals: grizzly and polar bears, wolves, musk oxen, Dall sheep, moose, golden eagles, and peregrine falcons. But its most famous inhabitants belong to the Porcupine caribou herd, which over the past decade has ranged from 130,000 to 180,000 members.

The oil issue

The Porcupine is North America's only international herd of caribou, with a range that encompasses tens of thousands of square miles in both Canada

and Alaska. But that isn't the herd's only – or chief – claim to fame. Since the early 1980s, it has been at the center of a national debate: whether to allow oil and gas development in the Arctic Refuge's 1½-million-acre (600,000-hectare) coastal plain.

The oil industry and its supporters – including most Alaskans – push hard for oil and gas development, while those desiring a wilderness designation fight just as hard to save the wild landscape, which is a seasonal home for dozens of species that use it for all sorts of activities: denning, breeding, nesting, spawning, hunting, grazing, and calving. During the Bush years the fight often tipped to the side of drilling, but with the election of Barack Obama conservationists can breathe a little bit easier – at least for now.

The caribou have become a symbol of what's at stake, largely because portions of the coastal plain serve as a traditional "core calving area" where caribou cows give birth each spring. It's also where the caribou gather in huge, densely packed crowds from mid-June to mid-July to get some relief from mos-

quitoes and parasitic flies. The largest single group seen by biologists numbered more than 94,000 caribou.

While fierce debates have raged over the Arctic refuge's coastal plain, relatively little attention has been given to the refuge's other 17½ million acres (7 million hectares), though they encompass some of the world's wildest Arctic lands, including the eastern third of the Brooks Range, Alaska's northernmost mountain chain.

The northern foothills

Stretching east–west across the state, the **Brooks Range** is a gently subdued mountain kingdom, with wave after wave of ridgelines and mountain tops – mostly under 5,000ft (1,500 meters) – that can be easily ascended in a day or less by hikers in good physical condition (this is no place for couch potatoes). Dissecting the mountains are wide, U-shaped, north-south trending river valleys that create a sense of wide-open spaces. The **Aichilik River Valley** is one of those.

Rather than backpack or float a river, as most refuge visitors do, this group of

BELOW: a polar bear comes calling.

BELOW: Sierra Club
hikers leave camp
in the wildlife
refuge.

explorers has established a "base camp"
on one of the Aichilik's many gravel
bars; from here they will explore the
surrounding landscape on day hikes.
By setting their four tents on the river's
sand and gravel, the campers avoid
trampling the tundra: such low-impact
practices are especially important in
fragile Arctic ecosystems.

It's equally important, on any Alaska
backcountry trip, to bring gear that can
withstand winter-like storms, which
may occur at almost any time of year,
and to keep a clean camp and store
food away from tents and in such a
way that animals – whether grizzlies or
ground squirrels – aren't likely to get
into it. There are no trees here, so the
group has brought plastic bear proof
food canisters, and build a rock cairn
around them.

Tell-tale signs

This Aichilik River camp is nestled
among the Brooks Range's northern
foothills, within 3 miles (5km) of the
coastal plain. The valley is one of many
corridors used by the Porcupine caribou herd during seasonal migrations
to and from the plain. The caribou
have already moved through, but their
signs are everywhere: hundreds of deep
rutted trails criss-cross the landscape,
thick clumps of caribou hair hang
from willow bushes, and whitened,
sun-bleached bones and antlers lay
scattered on gravel bars, tundra wetlands, and limestone ridges.

Their first morning in the wilds, the
hikers walk to a gray, nameless, cone-
shaped mountain overlooking the
coastal plain. Leaving the river, they
cut across lowland tundra. From a distance, it appears smooth and monotonous, a green rolling carpet spread
between gray and brown hills. Up
close, that monotone green is transformed into a complex mix of grasses,
shrubs, mosses, lichens, and wildflowers. And it's anything but smooth.
They pick their way through a maze of
sedge tussocks, mushroom-shaped
grass mounds that are the stuff of Arctic legend.

Narrow at the base and wide on top,
the tussocks are unstable to walk upon;
any step slightly off center makes them
lean this way or that. It's possible to

walk between the tussocks, but the boggy ground between them quickly soaks boots. There's no easy solution, but at least the day hikers don't have heavy packs to balance.

As the group gradually ascends, the tussocks give way to alpine tundra; this is pleasant, like walking on a dry, spongy cushion. After a stop for lunch – the usual mix of nuts, fruit, cheese, chocolate – on a wind-swept knoll, the three men and three women jump across a clearwater creek, and leave tundra for talus. Forty minutes of strenuous rock-scrambling brings them to the hilltop, where they look upon an immense landscape of lakes, tundra plains, braided rivers, and craggy peaks. It's a wild and ancient land, one that inspires reverence.

An abundance of wildlife

Returning to camp, the visitors spot two golden eagles soaring above the ridge they've just left. Later in the week they will see Dall sheep, red foxes, songbirds, ptarmigan, a couple of caribou – stragglers from the Porcupine herd – and a grizzly bear sow with two cubs. The anglers among them will also catch grayling and Arctic char in the Aichilik's cold waters.

Continued hot weather prompts some members of the group to switch from daytime to evening walk-abouts for their last few days in the refuge; temperatures here may drop 10, 20 or more degrees at night. Their final evening, a pair ascends a 2,500ft (760-meter) limestone hill southwest of camp and are again rewarded with expansive views in all directions. To the north, beyond a series of humpbacked hills, is the undulating coastal plain stretching to the Arctic coast, where earth and sky meet in a white line: the ice-covered Beaufort Sea. To the east, across the Aichilik, are lowland plains, grading gently into tundra-covered knobs.

To the south and west are row after row of rugged ridges, culminating in the snow-capped tops of 8,000- and 9,000ft peaks (2,400–2,700 meters), 30 miles (50km) away. The landscape invites further exploration; the hikers wonder what's over the next pass.

The couple descends as the sun drops behind the mountains. Above

Dressed to cope with the climate.

BELOW: Inupiat crafts made from marine animals including whale bone, walrus ivory, and seal intestines.

Alaska-Speak

Some expressions peculiar to Alaska:
Eskimo ice cream: favorite Eskimo treat traditionally made of whipped berries, fish or moose meat, and seal oil.
kuspuk *(KUS-puk)*: Eskimo woman's parka, made from seal, marmot, rabbit, or ground squirrel skins. The fur of the garment faces inward for warmth. A light, cotton outer garment is worn for cleanliness and to reduce wear.
muktuk *(MUCK-tuck)*; Eskimo delicacy made from the fresh, frozen, boiled or fermented outer skin and attached blubber of whales.
ulu *(OO-loo)*: Eskimo cutting tool, traditionally made from slate and bone. Modern versions, popular as souvenirs, are generally made of stainless steel and wood.
sourdough: someone who has lived in Alaska for many years.

BELOW: rafters
paddle down the
Hulahula River.

the darkening landscape a twilight
glow paints the northern sky yellow,
then orange, and crimson. Even at midnight, in mid-August, it's too bright for
stars. For much of the summer, the sun
never leaves the Arctic sky, though it
may briefly hide behind high peaks.
The pilot arrives on schedule and too
quickly the backcountry visitors are
headed south, back to pavement and
restaurants and hot showers. In seven
days they have seen no other humans.
The solitude and wildness have been a
blessing.

Float trips

One of the most popular ways to
explore the Arctic Refuge is by float
trip. Although hundreds of rivers and
creeks flow out of the mountains, both
north and south, only a few are large
and deep enough to permit easy travel
by raft, canoe, or kayak. These include
the Sheenjek, Coleen, Kongakut, Canning, and Hulahula. Most refuge visitors go on guided trips that last one to
two weeks.

Some trips combine river floating
with overland backpacking; nearly all

allow opportunities for hiking through
the mountains. Contact refuge headquarters in Fairbanks (101 12th Avenue, 99701; tel: 456-0250 or
800-362-4546; http://arctic.fws.gov) for a
list of commercial outfitters and guides
permitted to work here.

The **Hulahula** is the most challenging of the Arctic Refuge's floatable
streams, with a few stretches of Class
III whitewater (on a scale of VI). At
high water, some rapids might even be
graded higher. It therefore isn't a good
stream for unguided beginners, but it's
popular with guided groups.

Born near the Arctic Divide, the
Hulahula is one of the Arctic Refuge's
largest and most heavily used north-
flowing rivers. Fed by remnant glaciers
as well as numerous clearwater tributaries, it passes two of the Brooks
Range's three highest peaks (9,020ft/
2,749-meter Mount Chamberlain and
8,855ft/2,699-meter Mount Michelson)
while flowing 100 miles (160km) to
the sea.

The river was given its name – originally spelled Hoolahoola – by whalers
and was taken from a Hawaiian word

meaning "to dance." Exactly to what dance the whalers referred is unknown but the name stuck.

River-runners who travel the Hulahula, or other north-bound streams, are likely to see Dall sheep, grizzlies, and sometimes wolves while passing through the mountains. Depending on the time of year, floaters may also cross paths with migrating members of the Porcupine caribou herd. Once out on the rolling and swampy coastal plain, rafters and other river travelers may see musk oxen, large prehistoric-like beasts with curved horns and long shaggy coasts. These living relics of the ice age disappeared from Alaska's North Slope in the late 1800s, probably because of human overhunting. Reintroduced to the Arctic Refuge in 1969 and 1970, the species population now numbers in the hundreds.

Most river trips into the refuge are done between early June and mid-July, when the streams are running highest. Even then, rivers don't always have enough water for easy floating. It's sometimes necessary to lift and carry rafts through shallow, riffled sections of rivers. Not only does early summer offer the best river-travel conditions, it also features prime wildlife viewing opportunities, especially on the coastal plain. And mosquito numbers are usually still low, particularly in June.

Getting to the refuge

Nearly all visitors enter the refuge by plane, using air-taxi services. The two most popular jumping-off spots are **Kaktovik ⑬**, an Inupiat Eskimo village along the Beaufort Sea on the refuge's northern border, and **Fort Yukon**, a small, predominantly Athabascan village 140 air miles (225km) from Fairbanks and about 450 miles (720km) from Anchorage. Both Kaktovik and Fort Yukon are served by commercial flights out of Fairbanks.

Once inside the refuge, visitors traveling on their own must be self-sufficient. There are no campgrounds or other facilities and backcountry travelers are expected to practice low-impact camping techniques. Here, as in other parts of the Arctic, it's also wise to come prepared for a wide range of weather conditions.   ❑

BELOW: first you carve your blocks of ice, then you build your igloo.

GATES OF THE ARCTIC

If you hear the call of the wilderness, the Gates of the Arctic may be the place you are looking for, but plan your trip with care, because you really are on your own

Main attractions
ANAKTUVUK PASS
BETTLES
COLDFOOT
WISEMAN
WALKER LAKE

BELOW: hikers head into Anaktuvuk Pass, whose name means "the place of caribou droppings."

In 1929, Robert Marshall, a founder of the Wilderness Society, proposed that most of Alaska north of the Yukon River be preserved as wilderness. His vision wasn't realized, but much of northern Alaska is in fact now so protected; and the place most dear to Marshall, the central Brooks Range, is preserved in **Gates of the Arctic National Park and Preserve ⑭**. In the heart of northern Alaska, the park is 200 miles (320km) northwest of Fairbanks, and 200 miles southeast of Barrow, Alaska's largest Eskimo community.

No maintained roads or trails exist within the park – no phones, TVs, radios, gas stations, restaurants, stores, or hotels. No emergency services are available: no hospitals, first-aid stations, ambulances, police, or fire stations. There is one permanent ranger station at **Anaktuvuk Pass**, a Native village in the middle of the park. Other park staff operate out of Bettles and the Fairbanks headquarters.

The culture of the Nunamiut Inupiat is being documented in the **Simon Paneak Memorial Museum** (Anaktuvak Pass; tel: 907-661-3413; www.co.north-slope.ak.us/nsb/55.htm). Emphasis is put on the importance of the caribou in determining the Nunamiut people's nomadic lifestyle. Local artwork and crafts are on sale.

Outdoor activities

Such wilderness provides freedom from the trappings of civilization – one that only about 2,000 experience each year. In summer, there are opportunities for mountaineering, backpacking, hiking, and camping. The lakes, rivers and streams allow for rafting, canoeing, kayaking, and fishing. Also popular are birding, flightseeing and wildlife viewing.

Fall activities include blueberry and cranberry picking, and hunting for bear, Dall sheep, caribou, moose, ducks, geese, rabbits, and ptarmigan (non-subsistence "sport" hunting can be done only in the preserve). In win-

ter, however, the park is quiet. The sun drops below the horizon in December and doesn't appear again until January. The temperature can fall to as low as –70°F (–57°C). In March and April, as daylight hours again exceed darkness, a few hardy adventurers use the park for cross-country skiing, dog sledding and snowshoeing.

The Gates of the Arctic area is known as "inhabited wilderness." Visitors, floating past a Native fish camp, may see orange-red salmon strips drying on birch poles or a fish net bobbing with the flow of the river. They may even encounter a trapper's secluded log home with a snow-machine outside, traps and a bearskin hanging from the cabin walls. But people are rarely seen. The area's population density is less than one person per 5,000 acres (2,000 hectares).

Gateway to Gates

Gates of the Arctic National Park and Preserve is remote, pristine wilderness. The meaning of "remote" becomes immediately evident when trying to get here. **Bettles ⓯** is the primary gate-

way to Gates. You can take a scheduled flight from Fairbanks to this friendly little outpost, then hire an air taxi to fly into the park. Before going, check in at the park's ranger station and discuss your itinerary with staff. Bettles also provides visitors to Gates with potential outfitters, guides, and a lodge.

From here, any number of trips are possible into the park, but they all cost a lot. If you want to cut costs, it's sensible to travel in a group. A trip for six from Bettles can cost less than half what it costs for two. Compare services to prices and ask for references. Reputable guides will have names of people to contact who have taken their trips.

If you are short of money but have the time and the physical stamina you can backpack the many miles to the park, after driving along the Dalton Highway, built during the creation of the trans-Alaska pipeline *(see page 279)*. Check for road conditions on the Highway by calling 511 (within Alaska, or 866-282 7577; http://511.Alaska.gov).

Fairbanks is also a recommended stop for maps, information and supplies. The **Alaska Public Lands Infor-**

TIP

Be prepared
When you meet a bear in 8 million acres (3.2 million hectares) of this wilderness, you're on your own. People still freeze and starve to death in remote cabins in the Brooks Range wilderness; months may pass before their bodies are found. If you don't arrange for someone to rescue you, no one will. This is self-reliance – or, for the unprepared, suicide.

BELOW: Anaktuvuk Pass, with 300 residents, is the only community within the national park.

Hiding from mosquitoes.

BELOW: caribou bulls cross the Alatna River in the Brooks Range.

mation Center (101 Dunkel Street; tel: 459-3730; www.nps.gov/aplic) has a complete list of air services, commercial services, information books, and maps. Information is also available directly from park headquarters (tel: 692-5494; www.nps.gov/gaar), the Alaska Department of Fish and Game, the Department of Transportation, the Alaska State Troopers, and the State Department of Tourism.

Fairbanks is generally the last stop to shop for supplies, including stove fuel and food. Since all fuel must be flown in, many communities have erratic or non-existent supplies; camp stove fuel is not allowed on scheduled airlines. Villages are often not equipped with facilities for visitors, so travelers should have adequate food supplies and should have arranged return transportation in advance.

The Dalton Highway winds through wild and beautiful wilderness and nears Gates's eastern boundary at **Coldfoot ⑯**, approximately 250 miles (400km) north of Fairbanks. In early September, when the birch leaves are golden in the hills and the weather is sunny and dry, the drive alone is worth the trip – though early winter snowstorms may temporarily block the road in September or even August. A stop at the **Coldfoot Services Truckstop** is a must for any visitor. In the lodge-style dining hall restaurant, meals are eaten on oilcloth-covered tables with wooden benches, mining camp-style. Motel rooms are available.

The National Park Service and other federal agencies jointly operate a summer visitor center at Coldfoot. Another visitor center, the **Arctic Interagency Visitor Center**, is located just north of the Yukon River Bridge (tel: 678-5209; summer daily 10am–10pm).

Trips and trails

The most easily accessed trail into the park is in **Wiseman**, 15 miles (24km) north of Coldfoot. Wiseman is a turn-of-the-20th-century mining community. Its weathered buildings are still home to a few miners. The road from Dalton Highway to Wiseman extends on to several trails that enter the park. The **Nolan-Wiseman Creek Trail** goes through the historic mining area to the

Glacier River. Another approved trail follows the Hammond River north from Wiseman.

One of the most popular areas in Gates is the North Fork of the Koyukuk River, where the peaks, **Frigid Craigs** and **Boreal Mountain**, form "The Gates" for which the park is named. The Gates can be reached either by backpacking out of Anaktuvuk or by floating the North Fork from Summit Lake. Another favored excursion involves flightseeing out of the village of Bettles.

Float trips – and combination backpacking/float trips – can be arranged throughout the park. Or seek fish-filled **Walker Lake**, a blue jewel nestled in the deep forested hills in the southern part of the park. Winter cross-country ski trips, dogsled rides and ice fishing are available here. A few private cabins and lodges are the only places where a visitor can sleep indoors in or near the park.

Sport hunting is allowed only in the park's preserve section, and non-Alaskans must have a guide if they want to hunt for certain big game animals. A guide familiar with local conditions is recommended even if not required. Some game can be taken only by permit. Contact the Alaska Department of Fish and Game for specifics (tel: 465-4190; www.adfg.state.ak.us).

The mosquito menace

As well as being home to grizzlies, wolves and caribou, Gates is also host to hordes of mosquitoes. During certain times of the year – July in particular – wilderness travelers can best endure the ever-present swarm of bugs by keeping their entire body, including their hands, completely covered, and wearing a headnet. Always carry a good mosquito repellent, preferably one with a high DEET concentration, and a finely screened tent.

Another wilderness creature that inhabits Gates is *Giardia lamblia*, a microscopic water organism that causes "beaver fever," an unpleasant intestinal disorder. The best prevention is to boil all drinking water or use chemical disinfectants such as iodine.

July and August are the wettest months. Thunderstorms are common. Rain has been known to start in mid-August and not stop until it turns to snow in September. Temperatures range from –70°F (–57°C) to 92°F (32°C). Snow may fall in any month. The average summer temperature ranges from freezing to 85°F (29°C), prime hypothermia (body-chilling) conditions. Wool or synthetic clothing such as fleece keeps you warm and dry, and high-quality hiking boots are needed in rocky and soggy conditions.

People have drowned sleeping on sandbars; others have found that a gentle stream can become a raging whitewater river after a downpour. Three to 10 days' leeway should be allowed for water level changes if any river or creek crossings are involved. Anyone who wants to visit the Gates of the Arctic needs to do considerable research beforehand: topographical maps are vital, and every problem must be anticipated and planned for. ❏

Portrait of Wiseman
In the 1930s the mining community of Wiseman had a population of 80 men, 22 women and 25 children. Its raw life was vividly captured by Robert Marshall in his book "Arctic Village: A 1930s Portrait of Wiseman, Alaska."

BELOW: a fortified supply hut, known as a *cache*.

CAPE KRUSENSTERN

Alaska
Anchorage

The remote lands of Cape Krusenstern, whose archeological treasures reach back 4,000 years, are only for the self-sufficient and intrepid traveler, but the rewards are great

Main attractions
CAPE KRUSENSTERN
  NATIONAL MONUMENT
KIVALINA
NOATAK
SHESHALIK
KOTLIK LAGOON
KRUSENSTERN LAGOON

BELOW: Eskimo snow goggles dating to AD 50 found on a ridge at Cape Krusenstern.

It's hard to imagine a less likely place for buried treasure. There's nothing particularly conspicuous about **Cape Krusenstern** – no towering mountains, magnificent waterfalls, verdant forests. Only a low, ridged spit with deep furrows, dotted with countless ponds, and bordered by a relentless sea on one side and a large lagoon on the other.

Clipping the waves of the Chukchi Sea, Cape Krusenstern stretches into polar waters in northwestern Alaska just north of Kotzebue. Hidden beneath beach ridges on the cape are archeological treasures dating back at least 4,000 years. This earthbound chronicle of early man in Alaska brought about the establishment in 1980 of the 560,000-acre (226,600-hectare) **Cape Krusenstern National Monument** ⑰ (tel: 442-3890, or 442-3760 in summer only; www.nps.gov/cakr).

Charter planes and boats headquartered in **Kotzebue** take infrequent visitors to the monument, 10 miles (16km) northwest across Kotzebue Sound at its southern border. The monument lacks visitor services and receives only a few thousand visitors a year.

Remote villages

The small village of **Kivalina** stretches out along the Chukchi shore north of the monument and to the east of Krusenstern, across the Mulgrave Hills, lies the village of **Noatak**. Kivalina and Noatak have airstrips but most visitors arrive via Kotzebue, which has a regular jet service from both Anchorage and Fairbanks.

Cape Krusenstern is a bring-your-own-shelter place, and that goes for stove, food and water. Highlands beyond the beaches have freshwater streams, but it's still best to take some – and either boil or treat any local water you do use, to prevent the risk of giardia. The Krusenstern tableau is waiting, but come prepared to be self-sustaining. Planes can land on some beaches of the monument, and float-

planes put down on nearby lagoons. Many beach areas are privately owned; visitors should check with monument headquarters staff in Kotzebue for specific locations of private property, as they are not marked. Travelers are free to explore archeological zones, but no digging for artifacts or causing other disturbances are allowed.

Winds sweep almost constantly across the lowlands of Cape Krusenstern. In winter they bring instant freezing to an already cold land. In summer, fog blankets coastal areas, although temperatures are 40–65°F (4–18°C). Inland, the skies are often clear in June and July, but visitors should always carry rain gear and be alert for hypothermia.

Formation of the cape

The cape at Krusenstern didn't always exist. About 10,000 years ago, the coastline angled straight southeast from Point Hope, skirted a small mountain, and turned east. Kotzebue Sound was mostly a giant sandy lowland, not the open waterway it is today. During the Pleistocene Era, from approximately 2 million to 10,000–15,000 years ago, great ice sheets covered much of the northern hemisphere. These ice masses absorbed water, causing the sea level to recede. As the sea shrank away from the shore, it exposed a land bridge connecting North America and Asia. When the ice sheets melted, the sea level rose once again and covered the so-called Bering Land Bridge.

Sweeping down the newly aligned coastline, prevailing winds from the northwest propelled waves, which carried bits of gravel in their churning surf, down the beach. When the waves hit the turn where the coastline swung east, they dropped the gravel offshore. Every so often, usually in the spring, the winds shifted to the southwest. Great chunks of ice were driven onshore, but not before the ice scooped up gravel from shallow offshore beds and deposited it on the beach beyond the surf. Ridge after ridge built up on the outer shore of the cape.

Slowly the cape pushed seaward. Hardy beach plants colonized the ridges, their root systems helping to stabilize the gravels. Year after year the

Mineral wealth
A road to the Red Dog Mine crosses the northern boundary of Cape Krusenstern National Monument. Trucks haul zinc from open pit mines to a tidewater port. Cominco Alaska operates the mine, along with the NANA Regional Corp., a Native corporation based in Kotzebue.

BELOW: a lake at Cape Krusenstern National Monument.

An Inupiat woman making parka hood ruffs from wolf skins.

BELOW: a seal hunter on the Cape.

birth and death of beach plants built up a thin layer of soil, creating suitable habitat for other plants. Over the centuries, a carpet of green followed the shoreline, advancing seaward, until 114 ridges lined an approximately 3-mile (5km) wide spit. Lt Otto von Kotzebue, sailing with the Imperial Russian Navy, gave geographical recognition to the cape by naming it Krusenstern after the first Russian admiral to circumnavigate the globe in 1803–4.

The Old Whalers

Every once in a while the continuity of the archeological record was broken when scientists unearthed artifacts from a culture that did not fit in to the spectrum of early man in northwestern Alaska.

One such find was the record of Old Whalers on the beach ridge inland from the Choris remains. These prehistoric people, who lived for a brief time at the cape sometime between 1800 and 1500 BC, relied almost exclusively on the sea for sustenance. Their record indicates a greater use of whales than either preceding or subsequent cultures.

The cape today

Each spring, the rivers and streams of Kotzebue basin cleanse themselves when snow melt fills the channels which dump their load into Kotzebue Sound. Whitefish join this migration, leaving their inland wintering grounds and moving into summer feeding areas in coastal estuaries. This annual flooding acts as a catalyst for one of the region's major subsistence hauls.

As the floodwaters fan out into Kotzebue Sound, several species of whitefish swarm into sloughs along the Krusenstern coast, fattening throughout the summer in the brackish waters. Local residents congregate at the sloughs each fall when groundswells from the Chukchi Sea push gravel and sand across the channels by which whitefish exit the salt-water areas on their return migration. Residents harvest the fish trapped in the sloughs, to add to their winter staples.

Travelers should take extra care not to disturb fishing nets, boats or other gear on which local residents rely.

Also crucial is the 6-mile (10km) flatland at the monument's southern

tip, **Sheshalik**, "Place of White Whales." Several families maintain year-round homes at Sheshalik, which is a traditional gathering place for hunters of beluga, the small, white, toothed whale. Life in the community revolves around stockpiling the meat, fish, berries, and greenstuff that see these families through nine months of harsh winter.

Kotlik and Krusenstern Lagoons

For centuries, hunters have gathered at **sealing points** on the narrow isthmus separating the Chukchi from these inner lagoons. Returning, their boats loaded with sea mammal carcasses, the hunters portage the isthmus and continue their southerly journey over calm lagoon waters rather than fighting the waves of the open sea.

In May, waterfowl return from their winter sojourn and head for Krusenstern where snow melt has weakened the ice and open water spreads early throughout the lagoons. Several species of geese and ducks nest on the ponds, joined by their cousins on stilts, the sandhill cranes.

Later in the summer residents harvest salmonberries, cranberries, and blueberries. Women pick greens, preserving some in seal oil for later use. Fish are hung to dry on wooden racks. Chum salmon are taken for subsistence as well as for the commercial fishery in Kotzebue Sound.

Hunting territory

After waterfowl leave in the fall, hunters turn to caribou, ptarmigan, and sometimes walrus or – rarely nowadays – bear. Both black and brown bears have been found on the cape; polar bears roam offshore ice in winter and spring and occasionally come ashore.

Agile Arctic foxes follow behind these northern barons, ready to inspect any tidbit they leave behind. Onshore, elusive fur-bearers – wolves, wolverines, red foxes, lynx, mink, weasels, snowshoe, and tundra hare, and Arctic ground squirrels – patrol the tundra.

Hunters take moose in low-lying areas or Dall sheep in the Igichuk Hills. A small group of musk ox, descendants of the shaggy mammals which once roamed all arctic North America but were wiped out by hunters in Alaska in the mid-1800s, thunder across the tundra of the Mulgrave Hills.

Other species, generally not part of the subsistence catch, share Krusenstern's bounty. Birds such as the lesser golden-plovers, sandpipers, whimbrels, Lapland longspurs, and Savannah sparrows add their beauty and song. Arctic and Aleutian terns float gracefully above the tundra, ready to defend their nests from the purposeful forays of glaucous gulls and jaegers. An Asian migrant, the handsome yellow wagtail, builds its nest in tiny cavities in the beach ridges. Overhead, rough-legged hawks soar from their nests in the highlands to hover over the tundra.

The ambiance at Krusenstern is understated, but for the curious and the thorough, the history of early man in the north and its modern translation in the subsistence world of local residents are only a step away.   ❏

More than 10 million ducks, swans, and geese nest in Alaska.

BELOW: an Eskimo examines the remains of a whale as they dry out.

NATIVE ART AND ARTIFACTS

Items which once had specific purposes are now highly prized as tourist souvenirs, although to the Native people their traditional cultural values are still important

In early times, all Alaska Native art served a definite purpose. The items created had either a practical or a cultural use. For instance, carvers created masks for ceremonies, totem poles to tell the histories of clans, and Chilkat blankets for special dancing, or to present as tokens of esteem.

These days, although much Native art continues to serve traditional purposes, many objects are sold into private hands. Dance fans and masks, for example, are still used in ceremonies today, but they are regularly sold as souvenirs. Often, these sales are a welcome source of income for the villages. Visitors to Alaska eagerly seek ivory scrimshaw, carvings of bone, wood, and stone, and baskets woven with colorful grasses or formed from birch bark.

Regional differences

Natives from different parts of Alaska excel in various types of art. Doll making has been an Eskimo art form for at least 2,000 years. The Athabascans are known for colorful beadwork, usually flowers created on tanned moose hide, and incorporating porcupine quills and buttons. The Aleuts are masters at making tightly woven grass baskets, decorated with multicolored embroidery. Some baskets can take up to 15 hours an inch to complete. Southeast tribes are known for their blankets and totem poles.

ABOVE: this totemic symbol is a detail from a pole in the popular Sitka National Historic Park. It is typical of the traditional designs used by the Tlingit people when carving their ceremonial masks, rattles and everyday utensils, each with its own story to tell.

BELOW: these Yup'ik dolls have faces of moose skin and miniature parkas with wolverine ruffs and beaver mitts.

ABOVE: Chilkat blankets can take over a yea to make, and were once highly sought after Native nobility. Each told a legend and was u for a special occasion: to cover a body lying in state, or as a gift to an honored guest.

TEM POLES: LEGENDS IN WOOD

Totem poles, some as high as 60ft (18 meters) tall, are one of the most popular examples of Northwest Native woodworking. Figures, or totems, on the poles are comparable to family crests and are used to tell a story, legend or event. The totemic symbols are usually animals, such as bears, eagles or killer whales. Their significance lies in myth – stories passed down through generations about how certain animals may have affected the destiny of ancestors.

Poles could usually be found clustered along the village's shore in front of clan houses or directly on the fronts of private houses, or in meteries. According to early accounts of Tlingit life, deceased clan members were cremated and their les placed in these poles.

Missionaries and other outsiders contributed to the destruction and neglect of many totem poles. ce the 1930s, many have been restored, some of which now stand in totem parks near villages Klawock and Saxman and at the Totem Heritage Center in Ketchikan.

LEFT: this Native house in Sitka has been covered with numerous yellow cedar plaques, all carved and painted with different Tlingit designs. The distinctive style relies heavily on the portrayal of birds, animals and fish, often in a highly stylized way. The Tlingit people's carving skills were also turned to practical use in making eating utensils and large canoes.

BELOW: the Oomingmak Co-Op in Anchorage is decorated with this musk ox mural and is a good place to buy articles made from the fine, soft musk ox wool called qiviut. Today's musk oxen are of the Greenland sub-species. The native animals were hunted to extinction by 1860; forming defensive circles to protect their young had been effective against wolves, but not against guns.

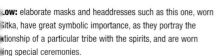

OW: elaborate masks and headdresses such as this one, worn itka, have great symbolic importance, as they portray the tionship of a particular tribe with the spirits, and are worn ing special ceremonies.

NOME AND THE SEWARD PENINSULA

Once a Wild West gold mining boom town, Nome is now best known as the end of the Iditarod Trail and the Seward Peninsula's commercial hub

BELOW: displays in Nome's oldest saloon, the Board of Trade.

This remote community has long been known as the city that wouldn't die, although it has had more than enough reason to disappear many times since its founding in 1899. **Nome** ⑱ has been burned to the ground; pounded by relentless gales; attacked by flu, diphtheria and countless other maladies; and almost starved out of existence, yet its population has always rebuilt and struggled on. Nowadays, this one-time boom town is best known for its connection to the Iditarod Trail Sled Dog Race; and it's the commercial center of the Seward Peninsula, whose wind-whipped tundra landscape was first inhabited thousands of years ago by peoples migrating from Asia into northwest Alaska.

It was gold, discovered in 1898, that brought men, and later women, to this windswept, wave-battered beach on the Seward Peninsula, 75 miles (120km) or more from the nearest tree. Of all the Alaska gold-rush towns, Nome was the largest and the rowdiest. Best estimates put the population in excess of 20,000 people by the summer of 1900, but nobody knows for sure.

By the time gold-bearing creeks around the area were discovered, claim jumping and other less-than-ethical mining practices were well advanced in Alaska. Claim-jumping was so rampant that it took a dozen years or more before everything was straightened out. By then the boom was dying and Nome had little more than 5,000 residents. Over the years the permanent population has shrunk as low as 500. It has more or less stabilized in recent years at about 3,500 residents.

Precious beaches

Nome hosted a whole series of gold rushes, each almost blending into the next. The first gold came the traditional way – it was found in the streams flowing into Norton Sound. The thousands of prospectors who rushed to Nome set their tents on the beach and explored the nearby gullies, not realiz-

ing that all they had to do was sift the sand that was their floor for the precious yellow metal.

The famed black-sand beaches of Nome count as the "second" gold rush. Since nobody could legally stake a claim on the beach, a man could work any ground he could stand on near the shoreline. The sands were turned over dozens of times and yielded millions of dollars in gold.

Then geologists pointed out that Nome had more than one beach. Over the centuries, as rivers carried silt away to the ocean, the beach line had gradually extended out to sea. The geologists predicted that under the tundra a few yards back from the water, miners would find an ancient beach and, with it, more deposits of gold. And so it was that later years saw yet a third gold rush as ground behind the sea wall was dug and re-dug to extract the precious metal.

Fortune seekers still sift the sands in front of Nome. In 1984 a Nome resident walking on the beach picked up a gold nugget weighing over an ounce from under a piece of driftwood. Such are the rewards of fresh air and exercise. The beach at Nome is still open to the public. Anyone with a gold pan or a sluice box can search for gold along the waterfront, and camping is permitted. If you're serious about finding more than a trace of gold, it's hard, back-breaking work, but then riches have never come easy for miners. Perhaps the only ones who found easy money were the gamblers and the tricksters who made their living relieving miners of their hard-earned gold.

Wyatt Earp visits

Some shifty characters who learned their crafts in the boom towns of America's Wild West converged on Nome as practiced, professional con-artists – men like Wyatt Earp, the frontier marshal, who arrived in Nome as a paunchy, 51-year-old saloon keeper.

Yet Nome's gold-rush years spawned a hero or two amid the unscrupulous. Shortly after Wyatt Earp arrived, a family named Doolittle moved to the town. One of the boys, Jimmy, delivered newspapers for the Nome Nugget, the oldest continually published news-

Pizza to go
Residents of Nome enjoy the luxury of hot, gourmet pizza delivered to their door. Those living in remote villages can also order the same pizza to be delivered via airplane. Airport Pizza, located near Nome airport, bakes and sells the pizza, and Bering Air Operations delivers it to the local air strip – not piping hot, but free of charge. (See listing, page 301.)

BELOW: Unalakleet, a Native village on the Norton Sound of the Bering Sea.

paper in Alaska. Young Jimmy grew up to lead "Doolittle's Raiders," the daring group of army pilots who launched their over-sized, overloaded bombers from the decks of a Navy aircraft carrier in the darkest days of World War II.

Energetic celebrations

The ability to face all comers, whatever the odds, is what makes Nome the rollicking place it is today. Nomites bring a special energy to every project they take on.

Tourists pan for gold.

The **Midnight Sun Festival** is a good example. Held on the weekend closest to the solstice (June 21), the two-day festival includes a late-night softball tournament, a street dance, a chicken barbecue, foodstalls (selling reindeer hot dogs and cotton candy), and a darts tournament. The **Nome River Raft Race** is part of the Midnight Sun Festival, and its only rule seems to be that there are no rules.

Less than two weeks later, Nome gets ready to party again with the 4th of July celebration. This event includes street games, a raffle, free ice cream (provided by the fire department) and

BELOW RIGHT: the Bering Sea Ice Golf Classic.

the **Anvil Mountain Run**. Participants are required to run up the mountain on the road, but are allowed to take any path they want on the way down; the tundra is a shorter route, but it's not as smooth going.

As with most civic celebrations, each event has its own parade. There are hardly any spectators because most of the local residents are in the parade. And what would the 4th of July be without fireworks? In the early 1980s Nome's city council wanted to stop such devices being sold within the city limits because of the fire hazard. This particularly affected the mayor of the time, as he was one of the largest fireworks dealers in the area. He solved the problem by setting up his firework stand a few steps outside the city line and gleefully sold all manner of pyrotechnics to the people, who were more than willing to use them.

There are advantages to living in a remote frontier town. Nome is a close community, with almost anyone available to lend a hand. Consider Christmas. Christmas trees are traditional decorations in local homes just as else-

Seward Peninsula Road Trips

Though travel to Nome must be by air or sea, the area boasts the second-largest city road system in the state. Three unmaintained gravel roads extend for a total of 300 miles (480km) across broad regions of the southwest portion of the Seward Peninsula.

These roads allow visitors opportunities – uncommon in remote bush communities – to drive or bike past small, outlying Native villages or through prime birding or wildlife-sighting areas. The visitor center (tel: 443-6624; www.nomealaska.org/vc) provides a road guide and a list of businesses offering car rentals. Check with the Alaska Department of Fish and Game (tel: 465-4190) for local information on roadside fishing or wildlife-viewing opportunities.

There are no services available along any of these remote roadways, so be sure to bring along adequate fuel, food, a spare tire and bug repellent. Current weather and driving conditions for any Alaska roadway are available from the Alaska Department of Transportation and Public Facilities by dialing 511; 866-282-7577; or online at http://511.alaska.gov.

In Alaska as a whole, only one-third of the 300 or so communities are located on the road system. Travel to the others, as well as deliveries of goods and tourists, must generally be via boat, airplane, all-terrain vehicle, and/or snow-machine.

where in the United States. The problem with this arises because the last ship of the season usually departs in October, just before Norton Sound freezes. Trees can be flown in, but that's expensive.

However, about 80 miles (130km) to the east is a convenient (at least by rural Alaska standards) forest, and in the weeks before Christmas residents band together and dispatch truck loads of volunteers along a bone-crunching road leading to the forest. The trucks are then filled with small spruce trees, enough to ensure that every household gets one. These aren't the magnificent Douglas firs that are favored in the Lower 48. Instead, they're straggly tundra spruces, but they fit the bill.

After the holidays, residents take their old trees out to "Nome National Forest" – a stretch of ice outside town – and "plant" them.

The Great Race

After Christmas, there's one more high point in the long winter, the combined **Spring Carnival** and **Iditarod Trail Sled Dog Race**, billed as "The Last Great Race on Earth" (*see pages 302–3*).

Also in March is the **Bering Sea Ice Golf Classic**. Participants, dressed in wacky outfits, play on artificial grass on top of the ice, next to the "Nome National Forest."

Today Nome is the transportation hub of western Alaska. It has a major airport with jet service to and from Anchorage, Fairbanks, and Kotzebue, and provides commuter plane service to every village in the region. Almost everyone touring northwestern Alaska must at least pass through Nome.

A small museum, the **Carrie McLain Museum** (in the public library at 233 Front Street; tel: 443-6630; free) concentrates mostly on gold-rush memorabilia. There are the gold dredges just outside town, and several shops selling ivory carvings and other Native artwork. And of course there's the gold panning.

Information on Nome's tourist businesses and rental companies can be

Ivory carvings are popular souvenirs.

BELOW: a team in the Iditarod Trail Sled Dog Race.

obtained from the Nome Convention and Visitor Bureau (tel: 443-6624; www. nomealaska.org/vc).

Adventures beyond Nome

The Seward Peninsula's road network can lead to all kinds of adventures: fishing, hiking, wildlife viewing, birding, mountain biking, to name a few. Roads connect Nome with other peninsula communities, including **Teller** (population 268) and the ghost town of **Council**. There's another ghost town, **Solomon**, along the Nome Council Road, and the "Last Train to Nowhere" is a rusting hulk of a gold-rush era train, stranded on the tundra.

The Anvil Mountain Road goes (appropriately) to the top of **Anvil Mountain**, which presents panoramic views of Nome, the surrounding countryside, and the Bering Sea. The Nome-Taylor Highway leads to **Pilgrim Hot Springs**; about 7 miles (11km) off the main road, this former Catholic mission and orphanage (*see margin note*) is open to the public, but visitors are asked to call ahead (tel: 443-5892) before visiting.

Bering Land Bridge Preserve

Another hot spot, the **Serpentine Hot Springs**, is located within the **Bering Land Bridge National Preserve**  (tel: 443-2522; www.nps.gov/bela), a 2.8-million-acre (1.1-million-hectare) parkland at the northern edge of the Seward Peninsula. Much closer to Siberia (55 miles/88km away as the raven flies) than Alaska's urban center, this preserve is among the most remote and least visited units in America's National Park System.

Its landscape is dominated by volcanic features such as lava flows and maars (former volcanic craters that are now lakes). Though barren in appearance throughout much of the year, the preserve is brightened each summer by bright tundra flowers.

Surprisingly, more than 250 species of flowering plants have been found here, enduring the region's harsh climate. And thousands of birds come each year to breed and raise their young. Over 100 species are known to migrate to the preserve, including sandhill cranes, loons, geese, swans, and a wide variety of shorebirds and songbirds.

Other residents include grizzlies, wolves, caribou, musk oxen, and moose. Also of interest is the culture of neighboring Inuits – their villages, reindeer herds, and arts and crafts.

Thousands of years ago, during the Pleistocene Ice Age, this region was part of the Bering Land Bridge, which connected what is today North America with Asia. Up to 1,000 miles (1,600km) wide, the bridge allowed humans to migrate from Siberia into what we now call Alaska.

The Bering Land Bridge National Preserve celebrates that past while protecting the present landscape and its wild inhabitants. As with most parklands in remote Alaska, this has no visitor facilities and is most easily reached by plane. Contact preserve headquarters or the Nome Convention and Visitor Bureau (see above) for up-to-date information on local air carriers.

Serpentine Hot Springs

This remote hot springs is located within the Bering Land Bridge National Preserve. You can't actually climb into the springs for a soak, because the water's too hot. There is nearby, however, a hot tub housed in a rustic bathhouse, with two pipes leading into it: one bringing hot water from the springs and the other cold water from a nearby creek. On days when the cold-water creek dries up, those hoping to enjoy a warm soak simply fill the tub early in the day, and let it cool.

You can also spend a few days hiking among huge granite outcroppings and sleeping in a bunkhouse.

It's not effortless to visit Serpentine Hot Springs, however. Summertime travelers must charter a fixed-wing aircraft (no helicopters) from Nome or Kotzebue to fly out to the Preserve. In winter, travel may be by snow-machine, as well.

For more information, contact the Bering Land Bridge National Preserve (www.nps.gov/bela), or to find an air charter service or tour operator in the area, contact the Nome Convention and Visitors Bureau (www.nomealaska.org) or the City of Kotzebue (www.cityofkotzebue.com). ❑

Native woman in splendid furs.

BELOW LEFT: the bleak tundra around Bering Land Bridge.

RESTAURANTS

Airport Pizza Restaurant & Coffee House
406 Bering Street (near Nome Airpprt)
Tel: (in Nome) 443-7992 or (outlying villages) 877-749-9270
www.airportpizza.com
$–$$$$
"You Buy! We Fly!' is the unique sales pitch of this one-of-a-kind restaurant featuring dine in, drive through or free delivery service, even to remote bush villages. Now open for breakfast, lunch, and dinner, this is perhaps the favorite eatery in Nome.

More than just pizza, it also features TexMex and sandwiches along with beer, wine and espresso.

Milano's Pizzeria
110 West Front Street, Suite 102
Tel: 907-443-2924
$–$$
A tasty assortment of Italian and Japanese dishes. The pizzas are a local favorite. Beer, wine.

Polar Café
201 Front Street
Tel: 443-5191 **$–$$$**
Classic American diner overlooking the Bering Sea. Great place for breakfast, a hot cup of coffee, and a taste of local flavor.

Twin Dragon
100 East Front Street
Tel: 443-5552 **$$**
With views of the Bering Sea, Mongolian barbecue is served here hot and to order, daily for lunch and dinner.

Price is for dinner excluding tax, tip, and beverages:
$ = under $15
$$ = $15–20
$$$ = $20–30
$$$$ = over $30

THE IDITAROD TRAIL SLED DOG RACE

They don't call it "the last great race on earth" for nothing. The Iditarod takes place over 1,150 grueling miles, taking 10 to 17 days to complete

The race starts officially in downtown Anchorage on the first Saturday in March, although this is strictly ceremonial, as mushers drive their teams 20 miles (32km) to Eagle River.

The following day, mushers and dogs begin the race for real in Wasilla. In all, teams travel a circuitous route of more than 1,100 miles (1,770km) before reaching the finish line in Nome (the distance from Anchorage to Nome by air would be 650 miles).

A wide range of mushers compete, from professionals with large kennels to adventurers making a once-in-lifetime sled dog trip through Alaska. Four-time winner Martin Buser holds the race's speed record, finishing in less than nine days in 2002. Mushers compete with teams of up to 16 dogs against themselves, each other and the wilderness.

The first fully-fledged race ran to Nome in 1973, recalling the 1925 "race for life," when 20 mushers relayed life-saving serum to Nome to fight a diphtheria epidemic. Many said it could not be done, yet 22 mushers got to the finishing line.

The **Knik Museum and Sled Dog Mushers Hall of Fame**, 40 miles (64km) from Anchorage, is located in a former pool hall at Knik (Mile 13.9 Knik Road, south of Wasilla; *see page 212 for details*). The museum tells the story of the Iditarod Trail and Alaskan mushers.

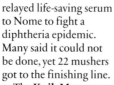

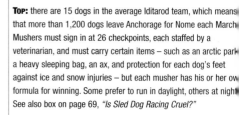

TOP: there are 15 dogs in the average Iditarod team, which means that more than 1,200 dogs leave Anchorage for Nome each March. Mushers must sign in at 26 checkpoints, each staffed by a veterinarian, and must carry certain items – such as an arctic parka, a heavy sleeping bag, an ax, and protection for each dog's feet against ice and snow injuries – but each musher has his or her own formula for winning. Some prefer to run in daylight, others at night. See also box on page 69, *"Is Sled Dog Racing Cruel?"*

TOP LEFT: Jeff King, a four-time Iditarod winner, was born in California but moved to Alaska in 1975 to seek adventure.

ABOVE: people crowd a hall in Nome for the awards banquet. With prize money totaling $400,000, the race boosts the local economy.

RIGHT: the end of the race is a cause for celebration in Nome. It's also an annual reminder that winter will soon come to an end.

THE MUSHERS WHO DEFIED THE ODDS

For the 60 to 70 racers who attempt the "the last great race", the trail is a grueling test of grit, stamina, and will. On the nine to fifteen day trek, mushers must contend with frostbite, violent moose encounters, blinding snow storms and temperatures that drop to forty below freezing. Dog injury is not uncommon, and sadly neither is death. In 2009, six dogs perished on the trail, the highest number since 1985. The fatalities renewed the debate over animal cruelty that has recently cast a shadow over the race.

Still, despite these tragedies, dozens of competitors are lured by the adventure and challenge of driving a sled dog team across Alaska each year. Since the race's start in 1973, five mushers have won the Iditarod title four times – Susan Butcher, Martin Buser, Jeff King, and Doug Swingley – while Rick Swenson holds the all-time record with five championships.

In 2005 Rachael Scdoris of Bend, Oregon upped the ante against the famously fierce competitors, hostile terrain and biting elements when she entered the race as its first blind musher. With the help of a guide who was under strict instructions to only provide visual assistance, Scdoris competed in three Iditarods. Despite scratching in 2005 and 2007, she crossed the finish line in Nome 2006, placing 57 out of the 71 finalists.

TOP RIGHT: Joe Redington, Snr. (1917–99), an Oklahoma-born dog musher, joined with Dorothy Page in 1967 to launch the first Iditarod race to commemorate the centenary of the US purchase of Alaska.

ABOVE LEFT: Lance Mackey, the 2007 Iditarod champion, hugs his lead dogs Larry and Lippy at the finishing line.

BELOW: four dogs wait in a truck before the race begins. Over 1,200 dogs take part in the race, and there's usually at least one fatality.

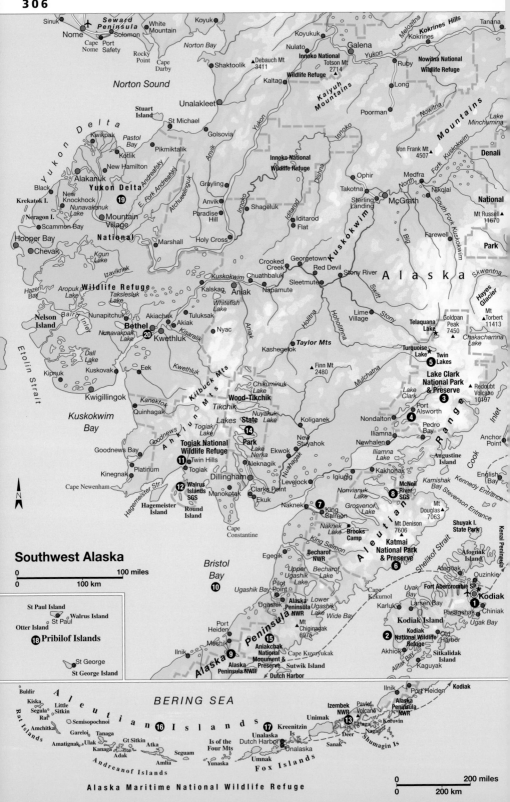

Sinuk
Nome
Cape
Nome
Port
Safety
Solomon
White
Mountain
Koyuk
Koyukuk
Kokrines Hills
Kokrines
Tanana
*Seward
Peninsula*
Melozitna
Yukon
Nowitna National
Wildlife Refuge
Galena
Ruby
Long
Nowitna
Mountains
Lake
Minchumina
Denali

Rocky
Point
Cape
Darby
Norton Bay
Nulato
Innoko National
Wildlife Refuge
▲Debauch Mt
3411
Totson Mt
2714
Norton Sound
Shaktoolik
Kaltag
Kaiyuh
Mountains
Poorman
Von Frank Mt
4507▲
North
Fork Kuskokwim
Mt Russell
11670▲
National

Stuart
Island
Unalakleet
St Michael
Golsovia
Yukon
Innoko
Ophir
Medfra
Nikolai
Park

Yukon Delta
Kwikpak
Pastol
Bay
Pikmiktalik
Anvik
Grayling
Shageluk
Iditarod
Takotna
Sterling
Landing
McGrath
Mt Torbert
11413▲

Kotlik
New Hamilton
Alakanuk
19
Marshall
Holy Cross
Paradise
Hill
Anvik
Flat
Iditarod
South Fork Kuskokwim
Farewell
Hayes
Glacier

Black
New
Knockhock
Nunavakanuk
Lake
Mountain
Village
E. Fork Andreafsky
Crooked
Creek
Georgetown
Red Devil
Stony River
A l a s k a
Skwentna

Krekatok I.
Neragon I.
Scammon Bay
National
Holy Cross
Chuathbaluk
Sleetmute
Swift
Goldpan
Peak
7450
Mt
11413

Hooper Bay
Chevak
*Kgun
Lake*
Izaviknek
Wildlife Refuge
Kalskag
Aniak
Napamute
Lime
Village
Hoholitna
Telaquana
Lake
Turquoise
Lake
5
Twin
Lakes

Hazen
Bay
*Aropuk
Lake*
Taksleluk
Lake
*Whitefish
Lake*
Akiachak
Akiak
Tuluksak
Nyac
Taylor Mts
Kashegelok
Holitna
Lake Clark
National Park
& Preserve
3
Redoubt
Volcano
10197

*Nelson
Island*
Nunapitchuk
Bethel
20 Kwethluk
Kisaralik
▲Finn Mt
2480
Chikuminuk
Lake
Lake
Clark
Port
Alsworth
4
Pedro
Bay

*Dall
Lake*
Kuskokvak
Eek
Kwethluk
Kilbuck Mts
Wood-Tikchik
State
Nuyakuk
Lake
Koliganek
Nondalton
Iliamna
Newhalen
Iliamna
Lake
Augustine
Island
English
Bay

Kipnuk
*Kuskokwim
Bay*
Quinhagak
Kanektok
*Tikchik
Lakes*
Park
14
New
Stuyahok
Kakhonak
Kamishak
Bay
Stevenson
Entrance

Kwigillingok
Goodnews
Ahklun Mts
Togiak
Lake
Lake
Nerka
Ekwok
Nushagak
Igiugig
Nonvianuk
Lake
Grosvenor
Lake
McNeil
River
SGS
8
Mt
Douglas
7063
Shuyak I.
State Park

Goodnews Bay
Platinum
Togiak National
Wildlife Refuge
11 Twin Hills
Togiak
Aleknagik
Dillingham
Levelock
King
Salmon
Naknek
Lake
Brooks
Camp
Mt Denison
7606
Afognak
Island

Cape Newenham
Hagemeister Str.
12 Walrus
Islands
SGS
Manokotak
Ekuk
Clarks Point
7 King
Salmon
Katmai
National Park
& Preserve
6
Afognak

Kinegnak
*Hagemeister
Island*
Round
Island
Cape
Constantine
Bristol
Bay
Egegik
Becharof
NWR
Mt
7063
Uyak
Bay
Fort Abercrombie SP
1
Kodiak

Southwest Alaska
Upper
Ugashik
Lake
Becharof
Lake
Cape
Kekurnoi
Karluk
Larsen Bay
Pasagshak
Chiniak

0 ___ 100 miles
0 ___ 100 km
10
Pilot
Point
Ugashik Bay
Ugashik
Lower
Ugashik
Lake
Alaska
Peninsula
NWR
Wide Bay
Kodiak
National Wildlife
Refuge
2
Old
Harbor

St Paul Island
St Paul
Walrus Island
Port
Heiden
Meshik
Mt
Chiginagak
6975
Cape Kuyuyukak
Akhiok
Alitak
Bay
Sitkalidak
Island

Otter Island
18 **Pribilof Islands**
Ilnik
9
Aniakchak
National
Monument &
Preserve
Sutwik Island
Kaguyak

St George
St George Island
*Alaska
Peninsula NWR*
Dutch Harbor
Ilnik
Port Heiden
Kodiak

A l e u t i a n
Buldir
Kiska
Little
Sitkin
Segula
Rat
Semisopochnoi
BERING SEA
Izembek
NWR
Pavlof
Volcano
Alaska
Peninsula
NWR

Rat
Islands
Amchitka
Garelol
Tanaga
I s l a n d s
16
Unimak
17
Kreenitzin
Is
13
Unga
Korovin

Amatignak
Ulak
Gt Sitkin
Atka
Kanaga
Adak
Amlia
Seguam
*Is of the
Four Mts*
Unalaska
Dutch Harbor
Unalaska
Deer
Sanak
Shumagin Is

Andreanof Islands
Yunaska
Umnak
Fox Islands

Alaska Maritime National Wildlife Refuge
0 ___ 200 miles
0 ___ 200 km

THE SOUTHWEST

Stretching from the Alaska Peninsula to the
Aleutian Chain, from the Kodiak Archipelago
to the Pribilofs, Alaska's Southwest is one
of the state's most remote regions

Far from Alaska's urban centers, Southwest Alaska is a broad and diverse region that includes the Kodiak Archipelago, Alaska Peninsula, Aleutian Islands, Bering Sea Islands, and Yukon-Kuskokwim Delta. It's a place of active volcanoes, wind-swept tundra, rugged coastal shores, and storm-wracked islands. It's also home to some of the world's largest bird rookeries and marine mammal populations, and the cultural center of the Aleut, Alutiiq, and Yup'ik Eskimo peoples, who have lived off the region's lands and waters for centuries.

Though often inhospitable to humans (and perhaps because of that), the Southwest region's landscape and climate support a diverse – and in some instances, rich – population of fish, birds, and mammals. Here is North America's largest nesting area for migrating waterfowl. Here too are the world's largest – and densest populations of – brown bears. And here are the continent's largest runs of sockeye; tens of millions of these salmon return each year to the region's river-and-lake systems, but the largest runs, by far, are centered in the Bristol Bay region.

Native villages

More than 80 communities are scattered through the region, most of them small, Native villages whose residents are still largely dependent on traditional subsistence lifestyles in which they hunt, fish, trap, and gather plants, just as they have for untold generations. Most towns and villages have 200 residents or fewer, though a few commercial centers have between 1,000 and 6,000 people. Few roads link any of the communities and travel is primarily by air or boat year-round, plus snowmobile or dog team in winter.

In the northern Gulf of Alaska, and separated from the mainland by stormy Shelikof Strait, the **Kodiak Archipelago** consists of a couple of

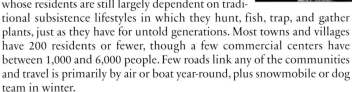

PRECEDING PAGES: brown bears beat anglers to a catch at McNeil River.
ABOVE: Aleut dancer; basket weaver.

dozen islands, most a few miles across or less. But Kodiak itself is the largest island in the US after Hawaii. Sometimes called Alaska's "emerald isle," **Kodiak** is 100 miles long and more than 50 miles across at its widest point (160 by 80km). Other large islands in the chain include **Afognak** and **Shuyak**, at the northernmost tip.

Approximately 14,000 people inhabit the Kodiak group; most are tied in some way to the fishing industry. The islands are ancestral homes to the Alutiiq people, close relatives of the Aleuts. Though the islands can be reached by either boat or plane, nearly all visitors arrive on commuter or air taxi flights, from Anchorage or Kenai Peninsula communities. The city of Kodiak is also visited year-round by the Alaska state ferry. Portions of the archipelago's coastal forests have been cut, but much of the landscape remains wild and protected by Kodiak National Wildlife Refuge and by state parks on Shuyak and Afognak islands. Kodiak island and city are discussed in greater detail on pages 311–17.

The Alaska Peninsula

Directly west of Kodiak, sandwiched between Shelikof Strait and Bristol Bay, the **Alaska Peninsula** stretches more than 500 miles (800km) from the southern boundary of Alaska's mainland to the beginning of the Aleutian Islands. A traditional home for Yup'ik Eskimo, Aleut, and Alutiiq peoples, the area also includes prime wildlife habitat.

To the northeast of the peninsula, **Lake Clark National Park and Preserve** covers 4 million acres (1.6 million hectares) of some of the most spectacular and least visited parkland in the state. At the intersection of coastal and Interior Alaska, the park has an astounding level of biological diversity and is also home to Mount Redoubt, an active volcano in the Aleutian Range. Since 1900, it has erupted five times; the most recent occurring in 2009 when plumes of ash and steam rose 15,000 feet (4,500 meters) to disrupt air travel for three days.

The **Izembek National Wildlife Refuge**, an "international crossroads" for migrating shorebirds and waterfowl, is located at the southern tip of the peninsula. Following the curve of land to the northeast, you'll find ample support for Alaska's inclusion in the North Pacific's "ring of fire" at the **Aniakchak Caldera** within the seldom-visited **Aniakchak National Monument and Preserve**.

Continuing on toward the mainland will take you to an area boasting the densest populations of brown bears in the world at **Katmai National Park and Preserve** and the **McNeil River State Game Sanctuary**. Both sites provide viewing platforms that enable visitors to observe bears congregating to grapple for salmon along remote streams.

The community of **King Salmon** (population 400) is the access point for many of the activities of the peninsula, including not only wildlife viewing, but also world-class sport fishing, hiking, backpacking and river-running.

Dillingham (population 2,300), serves as a hub for similar activities in the western Bristol Bay area. Trips can be arranged out of Dillingham to **Togiak National Wildlife Refuge** or to the nearby **Walrus Islands State Game Sanctuary.**

The Aleutian Islands

The **Aleutian Islands** extend southwest from the tip of the Alaska Peninsula in a 1,000-mile (1,600km) arc toward Asia. These islands are the traditional homeland of the Aleut people. Visitor services and information are centered at the communities of **Dutch Harbor** and nearby **Unalaska.** This area of Alaska is of particular interest to birders and sport fishers, as well as those interested in the islands' rich history of Aleut culture, Russian influence and remnants of Alaska's World War II involvement.

The **Yukon-Kuskokwim (Y-K) Delta** region of Southwest is mostly encompassed within the 19-million-acre (7.7-million-hectare) **Yukon Delta National Wildlife Refuge.** Both the Yukon and the Kuskokwim Rivers traverse the flat, treeless plains and tundra of the Delta and empty into the Bering Sea. Among the most populated regions of rural Alaska, the Yukon Delta is home to nearly 25,000 Yup'ik Eskimo people. Visitors to the area enjoy sport fishing, hunting, photography, rafting and, kayaking, and especially extraordinary birding and wild-life-viewing opportunities.

The Y-K Delta supports one of the world's largest aggregations of water birds and shorebirds. The rivers, streams, lakes, sloughs, and ponds of the region provide prime spawning and rearing habitat for 44 species of fish. Land mammals include caribou, brown and black bears, moose, wolves, and musk oxen. The gateway city to this roadless Refuge (as well as a transportation and services hub for the area) is Bethel (population 6,000), which has a regular airline service from Anchorage. Travel to outlying areas is by small plane or boat.

Pribilof Islands

Three hundred miles west of the Y-K Delta area, and 200 miles (320km) north of the Aleutian Islands in the Bering Sea lie the treeless **Pribilof Islands.** St Paul and St George are the only inhabited islands of the group, and fishing and tourism are their emerging economic mainstays. The islands are the summer home for a million fur seals, which may well be the largest gathering of marine mammals in the world. The nesting grounds along the rocky shores and steep cliffs of the Pribilofs draw hundreds of thousands of sea birds, and the relatively few birders who search for them.   ❑

LEFT: camping at McNeil River; the Russian Orthodox Church at Karluk, Kodiak Island. **ABOVE:** archeologist at work on Kodiak Island.

KODIAK

Two-thirds of mountainous Kodiak Island
is a wildlife reserve, famous for its brown
bears, while the city of Kodiak has a strong
and visible legacy from its Russian past

Alaska
Anchorage

A shift of the wind can change Kodiak Island from a desolate, windswept, rain-pounded rock isolated from the rest of the world by fog, to a shimmering emerald of grass, spruce trees, and snow-capped mountains glowing pink in the sunrise. But while the winds may shift, they remain predominantly from the north. Both the island itself and the city of Kodiak are places whose characters change with the weather, the seasons and the observer.

At first glance, the city of **Kodiak ❶** seems to be near world's end; it is a town of 5,900 people perched precariously on a small ledge of land between ocean swells and jagged mountains (another 2,700 people live in the "greater Kodiak" area and some 14,000 people inhabit the entire island). A look into Kodiak's economy reveals a major fishing port – one of the top three in the United States. Kodiak is home to a multi-million-dollar fishing fleet which ranges from the Pacific Northwest to Norton Sound.

Past cultures

Over 200 years of recorded history have swept across Kodiak, each one leaving traces of its passing. Artifacts of the indigenous Koniag culture surface near remnants of the Russian period or World War II bunkers, derelict whaling stations, collapsing herring-rendering plants, or fish-processing facilities. Just under the top soil is a layer of volcanic

ash which covered the town in 1912 and still drifts about, leaving a coating of fine, white dust. White spruce tree skeletons guard the salt marshes, monuments to the land subsidence which occurred during the 1964 earthquake and tidal wave.

From the air Kodiak Island, beyond the city, seems an untouched wilderness, 3,588 sq miles (9,293 sq km) of rugged mountains deeply indented by bays. The northern half is covered with spruce trees, the southern half with grass. Foresters say the spruce forest is

LEFT: a salmon
snack. **BELOW:**
Kodiak's harbor.

advancing down the island at the rate of a mile a century.

Landing in Kodiak (there are frequent commuter flights from Anchorage) can be an adventure. As the jet approaches the airport, it drops lower and lower over the water until its landing gear seems to skim the waves. Just beyond where the runway seems to emerge from the water, the plane sets down. At the other end of the runway sits **Barometer Mountain** (2,450ft/745 meters), so called because the peak is visible only in good weather.

The airport is about 5 miles (8km) from Kodiak City and there's a connecting bus. Spruce trees cast shadows across the highway, then the road twists in sharp turns around Pillar Mountain. In the winter bald eagles, sometimes 10 to a tree, perch in cottonwoods above the highway. The road then dips down into Kodiak.

The Russian legacy

Drawn by his search for sea otter pelts, Grigor Ivanovich Shelikof arrived in Three Saints Bay on the southeast corner of Kodiak Island in 1784 with two ships, the *Three Saints* and the *St Simon*. He was not welcomed by the indigenous Alutiiq people, who proceeded to harass the Russian party *(see page 46)*.

Having established his authority with brutal force, Shelikof founded the first Russian settlement in Alaska on **Three Saints Bay**, built a school to teach the Natives to read and write Russian, and introduced the Russian Orthodox religion.

In 1790 Alexander Andreyevich Baranov arrived at Three Saints Bay to take over leadership of the Russian settlement. He moved the colony to the northeast end of the island where timber was available, and which was closer to Cook Inlet and Prince William Sound. The site chosen by Baranov is now the city of Kodiak.

Russian members of the colony took Alutiiq wives and started family lines whose names still continue – Panamaroff, Pestrikoff, Kvasnikoff. Russian heritage in the city of Kodiak is also found on its street signs: Baranov, Rezanoff, Shelikof. The island's Native culture is also apparent, and can be seen at a performance by the Kodiak

Orthodox priests play a major role in the Kodiak community.

BELOW: Kodiak fishermen empty king crab traps.

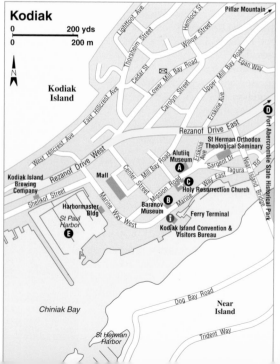

Kodiak

0   200 yds

0   200 m

N

Kodiak
Island

Pillar Mountain

Lightfoot Ave.
Thorsheim Street
Hemlock St.
Willow Street
Cedar St.
Lower Mill Bay Road
Upper Mill Bay Road
Egan Way
Carolyn Street
Erskine Ave.
East Hillcrest Ave.
West Hillcrest Ave.
Rezanof Drive East

D Fort Abercrombie State Historical Park

St Herman Orthodox
Theological Seminary

Alutiiq
Museum
A

Sargent Dr.
Tagura
Near Island Bridge
Near Island Rd.

Kodiak Island
Brewing
Company

Rezanof Drive West

Shelikof Street

Mall

Center Street
Mill Bay Road
Mission Road
Marine Way East

Holy Resurrection Church
C

Harbormaster
Bldg

Baranov
Museum
B

St Paul
Harbor

Marine Way West

Ferry Terminal

i

Kodiak Island Convention &
Visitors Bureau

E

Chiniak Bay

Dog Bay Road

Near
Island

St Herman
Harbor

Trident Way

Alutiiq Dancers, which includes 50 dancers who wear traditional dress and perform ethnic songs and dances. The troupe performs throughout the state, with daily summer performances in Kodiak (tel: 486-4449; www.sunaq.org).

Museums in Kodiak

Much of the rich culture of the Alutiiqs was absorbed by the Russian culture and can only be guessed at through artifacts and the diaries of the early Russian settlers. The best window on the culture is at the **Alutiiq Museum**  (215 Mission Road; tel: 486-7004; www.alutiiqmuseum.com; summer Mon–Fri 9am–5pm, Sat 10am–5pm, Sun by appointment, winter Tue–Fri 9am–5pm, Sat noon–4pm; charge). This Native-owned research museum interprets artifacts from ongoing archeological digs. Visitors can also join digs at remote sites in the Dig Afognak program (tel: 486-6357; www.afognak.org/dig.php).

The **Baranov Museum** (tel: 486-5920; www.baranovmuseum.org; summer Mon–Sat 10am–4pm, Sun noon–4pm, winter Tue–Sat 10am–3pm; charge) is across from the Visitors Bureau on Marine Way and next to the ferry dock. It too contains displays of Alutiiq artifacts and clothing as well as items from the Russian and early American periods. The small museum, whose store sells Russian samovars and jewelry, is located in the **Erskine House**. Once a storehouse for furs, this was designated a National Historic Landmark in 1962, and is North America's oldest Russian building.

Holy Resurrection Church

When the US bought Alaska from Imperial Russia, the Russian citizens left, but the Russian Orthodox churches remained. The two blue onion domes of the **Holy Resurrection Church** on Mission Road are the town's most outstanding landmarks. Orthodoxy still plays a significant role in the Kodiak community, and is the predominant religion in the six villages in the island area.

In 1974, the **St Herman Orthodox Theological Seminary** was relocated to Kodiak: the white buildings stand near the church. Father Herman arrived in Kodiak in 1794 and settled on **Spruce Island**, where he established a school and became renowned as an ascetic and miracle worker. He was canonized in Kodiak in 1970, the first Orthodox canonization to take place on American soil. His remains are kept in the church and the Russian Orthodox faithful make pilgrimages every August to his shrine. Other treasures of the Holy Resurrection Orthodox Church

The Holy Resurrection Church is testament to the importance of the Russian Orthodox faith in Kodiak.

BELOW: the Baranov Museum.

Most sockeye salmon in Kodiak is canned and exported.

BELOW: remnants of a World War II cannon in Fort Abercrombie State Historical Park.

include many brilliantly colored icons. Visitors are welcome to attend services.

The Russian Orthodox Church follows the Julian calendar, making Kodiak a town of two Christmases, December 25 and January 7, and two New Years, January 1 and January 14.

Fort Abercrombie

During World War II, Kodiak served as a major supply center for the Aleutian campaign. Military personnel and construction workers changed the city from a fishing village of 500 residents to a boom town of 4,000 people with another 20,000 in nearby areas. The US Navy built a major base on the site, which is now used as a US Coast Guard facility. Today all that remains of the war years are moss-covered bunkers.

Fort Abercrombie State Historical Park ❶, some 4 miles (6km) from the city, is dedicated to the memory of those days. A large bunker and the remains of gun emplacements over-

look the sea from a cliff. Other bunkers can be found by walking through an alpine meadow and along the cliff edge. There are several guided tours a week, and some good facilities for camping within the park.

There are also bunkers on **Pillar Mountain** (1,270ft/385 meters) behind the city. Hikers working their way through the alders and spruce forests along the tops of shale cliffs often find others. Crowned with radar towers, Pillar Mountain also provides panoramic views of the surrounding area.

Earthquake and tidal wave

Natural events have left indelible marks on Kodiak Island. Twice in the 20th century the landscape was altered, first by a volcanic ash fall in 1912 when Mount Novarupta on the Alaska Peninsula exploded, and again by the great earthquake and tsunami in 1964.

The Good Friday earthquake in 1964, which devastated much of South Central Alaska, also set off a tidal wave that swept into the city of Kodiak and destroyed the downtown buildings, canneries and the docks. Many residents fled up Pillar Mountain and watched helplessly while the sea ran out, leaving the harbor dry, and then rolled back in across the land. Those who didn't reach high ground were swept away.

After the tidal wave, most of downtown Kodiak was redesigned and rebuilt. Residents who lived through the tidal wave and stayed to rebuild the town have formed a special bond. Though the tidal wave was a tragedy, it left behind a feeling of unity that still pervades the community.

A thriving fishing industry

Kodiak's economic dependence on the sea has been constant. The city of Kodiak provides temporary moorage and services for approximately 3,000 fishing boats a year. Fishermen deliver up to $100 million worth of fish and shellfish annually. Ask Kodiak residents what season it is and, if it is sum-

mer, they're likely to answer, "salmon season." Fall is king crab season; winter's marked by the Tanner crab, marketed as snow crab; spring is herring season; halibut and black cod are harvested in spring and summer, and whitefish species most of the year.

Kodiak's fishermen work year-round, switching from fishery to fishery as the seasons change. Between seasons the waterfront throbs with activity. Crane trucks and flatbeds move 500lb (230kg) steel crab pots from storage to the boat and back to storage. In spring, herring seines and gillnets are stretched out on the docks where crew men with shuttles can attach float and lead lines.

Visitors are welcome to wander down the ramp behind the Harbormaster Building and walk along the floats in **St Paul Harbor** Ⓔ. Across the channel, on **Near Island**, is **St Herman Harbor**. In St Paul Harbor there are two loading docks where skippers load gear on board their boats.

Like its fishing industry, Kodiak's population is diverse, and you'll overhear a mixture of languages and accents as you wander around the harbor.

Touring Kodiak Island

Except for several Native villages, the populated portion of Kodiak Island is confined to the road system, and there are fewer than 100 miles (160km) of it. Some stretches are only fit for four-wheel-drive vehicles. The six coastal villages on the island are accessible only by plane or boat; to visit one of them, you need to make arrangements in advance.

It takes about an hour to drive to the end of the road at Fossil Beach. The road heads out of town past the **Buskin River State Recreation Area** where the headquarters and visitor center for the Kodiak National Wildlife Refuge is located. The Buskin River is a popular sport-fishing stream for salmon and steelhead.

The road continues past the airport, the Coast Guard base, the fairgrounds, the neighborhood of **Bells Flats**, and then climbs headlands, curves around bays and crosses rivers. In summer, salmon can be seen jumping in the bays and swimming up the rivers; July and August are the best months for salmon watching or fishing. Occasionally sea

Scarce seafood
Visitors expect to come to a major fishing port and eat seafood, but most of Kodiak's fresh seafood is in refrigerated vans waiting to be loaded onto barges for shipment. The fishing industry is geared to large-volume production and sales, which has made it difficult for small, local buyers to establish a steady source of supply. The local supermarkets do offer fresh seafood in season, however, and some restaurants include it on their menus.

BELOW: a visitor greeting pinpoints one of the main local industries.

Fishing is the main industry around Kodiak Island.

lions come into the bays to feed on the fish. There are no restrictions on exploring the beaches, walking through the forests or climbing the mountains.

Eventually the road comes to a T-junction. To the left is the community of **Chiniak** (population 50), which contains a number of quaint lodges and B&Bs. To the right, the road travels through cattle country where Kodiak's ranchers run about 2,000 head of beef cattle. Ahead the ocean comes into view again by **Pasagshak**, a popular river for fishing silver salmon. There is a small campsite on its banks.

The road continues past a sand-duned, surf-beaten beach and ends at **Fossil Beach**, where fossil shells lie loosely in the clay and rocks. During the fall, gray whales pass Pasagshak and Fossil Beach on their migration to California from the Bering Sea. In spring, the whales pass the island again as they migrate to their northern summer feeding grounds.

Kodiak Wildlife Refuge

By traveling along the roads you will see some of the loveliest scenery on the island. But if you want real wilderness, and bears, you must visit the **Kodiak National Wildlife Refuge ❷** (tel: 907-487-2600; http://kodiak.fws.gov), which can be reached only by air or sea. This mountainous wilderness, covering two-thirds of the island, belongs to bears and foxes, rabbits and birds, muskrats and otters.

Most people come here to see the brown bears. For those who aren't experienced in traveling through bear country, the best and safest way to see them is to take one of the bear-viewing tours based in Kodiak, but be warned – they are not cheap. Information on local guides can be obtained from the refuge headquarters.

Wilderness hikers should always remember to walk noisily through Kodiak's backcountry to reduce the chances of any confrontations with bears. As well as berries and salmon, the Kodiak bear enjoys a diet of calves and deer – much to the dismay of local ranchers and hunters. ❑

RESTAURANTS

B & B Bar
326 Shelikof Street
Tel: 486-3575 **$**
This unassuming little watering hole has the distinction of being Alaska's oldest licensed bar. Near the harbor, this is a second home for most of Kodiak's fishermen, who conduct a good deal of their business over a cool pint of beer.

Chart Room
236 Rezanof Drive
Tel: 486-5712
www.kodiakinn.com/dining.htm **$$$–$$$$**
Gaze out on a harbor view as you enjoy breakfast, lunch or dinner in this restaurant, located in the Best Western Kodiak Inn. Spe-

cialties include Alaska king crab, prime rib, and filet mignon. Bar.

El Chicano
103 Center Street
Tel: 486-6116
www.elchicanos.com **$$–$$$**
Large restaurant serving generous portions of Mexican fare.

Galley Gourmet
PO Box 1694
Tel: 486-5079
www.kodiak-alaska-dinner-cruises.com **$$$$**
Take a dinner or brunch cruise aboard the 42ft (13-meter) yacht, *Sea Breeze*. Features world-class seafood and gourmet desserts. Dinner cruises

last about 3½ hours and include sightseeing and wildlife viewing, with information dished up as well.

Henry's Great Alaskan Restaurant
512 Marine Way
Tel: 486-8844 **$$**
Reasonably priced seafood, steaks, gourmet burgers and sandwiches served for lunch and dinner daily. Located in the waterfront mall. Bar.

Mill Bay Coffee & Pastries
3833 Rezanof Drive East
Tel: 486-4411 **$**
A coffeehouse featuring locally roasted coffee and gourmet desserts. Also now

offers breakfast and lunch featuring fresh vegetables, eggs from free-range hens, and local seafood.

Old Powerhouse Restaurant
516 East Marine Way
Tel: 481-1088 **$$$**
Fine Japanese cuisine served up in a richly renovated building that used to serve as a powerhouse for the city. Beautiful view of the sea.

Price is for dinner excluding tax, tip, and beverages:
$ = under $15
$$ = $15–20
$$$ = $20–30
$$$$ = over $30

Wildlife Refuges

In 2009, two of Alaska's wildlife refuges celebrated their 100th anniversary, making them among the nation's oldest.

Put aside by President Teddy Roosevelt in 1909, areas that are now a part of the Yukon Delta and Alaska Maritime National Wildlife Refuges were among the 53 original sites designated to become the bold new National Wildlife Refuge System. Protecting wildlife, it began to play a critical role in preserving sensitive habitat in the rapidly developing state. In 1980, Congress added millions of acres to America's protected land by creating nine new refuges and expanding several others. Alaska now has 16 National Wildlife Refuges, ranging in size from 300,000 to 19½ million acres (120,000–7.9 million hectares).

The refuges encompass some of the world's most spectacular wildlands and present all sorts of opportunities for backcountry adventure: from river running and sea kayaking, to mountaineering, backpacking, fishing, hunting, and great wildlife viewing. A few can be reached by road, but most are remote, easily accessible by plane and in some instances, boat. And though several are popular with hikers, others hardly ever see people, or are used primarily by subsistence hunters and fishermen. Suggest drilling for possible oil beneath one of them, though, and political storms will rage.

While the Arctic National Wildlife Refuge garners the most international attention, the Southwest has the greatest diversity and concentration of Alaska's refuges, including:

● The smallest national refuge in Alaska, 303,000-acre (123,000-hectare) **Izembeck** NWR, located on the lower Alaska Peninsula, is an international crossroads for migrating waterfowl and shorebirds. Its heart is Izembeck Lagoon, where hundreds of thousands of waterfowl converge each fall. Brown bears fish salmon-rich streams, caribou migrate across the tundra. And the Aghileen Pinnacles, a group of precipitous volcanic spires, present a little-known mountaineering challenge.

● The side-by-side **Alaska Peninsula** and **Becharof** refuges in Southwest Alaska encompass towering volcanic peaks, rugged coastal fjords, rolling tundra, and glacially carved lakes. There are 14 major volcanoes, including nine that have erupted in historic times. Best known for hunting and fishing opportunities, these refuges are also prime candidates for backpackers, climbers, and coastal kayakers seeking extreme challenges.

● The **Alaska Maritime** refuge consists of more than 2,500 islands and includes areas of the Pribilof Islands, the Aleutian Chain, and the remote coast of the Chukchi Sea. About 80 percent of the state's 50 million nesting seabirds gather here. Marine life also includes whales, sea lions, walrus, porpoises, and sea otters. The refuge is outstanding for birdwatching and for the kayak trip of a lifetime.

● The **Togiak** refuge in Southwest Alaska has more than 30 species of mammals and clearwater streams with some of the continent's finest salmon and trout fishing. Coastal areas are rich with brown bears and marine mammals. The uplands have 2.3 million acres 930,000 hectares) of designated wilderness to explore on foot or by boat.

● The **Yukon Delta** NWR covers over 21 million acres of mostly treeless waterlogged expanse. Home to the largest aggregations of water birds in the world, it is a popular place for boating, birding, fishing, and hunting. *(See pages 340–1).*

For more information contact the US Fish and Wildlife Service office (1011 E. Tudor Road, Anchorage, AK 99503; tel: 786-3309; www.r7.fws.gov). ❑

RIGHT: Alaska has five species of loon.

A SERENGETI OF THE NORTH

Wildlife watching draws many visitors to the state. They are rarely disappointed, for the seas, parks and wilderness areas contain a remarkable variety of wildlife

Alaska is sometimes called the "Serengeti of the North." That's a bit of an exaggeration, but not much. The seas are the habitat of humpback, beluga, minke and gray whales, porpoises and dolphins, walrus, sea lions, sea otters, and polar bears; while the land is inhabited by 105 species of mammals, including hoary marmots, Dall sheep, little brown bats, flying squirrels, and ferocious wolverines. The state is also seasonal or permanent home for more than 400 kinds of fish and nearly 300 bird species.

The Pribilof Islands in the Bering Sea are the summer home to a million fur seals and to millions of sea birds, while thousands of bull walrus haul out each year on Round Island, in Bristol Bay. The McNeil River, on the Alaska Peninsula, has the world's largest gathering of brown bears: more than 100 individuals have been observed at McNeil Falls during a single summer, feeding on the salmon runs.

Farther north, some 400,000 caribou roam the state's northwest region, perpetually on the move, while 130,000 or more form the Porcupine caribou herd, which ranges through northeastern Alaska and western Canada. And each fall between thousands of bald eagles gather in Southeast Alaska's Chilkat Valley near Haines to feed on a late run of salmon.

ABOVE: inhabiting open tundra, musk oxen are a relic of the Ice Age. If predators threaten, they defend themselves by standing in a circle side-by-side, heads pointed out, in protective rings. Unfortunately it makes them an easy target for hunters with guns.

ABOVE: two walrus bulls display their tusks as they engage in a territorial dispute along the rocky coast of Round Island, part of the Walrus Islands State Game Sanctuary in Bristol Bay. They're bulky creatures: an adult male may weigh up to 4,000lbs (1,800kg).

RIGHT: Alaska is home to some two dozen caribou herds, totaling more than 1 million animals. They are called "the nomads of the north" because they travel so extensively, and seem to be in constant movement.

BELOW: the largest members of the deer family, moose are the most important game animals in the state. They are herbivores and feed on a variety of plants, including aquatic weeds.

BEAR COUNTRY

There's a good reason why Alaska is called "bear country." It's the only one of the 50 states to be inhabited by all three of North America's bears: the black bear, the polar bear, and the brown bear – also called the grizzly.

Polar bears roam the ice of the Beaufort, Chukchi and Bering seas. Both black and brown bears are found throughout most of the state, though the smaller black bears tend to be forest creatures. Browns and grizzlies prefer open areas: mountain meadows, Arctic tundra, and coastal beaches.

Brown bears and grizzlies are members of the same species: the former are coastal creatures while the latter live in the interior. Grizzlies have longer claws and a bigger hump and are generally smaller than their coastal cousins. This is thought to be because brown bears have access to energy-rich foods, especially salmon. Though classified as carnivores, brown, grizzly and black bears eat both vegetation and meat; the polar bear is a true carnivore and its favorite prey is the ringed seal.

BELOW: gray wolves are the ultimate symbols of the wild. They range through much of Alaska but they tend to inhabit remote wilderness and avoid humans as much as possible.

LEFT: easily Alaska's most agile and graceful four-legged animals, Dall sheep delicately navigate some of the most perilous terrain in the state. Steep slopes of loose rock and sliding talus or scree are their safeguard against such indomitable predators as bears and wolves.

LAKE CLARK NATIONAL PARK

Alaska
Anchorage●

Lake Clark may be the quintessential Alaska parkland, with volcanoes, rugged coastline, several major river systems, and a wide diversity of plants and animals

BELOW: dawn by the shores of Lake Clark.

I t's 11pm on a late July evening. The sun has disappeared behind a gentle hill, but the northwest horizon remains brightened by an afterglow of rich pastels. A band of yellow gradually yields to orange, then rose and finally purple. Winds that swept in with an early evening rain shower have died, leaving the air utterly still yet surprisingly bug-free despite the midsummer warmth.

With the wind and rain's departure, a shroud of silence has fallen over **Turquoise Lake**. The quiet is broken only by the soft crunching of boots on beach gravel, the occasional splash of grayling, and the intermittent screeches of two young terns calling for their parents, out busily fishing for the evening meal.

It is a magical, paradisical evening along the lake – serene, yet bursting with life. Sandpipers and plovers prowl the shoreline, skittering and dipping in their frenetic search for food. Just a few yards offshore, a family of old squaws swims past. And across the lake, an eagle circles over a small group of caribou, crossing tundra brightened by multi-colored fields of wildflowers: blue monkshood and Jacob's ladder, yellow tundra rose, pink fireweed, and prickly rose.

Yet less than 10 miles (16km) to the east is an ominous and desolate world where the tundra's greens and yellows and pinks give way to the blacks and grays and whites of rock, snow, and ice. Rising darkly into the sky, 8,020ft (2,444-meter) **Telaquana Mountain** is a natural fortress of solitude, its upper reaches guarded by jagged spires and pale-blue glaciers that overhang sheer rock cliffs. It's forbidding and impenetrable. In fading light, it is a magnificent spectacle.

The essence of wild Alaska

The 4-million-acre (1.6 million-hectare) **Lake Clark National Park and Preserve ❸** may indeed be the quintessential Alaskan parkland. Within its boundaries are two active volcanoes, including one – 10,197ft (3,108-meter) Mount Redoubt – that erupted in 1990 and again in early 2009; rugged coastline whose rocky cliffs serve as rookeries for multitudes of puffins, cormorants, kittiwakes, and other seabirds; two major mountain systems, the Aleutian and Alaska ranges, which join to produce the Chigmit and Neacola mountains (snow-capped and glacially carved, most of the park's high peaks remain unclimbed and unexplored); and several major river and lake systems – including three designated wild rivers – that offer world-class sport-fishing opportunities for all five species of Pacific salmon and rainbow trout.

Lake Clark is also home to a remarkably diverse mix of plant communities. Along the coast is one of the northernmost stands of Sitka spruce rain forest, while inland are lowland boreal forests typical of Interior Alaska and several varieties of tundra, including Arctic tundra usually found in northern Alaska. Those varied ecosystems support more than 100 species of birds and nearly 40 species of mammals, including black and brown bears, wolves, Dall sheep, caribou, and moose.

"Lake Clark has a fantastic diversity of resources," says Paul Haertel, who served as the park's first superintendent after it was established in 1980. "It's a place that captures the essence of wild Alaska; it has everything you could imagine."

An undiscovered park

Here, then, is a national park with fantastic scenery, easy access by air, and diverse recreational opportunities. One would expect it to be among Alaska's most popular destinations. But it's not. In fact, Lake Clark is among the state's least-known and least-appreciated national parks. In a sense, it remains one of Alaska's undiscovered parks.

There are a few reasons why. For one thing, it doesn't have one or two major attractions. Denali, for example, has Mount McKinley and wildlife viewing. Katmai has its bears. Glacier Bay has its spectacular glacier-sculpted landscape and marine wildlife tours. An even bigger factor, perhaps, is that Lake Clark is

TIP

Getting There
The park can't be reached by road. Most visitors charter a flight from Anchorage, about 90 minutes from Lake Clark. Charter flights can also be taken from the Kenai Peninsula. Commercial airlines fly between Anchorage and Iliamna, a base for many charter airlines.

BELOW: an angler lands an Arctic grayling on Lake Clark.

A walk in the very remote woods.

BELOW: a family from Port Alsworth crosses the lake.

not accessible by road (or cruise line). Sure it's easy to reach by plane, and relatively inexpensive. But "bush plane" travel is still very foreign to most travelers. And most visitors don't like the idea of being dropped "in the middle of nowhere."

There's one other factor that likely acts as a crowd deterrent: the lack of visitor facilities. The National Park Service has intentionally kept development to a minimum. The park's main office is in Anchorage (tel: 781-2218; www.nps.gov/lacl), with a "field headquarters" at **Port Alsworth ❹**, on Lake Clark's southeast shore. There are no other public facilities within the park, although rangers may be seasonally based in the backcountry. Several privately owned wilderness lodges, most of them catering to hunters and anglers, are located in and around the park; several are at Port Alsworth, the entry point for many visitors. In addition, dozens of guide services operate within the park. The majority specialize in sport fishing, but other guided activities include backpacking, hiking, lake-touring, mountaineering, photography, and river running.

Several air-taxi operators offer flightseeing trips into the park and transport big-game hunters. Information on commercial visitor services authorized to conduct business within Lake Clark National Park and Preserve can be obtained from the park's Anchorage office. However, with no connection to Alaska's highway system, no singular attraction to catch the public's fancy, and minimal visitor facilities, Lake Clark is likely to remain a low-profile park, at least for the near future.

Wilderness lodges

Before Congress established Lake Clark National Park and Preserve in 1980, the region's resources were utilized by two main groups: local residents (most of whom lead a subsistence lifestyle in Dena'ina Indian villages near the park's southern edge); and "sport" hunters and anglers seeking trophy wildlife and fish.

Much of the fishing pressure comes from wilderness lodges. Prime fly-in fishing grounds include the Chilikadrotna and Mulchatna rivers – also popular with river floaters – as well as the Stony, Crescent, Silver Salmon and Nondalton rivers and Telaquana, Crescent and Tazmina lakes.

And then there's Lake Clark: 42 miles long (68km), up to 860ft deep (262 meters) and covering 110 sq miles (285 sq km), Alaska's sixth-largest lake is a critical sockeye salmon spawning ground. Many of the park's lake and river systems contribute significantly to Bristol Bay's world-famous commercial sockeye salmon fishery. In fact, one of its primary functions is to protect watersheds that feed the salmon fishery. Rainbows and salmon get most of the angling attention, but lake trout, pike, Dolly Varden, Arctic char, and Arctic grayling are also popular target species.

While sport fishing is permissible anywhere within the parkland, trophy hunting is restricted to Lake Clark's 1.4-million-acre (570-hectare) preserve, where tundra-covered foothills and lowland forests support healthy populations of caribou, moose, and brown bear. Prior to 1980, however, the Chigmit Mountains' Dall sheep populations were also fair game. "Back before the park was created, people would come in and take one – or two – of everything," says former Lake Clark ranger Jordan Fisher-Smith. "In some of the older cabins (within the park), people actually recorded their exploits on the walls." One such cabin overlooks upper Twin Lake (*see box*).

Exploring Twin Lakes

Nearly three decades later, **Twin Lakes** ❺ remains a popular backcountry destination, but it now attracts a different sort of crowd. Some visitors use it as a starting point for float trips down the Chilikadrotna, while others are more interested in backpacking. A few simply come to set up camp along the beach and relax.

Twin Lakes is a prime visitor destination for several reasons but access is probably the most significant one; it's only a half-hour flight from Port Alsworth. Founded in the 1940s by

When to go
Although the park is open year-round, most people visit from mid-June to early September, when temperatures average from 60 to 75°F (16–24°C). Coastal areas are about 10° cooler and are rainier and windier. Expect snowfall as early as September.

BELOW: a plane lands on the lake.

What the Hunters Claimed

Now off-limits to sport hunting, the Twin Lakes area once was popular with trophy seekers hoping to bag Dall sheep. These are a few samples of the scribblings found in one cabin:

"Shot 40-inch ram. Aug '65. Bill Silver, Castro Valley, Calif."

"Dr Norbert Conrad, Michigan. 1 sheep, 1 caribou, 1 black bear, 1 nice grizzly and lots of walking."

Some of the cabin's occupants got even more carried away with their boastful claims. Dr Chuck Finnell of Lapeer, Michigan, for example: "Record for eating most potatoes, 8-24-67 thru 9-8-67. Record double-shovel caribou, 8-26-67. Possible record sheep, 8-27-67. Assisted capture of record kangaroo mouse and 1 large shrew. 1 gut-shot squirrel. 7½ft grizzly, 9-2-67."

There's good fishing in the local lakes.

BELOW: a hiker heads for the Twin Lakes.

bush pilot Leon "Babe" Alsworth and wife Mary, Port Alsworth has become the region's "hub of activity" despite its small size (population about 100). For many visitors, this community on Lake Clark's southeast shore serves as the gateway to Lake Clark National Park and it's where the National Park Service has established its local headquarters.

The Alsworth family maintains its strong presence in the community; a structure first built by Babe and Mary Alsworth in the 1940s has been re-modeled and converted into "The Farm Lodge" (tel: 781-2208 or 888-440-2281), run by their son Glen and his wife Patty. The Alsworths also own Lake Clark Air (tel: 781-2208 or 888-440-2281; www.lakeclarkair.com) which runs daily commuter flights between Port Alsworth and Anchorage in the summer months.

Then there was Richard Proennicke, who settled at Upper Twin Lake in the 1960s and became something of an Alaskan legend when he wrote the book *One Man's Wilderness: An Alaskan Odyssey*. Now deceased, Dick Proen-nicke lived alone in the wilderness for three decades, and people would travel to Twin Lakes just to meet him. Though hospitable to those who passed his way, Proennicke sometimes second-guessed the wisdom of writing a book that so affected his solitary lifestyle. People are still drawn to the homestead where he lived.

Diverse wildlife

The scenery around Twin Lakes is spec-tacular, the wildlife diverse – every-thing from Dall sheep, moose, and grizzlies to beavers, eagles, shorebirds, waterfowl, ground squirrels, and voles. And the hiking is superb. Fed in part by glaciers born in the Neacola Moun-tains, the Twin Lakes are a vivid, pene-trating aquamarine hue. Much of their shoreline is bordered by boreal forest that offers easy walking – at least by Alaskan standards

Above the open white-spruce forest is dry alpine tundra, which in turn gives way to lightly vegetated or bare volcanic hills, whose canyons provide endless avenues for exploration and whose ridges offer awe-inspiring vistas of the Twin Lakes valley.

Kayaks, canoes or inflatables are wonderful means of exploring Lower and Upper Twin Lakes, 5 and 7 miles (8 and 11km) long, respectively. But beware: the valley often acts as a wind funnel and what had been a mirror-smooth lake surface may, in a matter of minutes, become a white-capped chop with waves 2ft to 3ft (60–90cm) high.

Turquoise and **Telaquana lakes** are the park's two other "destinations" most frequently visited by backpacker-hiker-camper types, again largely because of easy access and marketing strategies. Along with Twin Lakes, they've seen a substantial increase by wilderness explorers in the past 15 to 20 years. Yet even as Lake Clark's visi-tor-use curve moves slowly but steadily upward, vast expanses of the park remain terra incognita.

"You talk about natural resources that haven't been discovered; very few

people have set foot in the park's more remote mountainous areas. In fact, it's true to say that the park is largely unexplored north of Merrill Pass," says Paul Haertel, the park's first superintendent. "There are dozens of knife-edge ridges and steep-walled canyons where no one has ever walked, hundreds of mountains that have never been climbed. There's so much out there that remains to be discovered."

Some precautions

The weather often changes rapidly and quickly throughout Lake Clark because the park is located in a region where marine air masses from the Bering Sea and Gulf of Alaska frequently collide with drier, continental systems from Alaska's Interior. The result is extremely variable weather. The prime visitor season is June through August, when temperatures normally range from 50 to 65°F (10–18°C). Yet even in summer temperatures may drop into the 30s, especially at higher elevations. They may also, on occasion, climb above 80°F (27°C). Windy, wet weather is the rule, rather than the exception, espe-

cially in the park's eastern sections. The region's wettest months are August and September; winter is comparatively dry, but temperatures may plummet to –40° or colder.

Visitors exploring Lake Clark's backcountry on their own should plan to be totally self-sufficient. Quality clothing is a must, because hypothermia is a risk even in summer. Other "shoulds" include insect repellent, tents that can endure high winds and long spells of rain, and extra food. It's not uncommon for stormy weather to delay pick-up flights.

The Lake Clark region, like most of Alaska, is "bear country," and visitors should take appropriate measures to avoid close encounters with the park's ursine residents; that includes clean camping and noise-making when traveling in areas with low visibility. Bear-awareness brochures are available from the Park Service. Giardia may be a problem in some areas; when in doubt, it's best to treat drinking water. Before heading into the backcountry, it's also a good idea to leave a trip itinerary with someone reliable. ❑

A food and supplies cache at Twin Lakes.

BELOW LEFT: canoeing on Turquoise Lake.

Fishing on Lake Clark

Sport fishing is extraordinary in the lakes and streams of Lake Clark National Park, thanks largely to the abundance of rainbow trout, Dolly Varden, Arctic grayling, whitefish, lake trout, northern pike, and, particularly in the Cook Inlet drainage, silver and king salmon.

The Chilikadrotna and Mulchatna rivers offer some of the park's best prospects. Many anglers arrange to be dropped off in the upper reaches of one of these rivers and, after inflating a raft, drift and cast their way downstream for a few days. There's also good fishing in Kontrashibuna, Telaquana, and Turquoise lakes and in the streams that flow in and out of them. Lake Clark itself has given up trout larger than 50 pounds (23kg).

It takes years for the region's trout, grayling, and char to reach trophy size, so most anglers practice catch-and-release fishing, playing a fish as briefly as possible and avoiding removing it from the water as they remove the hook and let it swim away.

For many, that means fly-fishing. Spinning gear works well, too, particularly if anglers use single, barbless hooks, rather than treble hooks on spinners and spoons. Fish taken on bait tend to swallow hooks, damaging delicate gill tissue and internal organs, which leads to bleeding and, ultimately, death.

KATMAI NATIONAL PARK

Alaska
Anchorage

Take a trip to Katmai on the Alaska Peninsula
to fish and paddle, and see the strange lunar
landscape created by a volcanic eruption

Main attractions
KING SALMON
BROOKS RIVER AND CAMP
VALLEY OF TEN THOUSAND
  SMOKES
NOVARUPTA VOLCANO
KULIK LAKE
GROSVENOR LAKE

BELOW: river
canyons were cut
in the Valley of Ten
Thousand Smokes
after the 1912
eruption.

Nature in **Katmai National Park and Preserve** ⑥ is awesome. Here in this isolated location the scenery is breathtaking, the weather is unstable, the winds can be life-threatening, and the past is reckoned in terms of before and after the volcanic eruption of 1912.

Located 290 air miles (465km) from Anchorage on the Alaska Peninsula, the park is a haven for lovers of the unspoiled wilderness. No highway system touches this area; access is primarily by small plane, or by boat out of

King Salmon ⑦, the park's "gateway" community. Most visitors take a one-hour commuter flight from Anchorage to King Salmon, then fly by floatplane into Katmai's backcountry. It's also possible to arrange boat rides to some destinations, most notably **Brooks River and Camp**.

The park receives nearly 60,000 visits a year by sightseers and flightseers, fishermen, hikers, climbers and canoeists. The primary attraction is Brooks Camp, on **Naknek Lake**, where a large run of sockeye salmon each summer attracts dozens of brown bears, the coastal cousins of grizzlies.

You can pick up information at the Park Service's office in King Salmon or at the Brooks Camp Visitor Center (daily), where you're required to check in when visiting Brooks (be sure to ask about the evening ranger-led programs); or check the park's website before visiting (www.nps.gov/katm). Some people fly in for only a few hours, have a look at the bears, and then leave.

Viewing the bears

Book well in advance if you hope to stay in **Brooks Lodge** (tel: 243-5448 or 800-544-0551; www.bearviewing.net). Besides the lodge, there's also a campground that takes reservations on a first-come, first-served basis (tel: 877-444-6777 or 518-885-3639; www.recreation.gov). There are several easy walks in the immediate vicinity, and bears can be

viewed in summer from safe viewing platforms as they feed on spawning salmon in the Brooks River, particularly at Brooks Falls. The best time to see bears along the Brooks River is in July and again in September.

You can also book a place on a tour bus that provides transportation to the scene of volcanic devastation in the **Valley of Ten Thousand Smokes**. The bus takes visitors to Overlook Cabin, at the end of the road, from where you can see the valley and take a gentle, ranger-led hike, or set off on a more ambitious one on your own.

More than 90 years after the eruption, the valley remains awe-inspiring, though most of its "smokes" stopped steaming decades ago. Ash, pumice and rocks produced over 40 sq miles (100 sq km) of lunar landscape, sculpted by wind and water. The once-verdant valley floor, covered with shifting pumice, resists vegetation and quickly erases the imprint of hikers' boots.

Before the great eruption of 1912, a portion of the historic Katmai Trail passed through this valley. The trail was traveled by Russian fur traders and missionaries, then by a flood of gold seekers taking a shortcut to Nome. Prospectors and mail carriers used it to avoid a stormy sea passage around the Alaska Peninsula but by 1912 the gold rush had subsided and the trail was seldom traveled.

Today it is no longer visible and its ancient route is a path of obstacles. Blowing ash, rugged terrain, dense undergrowth, quicksand and narrow canyons challenge the most seasoned hiker. During severe weather, travelers are warned against the old route at Katmai Pass at the head of the valley. The interchange of air between the Gulf of Alaska and the Bering Sea streams through this pass and can cause winds of over 100mph (160kmh) – strong enough to blow hikers off their feet.

Tremors and eruptions

When the great eruption occurred, news was slow to reach the world outside Alaska because the area was so isolated, but its impact was felt hundreds of miles away. The closest account was given by a Native, American Pete, who was on the Katmai Trail only 18 miles

Grizzly Man
In 2003, Katmai gained unwelcome attention when Timothy Treadwell, famous for his "up close" documentation of its bears, was mauled to death. Two years later the incident was immortalized by Werner Herzog's movie, Grizzly Man. Most Alaskans believe that Treadwell behaved recklessly and brought the danger on himself.

BELOW: wildlife watching in Katmai.

Getting the campfire going.

(30km) northeast of Mount Katmai when the violent explosions began. Earth tremors that preceded the eruption were so severe that the residents of Katmai and Savonoski, small Native villages on the Alaska Peninsula, gathered their possessions and fled to Naknek, on Bristol Bay.

Later research gave credit for the devastation not to Mount Katmai, but to **Novarupta Volcano**, a volcano formed by the eruption itself. The explosion was heard up to 750 miles (1,200km) away in Juneau, and associated earth tremors caused immense avalanches on Denali (Mount McKinley), hundreds of miles to the north. Most heavily impacted were the Native villages of Katmai and Savonoski, later abandoned because of heavy ashfall, and the town of Kodiak on Kodiak Island, across Shelikof Strait.

BELOW: Katmai National Park's volcanic landscape.

The smoking valley

In the following years several expeditions were sent to the eruption site by the National Geographic Society to satisfy worldwide interest and carry out scientific research. Scientists were initially prevented from reaching the source of the eruption by seas of mud, ash slides as deep as 1,500ft (450 meters), and evidence of one of the most powerful water surges ever.

In 1916 the crater of Mount Katmai was reached and a smoking valley discovered at Katmai Pass. The valley was named by botanist Robert Griggs, who found it "one of the most amazing visions ever beheld by mortal eye. The whole valley as far as the eye could reach was full of hundreds, no, thousands – literally tens of thousands – of smokes curling up from its fissured floor." The landscape's fiery desolation prompted Griggs and his colleagues to call one stream the **River Lethe**, which in Greek mythology flows through the centre of Hades.

In 1918 the Valley of Ten Thousand Smokes was made a national monument in order to preserve an area important to the study of volcanism. In 1980 the monument was upgraded in status and greatly expanded: the new Katmai National Park and Preserve protected 4 million acres (1.6 million hectares) of coastal lands, forests, rivers, lakes, volcanic mountains, and alpine valleys.

When the Katmai monument was first created it was believed that the Valley of Ten Thousand Smokes would become a geyser-filled attraction to rival Yellowstone National Park in Wyoming, because scientists thought that the geyser field at Yellowstone was dying. But the reverse has come about. The Yellowstone geysers are still active, but the fumaroles at the Valley of Ten Thousand Smokes have subsided.

A rugged wilderness

Katmai National Park and Preserve makes available to visitors not only an area of amazing volcanic involvement but a representative and undisturbed portion of the Alaska Peninsula. Great varieties of terrain in Katmai include

the rugged coastal habitat of Shelikof Strait on one side of the Alaskan range and the rivers and lakes of the Naknek River watershed on the other. Mixed spruce and birch forests, dense willow and alder thickets, and moist tundra are found at lower elevations, with alpine tundra on the higher slopes.

A series of small lakes and rivers provide opportunities for canoeing, kayaking, and fishing. You can paddle to a group of tiny islands on Naknek Lake's north arm, but it's about a 60-mile (100km) round trip.

Varied wildlife

Rainbow trout, lake trout, char, pike and grayling are popular sport fish here, as well as sockeye, coho, king, pink, and chum salmon. Nearly 1 million salmon return each year to the Naknek River. Wilderness lodges at **Kulik** and **Grosvenor lakes** cater to serious fishing enthusiasts who want backcountry comfort and guided fishing, while other park visitors arrange their own fishing and float trips.

The brown bears are, of course, the main attraction, but there is a great deal of other wildlife that may be encountered elsewhere in Katmai – and you won't be quite so much part of the crowd as you would at the main bear-watching sites. Moose, caribou, land otter, wolverine, marten, weasel, mink, lynx, fox, wolf, muskrat, beaver, and hare all inhabit the park.

Offshore, in coastal waters, seals, sea lions, sea otters and beluga and gray whales can be seen. Birdwatching is also a popular pastime – the park has more than 40 songbird species.

The climate

The weather in Katmai is variable as this is a coastal region where different weather systems meet; heavy rain is characteristic of most areas in the summer months. The northwestern slope of the Aleutian Range has the most comfortable weather: at Brooks Camp the average daytime temperature is 60°F (15°C).

Here, skies are only expected to be clear or partially cloudy 20 percent of the time. Warm clothing, rain gear and boots are highly recommended at any time of the year. ❏

The 1912 eruption
As ash began to fall on Katmai in the great 1912 eruption, accompanied by nauseating gases, people feared they would suffer the fate of Pompeii and be buried alive.

BELOW: the Brooks River Falls, Katmai National Park.

MCNEIL RIVER STATE GAME SANCTUARY

Each summer, dozens of brown bears come to this Alaska Peninsula stream to feed on chum salmon that have returned to spawn. People, in turn, come to watch the fishing bears

The bears have always come first at **McNeil River State Game Sanctuary** ❽. Created in 1967 by the Alaska Legislature, the sanctuary is intended, above all else, to protect the world's largest known concentration of brown bears, the coastal cousins of grizzlies. The focal point of the gathering is **McNeil Falls**, where bears come each summer to feed on chum salmon, returning to the river to spawn. Typically, the salmon begin arriving in late June or early July and remain in large numbers until mid- to late August. As many as 144 individual bears (adults and cubs) have been identified along the river in a single season, while 72 bears have been seen feasting at the falls at one time.

By nature, adult brown bears tend to be fairly solitary creatures, with the exception of females that are raising families, or bears that temporarily pair up during mating season. For them to gather in such large numbers – and in such close quarters – is exceptional. For more than 35 years, Alaska's Division of Wildlife Conservation has enacted and enforced a series of restrictions to ensure that this unique gathering of bears is not disrupted by problems and conflicts with humans.

State regulations make it clear that brown bear viewing shall be the primary human activity in the sanctuary, which is located at the upper end of the Alaska Peninsula, just north of Katmai National Park and Preserve. Hunt-

ing and trapping are prohibited and all other use is allowed only as long as it does not significantly alter the bears' behavior. To limit human impacts, a permit system has been established to regulate the number of people who watch and photograph the bears.

A deadly encounter

Through the late 1960s, McNeil River was virtually unknown as a bear-viewing site. Jim Faro, a state biologist who managed the sanctuary in its early years, recalls that only a half-dozen or

Main attractions
MCNEIL FALLS
MIKFIK CREEK

LEFT: bears at play.
BELOW: cooling off.

Catch of the day.

BELOW: a family outing of brown bears.

so people visited in 1969. Because of that, there were few rules to govern visitor behavior. By 1970, however, the media had begun to bring McNeil to the public's attention. Vistation jumped. And because there were no rules to regulate public use, human activities got out of hand.

"We had people running up and down both sides of the river," Faro recalls. "There were even people fishing for salmon right at the falls, where the bears feed. If all the horror stories you heard about bears were true, we should have had lots of dead people."

Instead, the bears went into hiding. "It was like the bears were saying, 'We don't have to put up with this.' They took one look at all the people and left," Faro says. Only a handful of bears remained.

That same summer, a bear was killed by one of the sanctuary visitors. A photography guide decided to take some close-up pictures of a female with cubs, as they fed on the coastal mudflats. Crawling on his hands and knees, the photographer made his approach. The adult bear saw the movement and

charged. It's likely she thought another bear was approaching and threatening her young. The bear came more than 300ft across the flats. Expecting a false charge, the photographer remained on his hands and knees, rather than standing and identifying himself as human. Finally, when the bear was only 60 to 70ft (18–21 meters) away, the man made his move: he shot the sow with a .44 pistol. On being hit, the bear turned and fled, shot fatally in the lungs.

Tighter controls were needed, both to prevent future injurious encounters between bears and humans and to bring the bears back to McNeil in large numbers. In 1973, the Alaska Board of game approved proposals to regulate visitor activities in the sanctuary during the prime-time bear-viewing period.

The permit system

Since 1973, the primary visitor control has been a permit system that limits viewing and photography opportunities. No more than 10 people a day are allowed to visit the sanctuary's bear-viewing areas; and they may do so only when accompanied by one or two state

biologists. The permit period initially ran from July 1 through August 25, but it has been expanded to include June.

That permit system *(see page 334)* has been extraordinarily successful. Since the state enacted its visitor restrictions, the number of bears visiting the falls has increased nearly tenfold. Just as important, no bears have been killed within the sanctuary and no humans have been injured by bears – this despite thousands of human-bear encounters, often at close range.

Normally, bear "trespass" within the campground is not a problem. But occasionally a local resident – usually an adolescent bear – has to be taught the campground is off limits. The education proceeds in stages. Stage One is usually limited to loud, aggressive yelling. If that doesn't work, sanctuary staff "step it up a notch." That next step involves the use of a "shell cracker," which gives off a loud bang much like a firecracker. If there's still a problem, rubber pellets or even bird shot are used. But only rarely – and never in recent years – have the sanctuary staff had to go as far as Stage Three.

Mikfik Creek

Until the mid-1980s, few people visited McNeil sanctuary before July 1. That's when the chum salmon – and the bears – began to arrive at McNeil River. But in 1982, a new pattern began to emerge, because of changes at **Mikfik Creek**, a small, shallow, clearwater stream that flows through the sanctuary and enters a saltwater lagoon less than a mile from McNeil River. It hosts a run of sockeye salmon from early to mid-June, but historically the run has been so small that bears largely ignored the fish.

Then, mysteriously, Mikfik's sockeye return began to increase dramatically in size. Tens of thousands of sockeye (or red) salmon entered the creek each year. Not surprisingly, increased numbers of bears have been attracted to Mikfik's increased fishing opportunities. And following closely behind the bears were bear watchers and photographers.

The scene at the falls

While Mikfik has made the sanctuary's bear viewing more diverse, **McNeil Falls** remains the primary focus in July

The hunting issue
Controversy erupted in 2005 when the Alaska Game Board voted to allow bear hunting on two parcels of land near the McNeil River sanctuary. Opponents said this was unethical because the bears, being used to people in the area, wouldn't flee from hunters. After a flood of protest, the board reversed its decision in 2007.

BELOW: stalking a brown bear.

Be Prepared

Nearly all visitors reach the sanctuary by air, using air charters based in Homer. McNeil visitors must be self-sufficient and prepared for a wilderness experience; no commercial facilities are available. Visitors must bring their own tents, camping gear, and food.

Even in mid-summer, equipment and clothing must be suitable for cold, wet weather. Visitors are also cautioned that bad weather can delay flights for several days. Visitors should also be in good physical shape; the 4-mile (6.4km) round-trip hike to McNeil Falls is not especially hazardous, but it does require strenuous "slogging" across mud flats and crossing Mikfik Creek. A typical day at the falls lasts six to eight hours, on a narrow gravel pad that's about 15ft (4.6 meters) long.

TIP

Getting Around

To obtain an application packet for McNeil River State Game Sanctuary, contact the Alaska Department of Fish and Game, Division of Wildlife Conservation, (333 Raspberry Road, Anchorage, AK 99518-1599; tel: 267-2532; www.state.ak.us/adfg).

and August. Located a mile above the river's mouth, the falls is actually a step-like series of small waterfalls, pools, and rapids that stretch along the stream for several hundred yards. Individual bears take up their fishing positions based on their place in the ursine pecking order. The prime spots are located along the western bank, opposite the two viewing pads used by humans. Here the most dominant bears – adult males, some weighing 1,000lbs (450kg) or more – jockey for position.

The bears use a variety of fishing techniques. Some stand motionless in mid-stream. When a chum salmon swims by, the bear pins it to the river bottom with its paws, then bites into it. Others use snorkeling techniques, and a few even dive for fish. Cubs watch their mothers from the shore, closely observing mom's technique; now and then an especially bold cub will make its own attempt. But normally they'll wait until their mother brings a fish to shore. Adolescent bears – the equivalent of teenagers – that have been weaned from their mothers patrol the

shorelines, hoping to find a scrap or two. Gulls and bald eagles, too, crowd the river, fighting over carcasses.

The best fishers may catch dozens of salmon in just one day. One particularly adept male once caught more than 70 fish in less than eight hours. When hungry, bears will consume the entire fish, including head and bones. But as they become satiated, bears will go for the highest calorie parts: the brain, eggs, and skin.

The chum run ends in mid- to late August, but bears begin to disperse even before then, as they go in search of another nutritious food: berries.

Applying for permits

The permits are issued through a lottery held each year in late March. Applications must be postmarked or sent in online by March 1 and accompanied by a nonrefundable application fee of $25 per person (group applications are limited to three people).

Non-resident permit winners must pay $350 per person to visit the sanctuary for the four-day permit period, while Alaskans must pay $150. ❑

BELOW: viewing platform at McNeil Falls.

Mixing bears and people

Getting close to bears allows you to recognize their individuality – some are aggressive by nature but others are mild-mannered or even timid.

It's widely assumed that bears and people don't mix," says Larry Aumiller, the sanctuary's former long-time manager. "But here we've shown that they can mix, if you do the right things. To me, that's the most important message of McNeil: humans can peacefully coexist with bears. "

Such peaceful coexistence is possible because of a simple fact: McNeil bears are habituated to humans, but view them as neutral objects – almost a part of the landscape. People do not pose a threat; nor are they a source of food. To prevent any such association, feeding of bears is prohibited at McNeil (as it is throughout Alaska). Furthermore, a designated wood-frame building is provided for food storage, cooking, and eating. And a no-bears-allowed policy is strictly enforced within a well-defined campground area.

Aumiller's education of McNeil's bears went beyond campground discipline. Through the years he made it easier for the bears to "read" people. The close supervision of sanctuary visitors is, in part, intended to make humans more predictable to the bears. For example, visitors are permitted to watch and photograph bears from a single, defined viewing area; only 10 per day are allowed there; and viewing is done from late morning through early evening. Such routines and restrictions have made it easier for McNeil's bears to tolerate people.

The truth about bears

Bears aren't the only ones to receive an education at McNeil. The sanctuary is a valuable learning ground for humans as well. Many visitors come to McNeil filled with irrational fears born of ignorance or sensationalized accounts of bear attacks. They carry the simplistic and inaccurate image of bears as menacing, dangerous creatures – unpredictable killers lurking in the shadows and waiting to attack. McNeil helps to change such misconceptions. Visitors discover first-hand that bears aren't man-eating monsters as so often portrayed in literature and news accounts.

"The first day people come here," says Aumiller, "many are fearful, usually because of things they've heard or read. But after they've seen a few bears up close and the bears go about their business, people get incredibly blasé about them. After that, they have to be cautioned about getting too careless. The transformation is almost universal."

Aumiller believes that McNeil's visitors feel safe around the bears largely because the sanctuary provides a controlled situation. The biologists act as guides. And they're armed, though they've never had to shoot a bear. The removal of irrational fears makes it easier to accept the bears on their own terms. And there's no better place to watch "bears being bears."

Watching them for hours each day, for up to four days in a row, visitors gain glimpses into the animals' lives. People start to recognize the bears as individuals, with different mannerisms and personalities. Some are aggressive, even bullies, others mild-mannered or timid around their own kind. Some are excellent fishers, others fare poorly. ❏

RIGHT: bear-hunting photographers at Mikfik Creek.

REMOTE COMMUNITIES AND WILDLANDS

Part of the north Pacific's volcanic "ring of fire," the Alaska Peninsula has many settlements of Natives as well as some notable wildlife reserves

BELOW: Bristol Bay has large colonies of walrus.

Extending more than 500 miles (800km) from top to tip, the Alaska Peninsula ➒ is a rugged, storm-blasted, mostly treeless landscape inhabited by the world's densest population of brown bears: more than one bear per square mile. The greatest of these concentrations occur in **Katmai National Park and Preserve** and **McNeil River State Game Sanctuary** (*see pages 326 and 331 respectively*), at the upper end of the peninsula. Dozens of brown bears gather along peninsula streams each year to feed on the spawning salmon and both the National Park Service and Alaska Department of Fish and Game have established bear-viewing programs that give people unmatched opportunities to observe the fishing bears.

Bristol Bay

The largest salmon runs are those of the sockeye that return to **Bristol Bay** ➓ streams each summer; tens of millions of the salmon spawn here, providing nutrients for all manner of predators and scavengers, including bears, eagles, gulls, foxes, rainbow trout, and char. And humans, too. The Bristol Bay region is home to North America's largest commercial salmon fleet; and the streams that feed the bay are known around the world as a fisherman's paradise.

Though many anglers come to catch the region's salmon, rainbow trout are an even bigger draw. Dozens of fishing lodges are scattered through the Bristol Bay and Alaska Peninsula region. Other companies have fish camps or do guided day trips out of the region's communities.

Besides bears, salmon, and rainbows, Bristol Bay and the Alaska Peninsula are seasonal or year-round homes to numerous other species of mammals and birds; among the most spectacular concentrations are migrating herds of caribou, numerous colonies of sea birds and large marine mammal haulouts. Two of the world's greatest con-

centrations of walrus occur in Bristol Bay; one is at the **Togiak National Wildlife Refuge** ⑪; the other is at Round Island, within the **Walrus Islands State Game Santuary** ⑫ (tel: 842-2334; www.wildlife.alaska.gov/index. cfm?adfg=refuge.rnd_is). And on the lower Alaska Peninsula, the **Izembek National Wildlife Refuge** ⑬ (tel: 532-2419 in summer, or 267-2532 year-round; www.wildlife.alaska.gov/index.cfm? adfg=refuge.izembek) serves as an "international crossroads" for migrating waterfowl and shorebirds.

The refuge's heart is **Izembeck Lagoon**, where hundreds of thousands of migratory waterfowl converge each fall, including the entire world population of black brant.

Besides being home to large concentrations of wildlife, the Alaska Peninsula is also a seismically active place that is part of the North Pacific's "ring of fire." Dozens of volcanoes dot the landscape, several of them still considered active. **Pavlof Volcano**, on the lower peninsula, has erupted more than 40 times since 1790; in 1986 it sent volcanic ash more than 10 miles (16km) into the atmosphere and continued to belch smoke and ash and lava off and on for more than two years.

One of the more spectacular volcanic landscapes is **Aniakchak Caldera**, a 6-mile (10km) wide crater formed thousands of years ago by the collapse of a huge volcano. Within the caldera are all sorts of volcanic features: lava fields, warm springs, and cinder cones. The caldera is the dominant feature of **Aniakchak National Monument and Preserve** ⑮ (tel: 246-3305; www.nps.gov/ania), one of the least visited units of the National Park System.

The Alaska Peninsula and Bristol Bay region is home to the Aleut and Yup'ik Eskimo peoples. Here, as in much of rural Alaska, most residents continue to depend on subsistence harvests of fish, mammals, birds, and plants. Dozens of small villages are scattered along the coast; the area's two hubs are **Dillingham**, in Bristol Bay, and **King Salmon**, on the upper Alaska Peninsula. Both communities are served by daily commuter flights from Anchorage and are jumping-off spots for trips into the area's parks and

Getting to school
Students (grades 6 and above) in the Alaska Peninsula community of South Naknek (population 74) must cross the Naknek River each day to attend school. When the river is frozen, they travel by car, ATV or snowmachine; otherwise the daily school run is via bush plane.

BELOW: adding color to the fishing kit.

Finding the Best Fishing

There are several lodges and fishing guide operations in Katmai National Park (tel: 246-3305; www.nps.gov/katm) and **Wood-Tikchik State Park** ⑭ (tel: 842-2375 in summer, 269-8698 the rest of the year; http://dnr.alaska.gov/parks/units/woodtik.htm); at 1.55 million acres (630,000 hectares), Wood-Tikchik, north of Bristol Bay, is the largest of America's state parks, with two immense river-and-lake chains that are popular with boaters as well as anglers.

Guided sport fishing is also popular in three national wildlife refuges: the **Togiak refuge** is on Bristol Bay's northern edge (tel: 842-1063; http://togiak.fws.gov) while the **Becharof/Alaska Peninsula refuges** (tel: 246-3339; http://becharof.fws.gov) encompass much of the Alaska Peninsula.

BELOW: Mount Cleveland is a 5,675ft (1,730-meter) -high active volcano on Chuginadak Island in the western Aleutian Islands.

refuges. For information visitor services, contact the Dillingham Chamber of Commerce (tel: 842-5115; www.dillinghamak.com) or the King Salmon Visitors Center (tel: 246-4250).

The Aleutian Islands

Reaching southwest beyond the Alaska Peninsula, the **Aleutian Islands** ⑯ arc more than 1,000 miles (1,600km) in their bend toward Asia. More than 200 islands make up the chain, which separates the Pacific Ocean from the Bering Sea.

Nearly all of the islands are included within the **Alaska Maritime National Wildlife Refuge** (tel: 235-6546; www.alaska.fws.gov/nwr/akmar.index.htm), which protects the coastal lands and waters used by the many sea birds, shorebirds, waterfowl, and marine mammals that inhabit the chain.

While the volcanic, tundra-covered islands that make up the chain have a rugged, barren appearance, the waters surrounding the Aleutians are among the richest in the world, supporting a billion-dollar fishing industry. The area is also home to some of the world's largest bird colonies and marine mammal populations, from sea otters to seals and sea lions and whales. Yet even here, there is evidence of ecological stress: two once-plentiful species, sea lions and harbor seals, have experienced great declines in recent decades; the populations of some birds, too, have been greatly reduced. Scientists have been studying the declines, which may be tied to overfishing, climate change, or other factors.

The weather in the Aleutians is generally cool and wet, and often stormy. Annual precipitation ranges from 20 to 80 inches (50–200cm) a year. Summer temperatures rarely get much above 50°F (10°C) and in winter don't often drop below 20°F (–6.7°C). Winds seem to blow constantly and fog too is common. Visitors to the region must be prepared for weather delays, both coming and going.

Dutch Harbor

Aleuts have inhabited the island chain for centuries, depending on the marine ecosystem for their survival. Small numbers of Aleuts (and even smaller

numbers of non-Natives) still reside here, in several small communities. The Aleutians' largest city and commercial hub is **Dutch Harbor**, at the northern end of the chain on **Unalaska Island** ⓱. It is the No. 1 fishing port in the US, both in terms of poundage and value.

With a combined population of about 4,200 people, Dutch Harbor and neighboring **Unalaska** also serve as the Aleutians' tourism center, complete with the world-class Grand Aleutian hotel. Visitor activities here range from sport fishing for salmon and halibut to birdwatching, hiking, kayaking, and exploring World War II remnants. Japanese troops bombed Dutch Harbor during the war and also landed on Attu and Kiska Islands; the US military later retook those islands, in the only battles fought on American soil during World War II.

Those who travel to Dutch Harbor can learn more about local history at the **Museum of the Aleutians**, which has exhibits about the Aleut culture, Russian occupation, World War II, and the fishing industry. Contact the Dutch Harbor/Unalaska Convention and Visitors Bureau (tel: 907-581-2612 or 877-581-2612; www.unalaska.info) for more information about travel to and within the area.

The Pribilof Islands

Three hundred miles (480km) off the western coast of Alaska and 200 miles north of the Aleutians lie the **Pribilof Islands** ⓲, the nesting grounds for hundreds of thousands of sea birds of almost 200 different species, and the breeding grounds and summer home of nearly a million Pacific fur seals. Five volcanic, treeless islets make up the Pribilof group, but only two of those are inhabited by humans: **St Paul** and **St George**; with a population of about 500 people, nearly all Natives, the village of St Paul is the world's largest community of Aleuts. There are small hotels on both islands, but only St Paul has a restaurant. It also is visited

in summer by packaged tours, the easiest way to visit the Pribilofs (contact the Tanadgusix Village Corporation of St Paul Island for more tourism information, tel: 877-424-5637; www.alaskabirding.com).

Today, the fishing and tourism industries are being developed as St Paul's main economic supports. Past revenues were generated by the fur seal harvest and government aid. With the ending of the commericial harvest in 1985, the community was forced to find other means of support. The newly completed harbor is a boon to local fishermen, who had no safe haven for their boats, and is expected to attract new industry. Tourism also helps; the Pribilofs are known as a birders' paradise. Especially attractive to serious birders are the "accidental" Asian migrants that sometimes get blown to the islands by strong western winds. These birds are rarely, if ever, seen anywhere else in North America.

Unalaska Island, America's top fishing port.

BELOW: a fox cub in St George, Pribilof Islands.

BELOW: the First
Moravian Mission
building in Bethel.

Visitors to the Pribilofs should be prepared for cool and moist conditions. In June, the average daily high is 41°F (5°C) and nighttime lows fall into the 30s even in summer. And only rarely do the islands experience back-to-back sunny days.

Yukon-Kuskokwim Delta

Encompassing 76,000 sq miles (200,000 sq km) in remote Southwest Alaska, the **Yukon-Kuskokwim Delta** is home to Alaska's Yup'ik Eskimos and one of the world's great waterfowl-nesting areas.

Much of the delta is within the **Yukon Delta National Wildlife Refuge ⑲**. At 19.2 million acres (7.8 million hectares), this refuge is the nation's second largest (just slightly smaller than the Arctic National Wildlife Refuge). It's also the oldest refuge in Alaska; in 1909, President Theodore Roosevelt established the Yukon Delta Reservation. That reservation and some later refuges were then consolidated and expanded in 1980 to form the present Yukon Delta NWR. Within the refuge, waters from two of Alaska's

four largest rivers meander through immense, tundra wetlands. The Yukon flows 1,400 miles (2,250km) before emptying into the Bering Sea, while to the south, the Kuskokwim River winds 540 miles (870km) through Southwest Alaska.

This is as flat as Alaska gets: nearly 70 percent of the refuge is delta lands and waters less than 100ft (30 meters) in elevation. Innumerable streams and sloughs weave through this lowland, which is also dotted with tens of thousands of lakes, ponds, and marshes. In all, about a third of the refuge is covered in water. Higher and drier areas are covered by forests and range up to an elevation of 4,000ft (1,200 meters), in the gently rounded **Kuskokwim** and **Kilbuck Mountains**.

The refuge's wetlands are seasonal home to millions of birds: sea birds, shorebirds, waterfowl, songbirds, and raptors. In both diversity and numbers, the refuge is considered America's most important shorebird nesting area and is also critically important for ducks and geese. Birds come here from the Atlantic coast as well as Asia.

Spawning ground

The Delta's waterways also serve as important spawning and rearing habitat for more than 40 species of fish, including Alaska's five species of Pacific salmon, Dolly Varden char, northern pike, grayling, and rainbow trout. Mammals range from grizzlies and black bears to caribou, moose, wolves, and musk oxen. Coastal waters are important to several types of seals, walrus, and whales.

Few people visit the refuge; those who do come here largely for the sport fishing or birdwatching. For information on recreational opportunities, contact the refuge headquarters in Bethel (tel: 543-3151; http://yukondelta.fws.gov).

Bethel

The Delta's Yupik residents live in scattered villages along the coast and its main rivers. Most of the 50 or so communities are small, with few or no accommodations for travelers.

The commercial and social hub of the region is **Bethel** ❷⓿, a city of about 6,000 people on the Kuskokwim River.

Guarding the nest.

Here you'll find a theater, banks, restaurants, radio and TV stations, a college, a hospital, and lodging options. The Moravian Church established a mission here in 1884. Information on Bethel and outlying areas can be obtained from the Bethel Chamber of Commerce (tel: 543-2911; www.bethelakchamber.org).

From the flatlands of the Y-K Delta to the volcanic peaks and bear-rich salmon streams of the Alaska Peninsula and the wind-battered islands of the Aleutian chain and Pribilof Archipelago, the Southwest region presents adventurous visitors the opportunity to see parts of wild Alaska and aspects of the state's Native culture that few travelers ever encounter. ❑

RESTAURANTS

Dutch Harbor/Unalaska

Amelia's Restaurant
Biorka Drive
Tel: 581-2800 **$–$$**
Serving Mexican and American classics such as burgers and milkshakes, it opens early and is a perfect breakfast or lunch spot.

The Chart Room
Grand Aleutian Hotel,
498 Salmon Way
Tel: 866-581-3844 or 581-3844
www.grandaleutian.com
$–$$$$
Dutch Harbor's fine dining option has panoramic views of Margaret Bay, and features steak, pasta, and Alaska seafood. This elegant hotel also offers the bistro-style Margaret Bay,

on the first floor, and Cape Cheerful Lounge, a gathering spot for locals. Live entertainment. Bar.

Dillingham

Muddy Rudder
100 Main Street
Tel: 842-2534 **$–$$$$**
The favorite spot for locals and visitors alike is open for daily breakfast, lunch, and dinner from May through November. Steaks, seafood, burgers, sandwiches, and salads. Beer and wine.

Bethel

Arctic Sun Café
3551 Chief Eddie Hoffman Way
Tel: 543-3566 **$**
Located close to the Alaska Airlines terminal at Bethel

airport. Open 8am–10pm, this is a favorite spot for breakfast among the locals. Also serves standard burger, sandwich, soup, and salad type meals with occasional specials. No alcohol.

Brother's Pizzas and Subs
3551 Chief Eddie Hoffman Way
Tel: 543-3878 **$–$$$$**
Located in the same building as Arctic Sun Café. The locals say it's the best spot in town for pizza. Also serves burgers, sandwiches, and salads. Open daily 11am–11pm. No alcohol.

Dimitri's Restaurant
281 Fourth Avenue
Tel: 907-543-3434

Features Greek and Italian food, but also offers burgers, pork chops, salads.

V.I.P. Restaurant
1220 Chief Eddie Hoffman Highway
Tel: 543-4777
www.allanivik.com/VIP Restaurant.1html **$$–$$$**
Open daily for lunch and dinner. Specializes in sushi and Korean fare, but also serves American favorites such as burgers and salads.

Price is for dinner excluding tax, tip, and beverages:
$ = under $15
$$ = $15–20
$$$ = $20–30
$$$$ = over $30

✺ INSIGHT GUIDES   TRAVEL TIPS

ALASKA

TRANSPORTATION

ACCOMMODATIONS

ACTIVITIES

CONTACTS

A – Z

T RANSPORTATION

GETTING THERE AND GETTING AROUND

GETTING THERE

The 1½ million yearly visitors to Alaska arrive in one of three ways: by air, sea or road. The best choice for the individual traveler depends on the goals for the journey, the time available, and the costs involved. Arriving by train is not an option. No train system, neither US nor Canadian, connects with Alaska's railway service.

By Air

Generally speaking, the fastest and least expensive way to travel to Alaska is to fly. Several major airlines provide regularly scheduled flights into Anchorage's Ted Stevens International Airport (and some to Fairbanks International), especially during the summer season. Alaska Airlines offers, by far, the most comprehensive coverage, with daily direct flights to Anchorage from Vancouver (British Columbia), Seattle, Portland, San Diego, Los Angeles, Denver, and Chicago. Anchorage serves as the primary hub for travel to and within the state. Those wishing to travel to smaller, outlying towns and villages may do so from Anchorage by using Alaska Airlines, the smaller, regional airlines, or chartered air taxi companies.

The communities of Ketchikan, Wrangell, Petersburg, Sitka, Juneau, Glacier Bay/Gustavus, Yakutat, and Cordova may be reached directly from Seattle via Alaska Airlines. *(See page 347 for a list of airline contacts.)*

There are no airport taxes in Alaska, but each passenger is assessed a small fee that is attached to the price of the ticket. The fee usually amounts to only a few cents and at most, a few dollars.

Private pilots planning to fly to Alaska should have the latest federal government flight information publication, the Alaska Chart Supplement, available from the Federal Aviation Administration, 222 W. Seventh Ave., No. 14, Anchorage, Alaska, tel: 99513-7587 or at www.alaska.faa.gov.

Useful contacts

Airport Information (domestic or international airlines, terminal maps, ground transportation, visitor information):
Fairbanks International Airport: tel: 907-474-2500; www.dot.state.ak.us/faiiap
Juneau International Airport: tel: 907-789-7821; www.juneau.org/airport
Ketchikan International Airport: tel: 907-225-6800; www.borough.ketchikan.ak.us/airport/airport.htm
Ted Stevens International Airport (Anchorage): tel: 907-266-2526; www.anchorageairport.com

By Sea

Nearly half of all visitors to Alaska travel via **cruise ship**. There are several good reasons for this, beyond the effective marketing programs of the cruise industry. Most Alaska cruises begin – or end up – in Seattle or Vancouver, British Columbia, Canada. They offer one-way or round-trip voyages through the protected (and therefore generally calm) waterways of the Inside Passage. Passengers may go ashore and see the sights, experience the local culture and shop in various Southeast communities without having to repeatedly pack and unpack, or sleep in a different bed every night.

Passengers generally have the option of adding shore excursions – even extended land tours – to the basic package. The entire cost of the trip, while admittedly expensive, is known at the outset.

Cruising options

Big-ship cruise lines, such as Holland America, Princess, Celebrity, Norwegian, Regent Seven Seas, and Royal Caribbean transport thousands of passengers while offering not only luxurious travel to Alaska, but also an array of on-board entertainment for those who enjoy seemingly endless options of formal dinners (and formal dress), casinos, floor shows, spas, line dancing, art auctions, bingo, and kids' programs, to name a few.

Small-ship cruise lines, like Cruise West, Lindblad, Glacier Bay, American Safari, and American West Steamboat Company, carry 20–250 passengers, and specialize in excellent food, casual dress, close-up (sea-level) wildlife and glacier viewing, and educational lectures by on-board naturalists. These smaller ships have the added advantage of being able to offer stops in less-traveled areas such as Wrangell or Petersburg.

Whether you decide to go large or small, all cruise passengers must pay a $50 "head tax". While some of the money goes to monitoring the ship's environmental impact, most is used by local agencies for infrastructure upkeep. *(For more on cruising, see pages 87–93.)*

Those who are more adventurous (and have plenty of time) might want to consider one of the more unusual

Alaska cruises to the far north, around the Pribilof Islands (these are known to be superb for birdwatching) and into the Bering Sea. These are operated by the smaller, specialist expedition cruise companies.

Ferries

Independent travelers may choose another excellent option: traveling to Alaska aboard one of the **Alaska Marine Highway System** ferries. The state actually operates 11 ferries providing year-round service between Bellingham, Washington (or Prince Rupert, British Columbia, Canada) and Southeast and Southcentral Alaska's coastal communities. Seasonal service is available to those in Southwest.

Twice-monthly connections (cross-gulf) between the Southeast and Southwest routes are available in summer only. Most of these communities are located far from the road system; therefore ferry travel is basic transportation. The ferries range in size from the 180ft/149-passenger M/V *Lituya* to the 418ft/499-passenger M/V *Columbia*. The larger ferries offer comfortable (if not luxurious) staterooms, some with private baths.

During the summer, USDA Forest Service naturalists offer interpretive programs. There are large, clean public restrooms and showers (towels may be rented). Also, after 10pm, you may roll out a sleeping bag in one of the spacious lounges, kick back in a recliner, or pitch a tent (at any time) near the heated solarium, located on the upper deck. The ferries offer cafeterias or snack bars, gift shops, laundry facilities, video game rooms, occasional movies, comfortable lounges, and a play area for toddlers.

It is a low-key and user-friendly way to travel, but it doesn't come cheap. Walk-on passengers from Bellingham to Skagway, for example, will pay around US$350 (one way). They may bring along their bicycle or kayak, if they wish, for $56 and $86, respectively. If they want a stateroom (for two) with a bath, it will add about $350 more. If they drive a small automobile onto the ferry, add an additional $950 (considerably more for larger vehicles, including RVs).

Once on the ferry, the trip is surprisingly inexpensive: diners get a meal of fresh Alaskan seafood for under $10, the full bar serves pints of Alaskan beer for only $2 (other domestic brews are $3), free movies play once or twice daily, complimentary lectures commence

on the observation deck, and there is plenty of breathtaking scenery at no additional cost.

If you want to break up the trip and spend a few days in some of the towns along the way, the overall cost will not be greatly affected. However, you will need the luxury of time, as it may be two or three days before the next ferry comes along. There are two, new catamaran-styled fast ferries in the system, which add considerable flexibility between certain ports. One operates between Juneau, Sitka, Haines, and Skagway, and the other between the communities of Whittier, Valdez, and Cordova in Prince William Sound.

Travelers planning to use the ferry system during the busy summer tourist season should make reservations at least 6 months in advance. *(See also page 113.)*

Useful contacts

Alaska Marine Highway System: tel: 800-642-0066 or 907-465-3941; www.ferryalaska.com.
Northwest CruiseShip Association: http://alaska.nwcruiseship.org

By Road

Traveling the Alaska Highway is a great adventure. However, because of the great distance, only well-prepared drivers with plenty of time should consider it.

By Bus

Bus service and motorcoach tours are available to Alaska by way of the Alaska Highway. From Seattle, Washington, Greyhound connects with Greyhound Canada, offering service to Whitehorse in the Yukon Territory, Canada. From Whitehorse, Alaska Direct Bus Lines and Alaska/Yukon Trails connect with several Alaska communities, including Tok, Fairbanks, and Anchorage. Several companies offer motorcoach tours between the contiguous United States and Alaska. For more information, contact a travel agent.

By Car or RV

The new improvements to the Alaska Highway have made driving enjoyable and safe, but distance may be a drawback. It is 1,488 miles (2,395km) from Dawson Creek, BC to Fairbanks, and much of the trip will be through extremely remote, though spectacular, country. Make sure your vehicle is in dependable working order and bring along basic tools, flares, jack, spare tire, first-aid kit, and other emergency

equipment. If you're traveling the road in winter, be prepared with adequate food, water, warm clothing, and blankets in case of unexpected delays.

For essential information about driving Alaska's highways, refer to the latest edition of *The Milepost*, published and updated yearly, which gives detailed descriptions of points of interest, food, gas, and lodging options, as well as road conditions. Log onto http://milepost.com for additional information.

Useful contacts

Alaska Direct Bus Line: tel: 800-770-6652; www.alaskadirectbusline.com
Alaska/Yukon Trails: tel: 800-770-7275; www.alaskashuttle.com
Current driving, construction and weather conditions on Alaska highways: tel: 511 within Alaska, or 866-282-7577; http://511.Alaska.gov
Greyhound Canada Transportation Corp.: tel: 800-661-8747; www.greyhound.ca

GETTING AROUND

Because of Alaska's size, getting around is no small task. Destinations are dozens , if not, hundreds of miles apart and often separated by waterways, steep mountain ranges, and endless tracts of uninhabited terrain. For this reason, many travellers choose to see the state via cruise tours that take trips into the Interior. *(For more information on cruise tours see pages 90–1, and for contact info see pages 365–6.)*

For those who decide to go it alone, the state's few highways (six total), numerous airports, and direct train system make travelling easy, if time consuming. While cities in the Southeast are small and dense enough to navigate largely on foot, Anchorage and Fairbanks are sprawling and have limited public transportation. If you plan on spending any length of time in either, renting a car is advisable.

To and From the Airport

On arrival in Anchorage, or any other Alaska airport, you should expect to handle your own luggage. Ground transportation is usually available in the form of a local bus service (in Anchorage, Fairbanks and Juneau), taxis or car rentals. In Anchorage, the Alaska Railroad has a spur that connects cruise-ship passengers from the airport to downtown hotels.

However, most airports in Alaska are located within a few minutes' drive of the downtown area. A notable exception is Ketchikan, where the airport is located on a separate island, and a short ferry trip is necessary to reach the ground transportation – which you have to pre-arrange – to take you downtown. The ferry runs every half-hour and costs $5 per adult.

By Air

The secret to conquering Alaska's vastness is air travel. Commuter airlines and charter aircraft services are everywhere. More often than not, even the most remote cabins in the wilderness have some sort of airstrip nearby, or a stretch of hard-packed sand on a river bar to serve as a landing strip. Per capita, six times as many Alaskans have a pilot's license as do residents of the rest of the country.

Costs typically begin at $375 an hour (flight time) to charter a pilot and plane that can carry four passengers, depending on the amount of baggage. If you're traveling with a large group, it's even possible to charter a vintage DC-3, a twin-engine plane capable of hauling large loads for long distances. Also check local air-taxi operators for charter and commuter service to Alaskan communities.

On the facing page is a list of many of the carriers offering scheduled intrastate air service. Interline service is available to most rural Alaska points: check with carriers.

By Rail

The 470-mile (756-km) Alaska Railroad connects Anchorage with Fairbanks to the north and with Whittier and Seward to the south. There's daily service between Anchorage and Fairbanks in summer, but only weekly in winter. Service between Anchorage and Seward is seasonal (mid-May to mid-September).

For more information, contact: Alaska Railroad, tel: 907-265-2494 or toll-free 800-544-0552; www.akrr. com. Princess Cruises and Holland America/Grayline Alaska own several of the luxurious domed cars, including the McKinley Explorer, that travel as part of Alaska Railroads trains. Tours are available as are single trips to most Alaska Railroad destinations. To make reservations, contact Grayline Alaska at tel: (888) 452-1737; www. graylinealaska.com, Holland America at tel: (877) 932-4259; www. hollandamerica.com, or Princess Cruises at tel: (800) 774-6237.

By Sea

Besides sailing from Seattle to southeastern Alaska, the Alaska Marine Highway operates several ferries on the Gulf Coast. Homer on the Kenai Peninsula is connected to the Prince William Sound communities of Whittier, Valdez, and Cordova via the ferries. It's also possible to sail from Homer to Kodiak Island and onward to several Aleutian destinations. Check at the ferry office near the harbor if you're in any of the towns along the route, or get information in advance from the Alaska Marine Highway. *(For contact information, see page 345.)*

Public Transportation

Alaska's three largest cities offer municipal bus service.
Anchorage
Anchorage People Mover, tel: 907-343-6543; www.muni.org/transit1/mapping.
Fairbanks
Metropolitan Area Commuter System (MACS), tel: 907-459-1011; www. co.fairbanks.ak.us/transportation.
Juneau
Capital Transit System (CTS), tel: 907-789-6901; www.juneau.org/capitaltransit.

Private Transportation

Taxis

Taxis are nice for getting around town, but can be extremely expensive for long distances.
Anchorage
Alaska Checker Cab, tel: 907-274-3333
Alaska Yellow Cab, tel: 907-222-2222
Fairbanks
Alaska Cab, tel: 907-456-3355
Executive Cab, tel: 907-455-8899
Juneau
Capital Cab and Evergreen Taxi, tel: 907-586-2772

Car Rentals

If you are flying into Anchorage, Fairbanks, or Juneau, you can rent a car without ever stepping outside. The companies listed below have desks inside the airport terminals:
Alamo, tel: 800-462-5266; www.alamo.com
Avis Rental Car, tel: 800-331-1212; www.avis.com
Budget, tel: 800-527-0700; www.budget.com

Recreational Vehicles

Renting an RV camper has become increasingly popular. There are many businesses offering this service.

Anchorage
A & M RV Center, tel: 907-279-5508 or 800-478-4678; www.gorv.com
ABC Motorhome & RV, tel: 907-279-2000 or 800-421-7456; www. abcmotorhome.com
Fairbanks
Adventures in Alaska RV Rentals, tel: 907-458-7368, www.adventuresakrv.com

Motoring Advice

The speed limit on most Alaska highways is 55mph (88kmh), although speeds of up to 65mph (104kmh) are allowed on some sections. Speed limits are lower within cities, in residential areas and especially near schools. Alaska law requires drivers to pull over at the first, safe opportunity whenever five or more vehicles are following behind them.

A right turn is permitted against a red light unless otherwise posted, but only after you stop long enough to confirm there is no traffic with which you will interfere. All drivers in both directions are required to stop for a school bus with its warning lights operating. Drivers may not proceed around or past a school bus until the lights have been turned off.

Drivers in Alaska may see hitchhikers, but not nearly as many as in the past. Hitchhiking is most common during the summer season, when both residents and visitors seek rides when traveling to jobs or adventures along major routes. You pick up hitchhikers at your own risk.

Prudence dictates that you slow your speed during the winter months. Highways in Alaska are not the best in the world, and in combination with ice and snow, can be treacherous. For the latest information on road conditions, dial 511, or go to http://511.alaska.gov.

Car Breakdown

When driving the highways in Alaska, it's always a good idea to be prepared. While excellent, dependable towing and repair services are available in the cities and even smaller towns of the state, you may break down in the middle of nowhere. It's very important that your vehicle be in reliable condition if you're planning a drive to remote areas. Check to be sure you have a working spare tire, a jack, flares, a basic tool kit, jumper cables, and a first aid kit, as well as food and drink. An extra can of oil as well as transmission and brake fluids could be a godsend. If you do break down along the road, you'll likely find that other drivers in Alaska will probably stop and see if they can help.

Airline Contacts

Major Carriers for all towns and cities:
Alaska Airlines
Tel: 800-252-7522
www.alaskaair.com
Delta Airlines
Tel: 800-221-1212
www.delta.com

Anchorage

International Carriers
China Airlines
Tel: 800-227-5118
www.china-airlines.com
Condor
Tel: 0-180-5-707-202
www.condor.com
Korean Air
Tel: 800-438-5000
www.koreanair.com
Major Domestic Carriers
Air Canada
Tel: 888-247-2262
www.aircanada.com
American Airlines
Tel: 800-433-7300
www.aa.com
Continental Airlines
Tel: 800-523-3273
www.continental.com
Frontier Airlines
Tel: 800-432-1359
www.flyfrontier.com
Northwest Airlines
Tel: 800-225-2525
www.nwa.com
Sun Country Airlines
Tel: 800-359-6786
www.suncountry.com
United Airlines
Tel: 800-864-8331
www.united.com
US Airways
Tel: 800-428-4322
www.usairways.com
Local Carriers
Arctic Circle Air Service
Tel: 907-243-1380
www.arcticcircleair.com
ERA Aviation
Tel: 907-266-8394 or
800-866-8394
www.flyera.com
Frontier Flying Service
Tel: 907-450-7200 or
800-478-6779
www.frontierflying.com
Grant Aviation
Tel: 888-359-4726
www.flygrant.com
Hageland Aviation
Service
Tel: 907-245-0139 or
866-239-0119
www.hageland.com

Pen Air
Tel: 907-771-2640 or
800-448-4226
www.penair.com
Air Taxis
Alaska Air Taxi
Tel: 907-243-3944 or
800-789-5232
www.alaskaairtaxi.com
Ellis Air Taxi
Tel: 907-822-3368
www.ellisair.com
Iliamna Air Taxi
Tel: 907-571-1248
www.iliamnaair.com
Regal Air
Tel: 907-243-8535
www.regal-air.com
Rust's Flying Service
Tel: 907-243-1595 or
800-544-2299
www.flyrusts.com

Fairbanks

Major Carriers
Air North
Tel: 800-661-0407
www.flyairnorth.com
Local Carriers
Arctic Circle Air Service
Tel: 907-474-0112
www.arcticcircleair.com
Bettles Air
Tel: 907-479-7018 or
800-770-5111
www.bettlesair.com
ERA Aviation
Tel: 907-266-8394 or
800-866-8394
www.flyera.com
Frontier Flying
Tel: 907-450-7200 or
800-478-6779
www.frontierflying.com
Larry's Flying Service
Tel: 907-474-9169
www.larrysflying.com
Warbelow's Air
Tel: 907-474-0518 or
800-478-0812
www.warbelows.com
Wright's Air Service
Tel: 907-474-0502 or
800-478-0502 in Alaska
www.wrightair.net

Haines

Local Carriers
Mountain Flying Service
Tel: 907-766-3007 or
800-954-8747
www.flyglacierbay.com
Wings of Alaska
Tel: 907-789-0790
www.wingsofalaska.com

Homer

ERA Aviation
Tel: 907-266-8391 or
800-866-8394
www.flyera.com
Grant Aviation
Tel: 888-359-4726
www.flygrant.com

Juneau

Local Carriers
Wings of Alaska
Tel: 907-789-0790
www.wingsofalaska.com
Helicopter Services
Coastal Helicopters
Tel: 907-789-5600
www.coastalhelicopters.com
ERA Aviation
Tel: 907-586-2030
www.erahelicopters.com
Temsco Helicopters
Tel: 907-789-9501 or
877-789-9501
www.temscoair.com

Kenai

Local Carriers
ERA Aviation
Tel: 800-866-8394
www.flyera.com
Grant Aviation
Tel: 888-359-4726
www.flygrant.com

Ketchikan

Local Carriers
Promech Air
Tel: 907-225-3845 or
800-860-3845
www.promechair.com
Taquan Air
Tel: 907-225-8800 or
800-770-8800
www.taquanair.com
Helicopter Services
Temsco Helicopters
Tel: 907-225-5141 or
877-789-9501
www.temscoair.com

Kodiak

Local Carrier
ERA Aviation
Tel: 907-266-8391 or
800-866-8394
www.flyera.com

Nome

Local Carriers
Bering Air
Tel: 907-443-5464
or 800-478-5422
in Alaska
www.beringair.com

Frontier Flying
Tel: 907-450-7200 or
800-478-6779
www.frontierflying.com
Hageland Aviation
Tel: 907-443-7595 or
888-547-7595 in Alaska
www.hageland.com

Petersburg

Local Carriers
Nordic Air
Tel: 907-772-3535
Email: nordicair@gci.net
Pacific Wing Air Charters
Tel: 907-772-4259
www.pacificwing.com

Sitka

Local Carrier
Harris Aircraft Services
Tel: 907-966-3050 or
877-966-3050 in Alaska
www.harrisaircraft.com

Skagway

Local Carrier
Mountain Flying Service
Tel: 907-766-3007 or
800-954-8747
www.flyglacierbay.com
Promech Air
Tel: 907-225-3845 or
800-860-3845
www.promechair.com
Wings of Alaska
Tel: 907-983-2442
www.wingsofalaska.com
Helicopter Services
Temsco Helicopters
Tel: 907-983-2900 or
877-789-9501
www.temscoair.com

Valdez

Local Carrier
ERA Aviation
Tel: 907-266-8394 or
800-866-8394
www.flyera.com
Helicopter Services
ERA Aviation
Tel: 907-835-2595
www.erahelicopters.com

Wrangell

Local Carriers
Sunrise Aviation
Tel: 907-874-2319 or
800-874-2311
www.sunriseflights.com
Helicopter Services
Temsco Helicopter
Tel: 907-874-2010
www.temscoair.com

ACCOMMODATIONS

HOTELS, PUBLIC-USE CABINS AND HOSTELS

Choosing Accommodations

Accommodations vary greatly, as you would expect in a state with such diverse communities. Larger towns offer a range of hotels, many with international standards, while in the very smallest villages, facilities may be mediocre or non-existent.

Anchorage has seen a boom in hotel construction; many of the newer hotels offer rates which are lower than in the rest of the US, but often lack extras, like full-service restaurants.

Prices anywhere, especially in more remote areas, are high, especially during peak summer months. A "bed tax" is attached to all bills, but varies between 5 percent and 10 percent of the total depending on the city or borough.

Rates given here are for standard double rooms during peak summer months. Rates during the off-season are considerably lower.

Bed and breakfast These are very popular, with many offering outstanding service. For information about facilities statewide, write to **Alaska Private Lodgings/Stay With A Friend**, PO Box 1924, Homer, AK 99603, tel: 907-235-2148; www.alaskabandb.com

Free booklet The Alaska Travel Industry Association provides an extensive list of accommodations in the *Alaska Vacation Planner*. To get this free booklet, call them at 907-929-2200 or visit www.travelalaska.com

Public-Use Cabins

For a totally Alaskan experience, visitors can stay in remote wilderness cabins maintained by the US Forest Service (*see panel on page 85*). The

cost of rentals is low (around $25 to $75 a night), but getting there can be expensive. For more information on public-use cabins, contact the Alaska Public Lands Information Center, 605 W. Fourth Avenue, Suite 105, Anchorage, AK 99501, tel: 907-644-3661; www.nps.gov/aplic/center.

For reservations, call the National Recreation Reservation Service, tel: 877-444-6777 and website www.reserveusa.com. You can reserve cabins on federal lands on-line up to 180 days in advance, using a Visa, MasterCard or Discover card.

Information on Forest Service cabins can also be obtained at the websites for the Tongass and Chugach National Forests: www.fs.fed.us/r10/tongass and www.fs.fed.us/r10/chugach.

For National Park Service cabins: log on to: www.nps.gov.

For State Park Cabins write to: Department of Natural Resources, 550 W. Seventh Avenue, Suite 1260, Anchorage, AK 99501, or tel: 907-269-8400; www.dnr.state.ak.us/parks/index.htm.

BELOW: the relaxed way to tour Alaska.

Campgrounds

Federal, state, municipal, and private campgrounds vary from barely organized tent sites to full hook-up recreational vehicle parking sites. There are campgrounds along all of the major highways, but it may be some distance between them. And in summer, many of them are filled by early evening or even late afternoon, especially on weekends, so it's smart to plan ahead.

Most campgrounds charge fees for overnight use. Daily rates vary from $10 at rustic sites to more than $20 for full hook-up sites in private campgrounds. All the campgrounds are open in the summer only, but some RV parks are open year-round.

The best sources for listings are the *Alaska Vacation Planner* and *The Milepost*, available in bookstores. For private campgrounds and RV parks visit Alaska Campground Owners Association at www.alaskacampgrounds.net. For information about state and federally run campgrounds visit www.dnr.alaska.gov/parks/asp/access.htm, and www.nps.gov/aplic/camping.htm.

Hostel Information

Private hostel accommodations are available throughout the state. Information is available through online listings or in *The Hostel Handbook*, which is available at http://hostelhandbook.com.

Many hostels are members of the Alaska Hostel Association. For inexpensive lodgings around Alaska, visit their website at www.alaskahostelassociation.org, or contact them at Alaska Hostel Association, PO Box 92422, Anchorage, 99509-2422.

ANCHORAGE

Anchorage Downtown Hotel
826 K Street, Anchorage, AK 99501
Tel: 907-258-7669
www.anchoragedowntownhotel.com
Family run and within walking distance of downtown, this 19-room hotel offers refrigerators and microwave ovens in every room. **$$$**

Anchorage Marriott Downtown
820 West Seventh Avenue, Anchorage, AK 99501
Tel: 907-279-8000 or 888-236-2427
www.marriott.com
One of the newest downtown hotels, it accommodates many business travellers. With 395 rooms, restaurant, laundry, and lounge, it is luxurious and convenient. **$$$$**

Chelsea Inn Hotel
3836 Spenard Rd, Anchorage, AK 99517
Tel: 907-276-5002 or 800-770-5002
www.chelseainnalaska.com
Funky and friendly atmosphere in Midtown.

PRICE CATEGORIES

Price categories are for a summer standard double room without breakfast:
$ = under $90
$$ = $90–130
$$$ = $130–200
$$$$ = more than $200

Offers free airport and railroad shuttle buses, in addition to on-site laundry facilities. 34 rooms. **$**

Comfort Inn Ship Creek
111 Ship Creek Avenue, Anchorage, AK 99501
Tel: 907-277-6887 or 800-424-6423
www.choicehotels.com
Sitting on the scenic Tony Knowles Coastal Trail and just blocks from downtown, this 100-room hotel is centrally located. **$$$–$$$$**

Creekwood Inn
2150 Seward Highway, Anchorage, AK 99503
Tel: 907-258-6006 or 800-478-6008
www.creekwoodinn-alaska.com
Situated in midtown, this hotel is walking distance to shopping malls, movie theatres and 24-hour restaurants. All 26 rooms have microwave ovens and refrigerators. There is also a cabin and RV park. **$$**

Historic Anchorage Hotel
330 E Street, Anchorage, AK 99501
Tel: 907-272-4553 or 800-544-0988
Established in 1916, this is the city's oldest hotel. Now refurbished, it offers a taste of old-time downtown Anchorage. **$$$$**

Hotel Captain Cook
939 West Fifth Avenue, Anchorage, AK 99501
Tel: 907-276-6000 or 800-843-1950
www.captaincook.com

Among Anchorage's finest, all 547 rooms offer either mountain or inlet views. Restaurants, lounges, a coffee shop all on site, and an athletic club with pool. **$$$$**

Inlet Tower Hotel & Suites
1200 L Street, Anchorage, AK 99501
Tel: 907-276-0110 or 800-544-0786
www.inlettower.com
Located six blocks south of downtown's core, each of the 164 rooms and suites has a view of the city. Laundromat, free shuttle, and restaurant completes the package. **$$$$**

Millennium Alaskan Hotel Anchorage
4800 Spenard Road, Anchorage, AK 99517
Tel: 907-243-2300 or 866-866-8086 for reservations
www.millenniumhotels.com
Watch float planes land on scenic Lake Spenard just outside. This 248-room hotel has a rustic lodge motif, complete with a stone fireplace, and trophy heads in lobby. **$$$$**

Quality Inn & Suites Airport
4615 Spenard Road, Anchorage, AK 99517
Tel: 907-243-3131 or 800-221-7550
www.choicehotels.com
Near Spenard Lake, this 217-room hotel ranges from "economy" to "luxury." There are four buildings, but

ask for the most recently renovated. **$$$**

Sheraton Anchorage Hotel
401 E. Sixth Avenue, Anchorage, AK 99501
Tel: 907-276-8700 or 800-478-8700 for reservations
www.sheratonanchoragehotel.com
This downtown luxury 375-room hotel has acres of cream-colored marble, a winding jade staircase, restaurant, lounge, and café.**$$$$**

Voyager Hotel
501 K Street, Anchorage, AK 99501
Tel: 907-277-9501 or 800-247-9070
www.voyagerhotel.com
A favorite with business travellers, all 40 rooms have kitchens, queen beds, voicemail, and data ports. **$$$–$$$$**

Westmark Anchorage
720 W. Fifth Avenue, Anchorage, AK 99501
Tel: 907-276-7676 or 800-544-0970
www.westmarkhotels.com
Upmarket hotel with 200 rooms, each with its own balcony, while a bar and grill and Japanese sushi bar await downstairs. **$$$$**

FAIRBANKS

Bridgewater Hotel
723 First Avenue, Fairbanks, AK 99701
Tel: 907-452-6661 or 800-528-4916
www.fountainheadhotels.com
Located in downtown Fairbanks, this small 94-room hotel overlooks the Chena River. It offers free

airport and train depot shuttle, and a breakfast café. Closed in winter.
$–$$$$

Chena Hot Springs Resort
Mile 56.5 Chena Hot Springs Road, PO Box 58740, Fairbanks, AK 99711-0740
Tel: 907-451-8104
www.chenahotsprings.com

In a wilderness setting, 59 miles (95km) from Fairbanks, sits the only "ice hotel" in the United States. In addition to ice cold drinks and mineral hot springs open year-round, there are 81 rooms, eight rustic cabins, a Mongolian-style yurt tent, plus RV, and tent camping. (See also page 348.) **$–$$$$**

Fairbanks Princess Riverside Lodge
4477 Pikes Landing Road, Fairbanks, AK 99712
Tel: 907-455-4477 or 800-426-0500
www.princesslodges.com
In a wooded area on banks of the Chena River near the airport, this 325-room lodge is the standard for cruise accommodations: it features two restaurants, a lounge with live entertainment, laundry facilities, and a gift shop. **$$$**

Golden North Motel
4888 Old Airport Road, Fairbanks, AK 99709
Tel: 907-479-6201 or 800-447-1910
www.goldennorthmotel.com

Near shopping malls and airport, this 60-room budget motel is locally owned and offers free van service and continental breakfast. **$$**

Pike's Waterfront Lodge
1850 Hoselton Drive, Fairbanks, AK 99709
Tel: 907-456-4500 or 877-774-2400
www.pikeslodge.com
This complex of 28 cabins, 180 rooms, sauna and workout room, and three restaurants (including a sprawling deck along the Chena River), is a "green lodge" in an historic setting. **$$$$**

Regency Fairbanks Hotel
95 Tenth Avenue, Fairbanks, AK 99701
Tel: 907-452-3200 or

800-478-1230 (in Alaska) or 800-348-1340
www.regencyfairbankshotel.com
All 128 rooms have kitchens and digital phones with modem ports and voicemail. A dining room and lounge are located on the lower level. **$$**

Sophie Station Hotel
1717 University Avenue, Fairbanks, AK 99709
Tel: 907-456-3642 or 800-528-4916
www.fountainheadhotels.com
Elegant, all-suite hotel with 147 units. Gift shop, restaurant and lounge located on main commercial road near the airport and business district. **$$$$**

Wedgewood Resort
212 Wedgewood Drive, Fairbanks, AK 99701

Tel: 907-456-3642 or 800-528-4916
www.fountainheadhotels.com
Some of the 440 rooms are fully furnished condo-style one- and two-bedroom apartments, while others are recently built luxury hotel rooms. With easy access to nature trails, it is great for bird lovers. **$$$$**

Westmark Fairbanks Hotel
813 Noble Street, Fairbanks, AK 99701
Tel: 907-456-7722 or 800-544-0970
www.westmarkhotels.com
Recently remodeled with internet access, tour desk, shuttle service. Handy downtown location around a large courtyard; 400 rooms. Two restaurants, lounge, fitness center. **$$$**

OTHER CENTERS

Barrow

Barrow Airport Inn
1815 Momegana Street, PO Box 933, Barrow, AK 99723
Tel: 907-852-2525 or 800-375-2527 in Alaska only
Email: airportinn@barrow.com
A homey atmosphere across the street from the airport. 16 rooms, all but one with fridge and microwave, nine with kitchenettes. **$$**

King Eider Inn
1752 Ahkovak Street, PO Box 1283, Barrow, AK 99723
Tel: 907-852-4700
www.kingeider.net/eider
This 19-room, homey hotel has a sauna for all guests and two rooms with kitchenettes. **$$$**

Copper Center

Copper Center Lodge
Mile 101 Richardson Highway, Loop Rd, PO Box Drawer J, Copper Center, AK 99573
Tel: 907-822-3245 or 866-330-3245
www.coppercenterlodge.com
An historic log structure with an unspoiled country atmosphere. Includes restaurant and shuttle service to the Kennicott Mine. **$$**

Cordova

Reluctant Fisherman Inn
409 Railroad Avenue, PO Box 150, Cordova, AK 99574
Tel: 907-424-3272
www.reluctantfisherman.com
With 40 recently renovated rooms, many looking out on the mountains or the boat harbor. Common areas are lavishly decorated in a style reflecting the town's mining history. Restaurant and lounge are open daily in the summer. **$$$**

Delta Junction

Alaska 7 Motel
Mile 270.3 Richardson Highway, PO Box 1115, Delta Junction, AK 99737
Tel: 907-895-4848
www.alaska7motel.com
This budget hotel for highway travellers has 16 recently renovated budget rooms each with internet access. **$$**

Kelly's Alaska Country Inn
1616 Richardson Highway, PO Box 849, Delta Junction, AK 99737
Tel: 907-895-4667
www.kellysalaskacountryinn.com
A modern inn owned and operated by a "pioneer

family." In the town center, each of the 21 rooms has a refrigerator, TV and coffee maker. **$$**

Denali National Park

Camp Denali
PO Box 67, Denali National Park, AK 99755
Tel: 907-683-2290
www.campdenali.com
Offers 17 cabins in the Kantishna area, with views of Denali (Mount McKinley) and surrounded by wilderness. Shared bathrooms. Prices include all meals, lodging, transportation from park entrance, guided activities, and a unique, highly acclaimed program of naturalist-led activities deep within the national park. **$$$$**

Denali Princess Lodge
Mile 238.5 George Parks Highway, PO Box 110, Denali National Park, AK 99755
Tel: 800-426-0500
www.princessalaskalodges.com
Has 280 rooms and suites, with spacious common areas, off the highway, just outside Denali National Park, with access to many

park activities. Spas, gift shops, dining room, lounge, café, tour desk. **$$$$**

Kantishna Roadhouse
1 Doyon Place, Suite 300, Fairbanks, AK 99701
Tel: 800-942-7420
www.kantishnaroadhouse.com
Located in the heart of Kantishna, this lodge offers a variety of log cabins that include private baths. Gold panning and sled dog teams offer entertainment, as do the many outdoor activities nearby. Restaurant and full bar. **$$$$**

McKinley Village Lodge
Mile 232 George Parks Highway
For reservations, contact:
Denali Park Resorts, 241 North C Street, Anchorage, AK 99501
Tel: 907-276-7234 or 866-761-6631
www.denalinationalpark.com
This 188-room complex sits on 20 acres (8 hectares) above the Nenana River.

Has a full service restaurant, nearby hiking and interpretive trails, and shuttle service to Denali National Park, 8 miles (13km) away. **$$$$**

Dillingham

Dillingham Hotel
429 Second Avenue West,
PO Box 550, Dillingham, AK 99576
Tel: 907-842-5316
Fax: 907-842-5666
Right in the heart of town, this was one of the first hotels built in Dillingham; 31 rooms, some with private bath. Rebuilt in the mid-1970s. **$$$**

Dutch Harbor

The Grand Aleutian Hotel
498 Salmon Way, PO Box 921169,
Dutch Harbor, AK 99692
Tel: 907-581-3844 or
866-581-3844
www.grandaleutian.com
This 1993 hotel has won an architechtural award for its chalet-style design; it has 112 rooms and six suites. There's a stone fireplace in the three-story lobby, two restaurants, two bars, plus meeting rooms, travel services, and views of Margaret Bay. **$$$**

Girdwood

**The Alyeska Hotel/
Alyeska Resort**
1000 Arlberg Road, PO Box 249,
Girdwood, AK 99587
Tel: 907-754-1111 or
800-880-3880
www.alyeskaresort.com
This year-round resort 40 miles (64km) southeast of Anchorage in Girdwood, off the Seward Highway, is the height of luxury. Six chairlifts and tram, night skiing, convention facilities, restaurant, swimming pool, exercise room, and hot tub with a view of the mountain. There's also a ski school, alpine and telemark skiing, ski rental, and ice skating; dogsledding and sleigh rides can be arranged. Summer sightseeing tram lift ride. **$$$–$$$$**.

Glacier Bay/ Gustavus

Glacier Bay Lodge
241 W. Ship Creek, Anchorage,
AK 99501
Tel: 907-264-4600 or
866-761-6634
www.visitglacierbay.com
Only hotel within the park, situated above the dock where day boats begin trips to the glaciers; 55 rooms. Dining room and gift shop. **$$$–$$$$**

Gustavus Inn
PO Box 60, Gustavus, AK 99826
Tel: 907-697-2254 or
800-649-5220
www.gustavusinn.com
A luxurious 13-room country inn near Glacier Bay National Park offering all-inclusive packages for fishing, whale watching, sea kayaking, and other activities. Prices include family-style meals and shuttle from the airport. **$$$$**

Glennallen

Caribou Hotel
Mile 187 Glenn Highway,
PO Box 329, Glennallen, AK 99588
Tel: 907-822-3302
www.caribouhotel.com
The 25 rooms in the trailer-like annex in front of the main building are clean but spartan, with shared bath, while the 70 nicely

BELOW: the Alyeska Resort, Girdwood.

furnished rooms in the main building cost more. Restaurant and gift shop next door. Cabins are also available only a short distance away. **$–$$$**

Haines

Captain's Choice Motel
108 2nd Avenue North,
PO Box 392, Haines, AK 99827
Tel: 907-766-3111 or
800-478-2345
www.capchoice.com
Centrally located overlooking Portage Cove and Chilkoot Inlet, this 40-room motel offers car rental, a laundromat, and local tour bookings. Pet-friendly. **$$–$$$**

Hotel Halsingland
13 Fort Seward Drive,
PO Box 1649, Haines, AK 99827
Tel: 907-766-2000 or
800-542-6363
www.hotelhalsingland.com
Cozy and very affordable, this 50-room inn is housed in an historic Fort William Seward building facing the parade grounds. Five "budget" rooms share bathrooms while downstairs features a cocktail lounge, restaurant featuring locally caught seafood, and activity desk. **$–$$**

Mountain View Inn
57 Mud Bay Road, PO Box 62,
Haines, AK 99827
Tel: 907-766-2900 or

800-478-2902
www.mtviewinn.net
Within walking distance of downtown and Fort William Seward; 9 units, most with kitchens, all with refrigerators, pet-friendly, internet. **$$**

Homer

Bay View Inn
2851 Sterling Highway,
PO Box 804, Homer, AK 99603
Tel: 907-235-8485 or
877-235-8485
www.bayviewalaska.com
With 12 basic rooms, six with kitchens, plus a guest cottage, and magnificent views of the Kachemak Bay. **$$**

Driftwood Inn
135 W. Bunnell, Homer, AK 99603
Tel: 907-235-8019 or
800-478-8019
www.thedriftwoodinn.com
This clean and cozy inn with 21 rooms (some with shared bath) is just one block from Bishop's Beach. Complete with common sitting room, eating area, internet access and 22 RV hook-ups. **$–$$**

Heritage Hotel
147 E. Pioneer Avenue, Homer,
AK 99603
Tel: 907-235-7787 or
800-380-7787
www.alaskaheritagehotel.com
This 34-room hotel (including one with a jacuzzi, and a suite that includes a kitchen), is conveniently located downtown near Homer's restaurants, shopping and entertainment. The owners also have an RV park on the Homer Spit. **$$**

Land's End Resort
4786 Homer Spit Road, Homer,
AK 99603
Tel: 907-235-0400 or
800-478-0400
www.endofthespit.com
The hotel has 108 rooms in

PRICE CATEGORIES

Price categories are for a summer standard double room without breakfast:
$ = under $90
$$ = $90–130
$$$ = $130–200
$$$$ = more than $200

a variety of sizes; about three-fourths have views of the bay. Full-service restaurant which specializes in fresh seafood, gift shop/ espresso bar. **$$–$$$**

Juneau

Best Western Country Lane Inn
9300 Glacier Highway, Juneau, AK 99801
Tel: 907-789-5005 or 888-781-5005
www.countrylaneinn.com or www.bestwestern.com
Near the airport and Mendenhall Glacier, all 55 rooms have data ports and cable TV, and most have internet access. Free continental breakfast and shuttle. **$$–$$$**

The Breakwater Inn
1711 Glacier Avenue, Juneau, AK 99801
Tel: 907-586-6303 or 888-586-6303
www.breakwaterinn.com
Overlooking the small boat harbor, many of the 49 rooms have balconies, and kitchenettes. Freezers are also available. Restaurant, lounge. **$$$**

Driftwood Lodge
435 Willoughby Avenue, Juneau, AK 99801
Tel: 907-586-2280 or 800-544-2239
www.driftwoodalaska.com
Downtown; 63 rooms, many with kitchenettes and apartment-style floor-plans. Laundry facilities, and bike rentals; 24-hour airport shuttle. **$$**

Super 8 Motel
2295 Trout Street, Juneau, AK 99801
Tel: 907-789-4858 or 800-800-8000
www.super8.com
Near the airport, this motel has 75 rooms. Freezers available, plus 24-hour airport and ferry shuttle. **$$**

The Westmark Baranof Hotel
127 North Franklin Street, Juneau, AK 99801
Tel: 907-586-2660 or 800-544-0970
www.westmarkhotels.com
Nine-story art-deco structure; 196 rooms.

Coffee shop, lounge, restaurant, popular with politicians and state employees. **$$–$$$**

Katmai

Brooks Lodge
For reservations contact:
Katmailand Inc., 4125 Aircraft Drive, Anchorage, AK 99502
Tel: 907-243-5448 or 800-544-0551
www.bearviewing.net
Within Katmai National Park, on the Naknek Lake and Brooks River and accessible only by plane or boat; 16 rustic cabins. Main lodge, restaurant, bar, sport fishing, bear viewing, trips to the Valley of Ten Thousand Smokes. **$$$$**

Grosvenor Lodge
Katmailand Inc., 4125 Aircraft Drive, Anchorage, AK 99502
Tel: 907-243-5448 or 800-544-0551
www.katmailand.com
Three- to 7-night packages available at this wilderness fishing lodge in the heart of Katmai National Park, including everything from air fare from Anchorage to guided fishing and fishing gear. **$$$$**

Katmai Wilderness Lodge
Contact PO Box 4332, Kodiak, AK 99615
Tel: 907-486-8767 or 800-488-8767
www.katmai-wilderness.com
Located on Katmai's rugged outer coast, accessible only by plane or boat; seven rooms. Stays range from 3 nights to a week or more. Bear viewing, fishing, photography, kayaking. The cost includes air fare from Kodiak, guided activities and gourmet meals. **$$$$**

Kenai Peninsula

Gwin's Lodge
14865 (Mile 52) Sterling Highway, Cooper Landing, AK 99572
Tel: 907-595-1266
www.gwinslodge.com
Half a mile (1km) from Russian River fisheries, all of the 13 cabins have private baths, and most have kitchenettes or full kitchens. **$$$–$$$$**

Kenai Landing
2101 Bowpicker Lane, Kenai, AK 99611
Tel: 907-335-2500 or 800-478-0400
www.kenailanding.com
This complex of 47 rooms and one suite includes a restaurant, theatre, hiking trails, and a boat launch. Located at the mouth of the Kenai River. **$–$$$**

Kenai Princess Wilderness Lodge
PO Box 676, Mile 2 Bean Creek Road, Cooper Landing, AK 99572
Tel: 907-595-1425 or 800-426-0500
www.princesslodges.com
An 86-room luxury resort hotel near Cooper Landing overlooking Kenai River. Path from main lodge leads to cabins; some are four-plexes, others are bungalow style. Restaurant, lounge, spa, and indoor and outdoor hot tubs. **$$$$**

Sunrise Inn
Mile 45 Sterling Highway, PO Box 832, Cooper Landing, AK 99575
Tel: 907-595-1222
www.alaskasunriseinn.com
On Kenai Lake, 10 units each with TV and private bath. Restaurant and lounge. **$$$**

Ketchikan

Gilmore Hotel
326 Front Street, Ketchikan, AK 99901
Tel: 907-225-9423 or 800-275-9423
www.gilmorehotel.com
Built in 1927, this recently remodeled 38 room hotel is downtown on the waterfront. Restaurant and full bar. **$$$**

Super 8 Motel
2151 Sea Level Drive, Ketchikan, AK 99901
Tel: 907-225-9088 or 800-800-8000
www.super8.com
Situated near a shopping mall between ferry terminal and downtown; 83 rooms. Shuttle service and freezers available. **$$**

WestCoast Cape Fox Lodge
800 Venetia Way, Ketchikan, AK 99901
Tel: 907-225-8001 or

866-225-8001
www.capefoxlodge.com
Located above downtown Ketchikan and Tongass Narrows, access is by scenic tram from downtown or a driveway; 72 rooms. Dining room, lounge, meeting and banquet facilities. **$$$$**

Kodiak

Best Western Kodiak Inn
236 W. Rezanof Drive, Kodiak, AK 99615
Tel: 907-486-5712 or 800-780-7234
www.bestwestern.com
In town center above the waterfront; 81 rooms. Lounge, restaurant. **$$$**

Comfort Inn Kodiak
1395 Airport Way, Kodiak, AK 99615
Tel: 907-487-2700 or 877-424-6423
www.comfortinn.com
Located near the airport; 50 rooms with voicemail and data ports. Salmon fishing on nearby river, restaurant, and lounge. **$$$–$$$$**

Kodiak Treks
11754 South Russian Creek Road, Kodiak, AK 99615
Tel: 907-487-2122
www.kodiaktreks.com
Located on Aleut Island in the heart of bear country, this small ecolodge offers rustic accommodations. Sauna and private baths available. Meals, guided hikes, kayaking opportunities included. **$$$$**

Russian Heritage Inn
119 Yukon Street, Kodiak, AK 996015
Tel: 907-486-5657
www.russianheritageinn.com
This downtown 25-room motel is pet-friendly, and offers internet access and laundry facilities. **$**

Kotzebue

Nullagvik Hotel
308 Shore Ave, PO Box 336, Kotzebue, AK 99752
Tel: 907-442-3331
www.nullagvik.com
Overlooking Kotzebue Sound; 74 rooms. Restaurant, gift shop, and travel agency. Tours can be arranged. **$$$$**

Nome

Nome Nugget Inn
315 Front Street, PO Box 421,
Nome, AK 99762
Tel: 907-443-4189 or
877-443-2323
www.nomenuggetinnhotel.com
Decorated in gold-rush era
fashion, with frontier
memorabilia in lobby and
lounge. 47 rooms with
private baths. Restaurant,
lounge. Front Street and
Bering. **$$**

Palmer Area

Colony Inn
325 East Elmwood (check-in
handled at the neighboring Valley
Hotel – see address below)
Tel: 907-745-3330 or
800-478-7666 in Alaska
Lovingly restored historic
building with large
downstairs sitting area; 12
guest rooms decorated with
quilts and antique
reproductions. Restaurant.
$$–$$$

Hatcher Pass Lodge
Mile 17.5 Hatcher Pass Road,
PO Box 763, Palmer, AK 99645
Tel: 907-745-5897
www.hatcherpasslodge.com
Located near Independence
Mine State Historic Park ,
this cozy 3-room lodge
has nine additional
cabins, a restaurant, bar,
entertainment, sauna,
plus cross-country skiing
and excellent hiking
opportunities.
$$–$$$

Sheep Mountain Lodge
17701 West Glenn Highway,
Sutton, AK 99674
Tel: 907-745-5121 or
877-645-5121
www.sheepmountain.com
Ten cabins with bath and
shower and private deck.
Hiking in summer, nordic
skiing in winter on groomed
trails. Restaurant, hot tub,
sauna. **$$$**

Valley Hotel
606 S. Alaska, Palmer, AK 99645
Tel: 907-745-3330 or
800-478-7666 (in Alaska)
Downtown near visitor
center; hotel built in 1948
now remodeled with 43
rooms; 24-hour restaurant,
cocktail lounge. **$–$$**

Petersburg

Scandia House
110 Nordic Drive, PO Box 689,
Petersburg, AK 99833
Tel: 907-772-4281 or
800-722-5006
www.scandiahousehotel.com
This downtown hotel rebuilt
in 1995 has 33 rooms,
some with kitchenettes and
jacuzzis. Car, bike and boat
rental is available. **$$**

Tides Inn
307 N. First Street, PO Box 1048,
Petersburg, AK 99833
Tel: 907-772-4288 or
800-665-8433
Email: tidesinn@alaska.net
www.tidesinnalaska.com
This inn is located
downtown overlooking
Petersburg's North Harbor,
and has 45 rooms (some
with kitchenettes). **$–$$**

Seldovia

**Across the Bay Tent and
Breakfast**
PO Box 112054, Anchorage,
AK 99511 (winter)
Tel: 907-345-2571 (winter) or
907-235-3633 (summer)
www.tentandbreakfastalaska.com
Sturdy wall tents with twin
beds. Hearty meals served
at main house, hiking, bike
rentals, and guided
kayaking. Access is by water
taxi from Homer or you can
fly in. **$$**

**The Seldovia Boardwalk
Hotel**
234 Main Street, PO Box 72,
Seldovia, AK 99663
Tel: 907-234-7816
www.alaskacom/boardwalkhotel
www.seldoviaboardwalkhotel.com
On waterfront with a fine
view of water or mountains;
14 rooms. A sun-lit parlor
has wood stove. Coffee
service available. **$$$**

Seward

Breeze Inn Motel
303 N. Harbor Street, PO Box 2147,
Seward, AK 99664
Tel: 907-224-5238 or
888-224-5237
www.breezeinn.com
On the main road into town
right in the small boat
harbor, this 86 room inn
offers a restaurant, lounge,

espresso bar, gift shops,
and new atrium lobby. **$$$**

Hotel Seward
221 Fifth Avenue, PO Box 2288,
Seward, AK 99664
Tel: 907-224-8001 or
800-440-2444
www.hotelsewardalaska.com
Downtown, within an easy
walk of many attractions,
some of the 38 rooms have
bay views. Restaurant and
"Alaskan Victorian Lounge"
downstairs. **$$$–$$$$**

Marina Motel
Mile 1 Seward Highway,
PO Box 1134, Seward, AK 99664
Tel: 907-224-5518
www.sewardmotel.com
Across from the boat harbor,
one mile from downtown;
26 rooms. **$$–$$$**

Seward Windsong Lodge
31772 Herman Leirer Road,
PO Box 2301, Seward, AK 99664
Tel: 907-224-7116 or
800-478-8069
www.sewardwindsong.com
Forested setting near the
banks of Resurrection River;
108 rooms, most either
mountain- or river-view;
café and restaurant, TV,
VCR. **$$$$**

Sitka

Sitka Hotel
118 Lincoln Street, Sitka, AK 99835
Tel: 907-747-3288
www.sitkahotel.net
Located in the downtown
area and furnished in
Victorian-era decor; 60
budget rooms, some with
shared bathrooms. There
are also suites with
kitchenettes and an
attached restaurant. **$$**

Westmark Sitka
330 Seward Street, Sitka,
AK 99835
Tel: 907-747-6241 or
800-544-0970
www.westmarkhotels.com
Overlooking the Crescent
Harbor waterfront; 101
rooms. Restaurant; lounge,
high-speed internet.
$$–$$$$

Skagway

Historic Skagway Inn
655 Broadway, PO Box 500,
Skagway, AK 99840
Tel: 907-983-2289 or

888-752-4929
www.skagwayinn.com
Born as a bordello during
the Klondike Gold Rush, this
historic inn within Klondike
National Historic Park has
rooms named after the
ladies who once worked
here. There are 10 rooms,
some with private baths,
others shared. (The hotel
was remodeled in 2004.)
Free transportation to the
famed Chilkoot Trail.
$$–$$$

Sgt. Preston's Lodge
370 Sixth Street,
PO Box 538, Skagway, AK 99840
Tel: 907-983-2521 or
866-983-2521
http://sgtprestons.eskagway.com
This clean, newly renovated
establishment located in
downtown Skagway offers
38 rooms and two suites,
with TV, phones and private
baths. Good value, with
courtesy van service. Pet-
friendly. **$$**

Westmark Inn Skagway
Third and Spring streets,
PO Box 515, Skagway, AK 99840
Tel: 907-983-6000 or
800-544-0970
www.westmarkhotels.com
Near stores and attractions,
including national historic
park, this 151-room hotel
mostly serves package tour
passengers. Two restaur-
ants and lounge. Closed in
winter. **$$$**

Soldotna

**Hooligan's Lodging and
Saloon**
44715 Sterling Highway, Soldotna,
AK 99669
Tel: 907-262-9951
www.hooliganslodge.com
Located within walking
distance of the Kenai River.
Offers 34 large, clean rooms
and a bar. **$$–$$$**

Kenai River Lodge
393 Riverside Drive, Soldotna,
AK 99669

PRICE CATEGORIES

Price categories are for a
summer standard double
room without breakfast:
$ = under $90
$$ = $90–130
$$$ = $130–200
$$$$ = more than $200

Tel: 907-262-4292 or
800-977-4292
www.kenairiverlodge.com
Overlooking the famous
Kenai River, yet within
easy walking distance of
restaurants and
businesses; all 25
rooms have coffee pots,
refrigerators, and TVs. Free
continental breakfast.
Excellent sport fishing. **$$$**

Soldotna Inn
35041 Kenai Spur Highway,
Soldotna, AK 99669
Tel: 907-262-9169 or
866-262-9169
www.mykels.com
In the heart of downtown
Soldotna, within walking
distance of the Kenai River.
28 modern rooms with
refrigerators, some with
kitchenettes. Restaurant,
lounge, wireless internet,
and continental breakfast.
$$$

Talkeetna

**Mt. McKinley Princess
Wilderness Lodge**
Milepost 133 on the Parks
Highway, PO Box 13550, Trapper
Creek, AK 99683
Tel: 907-733-2900 or
800-426-0500
www.princesslodges.com
Modern lodge with large,
open "Great Room"
featuring a massive
fireplace, evening piano
music and cocktails. Deck
looks out towards the
Alaska Range, including Mt
McKinley; 460 bungalow-
style guest rooms; bar,
restaurant, café. About 45
minutes' drive north of
Talkeetna, lodge offers
regular shuttle from the
Talkeetna train station to
the lodge. Closed in winter.
$$$

Swiss-Alaska Inn
PO Box 565, Talkeetna, AK 99676
Tel: 907-733-2424
www.swissalaska.com
Family-run with 20 rooms all
decorated in bright, floral
motif, with DVD players.
Restaurant and lounge, with
views of Mount McKinley.
East Talkeetna by the boat
launch. **$$$**

Talkeetna Alaskan Lodge
23601 S. Talkeetna Spur Road,

PO Box 727, Talkeetna, AK 99676
Tel: 907-733-9500 or
888-959-9590
www.talkeetnalodge.com
Majestic, chalet-style lodge
with a large deck offering
sweeping views of the
Alaska Range and Mount
McKinley. 201 rooms,
including suites, many
"mountainside" with views;
restaurant, bar. **$$$$**

Tok

Westmark Inn-Tok
Mile 1315 Alaska Highway,
PO Box 130, Tok, AK 99780
Tel: 907-883-5174 or
800-544-0970
www.westmarkhotels.com
The 92 standard rooms are
in buildings connected by
boardwalks. Restaurant, gift
shop, and laundromat.
Closed in winter. **$$–$$$**

Young's Motel
Mile 1313 Alaska Highway,
PO Box 482, Tok, AK 99780
Tel: 907-883-4411
Email: edyoung@aptalaska.net
Along the Alaska Highway
behind the area's most
popular restaurant, Fast
Eddie's; 43 rooms in one-
story buildings. **$**

Valdez

**Totem Inn Hotel and
Suites**
144 East Eagan Drive, PO Box 648,
Valdez, AK 99686
Tel: 907-835-4443 or
888-808-4431
www.toteminn.com
Locally owned and operated
since 1972, each of the 70
rooms has a fridge and a
microwave. Cottages and
suites with kitchenettes are
also available. The hotel's
restaurant is a local
favourite serving breakfast,
lunch and dinner. **$$$**

Valdez Harbor Inn
100 Harbor Drive, Valdez,
AK 99686
Tel: 907-835-3434 or
888-222-3440
www.valdezharborinn.com
Located right on the harbor
in downtown Valdez, with 90
rooms. Restaurant, lounge,
coffee shop, exercise room,
laundry room, barber shop.
$$$

Wrangell

Sourdough Lodge
1104 Peninsula Street,
Wrangell, AK 99929
Tel: 800-874-3613
www.akgetaway.com/HardingsLodge
A small friendly local hotel
with lots of personal
touches and charm. The
owner is happy to arrange
activities and tours, while
also offering a shuttle
service from the airport and
ferry terminal. Freezers are
available for fishermen and
a full-service restaurant
serves three meals a day.
$$

Yakutat

Leonards Landing Lodge
PO Box 282, Yakutat,
AK 99689
Tel: 784-3245 or
877-925-3474
www.leonardslanding.com
This secluded lodge is on
the waterfront at the end of
the road (about 1½
miles/3km from the center
of town). With everything
from single rooms and
cabins, to two- or three-
room suites with
kitchenettes, it is very
popular with those seeking
to fish Yakutat's waters.
Fish processing also
available. **$$–$$$$**

BED & BREAKFAST

The following list gives the
central reservations
organizations in the main
towns. They will help you
find recommended Bed-
and-Breakfast accommo-
dation, and some will make
the reservation for you.
*(See also page 348 for
more information.)*

Anchorage

**Anchorage Bed &
Breakfast Association
Hotline**
PO Box 242623,
Anchorage, AK 99524
Tel: 907-272-5909 or
888-584-5147
www.anchorage-bnb.com

Fairbanks

**Fairbanks Convention &
Visitors Bureau**
101 Dunkel Street, Suite 111,
Fairbanks, AK 99701
Tel: 907-465-5774 or
800-327-5774
www.explorefairbanks.com

Homer

**Homer Bed and Breakfast
Association**
PO Box 2518,
Homer, AK 99603
Tel: 907-226 1114 or
877-296 1114
www.homerbedbreakfast.com

Juneau

B&B Locator
c/o Juneau Convention and Visitors
Bureau, One Sealaska Plaza,
Suite 305, AK 99801
Tel: 907-586 1737 or
800-587 2201
www.traveljuneau.com

Ketchikan

**Ketchikan Reservation
Service**
412 D-1 Loop Road,
Ketchikan, AK 99901
Tel: 907-247-5337 or
800-987-5337
www.ketchikan-lodging.com

Kodiak

**Visitors' Information
Center**
100 E. Marine Way,
Suite 200, Kodiak, AK 99615
Tel: 907-486-4782 or
800-789-4782
www.kodiak.org

Valdez

One Call Does It All
225 N. Harbor Drive,
PO Box 2197,
Valdez, AK 99686
Tel: 907-835-4988
www.valdezalaska.com

PRICE CATEGORIES

Price categories are for a
summer standard double
room without breakfast:
$ = under $90
$$ = $90–130
$$$ = $130–200
$$$$ = more than $200

ACTIVITIES

FESTIVALS, THE ARTS, NIGHTLIFE, SHOPPING, OUTDOOR ACTIVITIES, PARKS AND PRESERVES

HOLIDAYS AND FESTIVALS

Alaska celebrates all the traditional and official US holidays. In addition, there are many unusual festivals occurring year-round within the state. Some are created purely for amusement, while others are part of the cultural heritage.

Winter festivals are popular in Alaska, to help alleviate the long, cold, dark season. The largest is the Fur Rendezvous, held each February in Anchorage (see page 172). A highlight of the event is the World Championship Sled Dog Race. Homer also celebrates a winter carnival in February and the North Pole Winter Festival is held in March.

For a rare opportunity to observe the rich Native culture, visitors can attend the Savoonga Walrus Festival held on St Lawrence Island in May. This is not a tourist event, it is traditionally Eskimo. In June, Nalukataq (Whaling Feast) is celebrated in Barrow by the Eskimo community.

Other festivals are held tongue in cheek and for pure fun. Swimmers take to the icy waters of the Bering Sea in Nome for the annual Polar Bear Swim in May and locals join in the Moose Dropping Festival held in Talkeetna in July.

Dates change annually, so make sure you have a current schedule from the Alaska Travel Industry Association, tel: 907-929-2200 or 907-929-2842, www.travelalaska.com, or check the website of the local community's Convention and Visitors Bureau (see listing on page 369).

Annual Events

(National/state holidays in bold)

January

New Year's Day (1st)
Martin Luther King's Birthday (3rd Monday)
Polar Bear Jump Off Festival, Seward. The heartiest (and silliest) Alaskans don costumes to jump into the frigid Resurrection Bay. Events for all ages last all weekend. www.sewardak.org
Willow Winter Carnival, Willow. Events over two weekends include dogsled and cross-country races, a woodchopping contest, and talent shows. www.waco-ak.org

February

Presidents' Day (3rd Monday)
Cordova Ice Worm Festival, Cordova. Weekend-long activities include coronation of the Iceworm Queen, and the annual Survival Suit Race. www.iceworm.org
Fur Rendezvous, Anchorage. Ten-day long celebration of Alaska's fur-trapping and trading heritage. Many events, including the World Championship Sled Dog Race. www.furrondy.net
Iron Dog Gold Rush Classic Snow-machine Race, Wasilla to Nome. www.irondog.org
Yukon Quest International Sled Dog Race, Fairbanks to Whitehorse. www.yukonquest.com

March

Seward's Day (last Monday)
Iditarod Trail Sled Dog Race, Anchorage to Nome (see pages 302–3). www.iditarod.com
World Ice Art Championships, Fairbanks.

Spectacular sculptures made from Fairbanks' finest ice. Events for the whole family. www.icealaska.com

April

Alaska Folk Festival, Juneau. Free folk music festival. www.akfolkfest.org
Piuraagiaqta (Spring Festival), Barrow. Community parade and winter games in celebration of spring's arrival. www.cityofbarrow.org

May

Memorial Day (last Monday)
Kodiak Crab Festival, Kodiak. Carnival rides and activities throughout the weekend. www.kodiak. org/crabfest.html
Little Norway Festival, Petersburg. Complete with a parade and weekend-long activities. Residents dress in traditional Norwegian garb in celebration of their heritage. www. petersburg.org

June

Colony Days, Palmer. Celebrating Palmer's agricultural roots. A parade, races, and other activities are held all weekend. www. palmerchamber.org/visiting/annual_events.php
Mayor's Midnight Sun Marathon, Anchorage.
26.2 miles, the race runs across Anchorage on the Summer Solstice. www.mayorsmarathon.com
Midnight Sun Festival and Softball Tournament, Nome. Events include a softball tournament, a river raft race, and a folk music festival. www.nomealaska.org/vc/festivals.htm
Midnight Sun Run, Midnight Sun Baseball Game, Fairbanks. Both events start around 10pm, lasting through the white night. www. fairbanks-alaska.com/midnight-sun-run.htm

Summer Solstice, Statewide.
Events are held in cities and
communities across the state to
celebrate the longest day of the year.

July
Independence Day (4th)
Mount Marathon Race, Seward.
4th of July race up Mt Marathon.
www.sewardak.org
Southeast Alaska State Fair, Haines.
www.seakfair.org
World Eskimo-Indian Olympics,
Fairbanks.
The four-day event includes
competitions in hunting and survival
skills, as well as in dance and storytelling. www.weio.org

August
Alaska State Fair, Palmer.
Take in giant cabbages and plenty of
food on a stick at this lively annual
event. www.alaskastatefair.org
Talkeetna Bluegrass Festival,
Talkeetna.
Three-day campout music festival
with a wide variety of acts. www.
eideticimage.com/bluegrass/03/indexold.html

September
Labor Day (1st Monday)
Klondike Trail of '98 Road Relay,
Skagway and Whitehorse.
Foot race relay retracing the famous
path to the Yukon territory .www.
klondikeroadrelay.com

October
Alaska Day (18th)
Parades and festivals are held
statewide to celebrate the transfer of
Alaska from Russia to the US.

November
Veterans' Day (11th)
Thanksgiving (4th Thursday)
Alaska Bald Eagle Festival, Haines.
Weekend-long events include
lectures, workshops, and tours to the
Alaska Bald Eagle Preserve, where the
raptors gather every year. www.
baldeaglefestival.org
Whalefest, Sitka.
Activities include a 6-mile (10-km)
run, lectures, art shows, and whale-
watching tours. www.sitkawhalefest.org

December
Christmas (25th)
Bachelor Society Ball/Wilderness
Women's Contest, Talkeetna.
Fun local fundraiser with wilderness
competitions for women during the
day, and a bachelor auction at night.
www.bachelorsoftalkeetna.org
Colony Christmas Celebration, Palmer.
Horse-drawn wagon rides, reindeer

petting, and craft fair all with nod to a
Normal Rockwell Americana. www.
cityofpalmer.org
Harbor Stars Boat Parade, Kodiak.
Parade of brightly decorated boats
cruise along the coast. www.kodiakisland.
net/events.html

MUSIC, DANCE, DRAMA

Communities across Alaska have
much to offer in the way of
entertainment, although many of the
major performing groups take the
summer off to prepare for their
regular fall and winter seasons.
Check with local information centers
or scan local newspapers to find out
what's playing in the communities
you plan to visit.
Alaska Native Heritage Center
The center features Native dancers,
artists, cultural displays, and story-
tellers. 8800 Heritage Center Drive,
Anchorage, AK 99504, tel: 907-330-
8000 or 800-315-6608; www.
alaskanative.net
Anchorage Symphony Orchestra
Performs classic and contemporary
work, along with community-geared
programs. Season generally runs from
October to May. 400 D Street, Suite
230, Anchorage, AK 99501, tel: 907-
274-8668; www.anchoragesymphony.org
**Crown of Lights Northern
Lights Show**
LeRoy Zimmerman's award-winning
Northern Lights show, "The Crown of
Light," at Ester Gold Camp Historic
District is a spectacular blend of
Northern Lights photography and
symphonic music. PO Box 109, Ester,
AK 99725, tel: 907-452-7274 or
800-354-7274; http://fairbanks-alaska.
com/ester-gold-camp.htm
Days of '98 Show with Soapy Smith
Good family fun for all. Spend an
evening gambling with phoney money
and see the gold-rush history of
Skagway unfold on the stage of a
250-seat theater. Shows nightly mid-
May through mid-September. Matinees
for cruise ships. Tickets at the door.
Sixth Avenue and Broadway, PO Box
1897, Skagway, AK 99840-0215, tel:
907-983-2545 or 808-328-9132;
http://thedaysof98show.eskagway.com/index.htm
Fairbanks Summer Arts Festival
Two weeks of workshops, rehearsals,
performances, and concerts with
studies in music, dance, theater,
opera, ice skating, and visual arts in
July and/or August – an arts camp for
adults, as well as younger dancers
and ice skaters who are experienced
in those areas. PO Box 82510,

Fairbanks, AK 99708, tel: 907-474-
8869; www.fsaf.org
Kodiak Alutiiq Dancers
Daily summer performances of
traditional Alutiiq songs and dances;
cultural demonstrations and Native
arts and crafts. 312 West Marine Way,
Kodiak, AK 99615, tel: 907-486-
4449; www.sunaq.org
New Archangel Dancers
Folk dances from various parts of
Russia. Performances in Centennial
Hall near the harbor, timed to docking
of cruise ship or by special
arrangement. 208 Smith Street, Sitka,
AK 99835, tel: 907-747-5516; www.
newarchangeldancers.com
Northern Lights Theatre
A spectacular movie of the Northern
Lights accompanied by a symphony
on a wide screen with digital surround
sound. Mile 238.9, Parks Highway, PO
Box 65, Denali Park, AK 99755, tel:
907-683-4000; www.akpub.com/akttt/
lights.html
Pier One Theatre
Local talent lights up an intimate
stage in a "come-as-you-are"
warehouse on the Homer Spit. Dance,
drama, musicals. Seasonal service,
Memorial Day through Labor Day.
PO Box 894, Homer, AK 99603, tel:
907-235-7333; www.pieronetheatre.org

NIGHTLIFE

Like all good frontiers, Alaska has a
colorful nightlife centered on hearty
pints of local brew and live music.
Nearly every town, with the exception
of some "dry" native villages, has its
own favorite watering hole on the
main drag that often predates the
town itself. There, residents mix easily
with tourists, sometimes until the wee
hours of the morning. Alaska's last
call is 5am, but many smaller
communities stop serving alcohol
much earlier to combat drinking and
driving, a chronic Alaskan problem.
The students at University of Alaska
both in Fairbanks and Anchorage
attract a more varied nightlife that
includes some nightclubs. Larger
musical acts from the Lower 48
generally limit their Alaskan
engagements to Anchorage.
  While there is no statewide
smoking ban, Anchorage and Juneau
both prohibit smoking in bars,
restaurants, and nightclubs.

Music Venues

Bear Tooth Theatre Pub and Grill
1230 W. 27th Avenue, Anchorage,

AK 99503, tel: 907-276-4200; www.beartooththeatre.net Primarily a second-run movie theater that serves beer and pub food, the Bear Tooth frequently features well-known musical acts from the Lower 48.

Chilkoot Charlie's
2435 Spenard Road, Anchorage, AK 99503, tel: 907-272-1010; www.koots.com
Affectionately called "Koot's" by the locals, this labyrinth of a bar and nightclub features food and live music from around Alaska and the Lower 48, including nightly doses of swing.

Bars and Nightclubs

Barracuda's
1351 Cushman Street, Fairbanks, AK 99701, tel: 907-452-7977
Fairbanks' only hip-hop club. Features DJs, dancing, and karaoke. Small cover fee.

Darwin's Theory
426 G Street, Anchorage, AK 99501, tel: 907-277-5322; www.alaska.net/~thndrths
Share free popcorn and stiff drinks with locals in the small, downtown dive.

Doc Water's Pub
2 Marine Way, Suite 125, Juneau, AK 99801, tel: 907-586-3627; www.docwaterspub.com
Chow down on pub food until the wee hours of the morning as this bar serves food until last call. Live music, TVs turned to sporting events, and patio seating overlooking the Gastineau Channel available.

Humpy's Great Alaskan Alehouse
610 W. Sixth Avenue, Anchorage, AK 99501, tel: 907-276-2337; www.humpys.com
With food, live music, and plenty of Alaskan brewed beer, this is a favorite downtown hotspot.

Imperial Bar & Billiards
241 Front Street, Juneau, AK 99801, tel: 907-586-1960
Officially the oldest bar in Juneau (opened in 1891), the Imperial offers plenty of pool, darts, and poker. Thursday through Saturday a DJ plays hip-hop.

Kodiak Jack's
537 Gaffeny Road, Fairbanks, AK 99701, tel: 907-374-3373; http://kodiakjacks.alaskansavvy.com
If you are itching to ride a mechanical bull and dance to some country-and-western tunes, this is the place. Also doubles as a sports bar serving burgers, pizzas, and sandwiches.

The Marlin
3412 College Road, Fairbanks,

AK 99709, tel: 907-479-4646; http://themarlin.alaskansavvy.com
Cavernous and dark, this is a great place to mix with locals, enjoy live music, and eat some grilled hotdogs.

Pioneer Bar
739 W. Fourth Street, Anchorage, AK 99501, tel: 907-276-7996; www.pioneerbaralaska.com
Open since 1916, this is one of Anchorage's oldest bars. Often crowded, it also features an outdoor beer garden.

SHOPPING

What To Buy

Many rare crafts and products are available to buy throughout the state. Popular items include jade jewellery, canned food products and Alaska Native crafts. Gold nugget jewelry is also a local speciality and makes a wonderful Alaskan souvenir or gift. Somewhat expensive, Alaskan goods are generally of high quality.

Although opportunities to pick up bargains from the actual artisans have declined markedly in recent years, it is occasionally possible to strike a good deal in the villages. Alaska is still sufficiently folksy for many of the most interesting shopping places to be "Mom and Pop" operations. Your best bet for finding such establishments is to wander slowly through whatever town you're in and take time to check out the stock in even the most rundown-looking stores. Alaska is also home to many talented artists whose work can be purchased at local galleries and shops. Museums and major hotels all have gift shops hawking Alaskan products.

There are two ways to ensure you're buying authentic goods. If an item was manufactured in Alaska, the tag features a polar bear and the words, "Made in Alaska." Authentic Native-made products show a silver hand with the designation "Native Handicraft." Recently, Russian goods reading "Alaskan made" have seeped into the state, becoming a popular scam. Make sure that the label has the proper insignia.

Native Crafts

Native crafts are abundant and include items carved from walrus ivory, soapstone and jade. Also look for seal-oil candles, carved wooden totem poles, and clothing.
Alaska Native women make some

Nightlife by Night Light

Baseball games at midnight. Camping on Flattop Mountain to honor the summer solstice. Backyard gardening into the wee hours. City workers leaving jobs in the afternoon to fish prime salmon streams all night, then driving back to work in the morning. These are symptoms, one and all, of a curious relationship Alaskans have with light in summer.

Alaska's far-north place on the globe ensures that as the Earth's axis tilts closer to the sun in June, July, and August, the state basks in hours and hours of rich summer light. So significant is the annual ebb and flow of light to Alaskans that newspapers and radio commentators report how many minutes of light the state gains (or loses) each day.

Anchorage sees a late-night sunset throughout the summer. At and above the Arctic Circle, night disappears. In Barrow, almost 300 miles north of the Circle, the sun rises on May 10 and does not set again until August 1.

of the most intricately woven baskets in the world. Materials used for the baskets include beachgrass, birch bark and whale baleen. These items have become very popular over the years and command a high price, some selling for several hundred dollars. Beaded slippers from seal skin and wolf hair are also hand-made. Unusual porcupine quill earrings are affordable and attractive.

Jade and Ivory

Jade is found locally in Alaska, and is made into carvings as well as jewelry. Jade stones come in various shades of green, brown, black, yellow, white and red.

Scrimshawed walrus ivory – scenes are etched on the ivory – is another authentic handicraft. Visitors who wish to take ivory to a country other than the United States must obtain an export permit from the US Fish and Wildlife Service. Be sure to ask about restrictions when your purchase is made.

Fur

Furriers remain a popular business, particularly in larger cities like Anchorage and Fairbanks. Most fur comes from trappers who live in the bush and are regulated by the state's Fish and Wildlife Department. Still, fur remains a controversial trade, particularly with regard to animal cruelty, but in this state of extreme cold and back-to-the-land self-reliance, it is much more accepted. If you plan on purchasing fur, ask its origin and any customs regulations that may apply when taking it out of the US.

Shopping Areas

While downtown areas remain a popular place to shop, the suburban shopping mall has come to Alaska's larger cities to stay, and smaller communities are building mini-malls.

Anchorage
Fourth Avenue, and other streets downtown are still the most popular places to shop, with a variety of stores and heated sidewalks in the winter. Anchorage Fifth Avenue Mall, 320 W. Fifth Avenue, includes department stores, several national chain outlets, and a wide variety of specialty shops.

Dimond Center, located at the corner of Dimond Boulevard and the Old Seward Highway in south Anchorage, is the largest mall in Alaska. Besides major department and chain stores there are a variety of smaller shops. An ice rink is located at the southern end, in addition to several fast-food restaurants and a multi-screen movie theater. The area also includes many of the national chains in their own buildings, including office supply, sporting goods, book, and electronics stores. In the summer, one of Anchorage's small farmers' markets opens in the southwest corner of the parking lot.

Fairbanks
The main downtown shopping district runs along Cushman Avenue.

Bentley Mall, on the corner of College Road and the Old Steese Highway, is Fairbanks' largest. That and other local malls were an outgrowth of the building boom of the mid-1970s.

SPORTS

Spectator Sports
Baseball
Alaska has one of the best semi-pro baseball leagues in the country. The Fairbanks Gold Panners, the Anchorage Glacier Pilots, the Anchorage Bucs, the Mat-Su Miners, and the Kenai Peninsula Oilers are comprised of college players lured

north by the long days and opportunity to play ball. Many have gone on to Major League careers. Games are played in modest stadiums with double headers played late into the evening – sometimes without artifical light. For game information, contact the Alaska Baseball League www. alaskabaseballleague.org.

Prices are low. A few dollars gets you into the bleachers (the wooden seating area). Be sure to carry insect repellent, especially to games in the Fairbanks area, as well as a light jacket for cool evenings.

A good bet is the Midnight Sun Game in Fairbanks, which starts late at night on June 21, without lights, in celebration of the summer solstice.

Basketball
Probably the most-watched spectator sport in Alaska is high school basketball. Every community with seven or more students has its own school and enough players to field a team. Regional tournaments abound in late winter, with the state championship played out in March. Pick-up games and adult city league games also are popular, especially in rural areas.

The Great Alaska Shoot-Out, held the fourth weekend in November at the Sullivan Arena and hosted by the University of Alaska Anchorage, attracts top-rate college teams from across the United States. And Fairbanks has its Top of the World Classic, which also draws Division I teams north in November. For more information, visit www.shootout.net

Hockey
Hockey teams from the University of Alaska Fairbanks (the Nanooks) and

the University of Alaska Anchorage (the Seawolves) play between October and March against college teams from the rest of the US.

The ECHL's Anchorage Aces, a professional team, also play during the fall and winter, drawing rowdy crowds that take their hockey seriously. To be a part of the madness, check out www.alaskaaces.com for scheduled games.

Mushing
Alaska's official winter sport draws spectators to races throughout the state, from tiny villages to Alaska's urban center, Anchorage. Among the biggest events are Anchorage's Fur Rendezvous World Championship Sled Dog Race in February; Fairbanks' North American Championship in March; the 1,000-mile (1,600km) Yukon Quest, between Fairbanks and Whitehorse in the Yukon Territory, in February; and the 1,100-mile (1,770km) Iditarod Trail Sled Dog Race, staged each March from Anchorage to Nome *(see page 302)*. For more details, contact the Alaska Dog Mushers Association at 907-457-6874 or at www.sleddog.org.

Participant Sports
Golf
While golf in Alaska may never be as popular a draw as in destinations such as Hawaii, there are a number of courses in Anchorage and Fairbanks, as well as ones in Wasilla, Palmer, Homer and Juneau.

The three most popular public courses are in Anchorage: Moose Run, the state's oldest course, owned by the Army; Eagle Glen, considered by many to be the best in the state,

BELOW: both fresh and saltwater fishermen need to have licenses.

on Elmendorf Air Force Base; and the Anchorage Golf Course, on Anchorage's lower Hillside. There are also two 9-hole courses: at Russian Jack Springs Park and south Anchorage's Tanglewood Lakes.

Golf tournaments in Alaska range from the serious to the hilarious, such as Nome's Bering Sea Ice Golf Classic, an annual fund-raising event played in March on a 6-hole course on the frozen Bering Sea, or Kodiak's par-70, *one-hole* spring contest which is held on the side of 1,400ft (430-meter) Pillar Mountain.

Outdoor Activities

Canoeing and Kayaking

For those not averse to the water, there is no better way to explore the Alaskan outdoors than in a lightweight craft you paddle yourself. Most rivers are navigable by canoe, at least to some extent, and there are enough whitewater thrills available for kayakers to last a lifetime.

Anyone setting out on an extensive canoe/kayak trip in Alaska should leave a detailed itinerary with the nearest Alaska State Trooper office or park/refuge/forest headquarters. People who don't come out of the woods when expected are certainly a lot easier to find if the rescue agencies have some idea of where to start looking.

A particularly good canoeing experience is the Swanson River system of canoe trails near Soldotna on the Kenai Peninsula. Weekend adventures or 2-week expeditions are possible in this region, just a 3-hour drive from Anchorage. Prince William Sound also offers endless paddling opportunities but be aware that the weather can often be overcast and rainy. For more details on the Swanson River system, contact: Kenai National Wildlife Refuge, PO Box 2139 MS 519, Soldotna, AK 99669; tel: 907-262-7021; www.r7.fws.gov/nwr/kenai/index.htm.

Kayakers use waterproof storage sacks known as "dry bags." A large bag is roomy enough for a sleeping bag, pad, and tent. Smaller bags are available for extra clothes, food, and personal items. Don't take the term "dry bag" literally. Always add extra protection by first wrapping everything in plastic.

Cycling

Hundreds of cyclists make long-distance trips by pedal power along Alaska's road system every year. These trips are often as much a test of the ruggedness of the bikes and riders as they are a pleasurable journey. Cyclists should be warned that in many places bike shoulders are narrow, and it is a long way between cities, even on the road system.

Anchorage and Fairbanks have elaborate networks of bike paths/jogging trails. These often are splendid, safe paths set well off the road. In summer they are used for biking and walking, in winter for skiing.

Diving

Recreational diving in Alaska is not for the faint-hearted as the waters are cold. Local divers prefer dry suits to the older, more common wet suits. Currents in the saltwater may be treacherous. Inquire locally before undertaking any dives.

Once underwater, the cold northern seas offer good diving. The water is clear, except near the mouths of major, silt-laden rivers. Seafood can be harvested while diving, to be enjoyed once you're on dry land.

Few recreational divers go diving in freshwater in Alaska – the major rivers are usually heavily laden with silt from headwater glaciers, and are best avoided.

There are dive shops in Craig, Sitka, Ketchikan, Juneau, Kodiak, in the Prince William Sound area, on the Kenai Peninsula, and in Anchorage. Some offer guided dives, along with opportunities to dive with Stellar sea lions and to see fresh- and salt-water fish.

Fishing

The number of people who have long dreamed of fishing Alaska's pristine waters for massive king salmon, leaping trout, and wily northern pike must surely be in the millions. All those fish are there, and more. But they're not inclined to just leap in your boat. Prime fishing takes planning; it also helps to get tips from locals.

Most roadside streams and lakes experience considerable fishing pressure and you're likely to find crowded conditions, particularly during the height of the salmon season. But a short walk upstream, or down, may put you in all-but-unfished territory. Remember that just as you and your fellow fishermen are angling for the best catch, so are the local bears. While fishing, whether on crowded streams or not, always exercise extreme caution, and give bears plenty of room.

Those wishing to catch a monstrous salmon or halibut would do well to enlist the services of a fishing guide, located near most of the major fisheries. Rates typically are $100 or more a day per person but should provide more adventure than most anglers can imagine. Your best bet for salmon fishing with guides is on the Kenai River near Soldotna, in the Matanuska Valley, the Bristol Bay region, or on a fly-out trip from Fairbanks or Anchorage to a remote lodge or camp. Alaska's salmon and rainbow trout fisheries are famed throughout the world.

Halibut fishermen flock to Homer and Seward every year for the opportunity to latch on to these bottomfish, which can weigh 300lbs (136kg) or more. Several fish of 100–200lbs (45–90kg) are caught every year by charter boats operating from the Homer Spit and other Kenai Peninsula towns. Anglers will likely have to spend at least $150 for a day's charter-boat fishing per person, though special deals are sometimes available. Many first-class fishing resorts and wilderness lodges are scattered around Alaska, particularly in the Southwest and Southeast regions. Most are in remote areas, accessible only via floatplane. For those who have the $3,000 or more per person for a week's fishing, these offer an unforgettable experience.

If you're dreaming of fishing but sitting in a downtown Anchorage hotel, you're in luck. Head down the hill to the shores of Ship Creek, Anchorage's urban fishing hole, for an outstanding chance to reel in a salmon. Or just go to watch the fun. It's within walking distance of several hotels, many of which will rent or loan you fishing gear. Equipment for rent is also available from a fishing shack down at the water's edge. Make sure you have a fishing license.

Anyone 16 or older must have a fishing license when angling on Alaska's waters; that includes both fresh and saltwater. Fishing licenses are available at almost all sporting goods stores, most variety stores, at several grocery stores or online. For more information, contact the Alaska Division of Sportfish at 907-465-4180 or www.adfg.state.ak.us.

Angling Tips

It takes years for the region's trout, grayling, and char to reach trophy size, so most anglers practice catch-and-release fishing. For many, that means fly-fishing. Spinning gear works well, too, particularly if anglers use single barbless hooks, rather than treble hooks on spinners and spoons. Fish that are taken on bait tend to swallow hooks, resulting in damage to their delicate gill tissue and internal organs, leading to bleeding and, ultimately, death.

When fishing catch-and-release, play a fish as briefly as possible and avoid removing it from the water. Use forceps or needle-nose pliers to grasp the hook and gently slip it from the fish's mouth. If the fish must be handled, make sure that your hands are wet. Dry hands are more likely to remove the slimy coating on the fish's body, leaving it prone to deadly fungal infections. Cradle the fish underwater for as long as necessary until it recovers and swims away.

Hiking

Extensive hiking trips into Alaska's backcountry differ significantly from backpacking trips in most of the rest of the US and any trip should begin with a stop at one of the state's four Public Lands Information Centers (in Anchorage, Fairbanks, Tok, and Ketchikan; check the website www.nps. gov/aplic for more details). Although there are extensive hiking trails in populated regions of the state, treks in remote areas often will be more of an overland-navigation experience, which can be both extremely rewarding and challenging. You should know how to use a compass and read topographic maps when traveling across untrailed wilderness.

Regardless of where you hike, even in some city parks, take precautions to avoid a surprise run-in with wildlife. Bears, as well as moose, can be very dangerous when startled. Do your best to discourage a curious bear from entering your campsite by keeping it clean and free of accessible food. *(For more wildlife precautions, see pages 84–5, 371.)*

Hikers and backpackers should also exercise great caution whenever crossing streams; many of Alaska's rivers are fed by glaciers and are therefore extremely cold and possibly turbulent, with loose gravel bottoms. For perspective, consider that more people die from stream crossings than bear attacks (the number of fatalities are small in both cases).

Those going on extensive hikes in the Alaskan wilderness should leave an itinerary with reliable friends or family members and the Alaska State Troopers or, when appropriate, at the headquarters and/or trailhead of the park, refuge, or unit being explored.

Horseback Riding

Recently, horseback-riding tours have been added to the mix of Alaska's

---

Hypothermia

One of the first signs of hypothermia is violent and uncontrollable shivering. As the core body temperature drops, shivering diminishes and muscles become rigid. The chief symptoms at this stage are what one outdoor writer calls "the umbles:" stumbling, mumbling, fumbling, bumbling. Speech is slurred, coordination poor, and comprehension dull. If not properly treated the victim quickly becomes irrational, drifts into a stupor, and loses consciousness.

If you suspect a member of your party is suffering from hypothermia, immediately try to find shelter. Put the victim into dry clothes, wrap him in blankets or sleeping bags, keep him off the ground, and provide whatever heat may be available. If the condition worsens, put the victim in a sleeping bag with another person. Alone, the victim will be unable to produce enough heat to warm the bag, much less his own body.

Sufferers of hypothermia often don't realize they're in danger and may even deny it. It only takes a few minutes to slip into the condition, and, if untreated, death can follow in less than two hours.

The best plan, of course, is prevention. Dressing properly truly can be a matter of life and death. Always bring extra clothing on outdoor adventures, and consider your options before you get into trouble.

---

ecotourism. Mostly located in Southcentral and the Interior, tours can last as little as an hour to as long as several weeks in the backcountry. Most operators allow for a range of riding experience. *(See page 366 for contact information.)*

Hunting

Citizens of countries other than the US must enlist the services of a licensed hunting guide for hunting any big game animal in the state. Guided hunts typically cost from $2,000 for some single-species hunts to $10,000 or more for particular high-quality or multi-species hunts. A typical $2,000 hunt buys a few days of hunting caribou. The $10,000 might buy two to three weeks of hunting from several lodges or camps. A complete list of registered and master guides is available for download, or a copy may be purchased for $5 from: Department of Commerce, Community and Economic Development, Division of Occupational Licensing, Big Game Commercial Services Board, PO Box 110806, Juneau, AK 99811-0806, tel: 907-465-2534; www.commerce.state. ak.us/occ/pgui7.htm

US residents of states other than Alaska may hunt big game without a guide, except for brown/grizzly bear, mountain goat, and Dall sheep. For these animals, non-Alaska residents and US citizens must engage a guide or be accompanied by a family member – only father, mother, sister, brother, son or daughter qualify – who is a resident of Alaska.

Regulations affecting hunting areas, bag limits, and methods and means are extremely complex and vary from region to region around Alaska. To get a license and copies of the hunting regulations contact: the state Department of Fish and Game at 907-465-4190 or www.adfg.state.ak.us.

Study the regulations carefully before hunting. If in any doubt, inquire locally with the Alaska Department of Fish and Game. License & Tag Fees: tel: 907-465-2376 for current charges.

Skiing

Both downhill and cross-country skiing are popular in Alaska from November through May (snowfall permitting). There are trails for cross-country skiing throughout the state's populated areas and several communities have developed ski facilities, including Juneau, Anchorage, and Fairbanks.

The state's largest ski area is Alyeska, 40 miles (65km) southeast of Anchorage in Girdwood. The resort offers 2,500 vertical ft (760 meters) of skiing, including, on occasion, night skiing. The resort has a high-speed aerial tram capable of carrying 60 passengers at a time, and the Aleyska Resort, with a pool, restaurants, exercise facilities and meeting rooms.

Closer to Anchorage is Alpenglow at Arctic Valley, which also offers downhill skiing. Hilltop Ski Area, in south Anchorage, is popular with local snowboarders and novice skiers. Several parks in the Anchorage area are popular for cross-country skiing, including Russian Jack Springs, Kincaid Park, Far North Bicentennial Park, Hillside Park, and Chugach State Park. Another favorite is the

Tony Knowles Coastal Trail.

In Juneau, alpine skiers head for Eaglecrest Ski Area on Douglas Island, 12 miles (19km) from downtown Juneau. Facilities include two chairlifts and a day lodge.

Fairbanks offers a few privately owned downhill areas, including Mt Aurora/Skiland and Moose Mountain.

Popular cross-country trails in Fairbanks include the Creamers Field trail near downtown, Birch Hill Recreation area, and those on the University of Alaska campus. Not far away is Chena Hot Springs Resort, with trails and after-ski relaxation.

Surfing

Given that Alaska's tidal shoreline covers 31,383 miles (50,506km), it offers opportunities for surfers. The most popular beach is at Yakutat (see pages 156–7), the northernmost community along the Inside Passage. More and more surfers have headed here since Outdoor magazine named Yakutat as one of America's top five surf towns. Contact www.yakutatalaska. com for details.

PARKS AND PRESERVES

With eight national parks (many with attached preserves), four national monuments, three separate national preserves, 16 wildlife refuges (see page 317), 25 wild and scenic rivers and 12 designated federal areas – plus a state parks system of more than 3.2 million acres (1.3 million hectares) – Alaska holds more land in the public trust than any other state, by far.

For more information on all Alaska's public lands visit: Alaska Geographic at

BELOW: the easiest way to reach many parks is by air.

www.alaskageographic.org; Alaska Public Lands Information Center, 605 W. Fourth Avenue, Anchorage, AK 99501, tel: 907-271-2737; www.nps.gov/aplic; or US Fish and Wildlife Service Alaska Regional Office 1011 East Tudor Road, Anchorage, AK 99503, tel: 907-786-3309; www.r7.fws.gov.

Alaska Chilkat Bald Eagle Preserve Approximately 20 miles (32km) from Haines on the Haines Highway. Winter feeding ground for thousands of bald eagles, when it holds the largest concentration of these birds in the world – the best viewing is in November to December. Contact: Alaska State Parks, Haines Ranger Station, PO Box 430, Haines, AK 99827, tel: 907-766-2292; www.dnr. state.ak.us/parks/units/eagleprv.htm

Alaska Maritime National Wildlife Refuge Scattered coastal units from Kodiak to the tip of the Aleutian Islands Chain. More than 2,500 islands in all. Marine mammals and marine birds, including 50 million nesting seabirds. Contact: 95 Sterling Highway, MS 505, Suite 1, Homer, AK 99603, tel: 907-235-6546; www.alaska.fws.gov/nwr/akmar/index.htm

Alaska Peninsula and Becharof National Wildlife Refuges Within these side-by-side refuges in Southwest Alaska are active volcanoes, towering mountains, rolling tundra, and rugged coastal fjords. The refuges are known for their fish and wildlife, particularly salmon, brown/grizzly bears, moose, caribou, wolves, and wolverines. Excellent fishing and big-game hunting. Contact: PO Box 277, MS 545, King Salmon, AK 99613, tel: 907-246-3339; www.alaska.fws.gov/nwr/akpen/index.htm

Admiralty Island National Monument Southeast Alaska island within the Tongass National Forest, located 15 miles (25km) west of Juneau across Stephens Passage. Primary access is by boat or floatplane from Juneau, but wheeled planes are allowed to land on beaches. Mountainous terrain in coastal rainforest. Contact: 8510 Mendenhall Loop Road, Juneau, AK 99801, tel: 907-586-8800; www.fs.fed. us./r10/tongass/districts/admiralty

Arctic National Wildlife Refuge One of the world's great remaining Arctic wilderness areas, in the extreme northeast bordering Canada. (See pages 280–5.) Contact: 101 12th Avenue, Room 236, Fairbanks, AK 99701, tel: 907-456-0250 or 800-362-4546; www.alaska.fws.gov/nwr/arctic/index.htm

Chugach National Forest Second-largest national forest in the US (behind only the Tongass), the Chugach includes much of the Kenai Peninsula and Prince William Sound, as well as the Copper River Delta. (See page 119.) Contact: 3301 C St., Anchorage, AK 99503, tel: 907-743-9500; www.fs.fed.us/r10/chugach

Chugach State Park Anchorage's "backyard wilderness," with nearly a half-million acres of land and waters within the Chugach Mountains east of town. (See pages 180–3.) Contact: Alaska State Parks, Mile 115 Seward Highway, HC 52, Box 8999, Indian, AK 99540, tel: 907-345-5014; www.dnr.alaska.gov/parks/units/chugach

Denali National Park and Preserve One of Alaska's most popular tourist destinations, with an average 350,000 visitors a year, it is home to Mount McKinley – also known by the Athabascan name Denali, The High One – at 20,320ft (6,195 meters), the highest peak in North America. (See pages 223–33.)

To explore the park, you can take the cheaper, no-frills shuttle bus, or the more expensive tour bus, which includes lunch and a driver who is also a natural history guide. Advance booking is advised. For more information, visit www.nps.gov/dena/planyourvisit/bus-reservations.htm or call 800-622-7275 (in US) or 907-272-7275 (international). Contact for general park information: Denali National Park, PO Box 9, Denali National Park, AK 99755, tel: 907-683-2294; www.nps.gov/dena

Denali State Park Smaller and less celebrated neighbor of Denali National Park, "Little Denali" nonetheless offers numerous

opportunities for backcountry recreation and some of the best views anywhere of Mount McKinley/Denali and other Alaska Range giants. Contact: Alaska State Parks, HC 32 Box 6706, Wasilla, AK 99654, tel: 907-745-3975; http://dnr.alaska.gov/parks/units/denali1.htm

Gates of the Arctic National Park and Preserve
The peaks and valleys of the central Brooks Range lie within the park and preserve 200 miles (320km) northwest of Fairbanks. *(See pages 286–9.)* The most convenient access is by air with scheduled service from Fairbanks to Bettles, 40 miles (64km) south of the park. Contact: Visitor Information, PO Box 30, Bettles, AK 99726, tel: 907-692-5494; www.nps.gov/gaar

Glacier Bay National Park and Preserve
Located 50 miles (80km) northwest of Juneau at the northern end of Alaska's Panhandle, Glacier Bay is an ever-changing wilderness of tidewater glaciers, towering peaks, coastal fjords, marine mammals and northern birds. Though cruise ships enter the bay, their number is limited to preserve the wilderness experience. *(See pages 140–3.)* Contact: PO Box 140, Gustavus, AK 99826, tel: 907-697-2230; www.nps.gov/glba

Izembak National Wildlife Refuge
At the tip of Alaska Peninsula in SW Alaska, between the Pacific Ocean and Bering Sea. Outstanding birding and wildlife viewing, including caribou. Access is usually from Cold Bay, which can only be easily reached by airplane. Contact: PO Box 127 MS 515, Cold Bay, AK 99571, tel: 907-532-2445; http://alaska.fws.gov/nwr/izembek/index.htm

Kachemak Bay State Park and Wilderness Park
Across the Bay from Homer, these side-by-side units are relatively unknown, yet they're a wilderness lover's delight, with everything from glaciers and snowfields to coastal rain forest, tidal marshes, sheltered bays, and storm-wracked outer coast. Contact: Alaska State Parks, Kenai Area Office, PO Box 1247, Soldotna, AK 99669, tel: 907-262-5581; http://dnr.alaska.gov/parks/units/kbay/kbay.htm

Katmai National Park and Preserve
Excellent fishing and brown bear viewing, plus opportunities to explore mountains, valleys, and rugged coast by boat or foot. *(See pages 326–9.)* Approximately 250 miles (400km) southwest of Anchorage. Contact: PO Box 7, King Salmon, AK 99613, tel: 907-246-3305; www.nps.gov/katm

Kenai Fjords National Park
Boat or floatplane charters from Seward, on the Kenai Peninsula, 130 road miles (210km) south of Anchorage, are the usual means of access. Features the Harding Icefield, one of the major ice caps in the United States, plus tidewater glaciers, and the steep, rugged coastal fjords for which the park is named. Abundant wildlife and marine mammal viewing. Has four public-use cabins for rent, three along the coast, one inland that's for winter-use only. Contact: PO Box 1727, Seward, AK 99664, tel: 907-224-7500; www.nps.gov/kefj

Kenai National Wildlife Refuge
Located on the Kenai Peninsula across Turnagain Arm south of Anchorage. Spruce and birch forests with hundreds of lakes and streams make this prime habitat for moose, bears and salmon. Contact: PO Box

2139 MS 519, Soldotna, AK 99669, tel: 907-262-7021; http://alaska.fws.gov/nwr/kenai/index.htm

Kobuk Valley National Park
This western Brooks Range park is 350 miles (563km) northwest of Fairbanks and 75 miles (120km) west of Kotzebue. Great Kobuk Sand Dunes cover 25 sq miles (40 sq km). Canoe, kayak and raft trips are the primary recreational opportunities. Contact: PO Box 1029, Kotzebue, AK 99752, tel: 907-442-3890; www.nps.gov/kova

Kodiak National Wildlife Refuge
Encompasses much of Kodiak and Afognak islands southwest of Anchorage. Excellent hunting and fishing, as well as wildlife viewing, rafting, and camping amid spruce forests. Contact: 1390 Buskin River Rd, MS 559, Kodiak, AK 99615, tel: 907-487-2600 or 888-408-3514; http://alaska.fws.gov/nwr/kodiak/index.htm; email: kodiak@fws.gov www.r7.fws.gov

Lake Clark National Park and Preserve
Across Cook Inlet from Anchorage, Lake Clark is one of Alaska's overlooked gems, though it has a grand mix of features, from rugged coastline to pristine lakes and rivers, active volcanoes, and rugged mountains. *(See pages 320–5.)* Contact: 240 W. Fifth Avenue, Anchorage, AK 99501, tel: 907-781-2218; www.nps.gov/lacl

Misty Fiords National Monument
About 22 air miles (35km) from Ketchikan, near the southern tip of Alaska's Panhandle. Wet, scenic region of steep mountains descending into deep fjords. Floatplane or boat access only. *(See pages 114–8.)* Contact: US Forest Service, Federal Building, 648 Mission Street, Ketchikan, AK 99901; tel: 907-225-3101; www.fs.fed.us/r10/tongass/forest_facts/resources/wilderness/misty.shtml

Noatak National Preserve
Just north of Kotzebue, this northwestern Alaska preserve has no road access. Flights from Kotzebue are the normal means of getting to the area. Fantastic float-trip opportunities within the wild Noatak Basin. Contact: PO Box 1029, Kotzebue, AK 99752, tel: 907-442-3890; www.nps.gov/noat

North Eastern Panhandle Wilderness Areas
Inside the Tongass National Forest surrounding Juneau sit four wilderness areas: the Endicott River Wilderness, roughly 100,000 acres (38,000 hectares), is 45 miles (72km) northwest of the capital and

BELOW: exploring the wilderness as the ice melts.

borders Glacier Bay National Park, while to the south, the wilderness areas of Kootznoowoo, Chuck River, and Tracy Arm-Ford's Terror cover over a 1½ million acres (675,000 hectares). All areas provide excellent camping and wildlife-viewing opportunities. Contact: 8510 Mendenhall Loop Road, Juneau, AK 99801, tel: 907-586-8800; www.fs.fed.us/r10/tongass/forest_facts/resources/wilderness/anmjrd.shtml

Petersburg Creek-Duncan Salt Chuck Wilderness
Kupreanof Island across Wrangell Narrows from Petersburg in southeastern Alaska. Contact: Tongass National Forest, PO Box 1328, Petersburg, AK 99833; tel: 907-772-3871; www.fs.us/r10/tongass/districts/petersburg/psgduncan.shtml

Russel Fjord Wilderness
Heavily glaciated fjord about 25 miles (40km) northeast of Yakutat. Contact: US Forest Service, 712 Ocean Cape Road, PO Box 327, Yakutat, AK 99689, tel: 907-784-3359; www.fs.fed.us/r10/tongass

Selawik National Wildlife Refuge
Straddles the Arctic Circle in Northwestern Alaska about 360 miles (580km) northwest of Fairbanks. Consists mostly of lakes, estuaries, river deltas, and tundra wetlands. Home to caribou in winter and huge numbers of nesting waterfowl in spring and summer. Activities include river floating, sport fishing, and hunting. Contact: 160 Second Avenue, PO Box 270, MS 565, Kotzebue, AK 99752, tel: 907-442-3799 or 800-492-8848; http://alaska.fws.gov/nwr/selawik/index.htm

Shuyak Island State Park
At the northern end of the Kodiak Archipelago 250 miles (400km) southwest of Anchorage, Shuyak can be reached only by plane or boat. With coastal rain forest and bountiful,sheltered bays, it's a kayaker's delight. Four public-use cabins come in handy, given the often stormy weather. Contact: Alaska State Parks, 1400 Abercrombie Drive, Kodiak, AK 99615, tel: 907-486-6339; http://dnr.alaska.gov/parks/units/kodiak/index.htm

Sitka National Historical Park
The site of the 1804 Battle of Sitka between Tlingits and Russians. Located in a woodland setting with a collection of totem poles, a footpath through the old-growth forest, and an interpretive center for Russian and Native history. Contact: National Park Service, Sitka National Historical Park, 103 Monastery Street, Sitka, AK 99835, tel: 907-747-0110; www.nps.gov/sitk

---

If You Should Meet a Bear...

"Bearanoia" is a term commonly applied to those with an unreasonable fear of bears. Others, usually inexperienced in the ways of the Alaskan wilderness, sometimes lack a healthy respect for these powerful, if generally shy, animals. Treading a middle ground, seasoned bear-country trekkers use common sense and a basic understanding of bear behavior to avoid close encounters. Here are some tips:
• Avoid surprising bears. Talk loudly or carry "bear bells," and hike in groups of three or more whenever possible. Announcing your presence clearly allows bears to avoid you.
• Don't camp on or near bear paths. Trails along salmon streams, for example, should be avoided.
• Don't keep food in or near tents. Store food in sealed containers well away from camp. If possible, hoist containers high up in a tree.
• Avoid bear kills. Bears can remain in the area of a kill for days and can be highly protective of it.
• Give bears their space. If you happen upon a bear, turn and give it a wide berth. Walk away; never run. Running can trigger a predatory reflex in an otherwise peaceful animal. *For more on bears, see page 335.*

South Prince of Wales Wilderness
Approximately 40 air miles (64km) southwest of Ketchikan on Prince of Wales Island. Contact: US Forest Service, Tongass National Forest, Craig Ranger District, 900 Main Street, PO Box 705, Craig, AK 99921, tel: 907-826-3271, www.fs.fed.us/r10/tongass/districts/pow/index.shtml

Stikine-LeConte Wilderness
Southeastern Alaska mainland, a short distance north of Wrangell. Boats capable of navigating the Stikine River are the most common means of access. Contact: US Forest Service, Stikine Area, Tongass National Forest, 525 Bennett, PO Box 51, Wrangell, AK 99929-0051; tel: 907-874-2323; www.fs.fed.us/r10/tongass

Tetlin National Wildlife Refuge
South side of Alaska Highway at the Canadian border. Waterfowl, moose, caribou, black bears and wolves. The area is especially critical to some 143 species of nesting birds. Two lakeshore campgrounds; duck, caribou and moose hunting. Contact: PO Box 779 MS 529, Tok, AK 99780, tel: 907-883-5312; http://alaska.fws.gov/nwr/tetlin/index.htm

Wood-Tikchik State Park
At more than 1½ million acres, Wood-Tikchik is the nation's largest state park. Located in the Bristol Bay region, it is dominated by two river-and-lake chains that make it a critically important salmon spawning grounds. Popular with sport fishers and boaters, it draws people from around the world. Contact: Alaska State Parks: PO Box 1822, Dillingham, AK 99576; tel: 907-842-2375; http://dnr.alaska.gov/parks/units/woodtik.htm

Wrangell-St Elias National Park and Preserve
This huge park/preserve is the largest in the nation, and totals more than 13 million acres (5 million hectares); sometimes called North America's "mountain kingdom" it includes four mountain ranges, the continent's largest ice field, and a glacier larger than Rhode Island. Access is by air, mainly from Glennallen or Yakutat. *(See pages 190–5.)* Contact: National Park Service, 106.8 Richardson Highway, PO Box 439, Copper Center, AK 99573, tel: 907-822-5234; www.nps.gov/wrst

Yukon-Charley Rivers National Preserve
Includes a section of the Yukon River near Eagle, 325 road miles (523km) northeast of Fairbanks by road. Also accessible by road is Circle, outside the western boundary, about 140 road miles (225km) from Fairbanks. Home to gold-rush relics, bear, Dall sheep, moose and a population of peregrine falcons. Contact: National Park Service, Eagle Visitor Center, PO Box 167, Eagle, AK 99738, tel: 907-547-2233; www.nps.gov/yuch

Yukon Delta National Wildlife Refuge
Deltas of the Yukon and Kuskokwim rivers in southwestern Alaska. Plenty of waterfowl and seabirds – 170 species seen in the area and 136 species known to breed here, plus moose, caribou, brown bear, and wolves. Fishing, hunting and back-country recreation are good, though access to most of the refuge is difficult and the landscape is mostly boggy – and mosquito-infested in mid-summer. Contact: 807 Chief Eddie Hoffman Road, PO Box 346 MS 535, Bethel, AK 99559, tel: 907-543-3151; http://alaska.fws.gov/nwr/yukondelta/index.htm

TRANSPORTATION
ACCOMMODATIONS
ACTIVITIES
CONTACTS
A – Z

C ONTACTS

ALL THE USEFUL ADDRESSES YOU'LL NEED

Adventure Tours

Adventure Alaska Tours
Wilderness and land excursions include sightseeing tours, hiking, canoeing, and biking. Specializes in small groups on trips of five to 16 days.
PO Box 64, Hope,
AK 99605
Tel: 907-782-3730 or
800-365-7057
www.adventurealaskatours.com

Alaska Adventures Unlimited
Offers a variety of guided tours from one day to ten, exploring a variety of natural and cultural sites. River rafting, gold panning, hiking, sled dog, and flightseeing available among others.
PO Box 871723
Tel: 907-373-3494 or
800-580-3494
www.alaskaadventureunlimited.com/index.html

Alaska Passages Adventure Cruises
Fishing, whale watching, glacier viewing, kayaking, photography, and charters for research expeditions. Features customized trips through the Inside Passage, with a maximum of six guests.
PO Box 213, Petersburg,
AK 99833
Tel: 907-772-3967 or
888-434-3766
www.alaskapassages.com

Alaska Wildland Adventures
Nationally recognized natural history and ecotourism operator offers outdoor-oriented "safaris" of varying lengths for a variety of ages to Denali, Kenai Fjords, Kenai River fishing, and elsewhere. Also can arrange stays at wilderness lodges.
PO Box 389, Girdwood,

AK 99587
Tel: 907-783-2928 or
800-334-8730
www.alaskawildland.com

Arctic Treks
Wilderness backpacking and rafting in the Brooks Range. Two-week combination trips and seven- to ten-day base camp hiking trips in the remote Arctic National Wildlife Refuge, Gates of the Arctic National Park, and other neighboring parklands. Recognized outfitters and guides used for all programs.
PO Box 73452, Fairbanks,
AK 99707
Tel: 907-455-6502
www.arctictreksadventures.com

Arctic Wild
Guided backpacking, hiking, canoeing, and rafting adventures in the Arctic National Wildlife Refuge and Gates of the Arctic National Park. Besides its scheduled trips, the company organizes custom expeditions into the wilderness.
PO Box 80562, Fairbanks,
AK 99708
Tel: 907-479-8203 or
888-577-8203
www.arcticwild.com

Great Alaska Safaris
Small-group safaris include Denali flightseeing, kayaking, bear viewing, fishing, and tundra hiking.
33881 Sterling Highway, Sterling,
AK 99672, or
in winter PO Box 2670, Poulsbo,
WA 98570
Tel: 907-262-4515 in summer or
800-544-2261 year-round
www.greatalaska.com

Iniakuk Lake Wilderness Lodge
Spend a slice of winter 60 miles north of the Arctic Circle in a fully equipped wilderness lodge in the Brooks Range.

Plenty of Northern Lights and opportunities for dogsledding, snowshoeing, and cross-country skiing. Packages include 3 or 5 day, all-inclusive stays and including ski plane service from Fairbanks.
PO Box 80424, Fairbanks,
AK 99708
Tel: 877-479-6354
www.brooksrangewintertours.com

Log Cabin Resort and RV Park
Log cabins, campgrounds and log house with suites. RV hookups, rustic beach cabins with modern kitchens and baths. Outboards, skiffs, canoes for fishing in rivers, lakes and saltwater for salmon or halibut. Licensed charters. Canoeing, hiking, bird- and whale-watching, and photography.
PO Box 54, Klawock,
AK 99925
Tel: 907-755-2205 or
800-544-2205
www.logcabinresortandrvpark.com

Nunivak Island Guide Service
Wilderness trips include sport fishing, musk ox sport hunting, and wildlife viewing in the Yukon Delta National Wildlife Refuge.
PO Box 31, Mekoryuk,
AK 99630
Tel: 907-827-8213

Wilderness Alaska
Brooks Range backpacking and river trips. Customized and scheduled trips through the Arctic National Wildlife Refuge and Gates of the Arctic National Park, with a special focus on wilderness skills and field biology unique to the high Arctic. Also guides kayak trips in Prince William Sound.
PO Box 113063, Anchorage,
AK 99511
Tel: 907-345-3567
www.wildernessalaska.com

Bear Viewing

Over the past decade, the demand to view bears has exploded. Prime viewing time runs from June through early September, when the salmon are running, depending on the location. Most bear-viewing areas feature brown bears (the coastal cousins of grizzlies), but a couple in Southeast Alaska also include black bears.

Most of these locales have visitor limits, so plan far ahead.

Anan Creek Bear Observatory
In Southeast Alaska's rainforest, Anan is a rarity in that both black and brown bears may be viewed here. Best viewing is in July and August, when salmon runs reach their peak. Managed by the US Forest Service, in the Tongass National Forest.
Wrangell Ranger District, PO Box 51, Wrangell, AK 99929
Tel: 907-874-2323
www.fs.fed.us/r10/tongass/recreation/wildlife_viewing/ananobservatory.shtml

Fish Creek Wildlife Observatory Site
Fish Creek has been a local attraction for decades, but only in the last decade, as ecotourism has blossomed, has the creek become a major visitor attraction. Located near Alaska's border with Canada, on the edges of the Tongass National Forest, this salmon stream is the only one of Alaska's prime bear-watching locales to be along the road system. Mostly brown bears, but occasionally a black bear will wander through.
PO Box 126, Hyder,
AK 99923
Tel: 907-225-2148 in Ketchikan year-round or 250-636-2367 in Hyder from April through September
www.fs.fed.us/r10/ro/naturewatch/southeast/fish_creek/fishcreek.htm

Katmai National Park and Preserve
Like McNeil, Katmai is on the upper Alaska Peninsula. Prime viewing time is in July and September. Dozens of brown bears are drawn into the Brooks River by sockeye salmon, with fishing concentrated at Brooks Falls. Campground, visitor center, viewing platforms, ranger station, and a lodge with a dozen small cabins that can be rented.
Contact the national park at:
PO Box 7, King Salmon,
AK 99613
Tel: 907-246-3305
www.nps.gov/katm

McNeil River State Game Sanctuary
Widely regarded as the premier place to view lots of brown bears –

sometimes up close – McNeil offers a wilderness adventure that requires a permit, which are awarded in a lottery fashion by the Alaska Department of Fish and Game every spring (see page 334). Staying in a designated tent camping area that includes a cooking-eating shack and a wood-fired sauna, visitors hike to either Mikfik Creek or McNeil River to watch brown bears feed. The prime gathering is at McNeil Falls, from early July through mid-August, when as many as four or five dozen bears may gather at one time.
Alaska Department of Fish and Game, Division of Wildlife Conservation, 333 Raspberry Road, Anchorage, AK 99518
Tel: 907-267-2253
www.wildlife.alaska.gov/index.cfm

Pack Creek
Brown bears fish for salmon returning to Admiralty Island, in Southeast Alaska, a short plane ride from Juneau. Day viewing only. Prime time is July and August.
Admiralty Island National Monument 8510 Mendenhall Loop Road, Juneau, AK 99801
Tel: 907-586-8800
www.fs.fed.us/r10/tongass/districts/admiralty/packcreek/index.shtml

Redoubt Bay Lodge
Located across Cook Inlet from Anchorage adjacent to Lake Clark National Park and Preserve, the lodge originally catered to fishermen, but is now seeing more bear viewers. Other activities include fishing, kayaking, hiking, flightseeing.
Contact: Within the Wild Adventure Company, PO Box 91419, Anchorage, AK 99509
Tel: 907-274-2710
www.withinthewild.com

Cruises

Abercrombie & Kent
Full luxury onboard the 118-passanger Clipper Odyssey. Sails from Prince William Sound to Vancouver, exploring seldom-visited parks and towns along route.
1411 Opus Place,
Executive Towers West II, Suite 300, Downers Grove, IL 60515
Tel: 800-554-7016 or
630-725-3400

American Safari Cruises
Cruise from the Inside Passage in a yacht holding no more than 40 people. This small cruise company specializes in a gourmet experience from the food and wine to kayak excursions and shore wildlife trips.
3826 18th Avenue West, Seattle, WA 98119

Tel: 888-862-8881
www.amsafari.com
Cruise West
Up-close, casual, small-ship cruises that range from the Inside Passage to the Bering Sea, with the option of multi-day motorcoach tours to Denali, Anchorage, gold-rush sites, or other destinations.
2301 Fifth Avenue, Suite 401, Seattle, WA 98121
Tel: 888-851-8133
Email: experience@cruisewest.com
www.cruisewest.com

Lindblad Expeditions
In partnership with Nation Geographic, this small-boat cruise company offers tours of the Southeast and motor tours throughout the Interior, including Denali.
96 Morton Street, 9th Floor, New York, NY 10014
Tel: 212-765-7740 or
800-397-3348
www.expeditions.com

Major lines visiting Alaska include:
Carnival Cruise Lines
www.carnival.com
Celebrity Cruises
www.celebrity-cruises.com
Holland America
www.hollandamerica.com
Norwegian Cruise Line/NCLAmerica
www.ncl.com
Princess Cruises
www.princess.com
Regent Seven Seas Cruises
www.rssc.com
Royal Caribbean Cruise Lines
www.rccl.com

Charters and Day Cruises
Central Charters
Wildlife tour aboard classic yacht Danny J across Kachemak Bay to Halibut Cove's artist community and other custom tours, including trips to the coastal community of Seldovia. Also specializes in halibut fishing charters.
4241 Homer Spit Road, Homer, AK 99603
Tel: 907-235-7847 or
800-478-7842
www.centralcharter.com
Phillips' Cruises and Tours
4½-hour, 135-mile (217km) cruise within protected waters of Prince William Sound. See whales, seals, sea otters, porpoises, bird rookeries and as many as 26 glaciers in College and Harriman fjords.
519 W. Fourth Avenue, Anchorage, AK 99501
Tel: 907-276-8023 or
800-544-0529
www.26glaciers.com

TRANSPORTATION

ACCOMMODATIONS

ACTIVITIES

CONTACTS

A – Z

Portage Glacier Cruises
Take a one-hour cruise to the face of Alaska's most-visited glacier on the Ptarmigan. Offered through Gray Line of Alaska.
745 W. Fourth Avenue, Suite 200, Anchorage, AK 99501
Tel: 907-277-5581 or 800-478-6388
www.graylinealaska.com

Prince William Sound Cruises and Tours
Daily tours out of Whittier, with opportunities to see marine wildlife and calving tidewater glaciers.
509 W. Fourth Ave, Anchorage, AK 99501
Tel: 907-277-2800 or 877-777-2805
www.princewilliamsound.com

Rainbow Tours
Boat tours include whale watching, halibut fishing, and shuttle across Kachemak Bay to Seldovia. Hotel accommodation in Seldovia can be arranged. Group rates.
PO Box 1526, Homer, AK 99603
Tel: 907-235-7272
www.rainbowtours.net

Viking Travel, Inc.
Bookings on Luxury- and Explorer-class cruise ships, ferries and cruise-tour itineraries available. Individual trip planning.
101 N. Nordic, PO Box 787, Petersburg, AK 99833
Tel: 800-327-2571 or 907-772-3818
www.alaskaferry.com

Fishing Tours

Alaska Outdoor Services
Guided fishing trips on the Kenai River and other Kenai Peninsula waters.
PO Box 1066, Soldotna, AK 99669
Tel: 907-262-4589 or 888-434-7425
www.aosalaska.com

Central Charters
This Homer-based outfit is a booking company that specializes in halibut and salmon-fishing charters in Kachemak Bay and lower Cook Inlet.
4241 Homer Spit Road, Homer, AK 99603
Tel: 907-235-7847 or 800-478-7847
www.centralcharter.com

Great Alaska Fish Camp
Deluxe adventure lodge on Kenai River. Fish the world's largest salmon, halibut and rainbow trout. Both fresh- and saltwater guided trips on Alaska's Kenai Peninsula. Retreat facilities.

33881 Sterling Highway, Sterling, AK 99672
Tel: 907-262-4515 in summer, 360-697-6454 in winter or 800-544-2261 year-round
www.greatalaska.com

Juneau Sportfishing and Sightseeing
"Cruise ship style" fishing aboard fully equipped luxury boats. Half- and full-day packages include transportation, bait, tackle, rain gear, food. Wildlife watching is a bonus.
PO Box 20438, Juneau, AK 99802
Tel: 907-586-1887
www.juneausportfishing.com

Silver Fox Charters
Sport fishing for halibut in Kachemak Bay and Cook Inlet. High-tech navigational gear, heated cabins. Gear and bait furnished, as are meals and lodging. Package includes filleting, vacuum, and freezing up to 50 pounds of fish per person.
PO Box 402, Homer, AK 99603
Tel: 907-235-8792 or 800-478-8792
www.silverfoxcharters.com

Sportfishing Alaska
Longtime Alaskan and retired lodge owner arranges personalized fishing trips statewide.
9310 Shorecrest Drive, Anchorage, AK 99502
Tel: 907-344-8674 or 888-552-8674
www.alaskatripplanners.com

Hiking Tours

Alaska Mountaineering School
Both a climbing school and guiding company. Leads mountaineering expeditions to Denali (Mount McKinley) and Mount Foraker, plus custom expeditions to other peaks. Also guides backcountry treks in the Alaska and Brooks Ranges and Talkeetna Mountains.
PO Box 566, Talkeetna, AK 99676
Tel: 907-733-1016
www.climbalaska.org

St Elias Alpine Guides
Specializes in custom trips for individuals or small groups, while leading a full spectrum of activities in Wrangell-St Elias National Park and Preserve, from glacial walks to mountain hikes, nature tours, backpacking treks, and mountaineering expeditions.
PO Box 92129, Anchorage, AK 99509
Tel: 888-933-5427 or 907-345-9048
www.steliasguides.com

Horseback-Riding Tours

Alaska Horsemen Trail Adventures
In the heart of the Kenai Peninsula, this full service guest lodge offers everything from half-day trail rides to overnight pack trips, and has something for the beginner as well as for the accomplished rider. Fishing, gold panning, and river rafting also available.
PO Box 857, Cooper Landing, AK 99572
Tel: 907-595-1806 or 800-595-1806
www.alaskahorsemen.com

Denali Saddle Safaris
See stunning views of Mt McKinley while trekking through the tundra at the edge of the park. Half-day, full-day, or pack trips available.
PO Box 435, Healy, AK 99743
Tel: 907-683-1200
www.farthernorth.com/denalisaddlesafaris/about_us.htm

Kayaking/River Trips

ABEC's Alaska Adventures
Backpacking and river running trips in the Brooks Range, primarily the Arctic National Wildlife Refuge and Gates of the Arctic National Park. Rafting, kayaking and canoeing trips ranging from wild water to relaxing float trips. Custom trips can also be arranged elsewhere in the state.
PO Box 10791, Fairbanks, AK 99710
Tel: 907-457-8907 or 877-424-8907
www.abecalaska.com

Alaska Discovery Wilderness Adventures
Wilderness tours by raft, kayak, canoe, and foot. Also one-day bear watching at Pack Creek. Completely outfitted expeditions into Glacier Bay, Admiralty Island, Icy Bay and other wilderness areas in Southeast Alaska. Also expeditions to the Noatak River in the Gates of the Arctic National Park, the Kongakut River in the Arctic National Wildlife Refuge, Denali National Park, and Kachemak Bay. Group size limited. Explorations can be lodge-based or wilderness camping.
1266 66th Street, Suite 4, Emeryville, CA 94608
Tel: 510-594-6000 or 888-831-7526
www.akdiscovery.com

Alaska Rivers Company
Scenic or whitewater raft trips and float fishing on the upper Kenai River, plus saltwater fishing in Resurrection

Bay. Lodging in log cabins.
PO Box 827, Cooper Landing,
AK 99572
Tel: 907-595-1226 or
888-595-1226
www.alaskariverscompany.com

Chilkat Guides
Half-day river trips in the heart of the Chilkat Bald Eagle Preserve and upper Chilkat River and extended multi-day raft trips down the Alsek and Tatshenshini Rivers in Southeast Alaska and the Kongakut River in the Arctic National Wildlife Refuge.
PO Box 170, Haines,
AK 99827
Tel: 907-766-2491 or
888-292-7789
www.raftalaska.com

Class V White Water
Day trips and extended wilderness floats, both scenic and challenging, from the Kenai Peninsula to the Talkeetna Mountains, in Southcentral Alaska.
PO Box 641, Girdwood,
AK 99587
Tel: 907-783-4354
www.alaskanrafting.com

Denali Raft Adventures
Two-hour, four-hour, and full-day raft trips. Mild water or whitewater, oared or paddle boats, on the Nenana River, which forms the eastern border of Denali National Park.
Mile 238 Parks Highway,
PO Box 190, Denali National Park,
AK 99755
Tel: 907-683-2234 or
1-888-683-2234
www.denaliraft.com

Kayak Adventures Worldwide
Kayak in Kenai Fjords National Park, Prince William Sound and Resurrection Bay. Year-round trips available all over the world.
328 Third Street, PO Box 2249,
Seward, AK 99664
Tel: 907-224-3960
www.kayakak.com

Keystone Raft and Kayak Adventures, Inc.
Wilderness whitewater adventures. Raft trips from two hours to two weeks. Kayak support trips and class III, IV and V kayak excursions.
PO Box 1486, Valdez,
AK 99686
Tel: 907-835-2606 or
800-323-8460
www.alaskawhitewater.com

Ouzel Expeditions
Guided river float trips in western AK and Brooks Range. Fishing trips, scenic float trips on whitewater and calm rivers. Superb fishing for salmon, grayling and trout, plus birding trips with an experienced

ornithologist. Custom-tailored tours.
PO Box 935, Girdwood,
AK 99587
Tel: 907-783-2216 or
800-825-8196
www.ouzel.com

Southeast Exposure
Guided sea-kayaking trips through local waters of the Inside Passage, including Misty Fiords National Monument. Rental, instruction and sales.
37 Potter Road, Ketchikan,
AK 99901
Tel: 907-225-8829
www.southeastexposure.com

Tongass Kayak Adventures
Day trips, base camps and week-long sea-kayak explorations on Alaska's Inside Passage. Specializes in small-group tours.
PO Box 2169,
Petersburg,
AK 99833
Tel: 907-772-4600
www.tongasskayak.com

Skiing

Alyeska Resort
Year-round resort 40 miles (64km) southeast of Anchorage on Seward Highway. Six chairlifts and tram, night skiing, condominium accommodation and luxury hotel with convention facilities, restaurant, lounge, swimming pool, exercise room and hot tub with a view of the mountain. There's also a day lodge, ski school, alpine and telemark skiing, ski rental and repair, ski shops and ice skating; dogsledding and sleigh rides can be arranged. Summer sightseeing tram lift ride.
PO Box 249, Girdwood,
AK 99587
Tel: 907-754-1111 or
800-880-3880 for reservations
www.alyeskaresort.com

Eaglecrest Ski Area
Twelve miles (19km) from downtown Juneau, there's a base lodge, food service, rental shop, ski school, mountain facilities, two chairlifts, a surface lift and tube lift and mountain-top warming hut. Winter offers 640 acres (259 hectares) and 31 runs for alpine skiing and snowboarding, 40 acres (16 hectares) of snow-making (where machines produce snow during periods of low snowfall) and 5 miles (8km) of nordic trails. Bus service weekends and holidays only.
3000 Fish Creek Road,
Juneau, AK 99801
Tel: 907-790-2000
www.eaglecrestskiarea.com

Special Interest

Alaska Icefield Expeditions
Take a dogsled ride in the middle of summer on top two of Alaska's most spectacular glaciers. Tours are lead by professional mushers and handlers, and driven by dog teams training for the competitive winter season. Trips include helicopter rides to the glacier that provide great sightseeing opportunities. Overnight trips at the dog camp are also available.
PO Box 788, Skagway,
AK 99840
Tel: 907-983-2299
www.akdogtour.com

Alaska Outdoors
Their Alaska Wildlife Tour travels from Prince William Sound to the heights of Denali in search of wildlife. Bears, moose, caribou, Dall sheep, as well as orcas, whales, and bald eagles are on the itinerary. Excellent hiking opportunities and side excursions include fishing, kayaking, dog-sledding, horseback riding, and flightseeing.
PO Box 875649, Wasilla,
AK 99687
Tel: 907-357-4020 or
800-320-2494
www.travelalaskaoutdoors.com

Alaska Photography Tours
Capture the beauty of the Alaska backcountry while staying at the homey Farm Lodge bordering Lake Clark National Park. Daily flights into the backcountry, fishing packages are also available, and all meals are included.
The Farm Lodge,
General Delivery,
Port Alsworth, AK 99653
Tel: 907-781-2208 or
888-440-2281
www.alaskaphotographytours.com

Center for Alaskan Coastal Studies
Environmental education, research field trips and natural history outings studying the marine and coastal ecosystems of Kachemak Bay; beach and coastal rainforest studies.
PO Box 2225, Homer,
AK 99603
Tel: 907-235-6667
www.akcoastalstudies.org

Crow Creek Mine
Historic gold-mining building with artifacts near Girdwood, now on National Register of Historic Places. Open to tourists to pan for gold – equipment supplied and gold guaranteed. There's also a gift shop, overnight camping, and nearby trails to explore the surrounding Chugach National Forest. Groups of up to 150.

TRANSPORTATION

ACCOMMODATIONS

ACTIVITIES

CONTACTS

A – Z

PO Box 113,
Girdwood,
AK 99587
Tel: 907-229-3105
www.crowcreekgoldmine.com

Dig Afognak
The Koniag Native village of Afognak offers professionally led archeological digs and "culture camps" at remote sites on Kodiak Island.
115 Mill May Road, Suite 201,
Kodiak, AK 99615
Tel: 907-486-6357
www.afognak.org/dig.php

Joseph Van Os Photo Safaris
Wildlife photography tours for beginners to professionals. Alaska destinations include Katmai and Denali National Parks.
PO Box 655, Vashon Island,
WA 98070
Tel: 206-463-5383
www.photosafaris.com

Redington Sled Dog Rides
Half-hour to overnight mushing trips along the historic Iditarod Trail.
PO Box 877653, Wasilla,
AK 99687
Tel: 907-376-6730
Email: redingtons@yahoo.com

Wilderness Birding Adventures
Bird watching expeditions throughout much of Alaska, from Prince William Sound and the Kenai Peninsula to Nome, the Bering Sea, and the Arctic National Wildlife Refuge.
5515 Wild Mountain Drive,
Eagle River, AK 99577
Tel: 907-694-7442
www.wildernessbirding.com

Tour Operators

El Dorado Gold Mine and Riverboat Discovery Tours
The mine has two tours daily, including a narrow-gauge train ride and gold panning, from mid-May through mid-September. The riverboat tours are 3½ hours long, on the Chena and Tanana Rivers.
1975 Discovery Drive, Fairbanks,
AK 99709
Tel: 907-479-6673 or
866-479-6673
www.riverboatdiscovery.com

Frontier Excursions
Skagway's oldest independent tour company features gold-rush tours and trips to White Pass and the Yukon. Also shuttle service to Chilkoot trailhead and, in winter, sled dog tours.
PO Box 473, Skagway,
AK 99840
Tel: 907-983-2512 or
877-983-2512
www.frontierexcursions.com

Explore Tours
Ecotourism opportunities throughout the state, including cruises through the Inside Passage, fishing, wildlife viewing in Denali National Park, and viewing of the aurora borealis.
999 E. Tudor Road, Suite 200,
Anchorage, AK 99503
Tel: 907-786-0192 or
800-523-7405
www.exploretours.com

Grayline Alaska
Offering everything from day trips to Portage Glacier to multiple day packages touring the Southeast and Denali, Grayline is an all encompassing travel company, operated by Holland America.
745 W. Fourth Street, Anchorage,
AK 99501
Tel: 888-452-1737
www.graylinealaska.com

Kenai Fjords Tours (Alaska Heritage Tours)
Explore Resurrection Bay, Kenai Fjords National Park and the Chiswell Islands bird rookeries aboard comfortable excursion boats. Trips feature wildlife watching and tidewater glaciers. Day trips, meals, kayaking and overnight stays at an island wilderness lodge can also be arranged.
509 W. Fourth Avenue, Anchorage,
AK 99501
Tel: 907-265-4501 or
877-777-2805
www.kenaifjords.com

Klondike Tours.
Conducts historic Skagway, Glacier Bay and Yukon tours, including fishing, kayaking, rafting, horseback riding, and flightseeing.
PO Box 1061, Skagway,
AK 99840
Tel: 907-983-2075 or

866-983-2075
www.klondiketours.com

Kodiak Tours
Half- or full-day tours of Kodiak. Bear-viewing, flightseeing, and remote wilderness lodge stays can also be arranged.
114 Mill Bay Road, Suite 15, Kodiak,
AK 99615
Tel: 907-486-3920
www.kodiaktours.com

New Directions Tours/Mayflower Tours
Escorted tours by motorcoach and air to destinations such as Anchorage, Valdez, Fairbanks and Denali, plus glacier cruises.
Box 490, Downers Grove,
IL 60515
Tel: 630-435-8500 in Illinois or
800-323-7604 outside Illinois
www.mayflowertours.com

Nome Discovery Tours
Offers tours of Nome and its environs, with an emphasis on the gold rush and Inupiat history of the region.
Box 2024, Nome,
AK 99762
Tel: 907-443-2814
www.nomechamber.org/discoverytours.html

Northern Alaska Tour Company
Conducts ecotours to the Arctic Circle, Brooks Range, and Prudhoe Bay and other Arctic locales that emphasize natural and cultural history, wildlife, and geology. Some tours are completely ground-based, others combine ground and air travel.
Box 82991-W, Fairbanks,
AK 99708
Tel: 907-474-8600 or
800-474-1986
www.northernalaska.com

Sitka Tours
During a ferry port stop or a day in Sitka, visit the totem park in

BELOW: nature tours are popular with hikers in summer.

Sitka National Historical Park, the Russian Cathedral, Russian dance performances, and the Alaska Raptor Center. Company also offers charter and whale-watching tours in addition to trips throughout the Interior and Southcentral Alaska. Shuttle service is available to and from airport and ferrry.
PO Box 1000, Sitka, AK 99835
Tel: 907-747-8443 or 888-801-9649
www.sitkatours.net
Skagway Street Car Company
Take an historical tour of the city in a vintage touring car from the 1930s with guides dressed in turn-of-the-20th-century attire.
270 Second Avenue, PO Box 400, Skagway, AK 99840
Tel: 907-983-2908
www.skagwaystreetcar.com
Tlingit Cultural Tours
Learn more about the history and culture of Southeast Alaska's Tlingit tribe while enjoying the songs, language, and dance regalia of their peoples. A variety of motor and walking tours available.
c/o Sitka Tribal Enterprises, 200 4 Katlian Street, Sitka, AK 99835
Tel: 907-747-7290 or 888-270-8687
http://sitkatours.com
Trans Arctic Circle Treks
Features custom highway treks in Alaska, including the Dalton Highway from Fairbanks to the Arctic Circle, through the Brooks Range, and on to the North Slope and Prudhoe Bay. Coastal cruises and Alaska Railroad trips can also be arranged.
PO Box 82720, Fairbanks, AK 99708
Tel: 907-479-5451 or 800-336-8735 (US only)
www.arctictreks.com
Tundra Tours
Experience Inupiat Eskimo culture, the Arctic Ocean and the midnight sun. Summertime at the northern-most point in America. Cultural program includes Eskimo arts and crafts.
PO Box 189, Barrow, AK 99723
Tel: 907-852-3900 or 800-882-8478
www.tundratoursinc.com
White Pass and Yukon Route Railroad
Built 1898–1900 during the Klondike Gold Rush, the railroad takes passengers on day

excursions past sheer rock cliffs and through solid granite tunnels to White Pass Summit.
231 Second Avenue, PO Box 435, Skagway, AK 99840
Tel: 907-983-2217 or 800-343-7373
www.whitepassrailroad.com
World Express Tours
Tour operator and custom trip planner organizes an array of Alaska tours and adventure programs including executive and private charters, fishing packages, rafting and sailing programs, independent car/motorhome packages, mountaineering and hiking trips.
PO Box 90188, Raleigh, NC 27675
Tel: 800-544-2235
www.worldexpresstours.com

Tourist Information

Anchorage Convention and Visitors Bureau
524 W. Fourth Avenue, Anchorage, AK 99501
Tel: 907-276-4118
www.anchorage.net
Fairbanks Convention and Visitors Bureau
101 Dunkel Street, Suite 111, Fairbanks, AK 99701
Tel: 907-456-5774 or 800-327-5774
www.explorefairbanks.com
Haines Convention and Visitors Bureau
PO Box 530, Haines, AK 99827
Tel: 907-766-2234 or 800-458-3579
www.haines.ak.us
Juneau Convention and Visitors Bureau
One Sealaska Plaza, Suite 305, Juneau, AK 99801
Tel: 907-586-1737 or 800-587-2201
www.traveljuneau.com
Kenai Convention and Visitors Bureau
11471 Kenai Spur Highway, Kenai, AK 99611
Tel: 907-283-1991
www.visitkenai.com
Ketchikan Visitors Bureau
131 Front Street, Ketchikan, AK 99901
Tel: 907-225-6166 or 800-770-3300
www.visit-ketchikan.com

Kodiak Island Convention and Visitors Bureau
100 Marine Way, Suite 200, Kodiak, AK 99615
Tel: 907-486-4782 or 800-789-4782
www.kodiak.org
Mat-Su Convention and Visitors Bureau
7744 E. Visitors View Court, Palmer, AK 99645
Tel: 907-746-5000
www.alaskavisit.com
Nome Convention and Visitors Bureau
PO Box 240 H-P, Nome, AK 99762
Tel: 907-443-6624
www.nomealaska.org
Petersburg Visitor Information Center
PO Box 649, Petersburg, AK 99833
Tel: 907-772-4636 or 866-484-4700
www.petersburg.org
Sitka Convention and Visitors Bureau
PO Box 1226, Sitka, AK 99835
Tel: 907-747-5940
www.sitka.org
Skagway Convention and Visitors Bureau
PO Box 1029, Skagway, AK 99840
Tel: 907-983-2854
www.skagway.com
Valdez Convention and Visitors Bureau
200 Chenega Street, Valdez, AK 99686
Tel: 907-835-4630
www.valdezalaska.org
Wrangell Convention and Visitors Bureau
PO Box 1350, Wrangell, AK 99929
Tel: 800-367-9745
www.wrangellalaska.org

A HANDY SUMMARY OF PRACTICAL INFORMATION, ARRANGED ALPHABETICALLY

A dmission Charges

The larger museums and attractions in Alaska's main cities usually charge $5 to $10. The Alaska Native Heritage Center charges by far the highest at $23.50 for general admission. Seniors (individuals 65 and older) generally get a one to two dollar discount at most places, as do students and children. Young children under the age of three frequently get in for free. In smaller, out of the way attractions, a donation is suggested. Here, a few dollars is usually sufficient. Check websites for any fee changes or special deals. Admission is often reduced in the winter season.

Age Restrictions

To drive a car in the US, you have to be 16 or over. 21 is the legal age for drinking and purchasing alcohol, while cigarettes can be bought at 18.

Alcohol

The legal age for purchasing and consuming alcoholic drinks is 21, and

identification is often needed. Alcohol is sold or served in liquor stores, lounges and restaurants licensed by the state. Unlike most of the US, grocery stores cannot sell alcohol, but they usually have a separate liquor store attached or nearby.

Alaska state law requires a mandatory 3-day jail sentence for drivers found to be driving under the influence of alcohol – even for first-time offenders. Some small rural communities have banned alcohol – and they take it seriously. You could be arrested, fined, jailed or deported for violating the local ordinances. Before traveling to a remote destination, make sure you know the local liquor laws.

B udgeting for Your Trip

Traveling within Alaska is expensive. And the further you range from urban locations, the more expensive travel, food, lodging and services may become. This is due, in part, to the transportation costs involved in shipping goods and services to far-

flung regions in a vast state. Here are some examples of what you might pay in US dollars when this book went to press.

Camping: A less-expensive option, once you and your vehicle have made the trip up. Expect to pay $6–25 per night at a state or federally managed campground.

Hotels: During the summer season, basic hotel rooms are generally over $100 per night, and can be as high as $300 (or more) per night during periods of highest demand. Advance reservations in summer are strongly recommended.

Meals: A fast-food meal for one will typically cost less than $10. A meal in a casual restaurant will likely run between $10 and $20. Evening meals in a nice restaurant may cost $20–30 per person, and that's just for the entrée. Add a dessert and a glass of wine, and the price is likely to be close to $40–50 for one, not counting the tip (see *Tipping, page 374*).

Transportation: Most Alaska cities, of even modest size, offer **taxi** service. A trip from Anchorage airport to the downtown area in a taxi will cost around $20 (before the expected tip). Larger cities offer municipal **bus** lines. In Anchorage, a ride on the People Mover costs $1.75 (one way) for adults, $1 for youth and is free for children aged 4 and under. **Rental cars** are available in larger cities, and you can expect to pay $50–150 per day, depending upon the size vehicle you want. Be sure to reserve early. In peak season it can be very difficult to find a rental car at any price. Regular travel on the Alaska **Railroad** between Anchorage and Denali National Park and Preserve costs about $146 per person, one way. If you care to ride in one of the glass-dome cars, make that $231. **Attractions.** Here's a sample of prices for Anchorage-area attractions: **The Imaginarium Science Discovery Center**: $5.50 adults, $5 children, **Anchorage Museum of History and Art** at the Rasmuson Center: $8 adults, $7 seniors, children under age 17 free, but $2 donation suggested, **Alaska Native Heritage Center**: $23.50 adults, $21.15 for seniors and military, $15.95 for children ages 7–16, **Alaska Zoo**: $10 adults, $8 seniors, $6 ages 3–18, and **H2Oasis Indoor Water Park**: $21.95 adults, $16.95 ages 3–13.

C hildren

Bringing your children along on an Alaska vacation is a wonderful idea, because most of the things that interest you will delight them as well. Whether planning to hike, cruise, fish, kayak or journey to Denali on the train, a trip to Alaska thrills young and old alike.
Accommodations: Many hotels in Alaska allow young children to stay for free in their parents' room.
Eating: Not only does Alaska have myriad standard fast-food options in the larger cities, many of Alaska's restaurants offer children's menus and even crayons and paper to help them wait for their food.
Places of Special Interest: Just getting to Alaska can be exciting, whether it's driving the highway watching for moose, or flying up and looking out the window at all those snow-covered mountains, even in summer. A trip to Alaska aboard one of the Alaska Marine Highway ferries is relaxing and fun for the whole family. Once you've arrived, the kids might enjoy camping, fishing, kayaking, or biking. Day-cruises out of any Southeast or Southcentral coastal community would likely involve

watching for marine mammals and glacier viewing.
There are also many exciting options within the larger cities. Here are some fun things to do with kids in the Anchorage area: The Imaginarium Science Discovery Center (737 West Fifth Avenue, tel: 907-276-3179) features a planetarium, hourly science demonstrations, a Alaska marine touch tank, a life-sized dinosaur, and more. The Alaska Zoo (4731 O'Malley Road, tel: 907-346-2133) gives kids (and their parents) a chance to get a close-up look at some of Alaska's wildlife. The H2Oasis Indoor Waterpark's (1520 O'Malley Road, tel: 907-522-4420) wave pool, lazy river, pirate-ship lagoon and Master Blaster 505ft water-coaster ride could make for an exciting day.
You could take a day trip south to Seward (by road or train) for a cruise into Kenai Fjords National Park, and while you're there visit the Alaska Sealife Center (301 Railway Avenue, tel: 907-224-6300) to check out the sea lions, puffins and seals. Or you could travel north to visit Denali National Park and Preserve. Spend the night in a nearby hotel (advance reservations essential) and the next day enjoy a bus tour into the park as you watch for bears, moose, sheep, wolves, and more.
Possible Concerns: Your children will enjoy their time in Alaska more if you remember to bring sun screen – yes, even here. The summer sun will still cause sunburn, even though the temperatures may seem mild. Another essential item is insect repellent. While Alaska has yet to have any problems with the West Nile Virus, mosquitoes are plentiful and may take much of the fun out of an otherwise splendid hike or picnic. If your plans take you onto the water, even in summer, dress your children (and yourself) warmly in layers. A T-shirt, then a light fleece jacket, topped with a wind/water-proof jacket, lightweight gloves and knit cap will allow for any changes in weather.

Climate

Alaska's vastness defies attempts to categorize its climate. For convenience, however, the state can be divided into five regions about which some climatic generalizations can be made.
Southeast: This is Alaska's Panhandle, a narrow ribbon of mountainous, mostly-forested mainland and islands extending along the western edge of British Columbia.

Wet and mild are the best terms to describe its climate. Certain communities in the region can receive more than 200 inches (5 meters) of precipitation annually. On rare, sunny days in summer, high temperatures might reach the mid-70s°F (21°C+) range. High 40s (4°C) to mid 60s (15°C) are the summer norms, under cloudy skies. Winter temperatures rarely fall much below freezing. Skagway and Haines are usually drier and cooler in winter.
Southcentral: Anchorage and most of the gulf coast comprise this part of Alaska. Some coastal communities are nearly as wet as southeastern cities, but the amount of rainfall lessens considerably just a short distance inland. Anchorage occasionally has summer highs in the 80s (26°C) but the 60s (15°C) and low 70s (21°C) are more common.
Interior: The broad expanse of inland Alaska, loosely centered on Fairbanks, gets an average of 10 inches (25 cm) of precipitation annually. Summer temperatures have reached 100°F (37°C) on occasions; 70s and 80s (21°C and 26°C) temperatures are common, with typical winter lows to −40°F (−40°C).
Northwest and Arctic Coast: This region encompasses Alaska's northern fringe and the west coast as far south as Kotzebue. High winds are common, and average temperatures are too cool to permit trees to grow. Near Nome, summer temperatures can climb into the 60s (15°C), but the high 30s (3°C) and 40s (4°C) are more common. Winter temperatures, though extreme, are never as low as some Interior temperatures. This is also an extremely dry area, receiving only minimal amounts of moisture every year. Barrow, for example, receives just 4.7 inches (11.5cm) of precipitation annually.

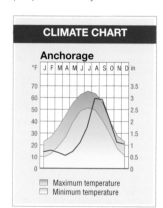

CLIMATE CHART

Anchorage

Maximum temperature
Minimum temperature

TRANSPORTATION
ACCOMMODATIONS
ACTIVITIES
CONTACTS
A – Z

Southwest and The Aleutians: The Aleutian Islands are justly known for some of the most miserable weather on earth. High winds (williwaws) can rise without warning and smash through the islands at speeds of 100mph (165kmh). Heavy fog is common, as are rain and cool temperatures. The southwestern mainland is the meeting point for Aleutian weather and Interior weather, and often experiences unsettled conditions, frequently accompanied by high winds.

Average Daily High Temperatures

Fahrenheit		
CITY	JANUARY	JULY
Anchorage	21.4°	65.2°
Barrow	−7.4°	45°
Cold Bay	33.1°	55.1°
Fairbanks	−1.6°	72°
Juneau	29.4°	63.9°
Kodiak	35°	60.5°
Nome	14.7°	57.7°

Centigrade		
CITY	JANUARY	JULY
Anchorage	−6°	18.4°
Barrow	−22°	7.2°
Cold Bay	0.6°	12.8°
Fairbanks	−18.6°	22.2°
Juneau	−1.5°	17.7°
Kodiak	1.6°	15.8°
Nome	−9.6°	14.3°

What to Wear

When packing for Alaska, remember you are traveling north. While Alaskans may describe the climate as warm in the summer, those from warmer climates find even the summer chilly. No matter what part of the state you are visiting, bring along a warm coat and a synthetic pile or fleece jacket. A wool or synthetic sweater, hat, and gloves or mittens, are also necessities.

Layering clothing is the best way to stay warm. While you may be able to run around in shirt sleeves on a warm summer day, the evenings often require a sweater or light jacket. Tour companies sometimes furnish specialty items such as parkas for overnight trips to Barrow, Kotzebue, Prudhoe Bay and other colder areas.

Since you will probably do a lot of walking, be sure to wear comfortable yet sturdy walking shoes.

No matter where you visit in Alaska, you are likely to run into periods of rain, so good-quality rainwear is needed. If your travel plans include flying to a remote area in a small plane, it is advisable to wear durable warm clothing; survival gear is required for cross-country

flights in small planes. Air services and charter flight operators normally carry sufficient survival gear as required by law; it's up to passengers to dress appropriately.

Because of its location on the Gulf of Alaska, weather conditions change rapidly. So, don't trust the weather reports and be prepared for everything.

Crime and Safety

Alaska is not crime-ridden, but occasional outbursts of violence are not unknown. Basic common sense should be followed: leave large amounts of money, jewelry and valuables in the hotel safe. Don't flaunt your money or display other valuables that could encourage a thief. Be careful where you leave handbags and luggage.

Sexual assault rates are quite high and women should not travel alone in secluded areas (such as wooded bike paths), near bars or other potentially troublesome areas. Use common sense and avoid dubious areas.

Anchorage, Fairbanks, Juneau, Homer, and Seward are among the cities and towns to have their own police departments and most villages have public safety officers. The Alaska State Troopers, a professional police force, respond to calls in most outlying areas.

Dialing 911 will put you in touch with a dispatcher who can provide an emergency service (police, fire or ambulance). Be specific about your problem and location. Bear in mind that Alaska's vast size may mean that help is many miles away.

Customs Regulations

Visitors entering Alaska from anywhere other than a US port of

embarkation will proceed through US customs. Personal effects, such as camping gear and fishing rods, are exempt from duties. Visitors who are over the age of 21 may also bring in small amounts (for personal use) of liquor, cigarettes and cigars (not from Cuba). You may also bring personal gifts, as long as the total value is not more than $100. These exemptions may only be claimed if you plan to spend at least 72 hours in the US, and if you have not claimed them within the preceding 6 months. A flat-rate duty of 3 percent applies to other goods brought into the US with you, and intended solely for personal use or personal gifts up to a $1,000 value limit (fair market retail in country of acquisition). The duty amount on items beyond the first $1,000 varies.

Don't wrap any gifts you bring into the country; they will need to be available for inspection. Don't try to bring raw food or plant material into the US without a special license. Don't bring more than $10,000 in cash (US or foreign) unless you want the hassle of filling out additional documentation. Don't try to bring a firearm into the country, except for a hunting trip. Foreign hunters must obtain a permit from the Bureau of Alcohol, Tobacco and Firearms 304-616-4550, www.atf.gov, before bringing along, buying or even possessing a gun. Your application must be accompanied by a valid hunting license, and the process could take months. *(See page 360.)* For more information, contact the nearest U.S. embassy or consulate, or the US Customs office, 877-227-5511 or www.cbp.gov.

When leaving Alaska, you will need to have a permit for any souvenir purchased that is made from protected mammals, such as certain native handicrafts. You can get a permit from the US Fish and Wildlife

BELOW: camping in Alaska is best reserved for the experienced camper.

Service in Anchorage 907-271-6198, a process that may take a few days. If your souvenir contains *marine* mammal parts, the permit must come from the Washington, DC office, and may take considerably longer. The simple solution is to have the store (where you purchase the item) ship it to your home, and handle all the needed documentation. Information is also available at www.commerce.state. ak.us/oed/nag/nativearts.htm.

For the latest information on what documentation you will need to cross any U.S/Canadian border, contact:
Canada Border Service Agency: tel: 800-461-9999; www.cbsa.gc.ca
U.S Customs and Border Protection: tel: 202-354-1000; www. cbp.gov/xp/cgov/travel

D isabled Travelers

Nearly all hotels, restaurants, tours and other businesses in Alaska's larger cities welcome visitors with disabilities. It is important to specify your particular special needs when making reservations. The US Coast Guard regulates tour-boat activities and therefore these vessels do not fall under the requirements of the Americans with Disabilities Act. While some smaller day-cruise boats are not structured to allow for wheelchair use, you will likely find that most tour operators make every effort to accommodate special-needs passengers.

A good contact is Challenge Alaska (3350 Commercial Drive, Suite 208, Anchorage, AK 99501; tel: 907-344-7399, TTY 907-344-7270, 888-430-2738; www.challengealaska.org). Challenge Alaska is a non-profit organization that specializes in providing sports and recreational opportunities for those with disabilities. The group operates an adaptive ski school at the Keil Center at the Alyeska Ski resort in Girdwood, just south of Anchorage. For more information, call 907-783-2925.

E mbassies and Consulates

Canada: 310 K Street, Suite 200, Anchorage, tel: 907-264-6734
Great Britain: University of Alaska, Anchorage College of Arts and Sciences, Room 362, 2311 Providence Drive, Anchorage, tel: 907-786-4848

Emergencies

In the event of any emergency requiring police, fire or ambulance

Electricity

The standard for electricity throughout the US is 110 to 120 volts (60 cycle) AC. The plugs have two flat, parallel pins. Foreign visitors who don't have dual-voltage appliances will need a 110-volt transformer and an adaptor plug.

service, go to the nearest telephone and dial 911. It is a toll free call; no coins will be needed for a public telephone. For less serious accidents, call the local police department or the state troopers non-emergency lines. Dial 907-555-1212 for directory assistance in locating the appropriate non-emergency police or trooper telephone number.

Etiquette

As when visiting any small town or community, be mindful that you are in someone's home, not a museum or exhibit. Ask before taking photos, and don't assume that it is okay to enter into people's houses. Be sure to introduce yourself, and ask permission to walk around the village. Generally friendly and welcoming people, a group will typically gather to share Native craft arts and home-cooked food. Buying something is a great way to strike up conversation. *(For additional tips, see pages 63–5.)*

G ay and Lesbian Travelers

In Alaska's "live and let live" spirit, homosexuality is widely accepted. However, it is important to exercise caution in some remote areas. Anchorage and Fairbanks have a fairly thriving gay and lesbian scene. To find gay-friendly bars, clubs, and other attractions, visit www.gayalaska.com.

In downtown Anchorage, Identity, Inc. runs the Gay and Lesbian Community Center at 336 East Fifth Avenue, PO Box 200070, Anchorage 99520-0070, tel: 907-929-4528, www. identityinc.org. A gay, lesbian, bisexual, and transgender organization, their mission is to build the Alaska GLBTA community through programs, education and collaboration.

H ealth and Medical Care

Two major hospitals serve the general public in Anchorage, and there is one in Fairbanks and another in Juneau. Additionally, there is a Native hospital

in Anchorage run by a number of Native-owned corporations. Treatment there is free for anyone who is one-quarter or more Native American. There is also a hospital on Elmendorf Air Force Base, in Anchorage, which serves military personnel and their families.

If you need to visit a doctor, larger cities in Alaska have walk-in clinics open daily with no appointment necessary. Clinics typically are staffed by some combination of physicians, nurses, health aids and, occasionally, dentists. The service will be expensive, and you will need to pay first, and then apply for any re-imbursement from your personal insurance company. Alaska hospitals will render 24-hour emergency aid to anyone in critical need, but short of that standard, payment will be required before care will be given. A trip to the emergency room due to an accident or serious illness can easily cost $1,000 or more. Adequate travel insurance is essential.
Alaska Native Medical Center
4315 Diplomacy Drive, Anchorage
Tel: 907-563-2662
www.anmc.org
Alaska Regional Hospital
2801 DeBarr Road, Anchorage
Tel: 907-276-1131
www.alaskaregional.com
Bartlett Regional Hospital
3260 Hospital Drive, Juneau
Tel: 907-796-8900
www.bartletthospital.org
Fairbanks Memorial Hospital
1650 Cowles, Fairbanks
Tel: 907-452-8181
www.bannerhealth.com
Providence Alaska Medical Center
3200 Providence Drive, Anchorage
Tel: 907-562-2211
www.providence.org

I nternet

Internet access is available at most public libraries, hotels, intenet cafés and airports. Even smaller cities generally offer some online access.

L ost Property

Here are some numbers you may need if you lose personal belongings:
Alaska Marine Highway System: tel: 800-642-0066
Alaska Railroad: tel: 907-265-2494
Fairbanks International Airport: tel: 907-458-2530
Juneau International Airport: tel: 907-789-9539
Ted Steven's International Airport (Anchorage): tel: 907-266-2623

Maps

An excellent source for topographic maps of Alaska is U.S. Geological Survey, 4210 University Drive, Rm 208, Anchorage, AK 99508, 907-786-7011, http://alaska.usgs.gov/science/esic/index.php. Maps may be viewed via the Alaska Travel Industry's website: www.travelalaska.com/Maps/Index.aspx

Media

Newspapers

The three major daily newspapers are the *Juneau Empire*, the *Anchorage Daily News* and the *Fairbanks Daily News-Miner*. Many smaller communities also put out newspapers, many of which tackle controversial local issues. For Native issues, the *Tundra Drums* (Bethel) is a good source.

Many bookstores and variety stores have one or more of the major Alaska dailies available for sale. In large cities, Seattle newspapers, the *New York Times*, the *Wall Street Journal*, and *USA Today* are normally available in bookstores and large grocery stores. The Loussac Library in Anchorage holds many of the country's largest newspapers.

Television

Only Anchorage has enough stations to affiliate actively with the four major television networks. These are CBS, Channel 11; ABC, Channel 13; NBC, Channel 2; and Fox Network, Channel 4. Other major cities will have one station or more, loosely affiliated with one of the networks, but usually offering a spread of programs from all three of the major networks along with a variety of locally produced shows. Public television (or "educational" television) is available in most of the state.

Again, most television programs are transmitted in English, although some regional shows may be broadcast in the area's Native dialect. The majority of these programs are on public television.

In the past few years, with the growing use of satellite communications equipment, even the most rural areas have gained access to television through the Alaska Rural Communications Services (ARCS).

Radio Stations

Some radio stations in Alaska still pass on messages to residents living in the bush. Regularly scheduled times are set aside for transmitting everything from messages of endearment to doctors' appointments.

The major radio networks have affiliates in all the larger cities, and most towns or villages will have a locally owned radio station. Quality varies from excellent to so-so. National Public Radio reaches communities throughout most of the state and is an excellent source of entertainment and information. For listings around Alaska, visit www.infoplease.com/ipea/A0758900.html.

The vast majority of radio programs are broadcast in English, though many of the public stations also offer a limited number of programs in Spanish, Russian or the Native dialect that is spoken in a particular village or region.

Money

Travelers' checks in US dollars are advised to ease problems in dealing with the currency. National banks in Alaska's major cities – Anchorage, Fairbanks and Juneau – can convert foreign currency at the prevailing exchange rate. Automatic Teller Machines (ATMs) can be found in just about every town on the road system.

Outside these metropolitan areas the opportunities to convert foreign money are dramatically reduced.

Tipping

Airport porters usually receive $1 for the first bag and 50 cents for each additional bag. (Don't expect porters outside of Anchorage.) Similar tips are appropriate for bellhops in the larger hotels.

Waiters and waitresses normally receive about 15 percent of the bill. Tipping can be as high as 20 percent for excellent restaurant service. Tips are inappropriate in most fast-food restaurants and cafés. Bartenders should get 10 to 15 percent of the bill depending on the quality of service.

See also Tax.

Opening Hours

Government offices (except for Post Office stations) are normally open from 8am to 4.30pm Monday through Friday, with banks and credit unions generally open from 10am to 6pm and, in some cases, during limited hours on Saturday. Except for necessary public services, most government offices and businesses are closed on public holidays (though the Post Office station at Anchorage airport is open every day from 6am to 11.59pm).

Retailers, especially in peak summer months, are the exception and often open seven days a week, well into the evening. Some grocery stores are 24-hour.

Postal Services

You can mail a letter at your hotel, at local post office, or in any of the official US Post Office's blue collection boxes located around town.

Public Holidays

Banks, offices, post offices, and state and federal agencies will probably be closed on the following state and national holidays:

January 1: New Year's Day
Third Monday in January: Martin Luther King, Jr. Day
Third Monday in February: Presidents' Day
Last Monday in March: Seward's Day

BELOW: Alaska isn't as remote as it can sometimes seem.

Last Monday in May: Memorial Day
July 4: Independence Day
First Monday in September: Labor Day
Second Monday in October: Columbus Day
October 18: Alaska Day
November 11: Veterans' Day
Fourth Thursday in November: Thanksgiving Day
December 25: Christmas Day

R eligious Services

Although a recent study concluded that Alaska was the least-religious state in the union, there are plenty of places of worship throughout the region. The Wasilla/Palmer area has recently become a growing center of Evangelical Christianity, and has perhaps the highest church per person ratio in Alaska. Protestant, Catholic, and Russian Orthodox are the dominant religions.

S moking

Like most of the US, Alaska is in a state of flux with regards to smoking. While it has long been popular here, recent restrictions have been voted in some cities and boroughs to limit smoking in restaurants and bars.

T ax

There is no state sales tax in Alaska. However, different boroughs and municipalities across the state may impose a sales tax on all or some goods and services, including hotel stays. If uncertain as to whether or not there is a local sales tax, ask any cashier or hotel clerk. All cruise passengers must pay a $50 "head tax" *(see page 344).*

Telephones

Public telephones can be found almost everywhere – hotel lobbies, stores, restaurants, bars, etc – and are usually reliable. Local calls cost around 50 cents.

Check the directory or dial 411 for local numbers. Information on telephone listings anywhere in the state can be obtained by dialing 1-907-555-1212. Information for other states and Canada can be obtained by dialing 1, followed by the appropriate three-digit area code and then 555-1212. The three-digit area code for all telephone exchanges within Alaska is 907.

Cell phones can be used in most major communities and several smaller ones, such as Barrow, Fairbanks, Tok, Valdez, Anchorage, Cordova, Juneau, Kenai, Homer, and Whittier. Check with your phone provider before arriving in Alaska.

Toilets

Gas stations, bars and restaurants have public restrooms available. So will some retail stores, but if not, the clerk will direct you to the nearest one. The farther you get from population centers, the more popular outhouses become due to concern over freezing water pipes. Most tourist areas have indoor plumbing, but it is likely you will encounter at least one Alaskan outhouse on your trip. For the large part, they are kept extremely clean, and contain covered receptacles close at hand to dispose of all paper waste.

Tour Operators

Alaska has countless tour operators throughout the state that offer everything from birdwatching to mountain climbing. *(See pages 364–9 in the Contacts section.)*

Tourist Information

For general information about travelling in Alaska, the Alaska Travel Industry Association provides a free guide upon request. You can contact them at:
2600 Cordova Street, Suite 201, Anchorage AK, 99503
Tel: 907-929-2842 or 800-862-5275
www.travelalaska.com
For information about visiting Alaska's parks, contact Public Land Information Centers at www.nps.gov/aplic. Every town and tourist destination has a visitors bureau that is generally located downtown. Below is a complete listing of visitors bureaus around the state, for additional information *see page 369 in the Contacts section.*

Websites

State of Alaska: www.state.ak.us
Visitor Information sites:
Anchorage: www.anchorage.net
Bethel: www.bethelakchamber.org
Cordova: www.codovachamber.com
Denali National Park and Preserve: www.nps.gov/dena
Dillingham: www.dillinghamak.com
Fairbanks: www.explorefairbanks.com
Gustavus: www.gustavusalaska.org
Haines: www.haines.ak.us
Homer: www.homeralaska.org
Juneau: www.traveljuneau.com

Time Zones

Alaska Standard Time (Pacific Standard Time minus 1 hour; Eastern Standard Time minus 4 hours; GMT minus 10 hours). The Aleutian Chain and St Lawrence Island are in the Hawaii-Aleutian Time Zone, which is 1 hour earlier.

Kenai: www.visitkenai.com
Ketchikan: www.visit-ketchikan.com
Kodiak: www.kodiak.org
Kotzebue: www.cityofkotzebue.com
Matanuska – Susitna (Palmer, Wasilla, Talkeetna, Sutton): www.alaskavisit.com
Nome: www.nomealaska.org
Petersburg: www.petersburg.org
Seldovia: www.seldovia.com
Seward: www.seward.com
Sitka: www.sitka.org
Skagway: www.skagway.org
Soldotna: www.soldotnachamber.com
Unalaska/Dutch Harbor: www.unalaska.info
Valdez: www.valdezalaska.org
Whittier: www.whittieralaskachamber.org
Wrangell: www.wrangellchamber.org
Yakutat: www.ptialaska.net

V isas and Passports

Visitors coming to the United States must have a valid passport, visa, or other accepted documentation. However, in an effort to attract more tourists, the US initiated the Visa Waiver Program for those coming on vacation for a maximum of 90 days. With 35 countries participating, the program allows for select travellers to enter the US with only a machine readable passport. Travellers under this program can also make short trips to Canada without an additional visa. As of 2009, participating travellers will need to register online three days before travel. To check eligibility for the Visa Waiver program, and for complete and up to date information for all travellers, visit the US State Department at www.travel.state.gov/visa/visa_1750.html.

W eights and Measures

Like the rest of the US, Alaska uses the Imperial system of weights and measures. Some conversions:
1 inch = 2.54 centimeters
1 foot = 30.48 centimeters
1 gallon = 3.8 liters
1 yard = 0.9144 meters
1 once = 28.40 grams
1 mile = 1.609 kilometers
1 pound = 0.453 kilograms

TRANSPORTATION

ACCOMMODATIONS

ACTIVITIES

CONTACTS

A – Z

FURTHER READING

General

It is surprisingly difficult to find books on Alaska in UK bookshops, but all those listed are available on Amazon at www.amazon.com or www.amazon.co.uk and are well worth seeking out.

Fiction

Call of the Wild; White Fang, by Jack London. Two classic tales, the first told through the eyes of Buck, a dog who makes the journey from pampered life to leader of a wolf pack, pulling sleds across Alaska before his return to the wild. White Fang tells the tale of a wild dog becoming tamed. Both stories give a good idea of both the hardship and the camaraderie inherent in the Alaskan experience.
Drop City, by T.C. Boyle. A funny and entertaining novel chronicling a group of hippies as they attempt to build a commune along the Yukon River deep in the Alaska bush.
Tisha: Story of a Young Teacher in the Alaska Wilderness, by Robert Specht. A popular, heart-warming story about Anne Hobbs, a young teacher living in the remote gold-rush settlement of Chicken in 1927, who was determined to treat people as equals, despite great prejudice.

Travel and Exploration

Coming into the Country, John McPhee. Still one of the best accounts of all that is Alaska, interweaving vivid characters and descriptive narrative to cover both urban life and the total wilderness.
Final Frontiersman: Heimo Korth and his Family, Alone in Alaska's Arctic Wilderness, by James Campbell. Campbell recounts the story of his cousin Heimo, who left his native Wisconsin and settled far north of the Arctic Circle, over 100 miles (160km) from his nearest neighbor. Hunting during spring visits to St Lawrence Island, Heimo's story is a glimpse into a dying way of life.
Green Alaska, by Nancy Lord. Alaskan writer and commercial fisherwoman, Nancy Lord, recounts the pivotal Harriman Expedition of 1899. Part history, part travel, part memoir, this is an entertaining and insightful read.

Into the Wild, John Krakauer. Made into a film in 2007 directed by Sean Penn, this is the story of Christopher McCandless, an idealistic young man who tried to survive in the wilderness, cutting off his middle class family and renaming himself Alex Supertramp. He was found dead by moose hunters, probably killed by eating toxic seeds.
Passage to Juneau, by Jonathan Raban. An interesting mix of natural and human history as the author sails solo along the Inside Passage.
Shadows on the Koyukuk: An Alaskan Native's Life along the River, by Sidney Huntington. A memoir simply told about growing up in the freezing north and the skills needed to survive.
Tracks across Alaska: A Dog Sled Journey, by Alastair Scott. This is a great read for anyone who romanticizes the great white north, or who dreams of abandoning the day job for a new life with a pack of huskies. In crisp, clear prose, the author describes how he took up dogsledding and followed the Iditarod trail.
Winterdance: The Fine Madness of Alaskan Dog Racing, by Gary Paulsen. No need to have an interest

in dogsledding to enjoy this book; an entertaining and touching account of Paulsen's training for and then running the Iditarod sled dog race.

History and Politics

Alaska: A History of the 49th State, by Claus M. Naske and Herman E Slotnick. A good history of Alaska up to the early 1990s.

Reference

The Milepost, edited by Kris Valencia. Known as the bible to Alaska with good reason, this is an incredibly detailed travel guide, listing gas stations, stream crossings, trash facilities, you name it. Excellent if you are planning on doing your own tour, probably too detailed if not.

Other Insight Guides

Insight FlexiMap: Alaska is a detailed illustrated map, laminated for ease of use and durability.

Insight Guide: US National Parks West provides full coverage, including striking photography, on all the main national parks in the west of the US, including Alaska and Hawaii.

Insight Guide: Canada gives a real insight into this vast country, from the Pacific-oriented west coast to francophone Quebec.

Send Us Your Thoughts

We do our best to ensure the information in our books is as accurate and up-to-date as possible. The books are updated on a regular basis using local contacts, who painstakingly add, amend and correct as required. However, some details are liable to change, and we are ultimately reliant on our readers to put us in the picture.

We welcome your feedback, especially your experience of using the book "on the road". We will acknowledge all contributions, and we'll offer an Insight Guide to the best letters received.

Please contact us at:
Insight Guides
PO Box 7910
London SE1 1WE
insight@apaguide.co.uk

ART AND PHOTO CREDITS

4Corners 172T
Accent Alaska 2/3, 112, 174, 215, 244
AKG-images London 36BR
Alamy 94, 209, 210, 213&T, 214&T, 216T
Alaska Division of Tourism 6L&BR, 7TCL, CR&BR, 8TR, 9B, 10CL, 11T&CL, 19T&B, 20T&B, 64, 101, 105L&R, 106L&R, 107, 121T, 127, 131, 142T, 150, 161L&R, 162L&R, 174T, 181, 198T, 203T, 204T, 220T&B, 221T&B, 235T, 238, 242, 260T, 265L&R, 266L&R, 267, 270T, 275T, 277T, 283T, 293T, 298T, 307T&B, 308B, 316, 324T, 328T, 348, 358, 361, 362, 368, 372
Alaska Stock 56, 57, 163, 204, 235, 239, 270, 280
Alaska Stock/Photolibrary 4T, 6CR, 16/17, 24, 29, 30, 39CL, 70, 75, 95, 114, 115T, 116, 118T, 120, 122, 133, 144, 156, 157, 158/159, 164, 173, 176, 177, 178, 179, 182&T, 183T, 184, 199T, 202, 203R, 208, 211, 222, 230, 236, 252, 253, 256, 258, 269, 272, 273, 299, 320, 321, 322&T, 328, 339, 340
Brian & Cherry Alexander 59, 110T, 241
Jon Arnold Images 203L
Roy Bailet 186/187
Bruce Bernstein Collection 256T
Bridgeman Art Library 36TL
Maxine Cass 151T
Julie Collins 275
Corbis 8BL,10B, 34/35, 37BR, 38BR, 41, 44, 47, 48, 49, 50, 51, 92/93, 98/99, 113T, 121, 123T&B, 124, 125, 126, 128, 218/219, 249, 259&T, 282, 290, 291, 292, 299, 308T, 309, 313T, 337
Celebrity Cruises 91
Cruise West 39TR, 55L, 89, 118, 141
Alex Demyan 136B
Mary Evans Picture Library 37TL, 152

Lee Forster 289
Getty Images 5B, 7TL, TR &BL, 9TR, 22, 38T, 62, 65, 80, 83, 86, 108, 109, 110, 117, 135, 137, 142, 143&T, 194T, 224, 225, 229T, 232, 233, 234, 237, 277, 278B, 317, 325, 331, 332
Hapag-Lloyd 87
Robert Harding World Imagery 240, 315, 323, 326
Kim Heacox 140, 227T
Holland America 7BCL, 25, 88, 90
iStockphoto.com 139, 180
Laif/Camera Press 145, 223, 226, 296
Tom & Pat Leeson 72
Kyle Lochalsh 205
Garry Lok 55R
James McCann 66, 68, 231T
Rick McIntyre 76R
Nana Museum of the Arctic 274
Nature Picture Library 10TR, 73, 74, 146L, 231
**Mark Newman/
Tom Stack & Associates** 78
PA Photos 39BR, 75, 257, 266, 286, 287, 298
Photolibrary 9CL, 12/13, 21, 31, 81, 84, 115, 116T, 132, 138&T, 146R, 147, 149, 151, 153, 170, 185, 186T, 189, 193, 195, 211T, 212, 217, 253, 271, 278, 333, 351
Jeff Schultz 14/15, 18, 26, 27, 28, 71, 82, 228, 245T, 297, 299T, 310, 330
Science Photo Library 341
Allan Seiden 32
Bill Sherwonit 23, 79, 85, 96/97, 119, 190, 191, 194, 198, 229, 279, 284, 288T, 324, 325T, 332T, 334, 335&T
Mark Skok 100
Still Pictures 63, 281, 283, 285L&R, 288
SuperStock 67, 76L, 77, 112T, 113B, 129, 134, 136T, 165, 166, 167, 168, 169, 175, 196, 197, 199, 200, 201, 205T, 216, 227, 240T, 254, 276, 304/305,

311, 312, 314, 327, 329, 336, 338
TopFoto 38BL, 130, 313
Travel Lounge 171
Unalaska 339T
University of Washington Library 4B, 36BL, 38, 42, 43, 45, 52, 53
Vautier-de-Nanxe 1, 40, 54, 207, 273T, 300
Harry M Walker 33, 60/61, 148, 168T, 169T, 171T, 172B, 183B, 188, 192, 206, 243, 245, 246, 248&T, 255, 261
Tom Walker 268
World Picture News 58, 176T, 262/263

154/155: Archive Photos 154/155T&C, 154BR, 155BR; **Corbis-Bettmann** 155TR&CR; **Corbis-Bettmann/UPI** 154BL

250/251: all pictures by **Brian & Cherry Alexander**

294/295: all pictures by **Harry M Walker**, except 295R (totem pole) **Bill Sherwonit**

302/303: Jim Dory 303TR; **Photolibrary** 302/303, 302BL&CR, 303CL; **Jeff Schultz** 303BL; **WpN** 302TL, 303BR

318/319: all pictures **Harry M Walker** except **Bill Sherwonit** 318CR and 319TR

Map Production: Original cartography Colin Earl, updated by Mike Adams

Production: Linton Donaldson

INDEX

Numbers in bold refer to main reference.

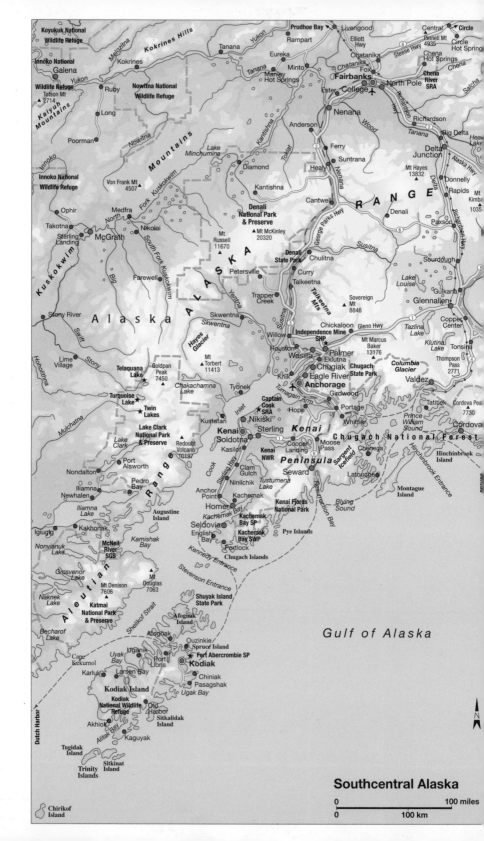

Southcentral Alaska

0   100 miles

0   100 km